*"But where shall wisdom be found? And where
is the place of understanding? Man knoweth not
the price thereof; neither is it found in the land
of the living... for the price of wisdom
is above rubies."*
— **The Book of Job,** *chapter 28, verses 12, 13, 18*

"D is for lots of things."
— **John Dee, All Fools' Day 1989**

THE SANDMAN™

PRELUDES & NOCTURNES

NEIL GAIMAN
writer

SAM KIETH
MIKE DRINGENBERG
MALCOLM JONES III
artists

DANIEL VOZZO
colorist

TODD KLEIN
letterer

DAVE McKEAN
covers

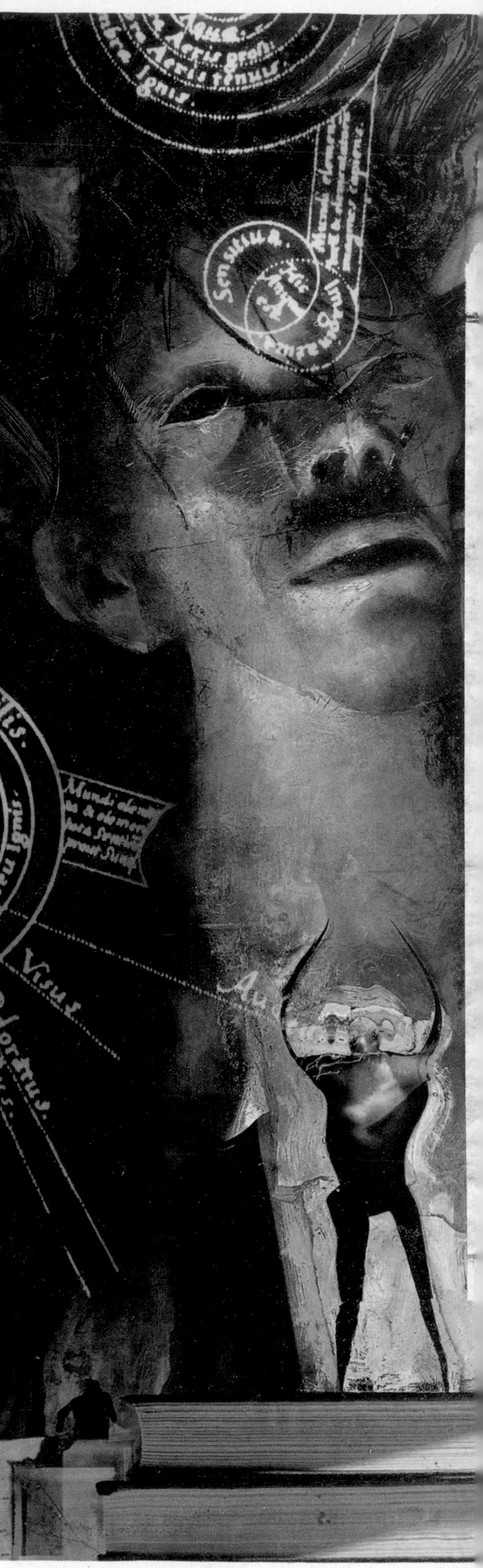

THE SANDMAN: PRELUDES & NOCTURNES

Published by DC Comics. Cover Copyright © 2010 DC Comics.
Compilation Copyright © 1991 DC Comics. Introduction Copyright
© 1995 DC Comics. All Rights Reserved. Afterword Copyright © 1991
DC Comics. All Rights Reserved.

Originally published in single magazine form as THE SANDMAN 1-8.
Copyright © 1988, 1989 DC Comics. All Rights Reserved.
All characters, their distinctive likenesses and related elements
featured in this publication are trademarks of DC Comics.
The stories, characters and incidents featured
in this publication are entirely fictional.
DC Comics does not read or
accept unsolicited submissions
of ideas, stories or artwork.

DC Comics,
1700 Broadway,
New York, NY 10019
A Warner Bros.
Entertainment Company
Printed in the USA.
Seventh Printing.
ISBN: 978-1-4012-2575-9

*Cover art and design
illustrations by Dave McKean.*

*Cover design by
Richard Bruning.*

SUSTAINABLE
FORESTRY
INITIATIVE

Certified Chain of Custody
At Least 20% Certified Forest Content
www.sfiprogram.org
SFI-01042
APPLIES TO TEXT STOCK ONLY

Library of Congress Cataloging-in-Publication Data

Gaiman, Neil.

*The sandman. Vol. 1, Preludes & nocturnes / Neil Gaiman, Sam
Kieth, Mike Dringenberg, Malcolm Jones III.*

p. cm.

"Originally published in single magazine form as The Sandman 1-8."

ISBN 978-1-4012-2575-9 (alk. paper)

*1. Graphic novels. I. Kieth, Sam. II. Dringenberg, Mike. III. Jones,
Malcolm, III. IV. Title. V. Title: Preludes & nocturnes. VI. Title:
Preludes and nocturnes.*

PN6728.S26G45 2012

741.5'973–dc23

2012027187

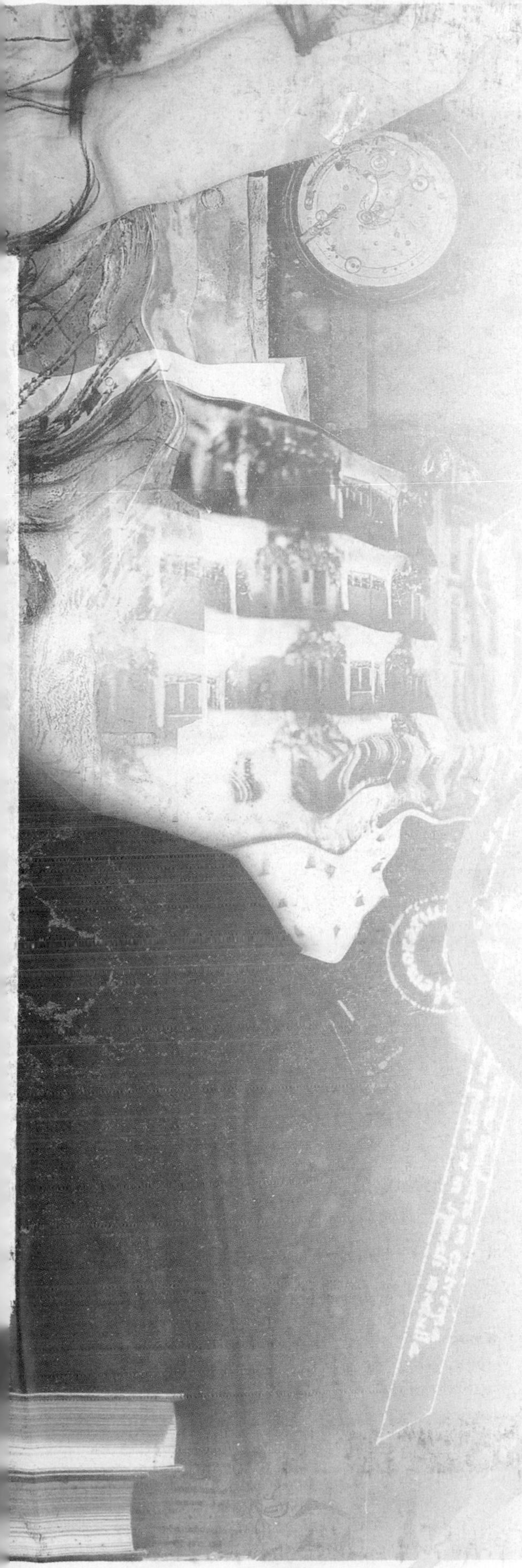

INTRODUCTION
KAREN BERGER

SANDMAN never lived up to my initial expectations. If it had, it wouldn't be the benchmark series it is today. Instead, it turned into something I never imagined: one of the best comics works ever produced.

Now, don't get me wrong. It's not that I didn't think the series had potential. The initial proposal is long gone, but my hazy memory recalls interesting characters, an intriguing, imaginative atmosphere and some hints at future storylines. It was evident that Neil Gaiman was a good "idea man," but whether he could execute those concepts was another story.

Back in 1987, Neil was a new writer to comics who had submitted a short SWAMP THING story to me a couple of years earlier. Journalism was his background and, like a good reporter, he hounded me every few months about that Swamp Thing tale. It wasn't until we first met in London during my first scouting mission for British talent that I realized that this was the same persistent but polite British guy who'd been bugging me all this time. It was at that meeting that Neil pitched the BLACK ORCHID miniseries, a SANDMAN series, and a series featuring John Constantine, among a host of others. The Sandman was already

spoken for in the Justice Society of America, and Constantine was on his way to being developed by Jamie Delano. It was decided that BLACK ORCHID made the most sense for us to see a proper proposal. Soon after we accepted Neil's final proposal, he and the silent, young, and formidably talented Dave McKean began work.

BLACK ORCHID was the second comics work that Neil had done. Like his first work, *Violent Cases*, it was technically solid but maybe, in a way, too precise. The craft was there, but there was a distance to Neil's writing that kept me from getting emotionally involved with the characters. However, there was enough of a spark in his work that we wanted to see if it would ignite with another project. That project would turn out to be a new Sandman series starring an entirely new character.

I've edited many start-up titles in my time, and SANDMAN, like most others, went through its share of birth and growth pains. In rereading the first storyline of the series, I was struck by a dichotomy. On the one hand, the first seven issues were a simple quest tale about the once-captive ruler of the dreamworld, featuring known DC characters and their haunts in

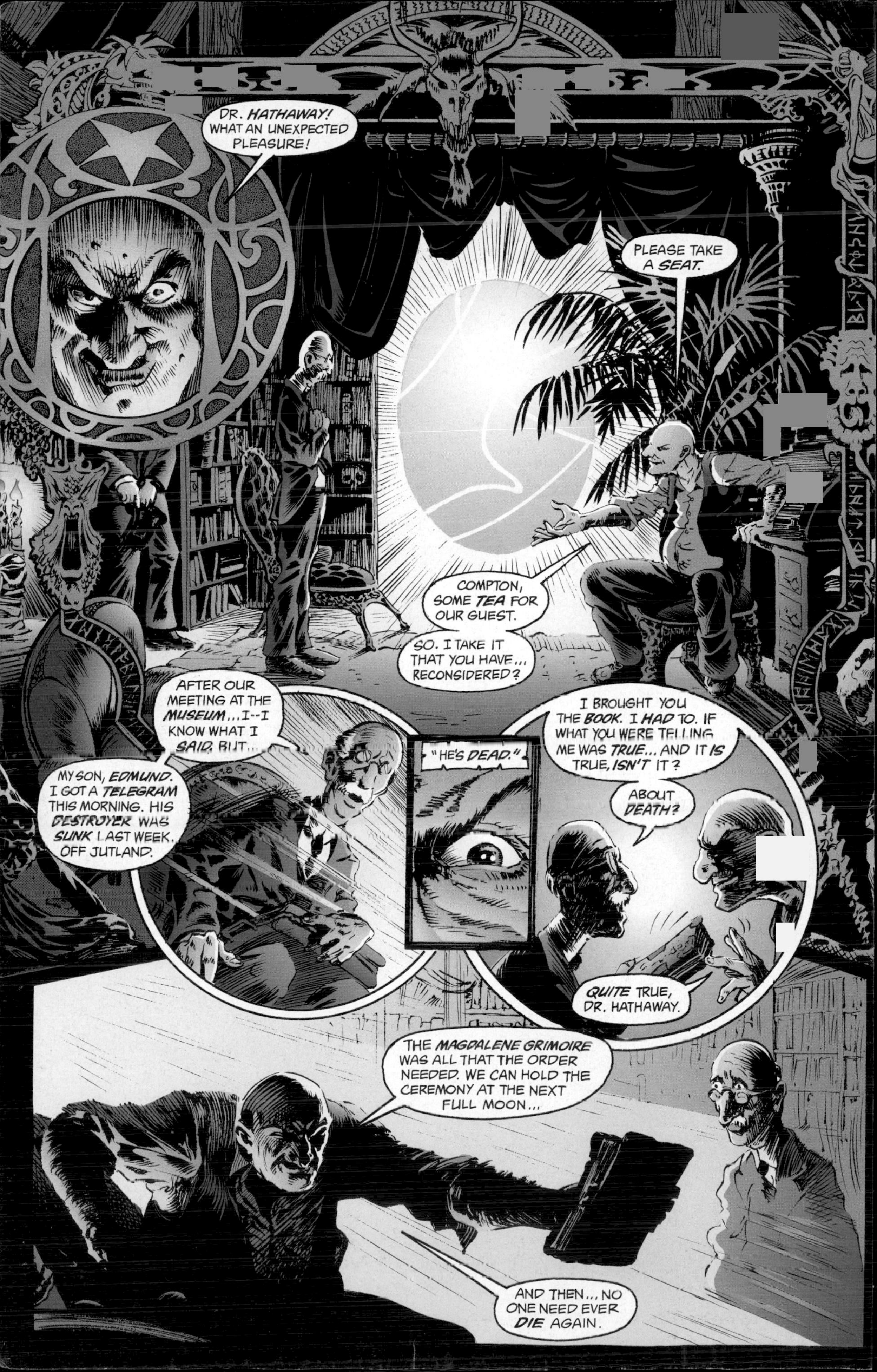
DR. HATHAWAY! WHAT AN UNEXPECTED PLEASURE!
PLEASE TAKE A SEAT.
COMPTON, SOME TEA FOR OUR GUEST.
SO. I TAKE IT THAT YOU HAVE... RECONSIDERED?
AFTER OUR MEETING AT THE MUSEUM... I--I KNOW WHAT I SAID, BUT...
MY SON, EDMUND. I GOT A TELEGRAM THIS MORNING. HIS DESTROYER WAS SUNK LAST WEEK, OFF JUTLAND.
"HE'S DEAD."
I BROUGHT YOU THE BOOK. I HAD TO. IF WHAT YOU WERE TELLING ME WAS TRUE... AND IT IS TRUE, ISN'T IT?
ABOUT DEATH?
QUITE TRUE, DR. HATHAWAY.
THE MAGDALENE GRIMOIRE WAS ALL THAT THE ORDER NEEDED. WE CAN HOLD THE CEREMONY AT THE NEXT FULL MOON...
AND THEN... NO ONE NEED EVER DIE AGAIN.

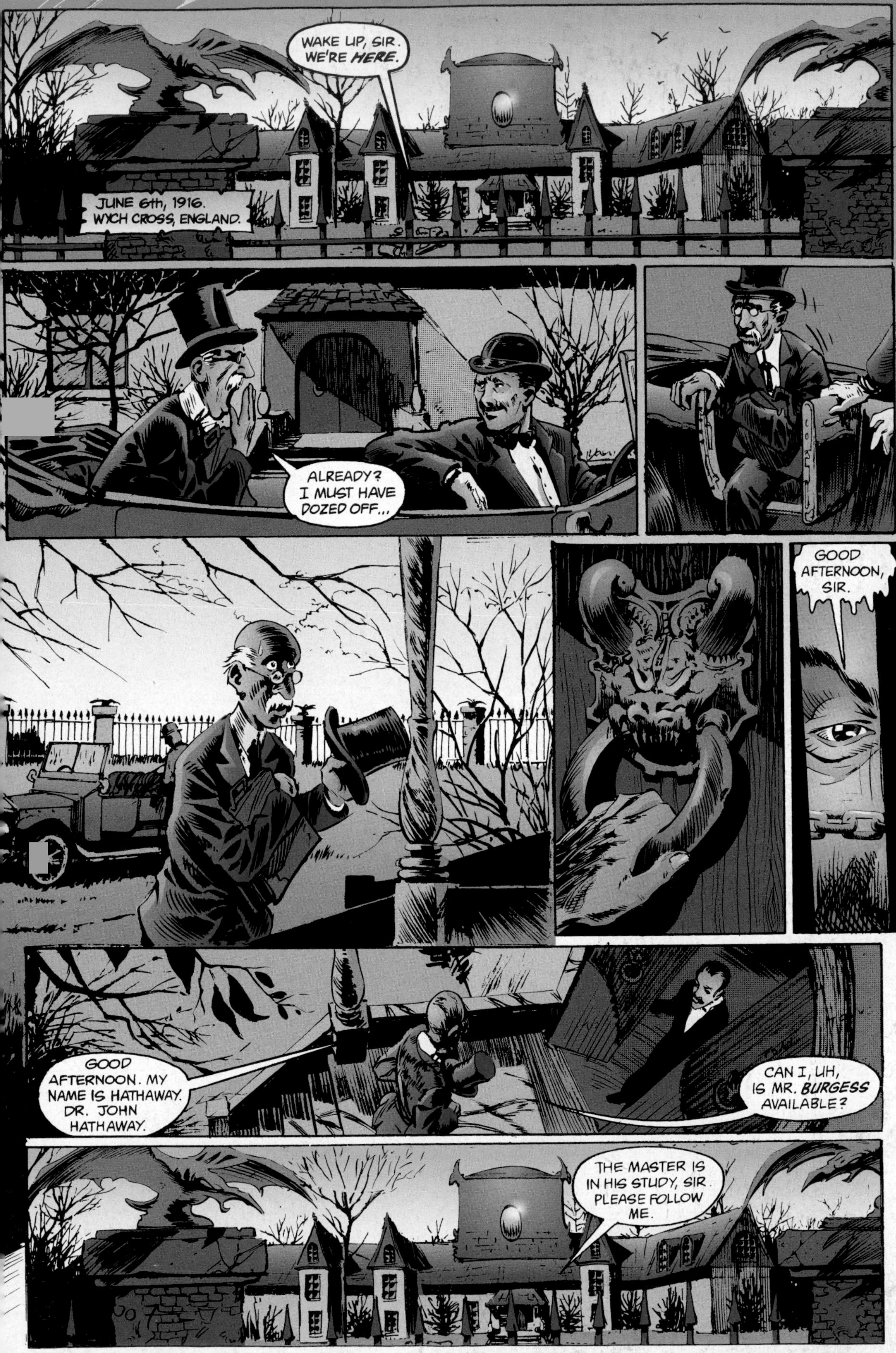
WAKE UP, SIR. WE'RE HERE.
JUNE 6th, 1916. WYCH CROSS, ENGLAND.
ALREADY? I MUST HAVE DOZED OFF...
GOOD AFTERNOON, SIR.
GOOD AFTERNOON. MY NAME IS HATHAWAY. DR. JOHN HATHAWAY.
CAN I, UH, IS MR. BURGESS AVAILABLE?
THE MASTER IS IN HIS STUDY, SIR. PLEASE FOLLOW ME.

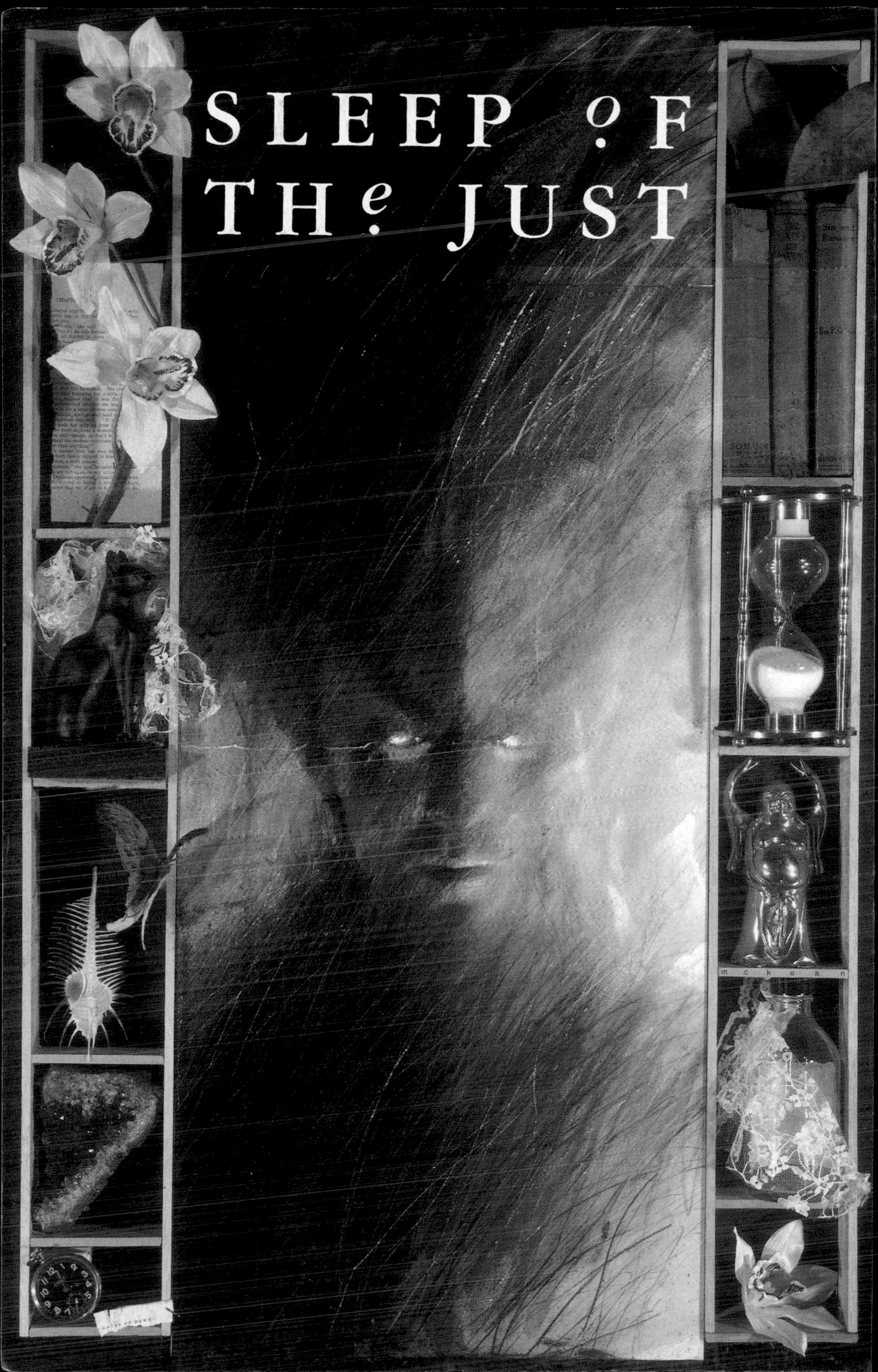
SLEEP OF
THE JUST
mckean

DƐDICATION

For Dave Dickson: oldest friend.

— Neil Gaiman

To my wife Kathy, my pal Tim, and

to everyone in jail.

— Sam Kieth

To friends and lovers. To Sam, Malcolm, and Neil;

may your talents never dim. You made working

on this book an indescribable pleasure. To Karen,

Tom and Art (without whom this book would

not have been possible), thanks for the time and

your super-human patience. Special thanks to

Beth, Matte, Sigal, the incomparable Barbara

Brandt (a.k.a. Victoria), Rachel, Sean F., Shawn S.,

Mimi, Gigi, Heather, Yann, Brantski, Mai Li,

Bernie Wrightson (for Cain and Abel) and,

as ever, to Cinnamon.

— Mike Dringenberg

To Little Malcolm.

— Malcolm Jones III

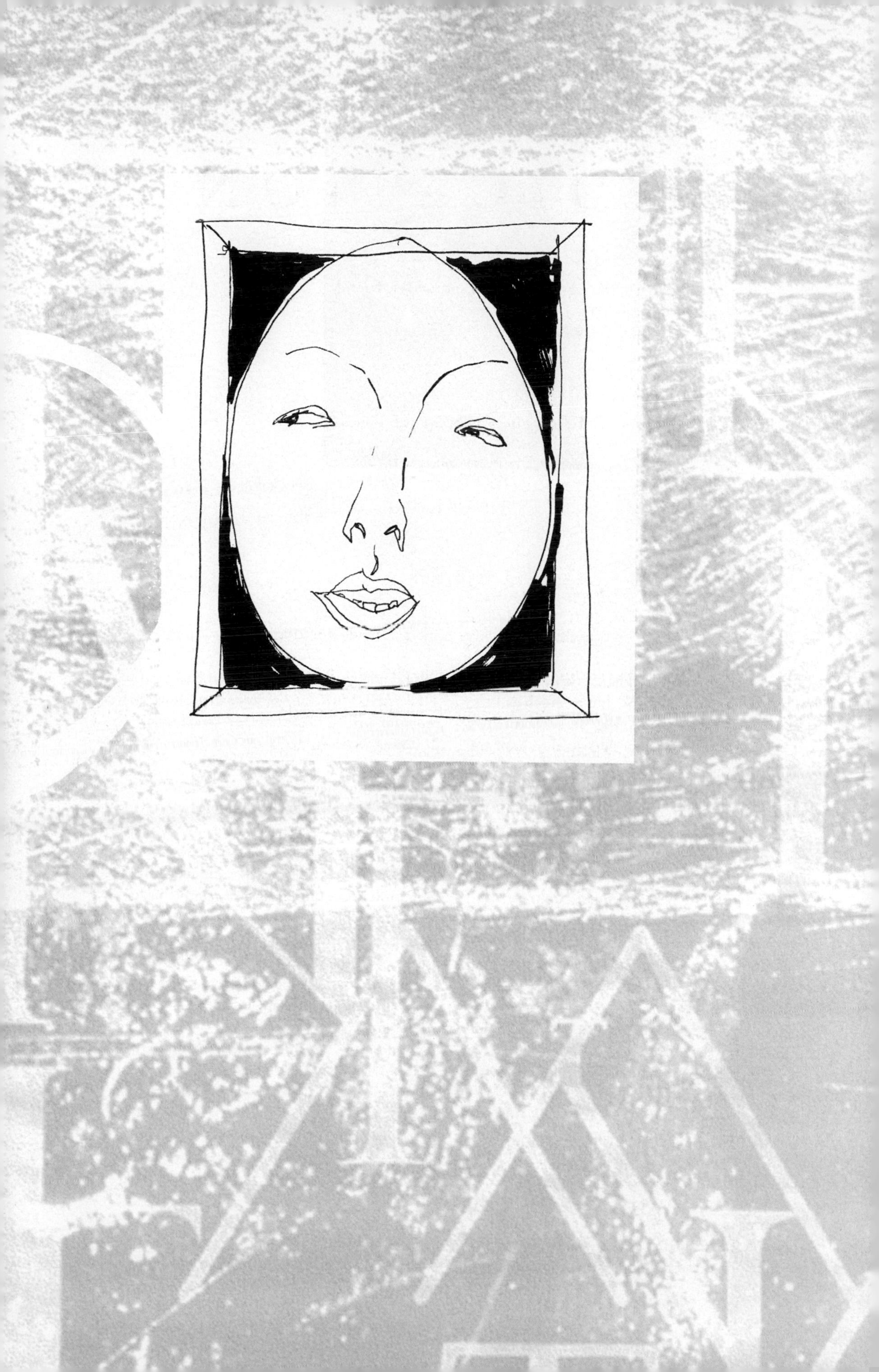

I knew early on that Neil had an ending for THE SANDMAN in sight, and as much as I would've loved for him to stay on indefinitely, it makes the only sense in the world to have a writer complete his work and see it through to its end, especially on a book that has achieved what it has. In the six years since its publication, THE SANDMAN has won more industry awards than any other comics series. It can also claim to its credit a World Fantasy Award for best short story ("A Midsummer Night's Dream") and an impressive list of quotes and introductions that includes Norman Mailer, Stephen King, and Tori Amos.

Neil's strength at creating singular and compelling characters is no more evident than in the Endless, who have proved to be just as popular as the Dream King himself. Each of the Endless will have their story told, which Neil and Chris Bachalo began with DEATH: THE HIGH COST OF LIVING, currently available in trade paperback, and continue in DEATH: THE TIME OF YOUR LIFE, the collection following in late 1996. Soon after the end of THE SANDMAN, its influence will be felt in THE DREAMING, a new monthly title that doesn't feature Morpheus or his siblings but highlights many of the super-

natural and horror characters that Neil used in THE SANDMAN. Just as important, it leaves room for writers to explore and create new dreaming territory, denizens, and dreamers alike.

It's been a poignant and strange feeling, writing this introduction to the first volume of the SANDMAN stories, now that the monthly series is winding down to its conclusion. It's interesting seeing the end of this complex and masterful epic saga while reexamining its more simple beginnings. Yet the foundation was strong in those early tales, firmly rooting the series and lining it with a potential that would sprout rich and fantastic worlds — a potential that took seed and blossomed into a phenomenon.

As I said in my opening, I never expected THE SANDMAN to become the landmark series that it has. But if there's anything to learn from one's expectations, it is that it's wonderful to be more than pleasantly surprised.

See you in your dreams,

Karen Berger
Executive Editor, Vertigo
January 1995

This first volume of the SANDMAN series is very much a work in progress; that of a talented writer who eventually honed and refined his skills and progressively developed his initial concept — a series about dreams: personal, nocturnal, and imaginary — and expanded it in ways that produced some classically modern and unforgettable stories.

Those stories to come — collected in THE DOLL'S HOUSE, SEASON OF MISTS, A GAME OF YOU, FABLES AND REFLECTIONS, BRIEF LIVES, WORLDS' END, the upcoming KINDLY ONES, and the final and still untitled volume — represent a wealth of narrative riches. There are the many tales that revolve around Morpheus — his dysfunctional pantheonic family the Endless, his lovers, his enemies, his kingdom, and his personal and far-reaching conflicts — though there are also a great number of tales where the Sandman is featured as a cameo player, or even sometimes not at all. It is in these stories (some of my favorites: "Soft Places," "Ramadan," "A Tale of Two Cities," and "Cerements"), where Neil's love of mythology, historical figures, and classical literature is woven into his own personal dream lore.

Like the landmark series before it — THE DARK KNIGHT RETURNS, WATCHMEN, and V FOR VENDETTA — THE SANDMAN's appeal has transcended the traditional comics market. And there's good reason for that. Ultimately, Neil Gaiman loves to tell stories, and the stories he tells are timeless, resonant, and universal. His work on THE SANDMAN appeals to people from different walks of life, attracting a constellation of readers who normally don't inhabit the same literary orbit. THE SANDMAN also has a disproportionate number of women who read the series, probably the most of any mainstream comic. In a medium that is still widely occupied by males, that in itself is a major achievement.

THE SANDMAN's popularity and success helped me to make an argument for forming a new imprint in 1992. I'd wanted to create a separate line of comics that would provide a place for the provocative and personal visions of comics' best talent. THE SANDMAN, along with a number of other highly regarded titles, formed the core of DC's newly-formed Vertigo imprint. THE SANDMAN's draw and reach both inside and outside of the comics market played an integral part in Vertigo's positioning and image.

known roles. Revenge, battle, quest fullfilled. Conventional stuff? Perhaps. On the other hand, the opening story also introduced a mysterious and powerful yet harebrained bunch of occultists and hangers-on, a bizarre "sleeping sickness" that affected seemingly random people — in an ambitious tale that took these characters through several decades of strange and tumultuous changes. Conventional stuff? Not at all. Still, in the hands of a different writer, the seeds that were planted in this fertile story ground could have borne a B-level fantasy/horror title.

As the series branched out in unexpected directions, THE SANDMAN developed into one of the most atypical books in comics. For me, the turning point was issue #8, "The Sound of Her Wings." It wasn't just the appearance of the adorable and ultimately pragmatic Death trying to cheer up her morose younger brother. Nor was it the fact that the too-familiar faces of DC characters were nowhere in sight. It was the element of humanity and interpersonal relationships that started coming through in Neil's work. Ironically enough, the catalyst for this emotional resonance was a character that traditionally represents the antithesis of all this.

The artists on PRELUDES AND NOCTURNES — Sam Kieth, Mike Dringenberg, and Malcolm Jones III — provided the right atmosphere for Morpheus' haunting origin story. Like Neil, they were relatively new to comics and were evolving their own distinctive styles. Sam did wonderful portrayals of Cain and Abel, and his visceral renditions of Hell and its gruesome inhabitants were truly horrifying. Mike, most notably, created the perky goth visual for Death, and his interpretation of Morpheus is probably one of the best ever done. Malcolm's illustrative line work brought a cohesive and definitive look to the overall series.

The covers for this first storyline (and all future ones) were illustrated, constructed and assembled by Dave McKean. An extraordinarily gifted artist at the ripe old age of 22, Dave was fresh out of art school when he worked on BLACK ORCHID. He's been most innovative on the SANDMAN covers, experimenting in different styles and techniques since the early portrait covers, complete with odd artifacts tucked away in the frames. Conceptually, Dave has been breaking with convention from the start. I still vividly remember his talking me into the idea of not having Sandman on every cover. (Believe me, it was a big deal back then.)

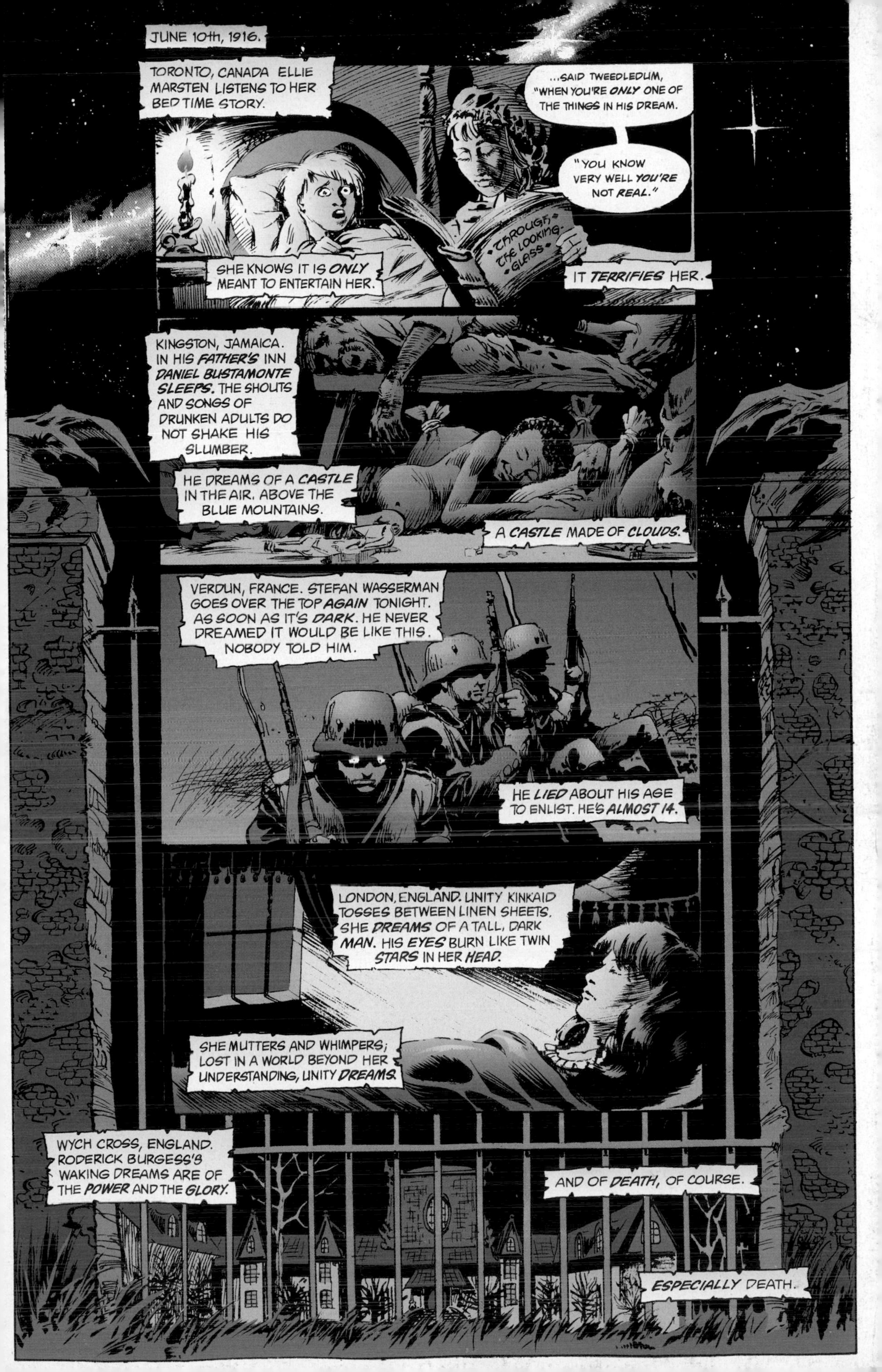
JUNE 10th, 1916.
TORONTO, CANADA ELLIE MARSTEN LISTENS TO HER BED TIME STORY.
...SAID TWEEDLEDUM, "WHEN YOU'RE ONLY ONE OF THE THINGS IN HIS DREAM.
"YOU KNOW VERY WELL YOU'RE NOT REAL."
THROUGH THE LOOKING GLASS
SHE KNOWS IT IS ONLY MEANT TO ENTERTAIN HER.
IT TERRIFIES HER.
KINGSTON, JAMAICA. IN HIS FATHER'S INN DANIEL BUSTAMONTE SLEEPS. THE SHOUTS AND SONGS OF DRUNKEN ADULTS DO NOT SHAKE HIS SLUMBER.
HE DREAMS OF A CASTLE IN THE AIR. ABOVE THE BLUE MOUNTAINS.
A CASTLE MADE OF CLOUDS.
VERDUN, FRANCE. STEFAN WASSERMAN GOES OVER THE TOP AGAIN TONIGHT. AS SOON AS IT'S DARK. HE NEVER DREAMED IT WOULD BE LIKE THIS. NOBODY TOLD HIM.
HE LIED ABOUT HIS AGE TO ENLIST. HE'S ALMOST 14.
LONDON, ENGLAND. UNITY KINKAID TOSSES BETWEEN LINEN SHEETS. SHE DREAMS OF A TALL, DARK MAN. HIS EYES BURN LIKE TWIN STARS IN HER HEAD.
SHE MUTTERS AND WHIMPERS; LOST IN A WORLD BEYOND HER UNDERSTANDING, UNITY DREAMS.
WYCH CROSS, ENGLAND. RODERICK BURGESS'S WAKING DREAMS ARE OF THE POWER AND THE GLORY.
AND OF DEATH, OF COURSE.
ESPECIALLY DEATH.

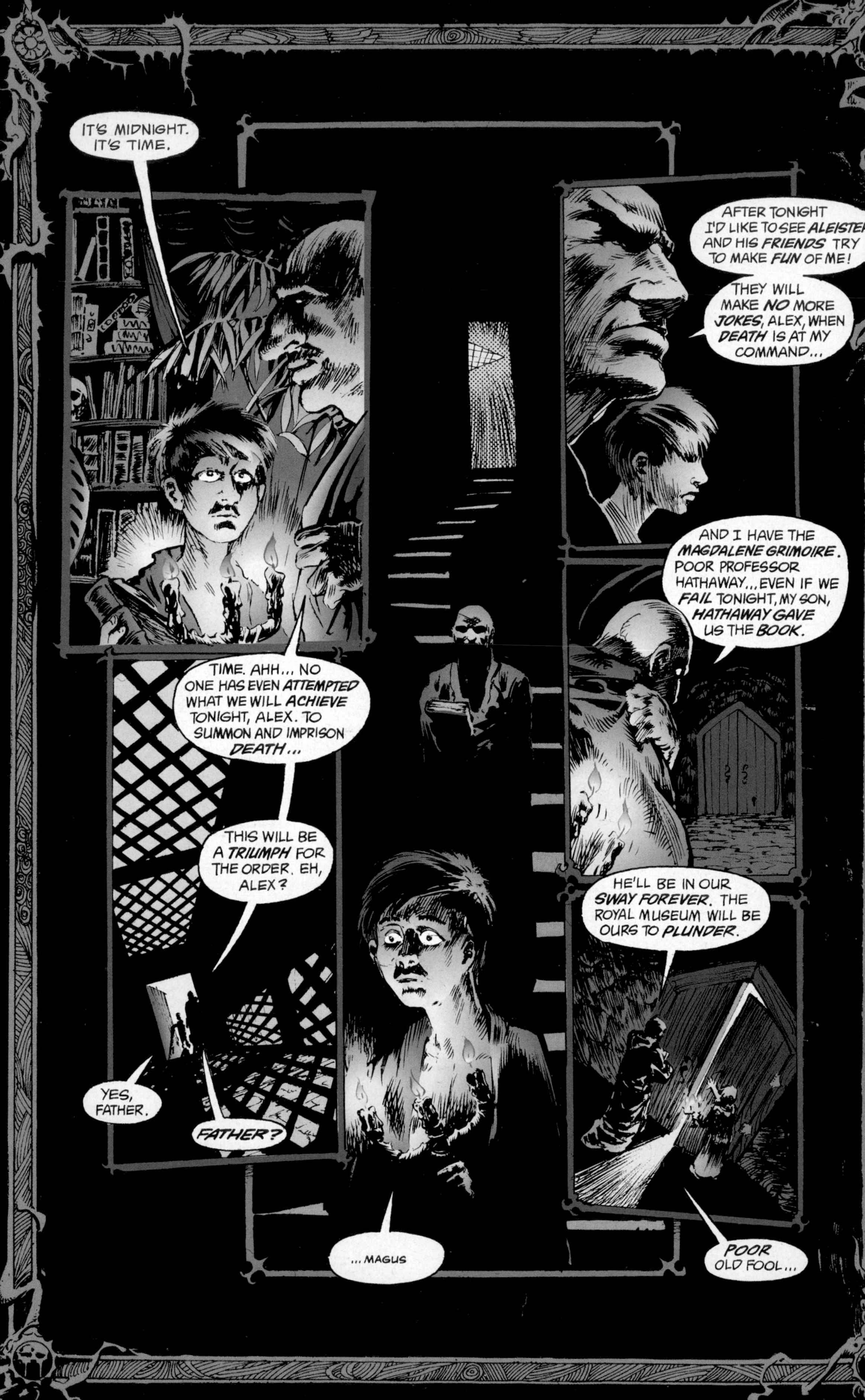
IT'S MIDNIGHT. IT'S TIME.
TIME. AHH... NO ONE HAS EVEN *ATTEMPTED* WHAT WE WILL *ACHIEVE* TONIGHT, ALEX. TO SUMMON AND IMPRISON *DEATH*...
THIS WILL BE A *TRIUMPH* FOR THE ORDER. EH, ALEX?
YES, FATHER.
FATHER?
... MAGUS
AFTER TONIGHT I'D LIKE TO SEE *ALEISTER* AND HIS *FRIENDS* TRY TO MAKE *FUN* OF ME!
THEY WILL MAKE *NO* MORE *JOKES*, ALEX, WHEN *DEATH* IS AT MY COMMAND...
AND I HAVE THE *MAGDALENE GRIMOIRE*. POOR PROFESSOR HATHAWAY... EVEN IF WE *FAIL* TONIGHT, MY SON, *HATHAWAY GAVE* US THE *BOOK*.
HE'LL BE IN OUR *SWAY FOREVER*. THE ROYAL MUSEUM WILL BE OURS TO *PLUNDER*.
POOR OLD FOOL...

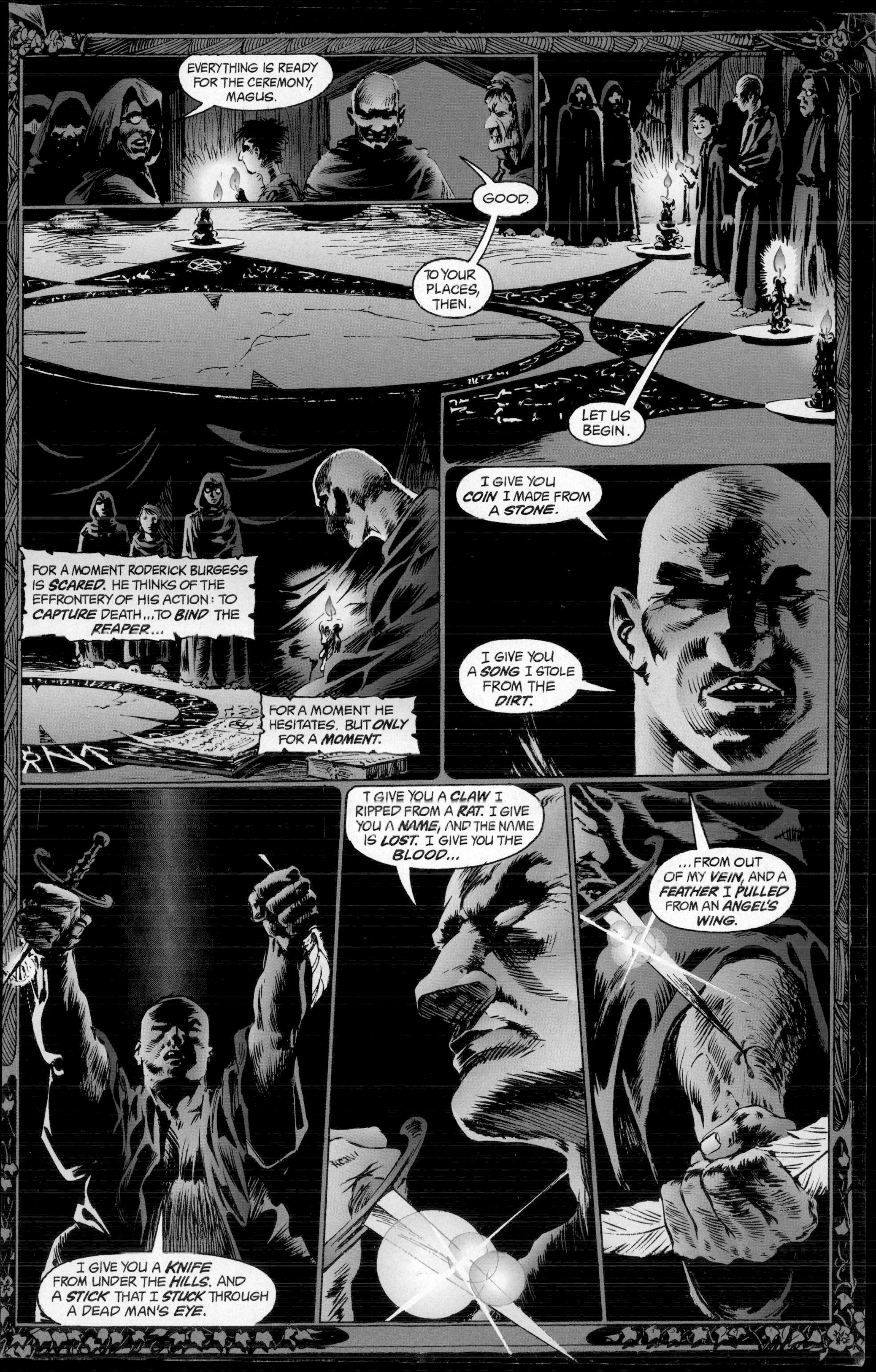
EVERYTHING IS READY FOR THE CEREMONY, MAGUS.
GOOD.
TO YOUR PLACES, THEN.
LET US BEGIN.
FOR A MOMENT RODERICK BURGESS IS SCARED. HE THINKS OF THE EFFRONTERY OF HIS ACTION: TO CAPTURE DEATH...TO BIND THE REAPER...
FOR A MOMENT HE HESITATES. BUT ONLY FOR A MOMENT.
I GIVE YOU COIN I MADE FROM A STONE.
I GIVE YOU A SONG I STOLE FROM THE DIRT.
I GIVE YOU A KNIFE FROM UNDER THE HILLS. AND A STICK THAT I STUCK THROUGH A DEAD MAN'S EYE.
I GIVE YOU A CLAW I RIPPED FROM A RAT. I GIVE YOU A NAME, AND THE NAME IS LOST. I GIVE YOU THE BLOOD...
...FROM OUT OF MY VEIN, AND A FEATHER I PULLED FROM AN ANGEL'S WING.

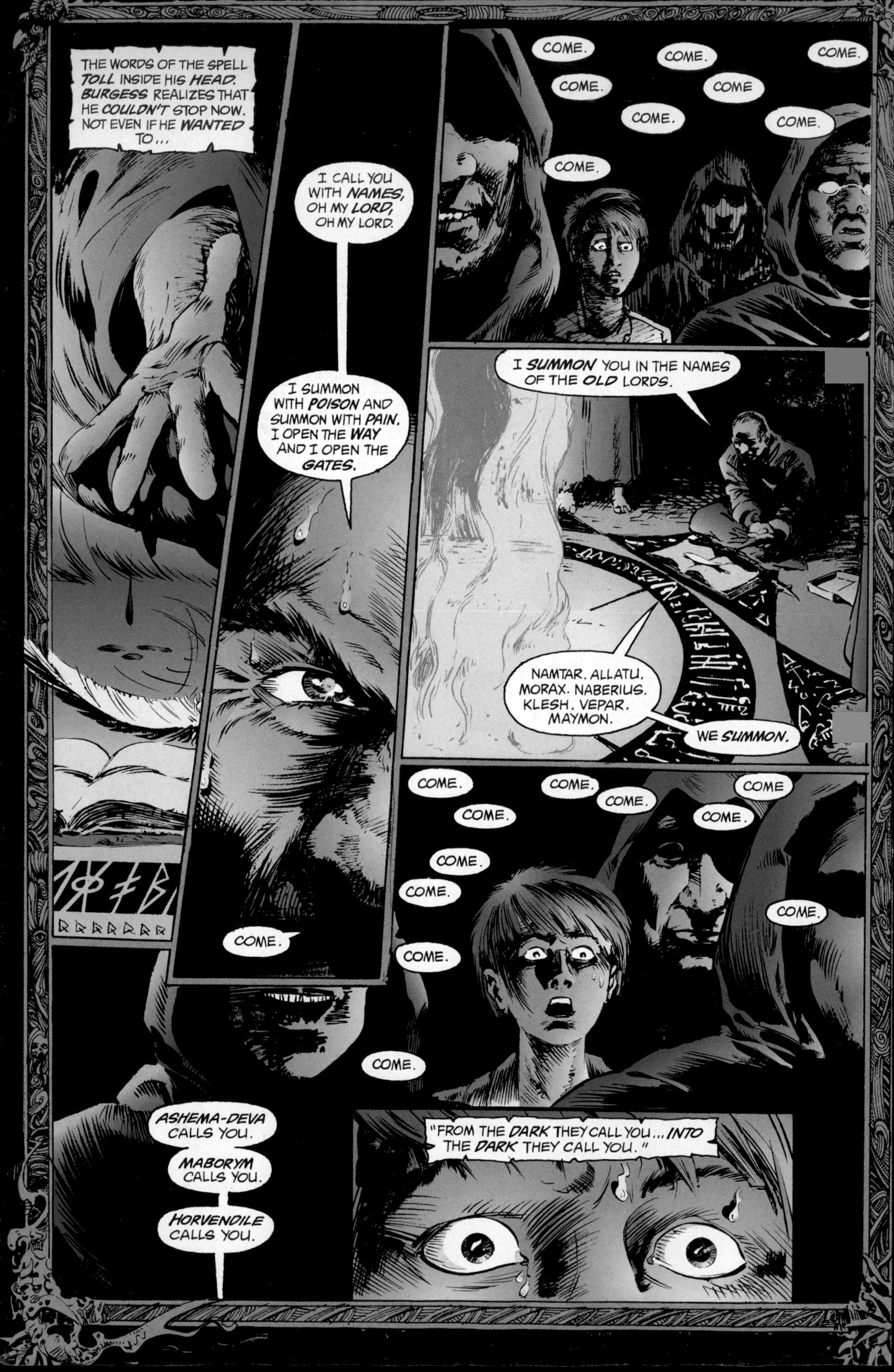
THE WORDS OF THE SPELL TOLL INSIDE HIS HEAD. BURGESS REALIZES THAT HE COULDN'T STOP NOW. NOT EVEN IF HE WANTED TO...
I CALL YOU WITH NAMES, OH MY LORD, OH MY LORD.
I SUMMON WITH POISON AND SUMMON WITH PAIN. I OPEN THE WAY AND I OPEN THE GATES.
COME.
COME.
COME.
COME.
COME.
COME
COME.
COME.
COME.
I SUMMON YOU IN THE NAMES OF THE OLD LORDS.
NAMTAR. ALLATU. MORAX. NABERIUS. KLESH. VEPAR. MAYMON.
WE SUMMON.
COME.
COME.
COME.
COME
COME.
COME.
COME.
COME.
COME.
COME.
COME.
ASHEMA-DEVA CALLS YOU.
MABORYM CALLS YOU.
HORVENDILE CALLS YOU.
"FROM THE DARK THEY CALL YOU... INTO THE DARK THEY CALL YOU."

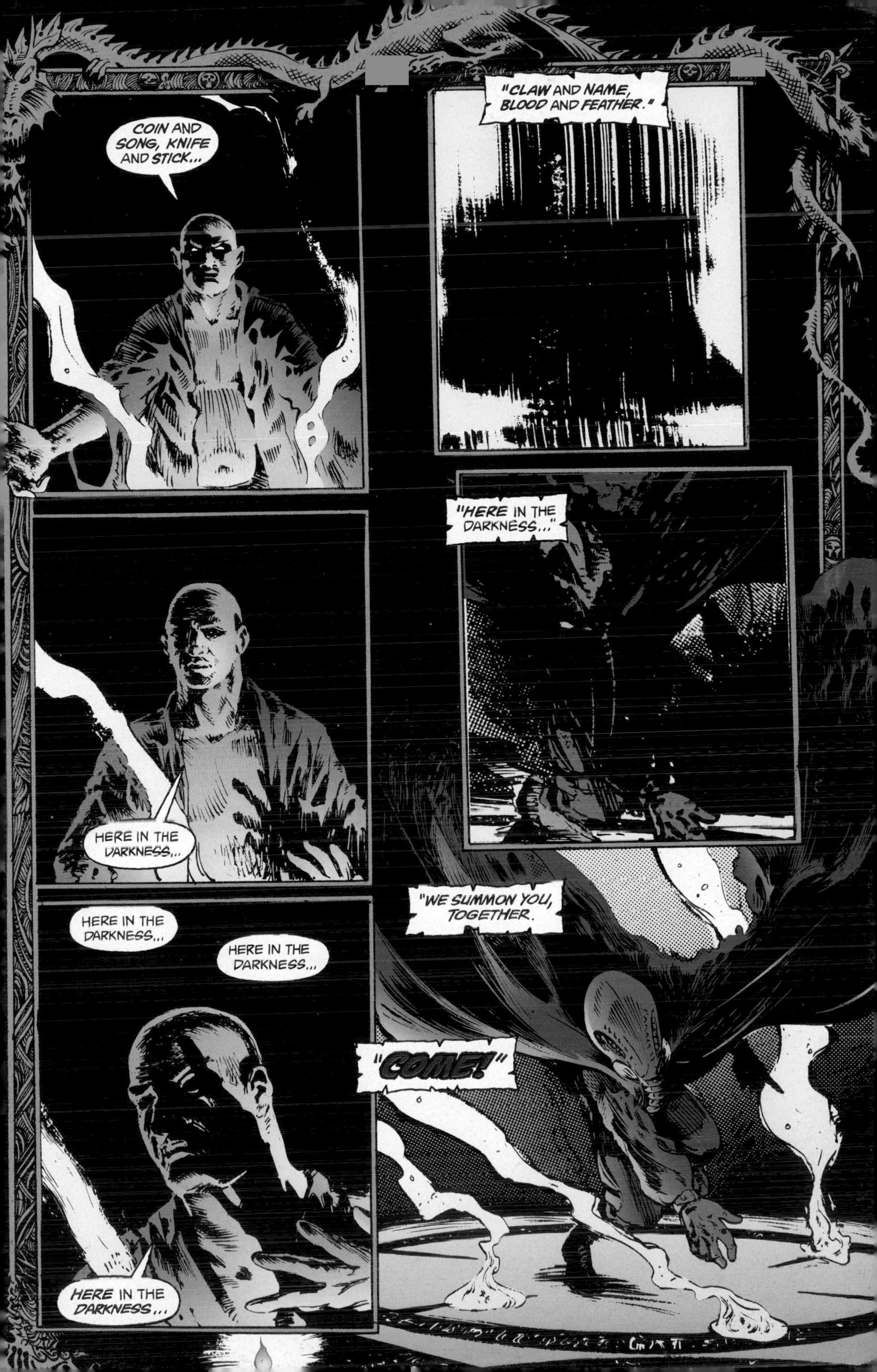
COIN AND SONG, KNIFE AND STICK...
"CLAW AND NAME, BLOOD AND FEATHER."
HERE IN THE DARKNESS...
"HERE IN THE DARKNESS..."
HERE IN THE DARKNESS...
HERE IN THE DARKNESS...
HERE IN THE DARKNESS...
"WE SUMMON YOU, TOGETHER.
"COME!"

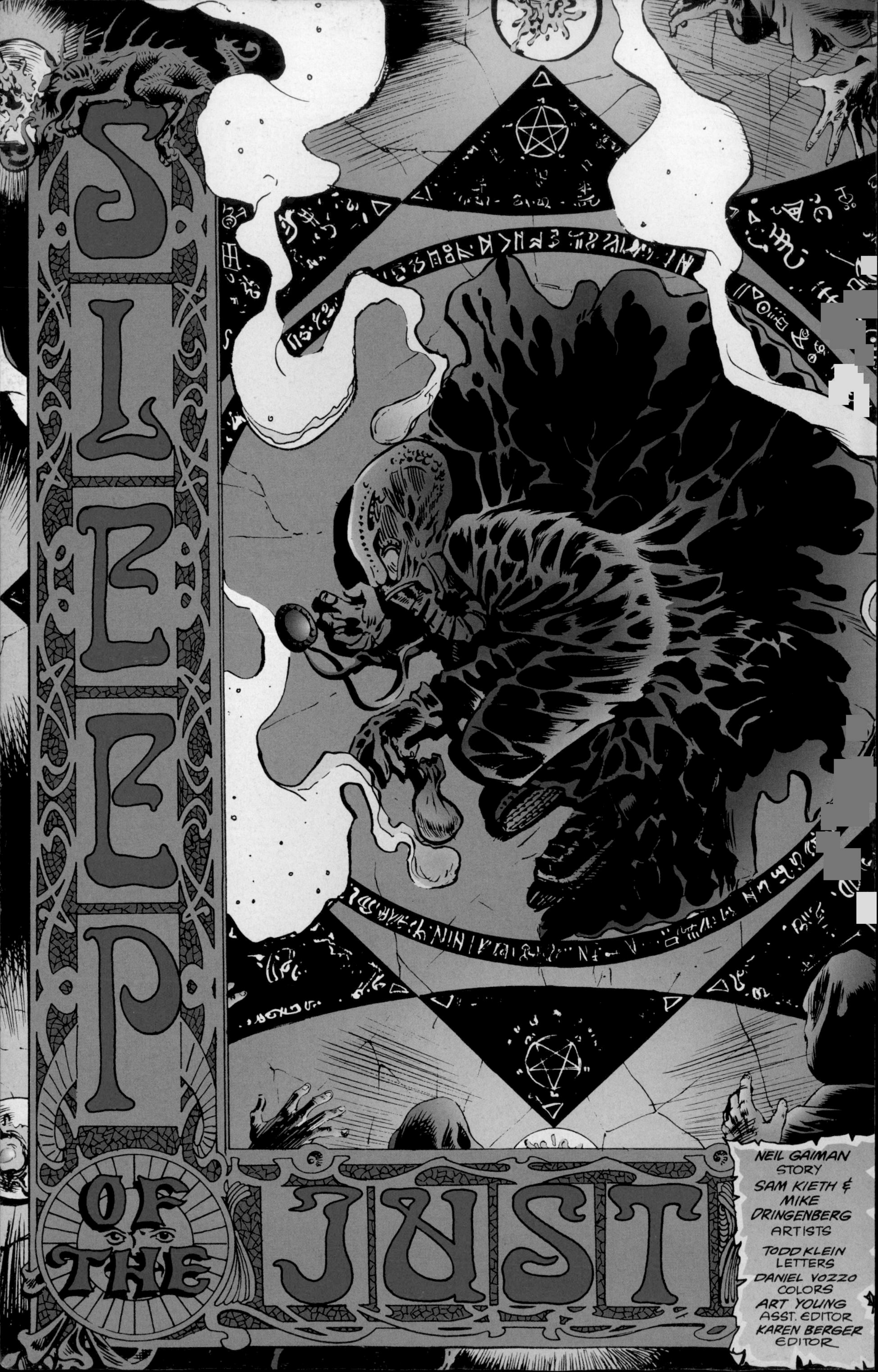
SLEEP OF THE JUST
NEIL GAIMAN STORY
SAM KIETH & MIKE DRINGENBERG ARTISTS
TODD KLEIN LETTERS
DANIEL VOZZO COLORS
ART YOUNG ASST. EDITOR
KAREN BERGER EDITOR

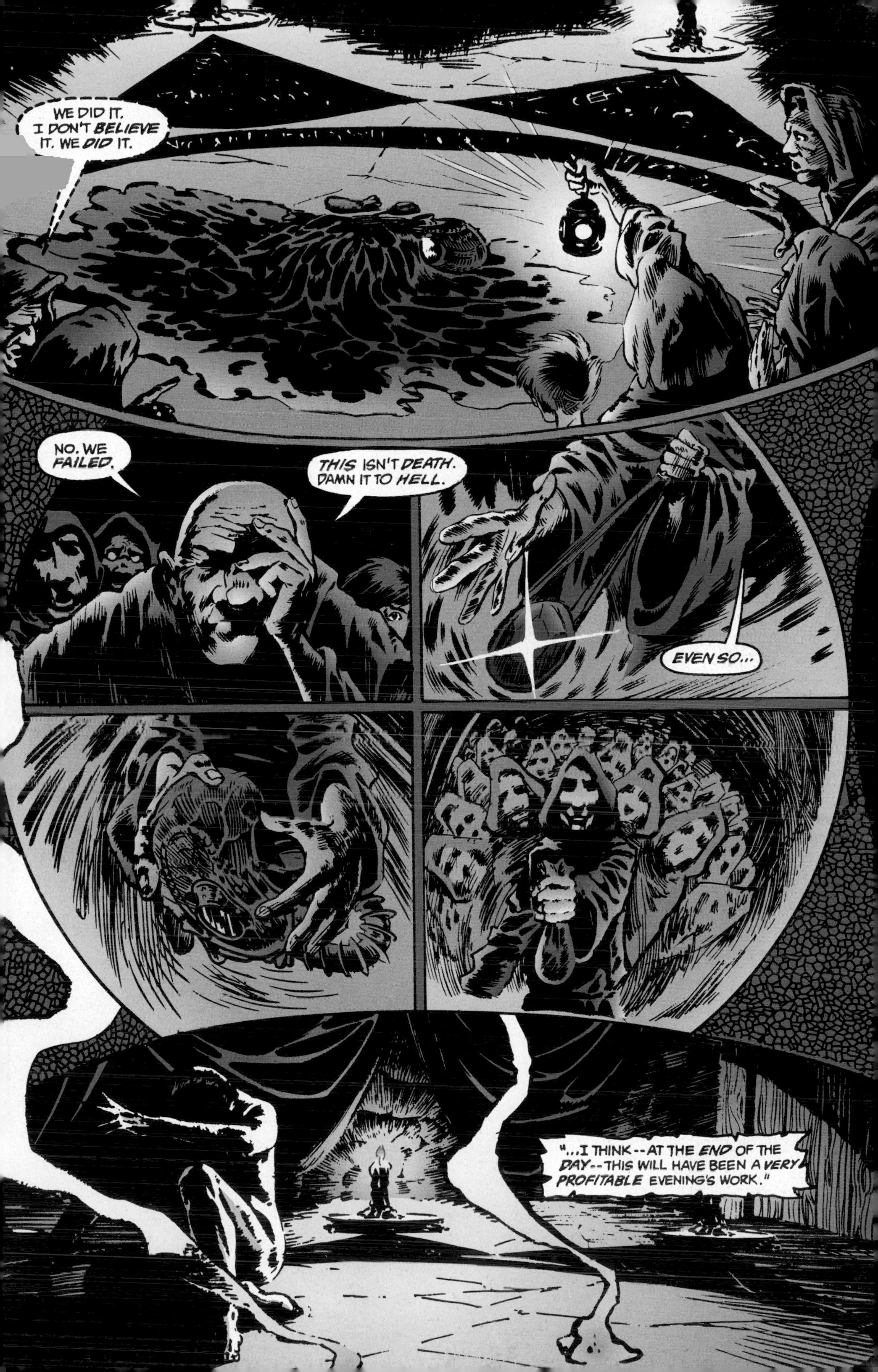
WE DID IT. I DON'T BELIEVE IT. WE DID IT.
NO. WE FAILED.
THIS ISN'T DEATH. DAMN IT TO HELL.
EVEN SO...
"...I THINK--AT THE END OF THE DAY--THIS WILL HAVE BEEN A VERY PROFITABLE EVENING'S WORK."

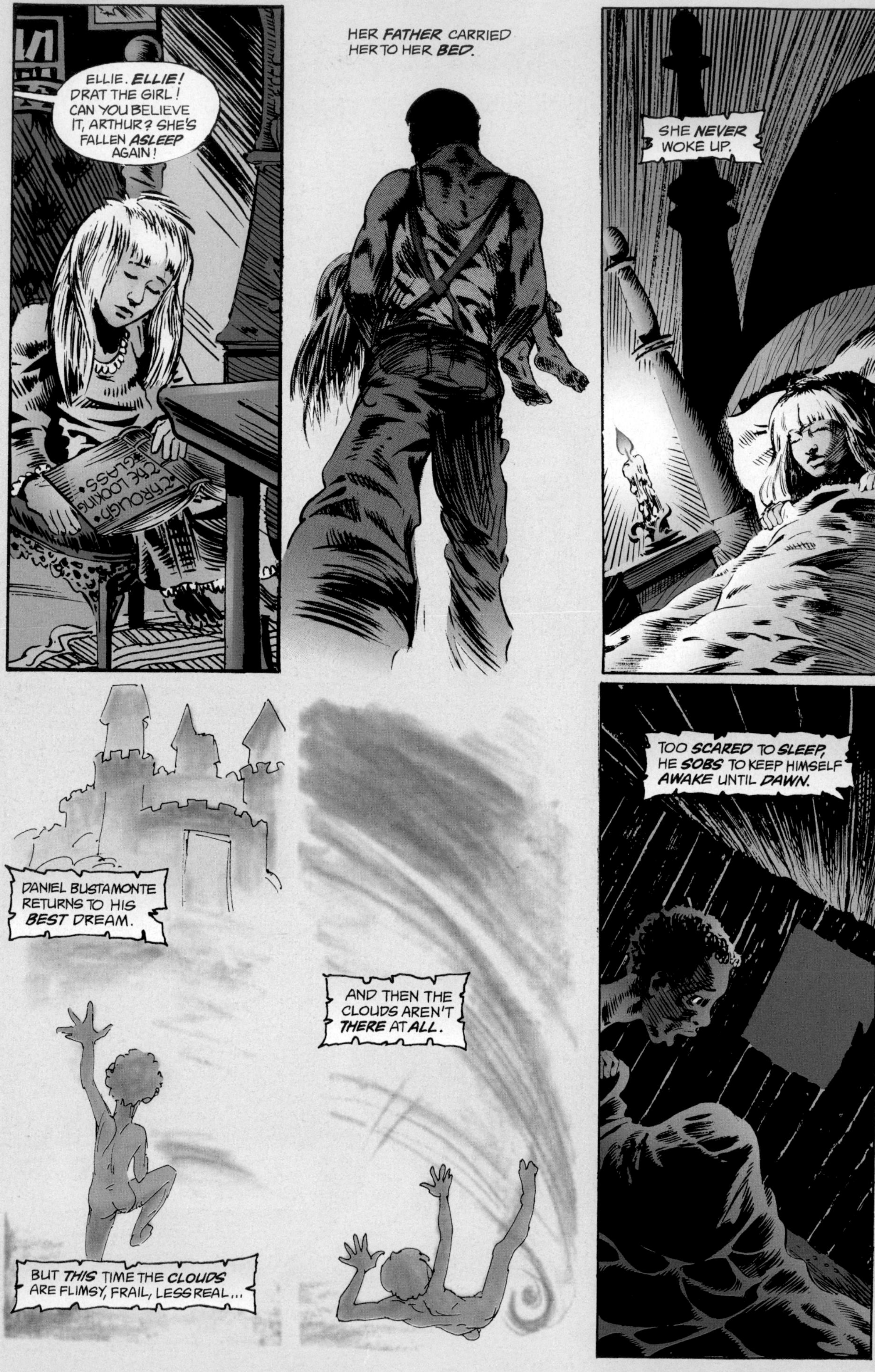

ELLIE. ELLIE! DRAT THE GIRL! CAN YOU BELIEVE IT, ARTHUR? SHE'S FALLEN ASLEEP AGAIN!
Through the Looking Glass
HER FATHER CARRIED HER TO HER BED.
SHE NEVER WOKE UP.
DANIEL BUSTAMONTE RETURNS TO HIS BEST DREAM.
BUT THIS TIME THE CLOUDS ARE FLIMSY, FRAIL, LESS REAL...
AND THEN THE CLOUDS AREN'T THERE AT ALL.
TOO SCARED TO SLEEP, HE SOBS TO KEEP HIMSELF AWAKE UNTIL DAWN.

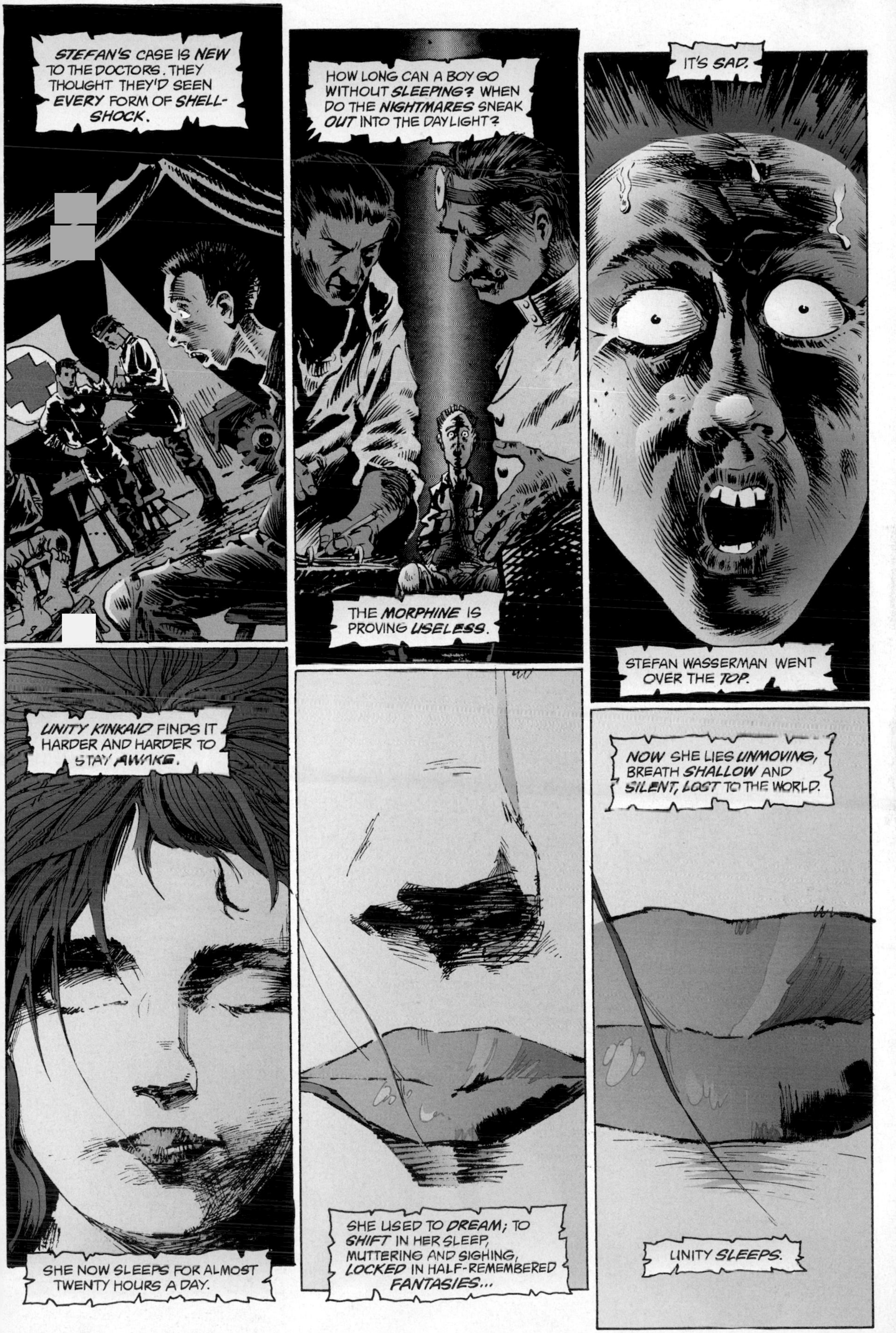
STEFAN'S CASE IS NEW TO THE DOCTORS. THEY THOUGHT THEY'D SEEN EVERY FORM OF SHELL-SHOCK.
HOW LONG CAN A BOY GO WITHOUT SLEEPING? WHEN DO THE NIGHTMARES SNEAK OUT INTO THE DAYLIGHT?
THE MORPHINE IS PROVING USELESS.
IT'S SAD.
STEFAN WASSERMAN WENT OVER THE TOP.
UNITY KINKAID FINDS IT HARDER AND HARDER TO STAY AWAKE.
SHE NOW SLEEPS FOR ALMOST TWENTY HOURS A DAY.
SHE USED TO DREAM; TO SHIFT IN HER SLEEP, MUTTERING AND SIGHING, LOCKED IN HALF-REMEMBERED FANTASIES...
NOW SHE LIES UNMOVING, BREATH SHALLOW AND SILENT, LOST TO THE WORLD.
UNITY SLEEPS.

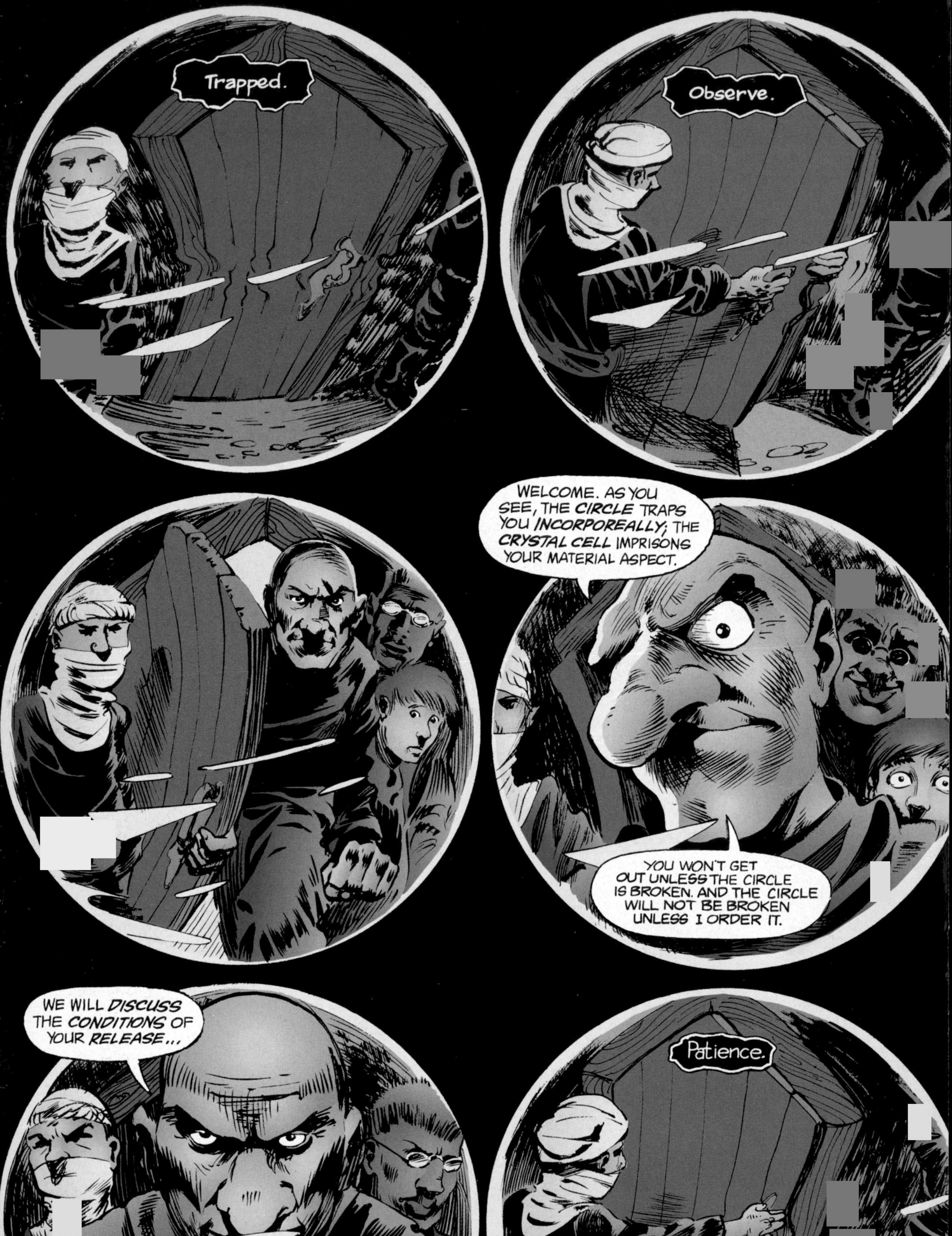

Trapped.
Observe.
WELCOME. AS YOU SEE, THE CIRCLE TRAPS YOU INCORPOREALLY; THE CRYSTAL CELL IMPRISONS YOUR MATERIAL ASPECT.
YOU WON'T GET OUT UNLESS THE CIRCLE IS BROKEN. AND THE CIRCLE WILL NOT BE BROKEN UNLESS I ORDER IT.
WE WILL DISCUSS THE CONDITIONS OF YOUR RELEASE...
Threats.
Patience.

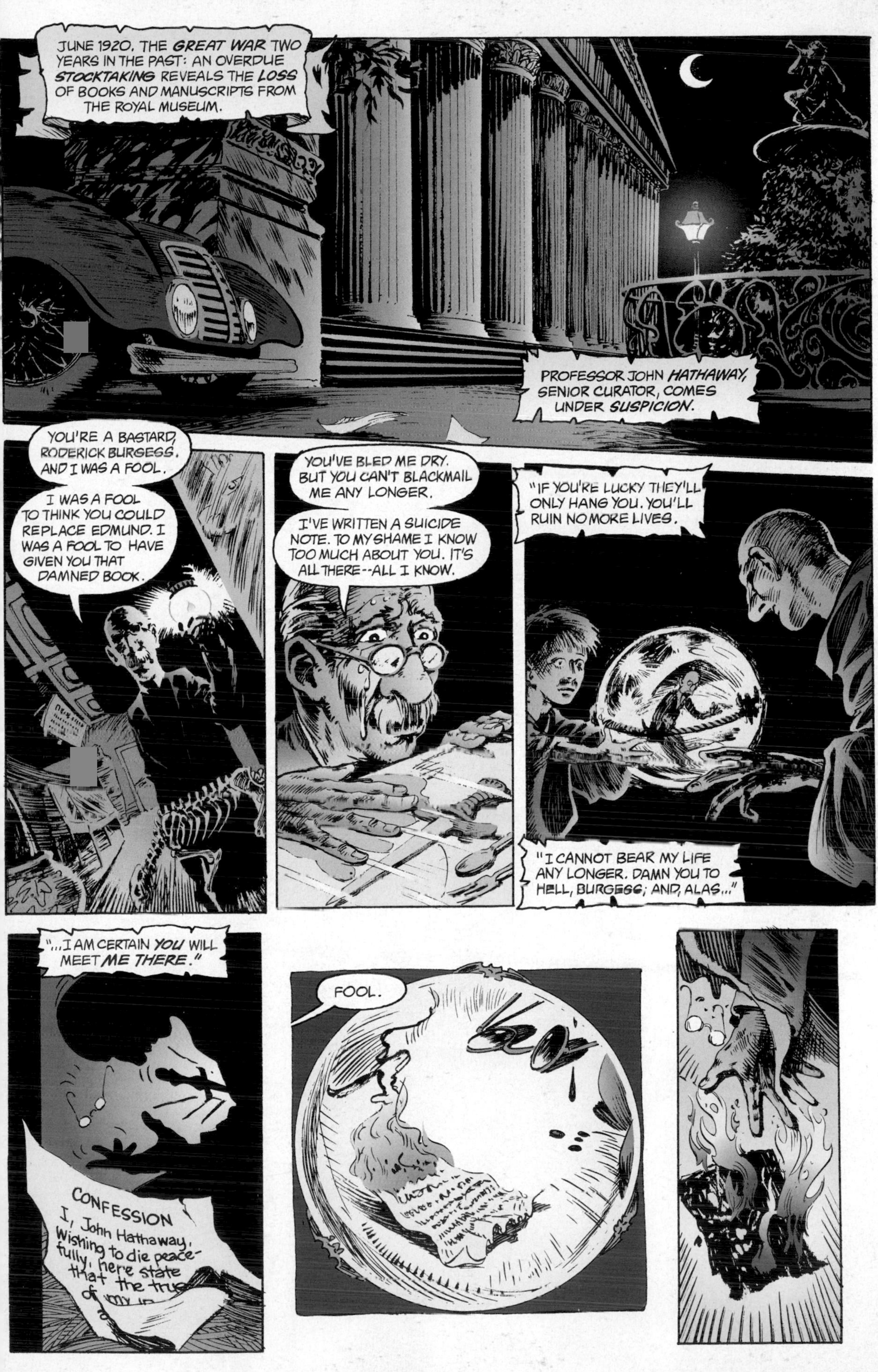
JUNE 1920. THE GREAT WAR TWO YEARS IN THE PAST: AN OVERDUE STOCKTAKING REVEALS THE LOSS OF BOOKS AND MANUSCRIPTS FROM THE ROYAL MUSEUM.
PROFESSOR JOHN HATHAWAY, SENIOR CURATOR, COMES UNDER SUSPICION.
YOU'RE A BASTARD, RODERICK BURGESS. AND I WAS A FOOL.
I WAS A FOOL TO THINK YOU COULD REPLACE EDMUND. I WAS A FOOL TO HAVE GIVEN YOU THAT DAMNED BOOK.
YOU'VE BLED ME DRY. BUT YOU CAN'T BLACKMAIL ME ANY LONGER.
I'VE WRITTEN A SUICIDE NOTE. TO MY SHAME I KNOW TOO MUCH ABOUT YOU. IT'S ALL THERE--ALL I KNOW.
"IF YOU'RE LUCKY THEY'LL ONLY HANG YOU. YOU'LL RUIN NO MORE LIVES.
"I CANNOT BEAR MY LIFE ANY LONGER. DAMN YOU TO HELL, BURGESS; AND, ALAS..."
"...I AM CERTAIN YOU WILL MEET ME THERE."
CONFESSION
I, John Hathaway, Wishing to die peace- fully, here state that the tru
FOOL.

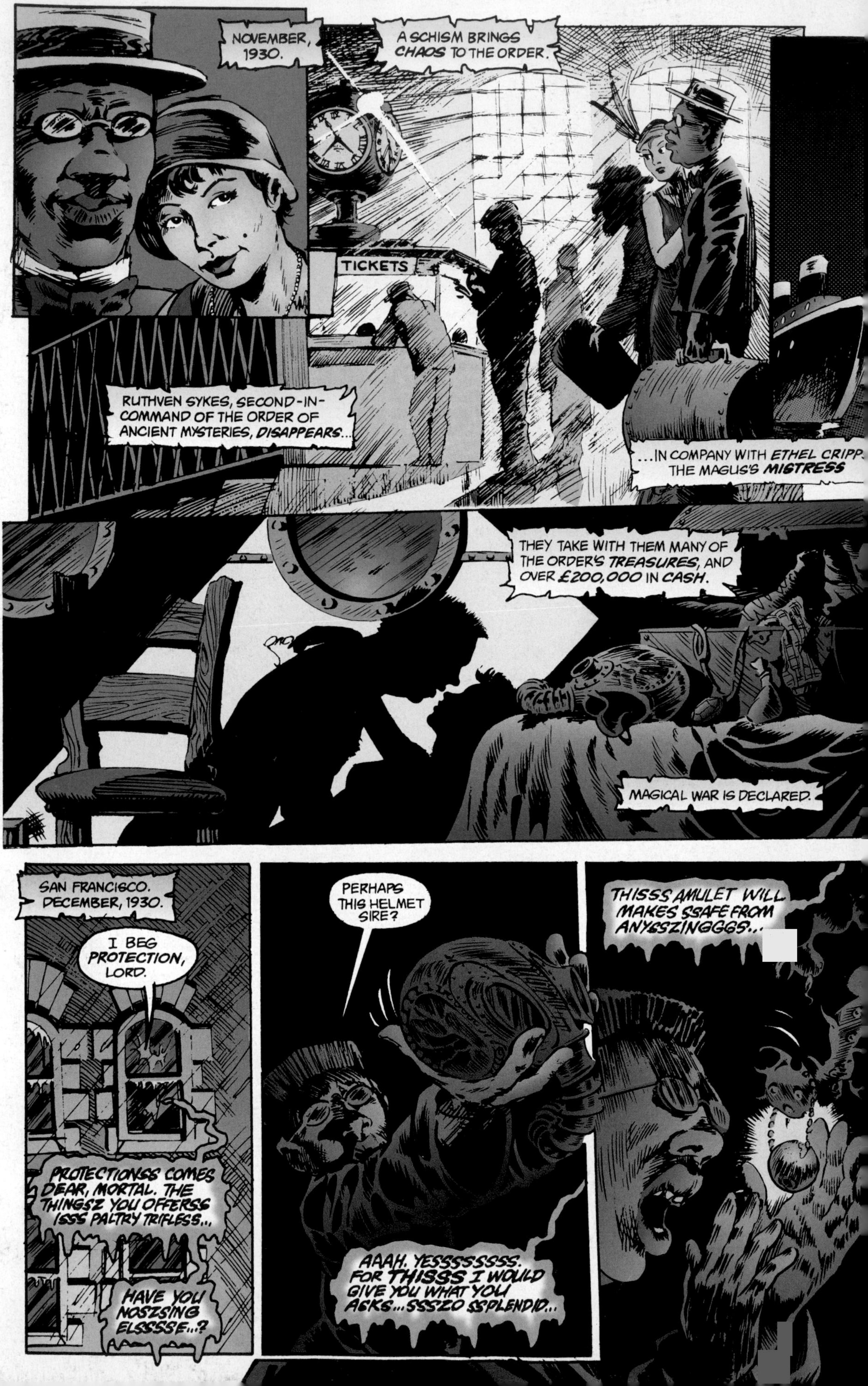
NOVEMBER, 1930.
A SCHISM BRINGS CHAOS TO THE ORDER.
TICKETS
RUTHVEN SYKES, SECOND-IN-COMMAND OF THE ORDER OF ANCIENT MYSTERIES, DISAPPEARS...
...IN COMPANY WITH ETHEL CRIPP THE MAGUS'S MISTRESS
THEY TAKE WITH THEM MANY OF THE ORDER'S TREASURES, AND OVER £200,000 IN CASH.
MAGICAL WAR IS DECLARED.
SAN FRANCISCO. DECEMBER, 1930.
I BEG PROTECTION, LORD.
PROTECTIONSS COMES DEAR, MORTAL. THE THINGSZ YOU OFFERSS ISSS PALTRY TRIFLESS...
HAVE YOU NOSZSING ELSSSSE..?
PERHAPS THIS HELMET SIRE?
AAAH. YESSSSSSSS. FOR THISSS I WOULD GIVE YOU WHAT YOU ASKS...SSSZO SSPLENDID...
THISSS AMULET WILL MAKES SSAFE FROM ANYSSZINGGGS...

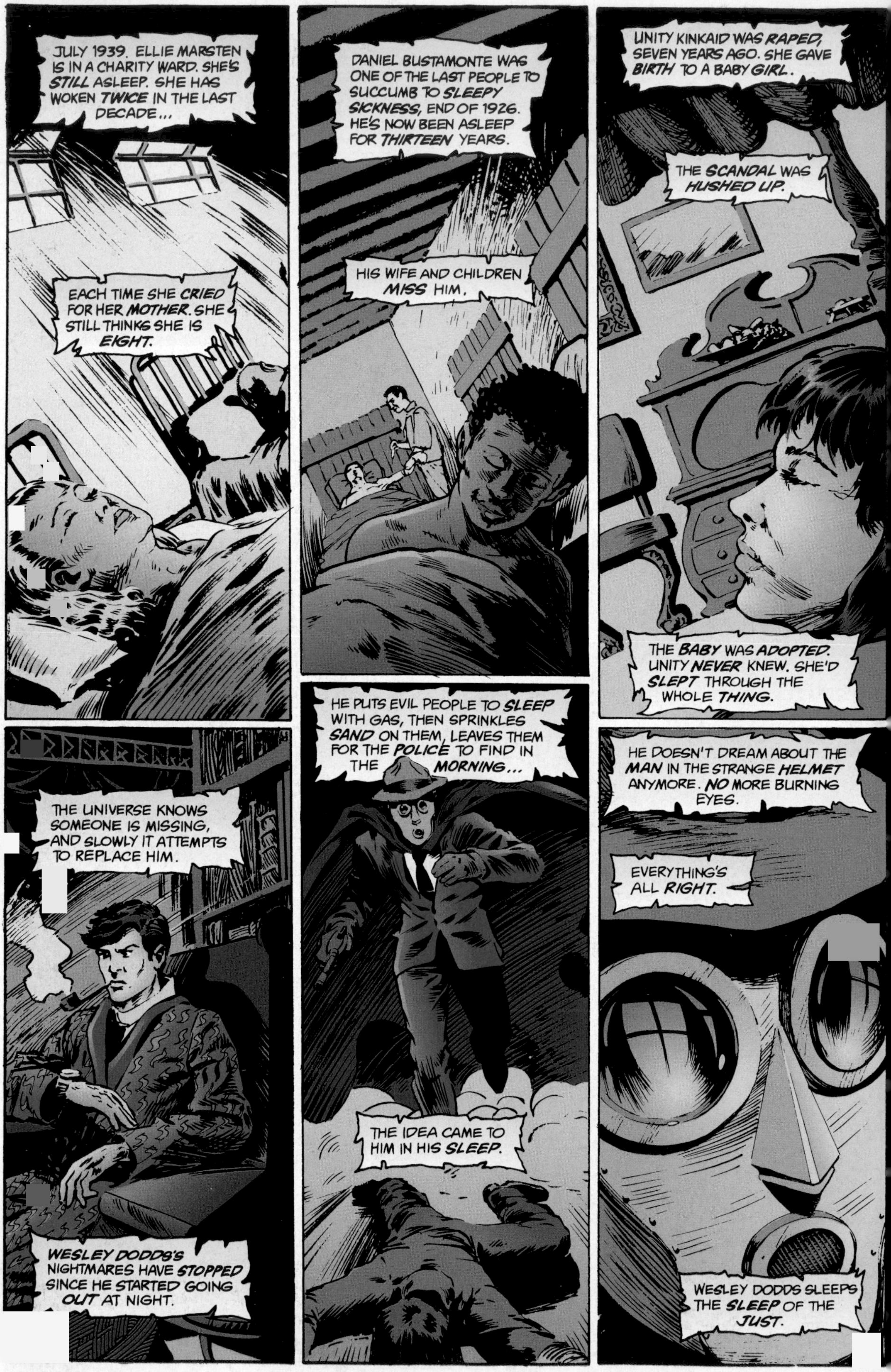
JULY 1939. ELLIE MARSTEN IS IN A CHARITY WARD. SHE'S STILL ASLEEP. SHE HAS WOKEN TWICE IN THE LAST DECADE...
EACH TIME SHE CRIED FOR HER MOTHER. SHE STILL THINKS SHE IS EIGHT.
DANIEL BUSTAMONTE WAS ONE OF THE LAST PEOPLE TO SUCCUMB TO SLEEPY SICKNESS, END OF 1926. HE'S NOW BEEN ASLEEP FOR THIRTEEN YEARS.
HIS WIFE AND CHILDREN MISS HIM.
UNITY KINKAID WAS RAPED, SEVEN YEARS AGO. SHE GAVE BIRTH TO A BABY GIRL.
THE SCANDAL WAS HUSHED UP.
THE BABY WAS ADOPTED. UNITY NEVER KNEW. SHE'D SLEPT THROUGH THE WHOLE THING.
THE UNIVERSE KNOWS SOMEONE IS MISSING, AND SLOWLY IT ATTEMPTS TO REPLACE HIM.
WESLEY DODDS'S NIGHTMARES HAVE STOPPED SINCE HE STARTED GOING OUT AT NIGHT.
HE PUTS EVIL PEOPLE TO SLEEP WITH GAS, THEN SPRINKLES SAND ON THEM, LEAVES THEM FOR THE POLICE TO FIND IN THE MORNING...
THE IDEA CAME TO HIM IN HIS SLEEP.
HE DOESN'T DREAM ABOUT THE MAN IN THE STRANGE HELMET ANYMORE. NO MORE BURNING EYES.
EVERYTHING'S ALL RIGHT.
WESLEY DODDS SLEEPS THE SLEEP OF THE JUST.

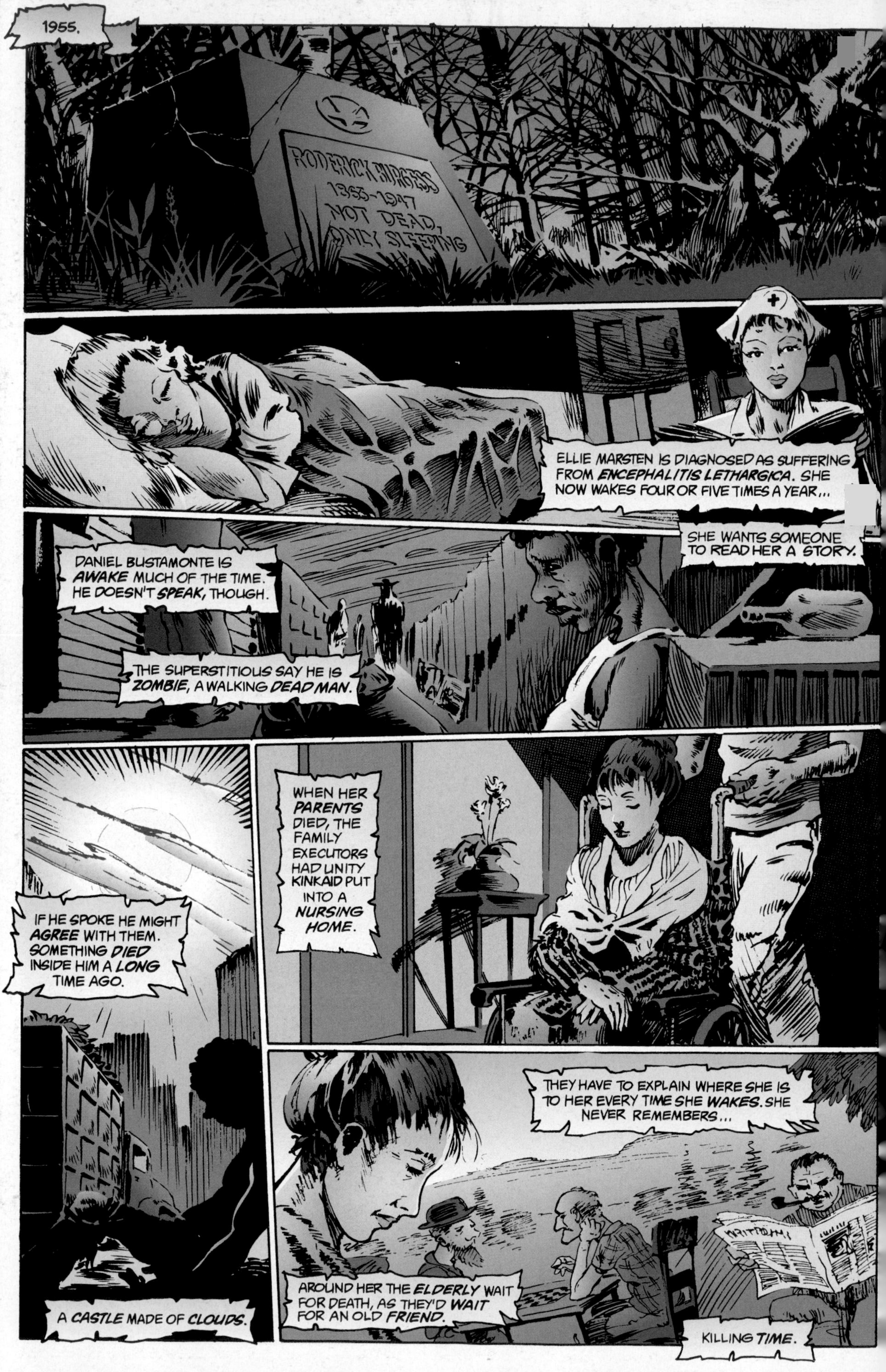
1955.
RODERICK BURGESS
1863-1947
NOT DEAD,
ONLY SLEEPING
ELLIE MARSTEN IS DIAGNOSED AS SUFFERING FROM ENCEPHALITIS LETHARGICA. SHE NOW WAKES FOUR OR FIVE TIMES A YEAR...
SHE WANTS SOMEONE TO READ HER A STORY.
DANIEL BUSTAMONTE IS AWAKE MUCH OF THE TIME. HE DOESN'T SPEAK, THOUGH.
THE SUPERSTITIOUS SAY HE IS ZOMBIE, A WALKING DEAD MAN.
IF HE SPOKE HE MIGHT AGREE WITH THEM. SOMETHING DIED INSIDE HIM A LONG TIME AGO.
A CASTLE MADE OF CLOUDS.
WHEN HER PARENTS DIED, THE FAMILY EXECUTORS HAD UNITY KINKAID PUT INTO A NURSING HOME.
THEY HAVE TO EXPLAIN WHERE SHE IS TO HER EVERY TIME SHE WAKES. SHE NEVER REMEMBERS...
AROUND HER THE ELDERLY WAIT FOR DEATH, AS THEY'D WAIT FOR AN OLD FRIEND.
KILLING TIME.

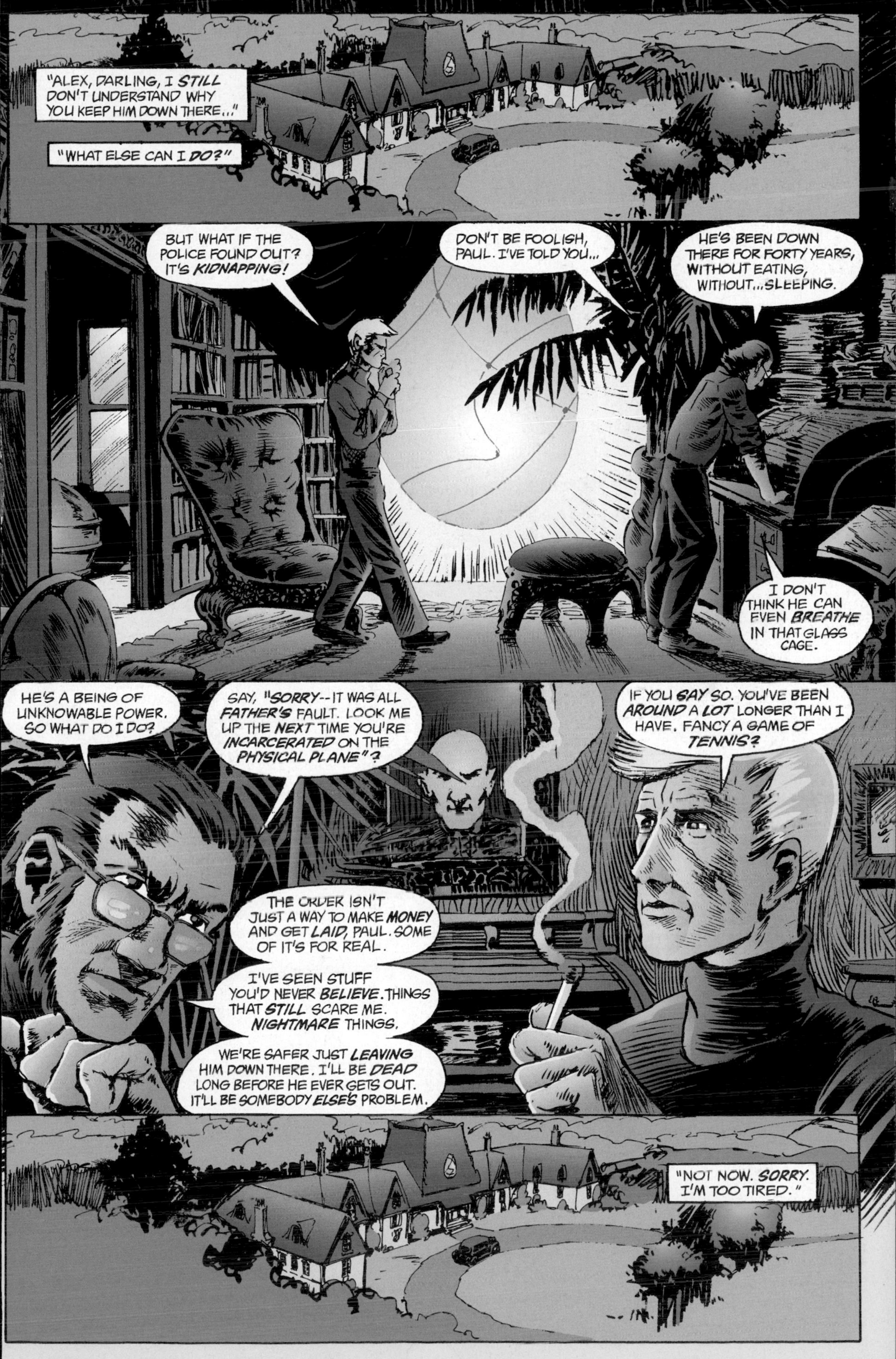
"ALEX, DARLING, I STILL DON'T UNDERSTAND WHY YOU KEEP HIM DOWN THERE..."
"WHAT ELSE CAN I DO?"
BUT WHAT IF THE POLICE FOUND OUT? IT'S KIDNAPPING!
DON'T BE FOOLISH, PAUL. I'VE TOLD YOU...
HE'S BEEN DOWN THERE FOR FORTY YEARS, WITHOUT EATING, WITHOUT...SLEEPING.
I DON'T THINK HE CAN EVEN BREATHE IN THAT GLASS CAGE.
HE'S A BEING OF UNKNOWABLE POWER. SO WHAT DO I DO?
SAY, "SORRY--IT WAS ALL FATHER'S FAULT. LOOK ME UP THE NEXT TIME YOU'RE INCARCERATED ON THE PHYSICAL PLANE"?
IF YOU SAY SO. YOU'VE BEEN AROUND A LOT LONGER THAN I HAVE. FANCY A GAME OF TENNIS?
THE ORDER ISN'T JUST A WAY TO MAKE MONEY AND GET LAID, PAUL. SOME OF IT'S FOR REAL.
I'VE SEEN STUFF YOU'D NEVER BELIEVE. THINGS THAT STILL SCARE ME. NIGHTMARE THINGS.
WE'RE SAFER JUST LEAVING HIM DOWN THERE. I'LL BE DEAD LONG BEFORE HE EVER GETS OUT. IT'LL BE SOMEBODY ELSE'S PROBLEM.
"NOT NOW. SORRY. I'M TOO TIRED."

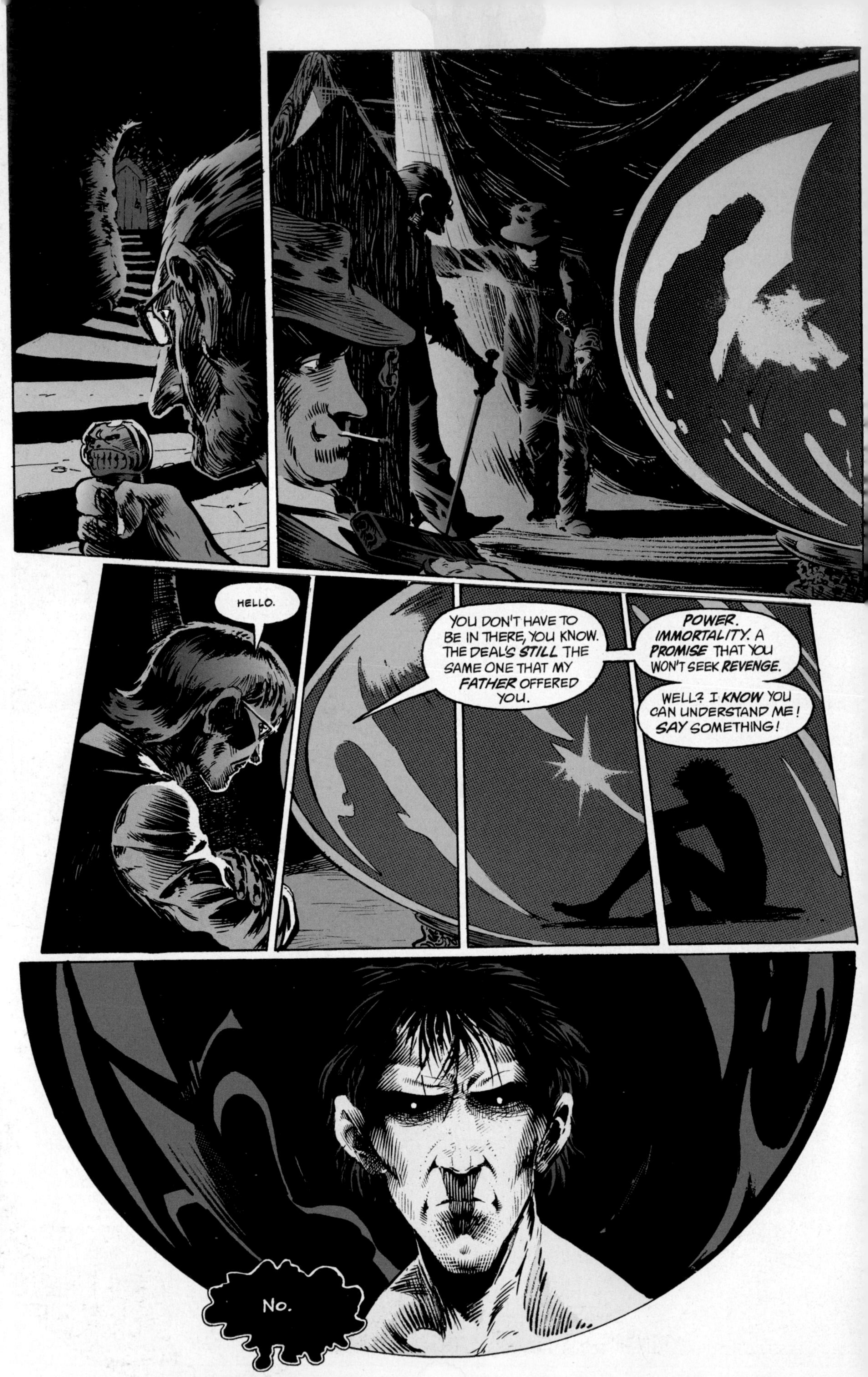
HELLO.
YOU DON'T HAVE TO BE IN THERE, YOU KNOW. THE DEAL'S *STILL* THE SAME ONE THAT MY *FATHER* OFFERED YOU.
POWER. IMMORTALITY. A *PROMISE* THAT YOU WON'T SEEK *REVENGE*.
WELL? I *KNOW* YOU CAN UNDERSTAND ME! *SAY* SOMETHING!
No.

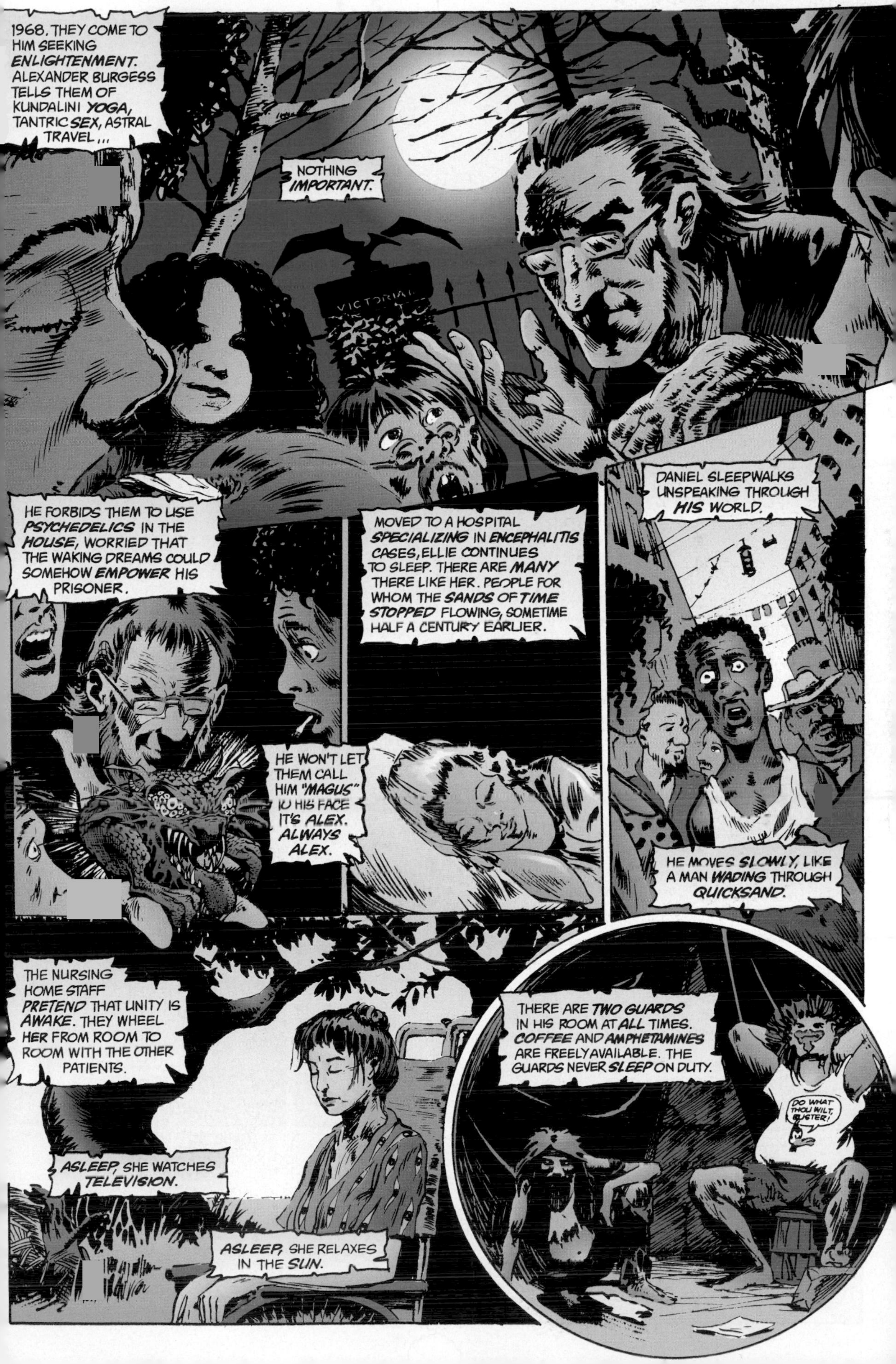
1968. THEY COME TO HIM SEEKING ENLIGHTENMENT. ALEXANDER BURGESS TELLS THEM OF KUNDALINI YOGA, TANTRIC SEX, ASTRAL TRAVEL...
NOTHING IMPORTANT.
HE FORBIDS THEM TO USE PSYCHEDELICS IN THE HOUSE, WORRIED THAT THE WAKING DREAMS COULD SOMEHOW EMPOWER HIS PRISONER.
HE WON'T LET THEM CALL HIM "MAGUS" TO HIS FACE. IT'S ALEX. ALWAYS ALEX.
MOVED TO A HOSPITAL SPECIALIZING IN ENCEPHALITIS CASES, ELLIE CONTINUES TO SLEEP. THERE ARE MANY THERE LIKE HER. PEOPLE FOR WHOM THE SANDS OF TIME STOPPED FLOWING, SOMETIME HALF A CENTURY EARLIER.
DANIEL SLEEPWALKS UNSPEAKING THROUGH HIS WORLD.
HE MOVES SLOWLY, LIKE A MAN WADING THROUGH QUICKSAND.
THE NURSING HOME STAFF PRETEND THAT UNITY IS AWAKE. THEY WHEEL HER FROM ROOM TO ROOM WITH THE OTHER PATIENTS.
ASLEEP, SHE WATCHES TELEVISION.
ASLEEP, SHE RELAXES IN THE SUN.
THERE ARE TWO GUARDS IN HIS ROOM AT ALL TIMES. COFFEE AND AMPHETAMINES ARE FREELY AVAILABLE. THE GUARDS NEVER SLEEP ON DUTY.
DO WHAT THOU WILT, BUSTER!

1970.

THE YOUNG PEOPLE HAVE DRIFTED AWAY.

ALEX HANDS OVER THE REINS OF ORGANIZATION TO *PAUL McGUIRE*, HIS LONGTIME PERSONAL *ASSISTANT*.

HE SEES THE ORDER OF ANCIENT MYSTERIES AS AN *EFFICIENT* METHOD OF PARTING THE *CREDULOUS* FROM THEIR *CASH*.

RODERICK BURGESS 1363 - 1947 NOT DEAD, ONLY SLEEPING

PAUL DOESN'T *BELIEVE* IN MAGIC.

ALEX SPENDS MOST OF HIS TIME IN HIS *STUDY*. HE WROTE A *MEMOIR* ABOUT HIS FATHER; WRITES LETTERS TO *NEWSPAPERS* DEFENDING HIS FATHER'S REPUTATION; IS EDITING A VOLUME OF HIS FATHER'S *LETTERS*.

ONE NIGHT HE *SLASHED* HIS FATHER'S PORTRAIT WITH A *KNIFE*.

ALEX WILL NO LONGER *READ* BOOKS ON *MAGIC*. EXCEPT FOR ONE. THE *LIBER FULVARUM PAGINARUM*. AND HE ONLY READS *ONE* PAGE OF THAT BOOK....

here is laid thee kinge of

OVER...

AND OVER...

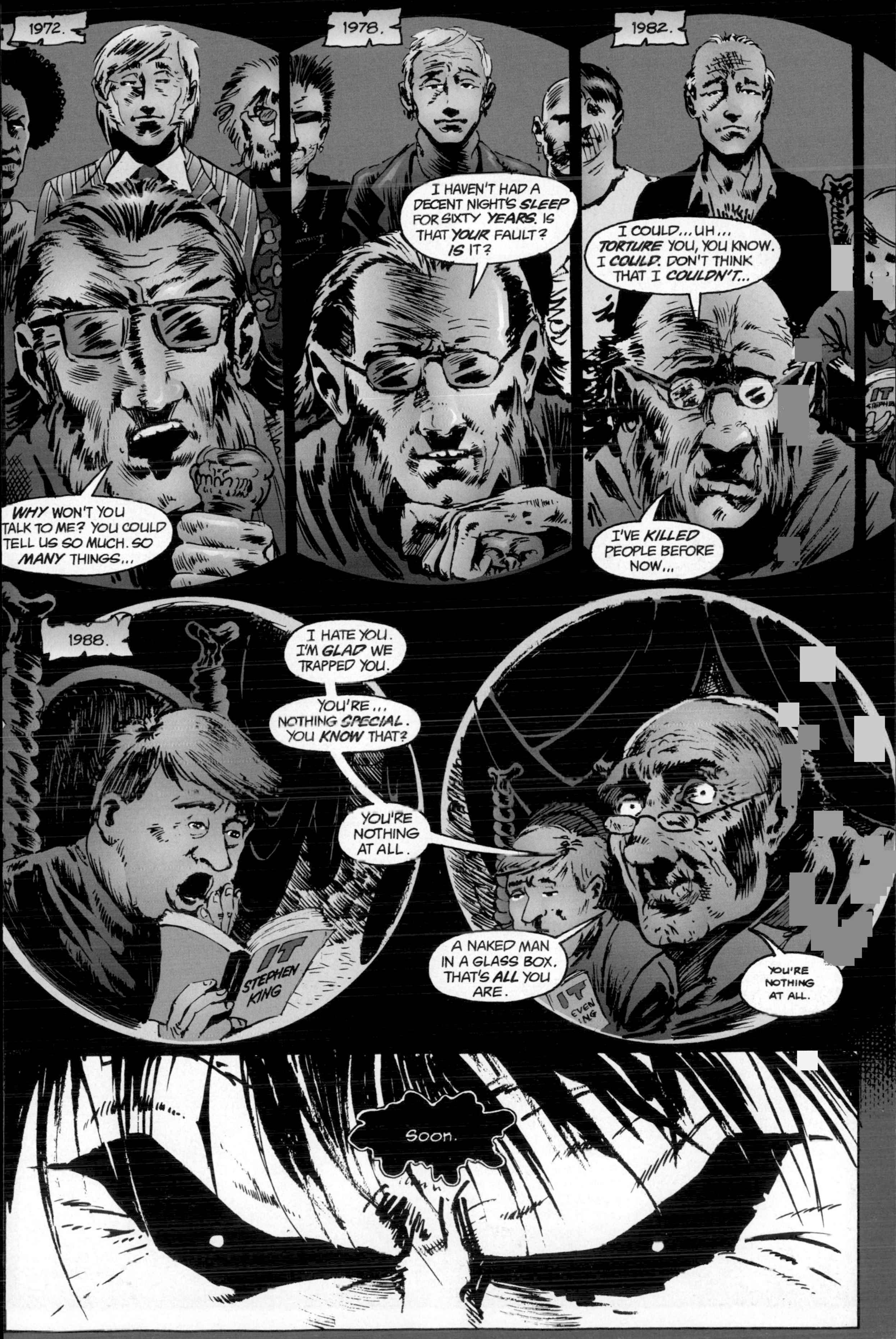
1972.
WHY WON'T YOU TALK TO ME? YOU COULD TELL US SO MUCH. SO MANY THINGS...
1978.
I HAVEN'T HAD A DECENT NIGHT'S SLEEP FOR SIXTY YEARS. IS THAT YOUR FAULT? IS IT?
1982.
I COULD... UH... TORTURE YOU, YOU KNOW. I COULD. DON'T THINK THAT I COULDN'T...
I'VE KILLED PEOPLE BEFORE NOW...
1988.
I HATE YOU. I'M GLAD WE TRAPPED YOU.
YOU'RE... NOTHING SPECIAL. YOU KNOW THAT?
YOU'RE NOTHING AT ALL.
IT STEPHEN KING
A NAKED MAN IN A GLASS BOX. THAT'S ALL YOU ARE.
YOU'RE NOTHING AT ALL.
Soon.

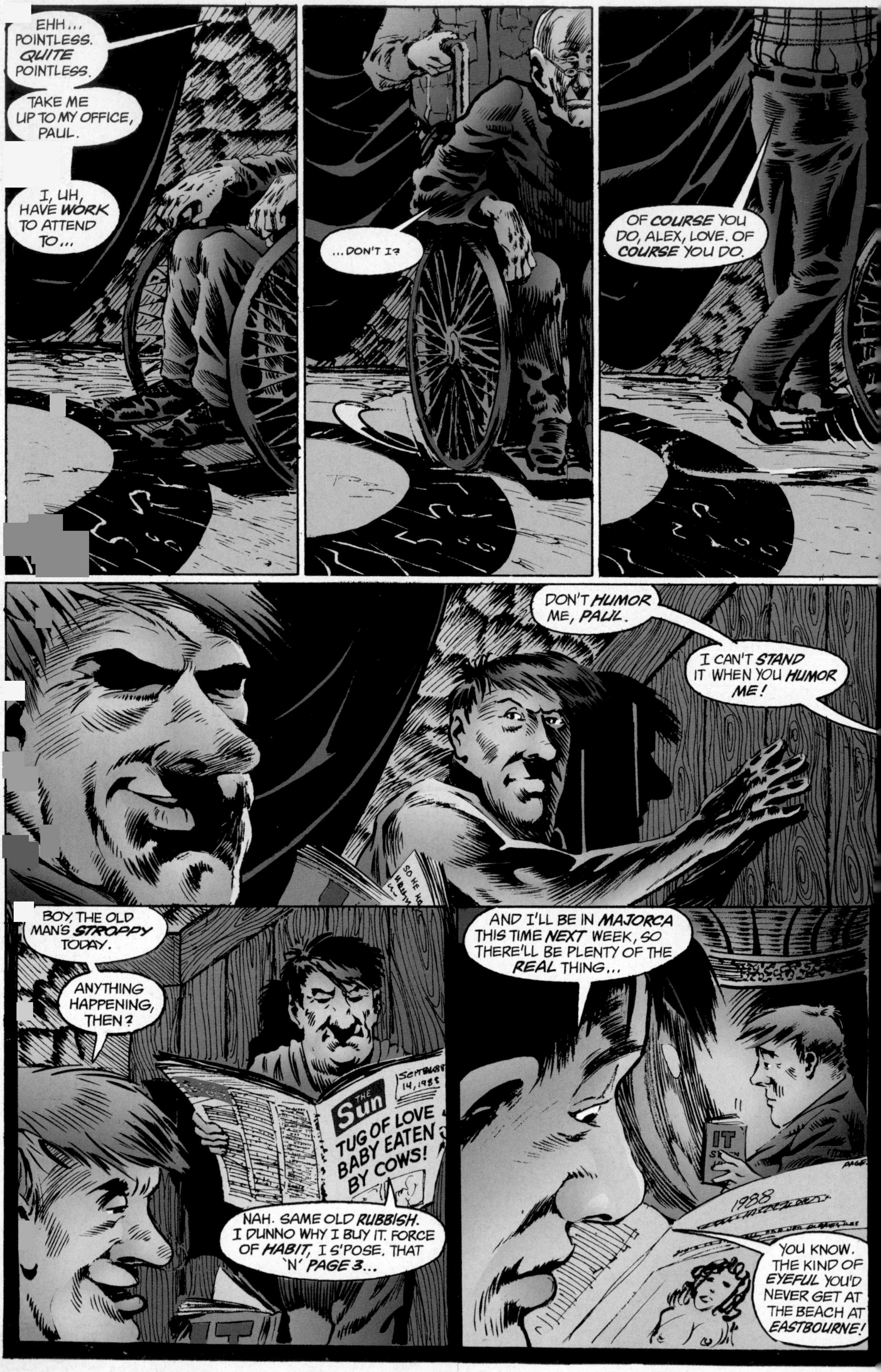
EHH... POINTLESS. QUITE POINTLESS.
TAKE ME UP TO MY OFFICE, PAUL.
I, UH, HAVE WORK TO ATTEND TO...
...DON'T I?
OF COURSE YOU DO, ALEX, LOVE. OF COURSE YOU DO.
DON'T HUMOR ME, PAUL.
I CAN'T STAND IT WHEN YOU HUMOR ME!
BOY, THE OLD MAN'S STROPPY TODAY.
ANYTHING HAPPENING, THEN?
THE Sun
TUG OF LOVE BABY EATEN BY COWS!
NAH. SAME OLD RUBBISH. I DUNNO WHY I BUY IT. FORCE OF HABIT, I S'POSE. THAT 'N' PAGE 3...
AND I'LL BE IN MAJORCA THIS TIME NEXT WEEK, SO THERE'LL BE PLENTY OF THE REAL THING...
1988
YOU KNOW. THE KIND OF EYEFUL YOU'D NEVER GET AT THE BEACH AT EASTBOURNE!

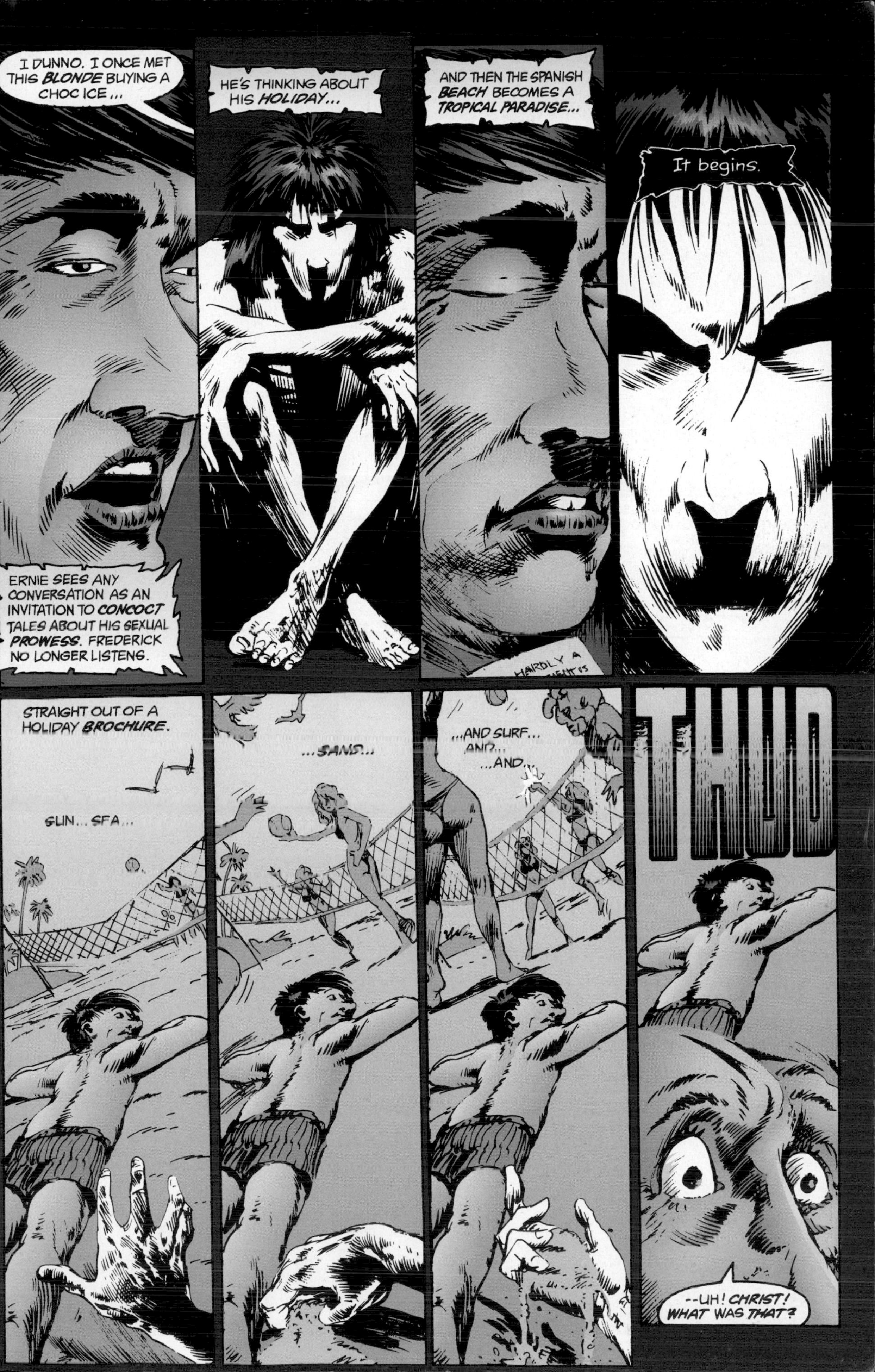
I DUNNO. I ONCE MET THIS BLONDE BUYING A CHOC ICE...
ERNIE SEES ANY CONVERSATION AS AN INVITATION TO CONCOCT TALES ABOUT HIS SEXUAL PROWESS. FREDERICK NO LONGER LISTENS.
HE'S THINKING ABOUT HIS HOLIDAY...
AND THEN THE SPANISH BEACH BECOMES A TROPICAL PARADISE...
It begins.
STRAIGHT OUT OF A HOLIDAY BROCHURE.
SUN... SEA...
...SAND...
...AND SURF... AND... ...AND...
THUD
--UH! CHRIST! WHAT WAS THAT?

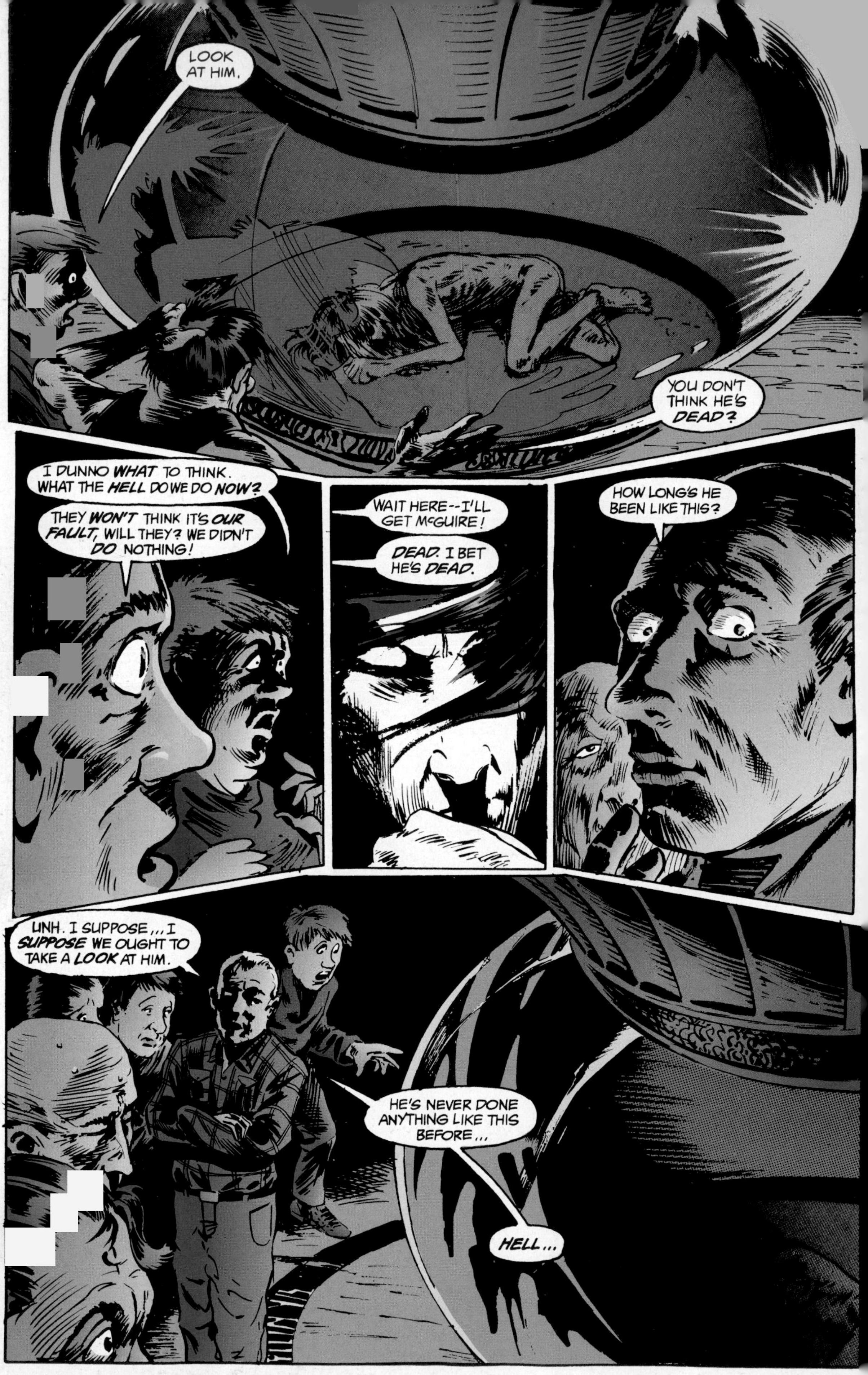
LOOK AT HIM.
YOU DON'T THINK HE'S DEAD?
I DUNNO WHAT TO THINK. WHAT THE HELL DO WE DO NOW?
THEY WON'T THINK IT'S OUR FAULT, WILL THEY? WE DIDN'T DO NOTHING!
WAIT HERE--I'LL GET McGUIRE!
DEAD. I BET HE'S DEAD.
HOW LONG'S HE BEEN LIKE THIS?
UNH. I SUPPOSE,,, I SUPPOSE WE OUGHT TO TAKE A LOOK AT HIM.
HE'S NEVER DONE ANYTHING LIKE THIS BEFORE...
HELL...

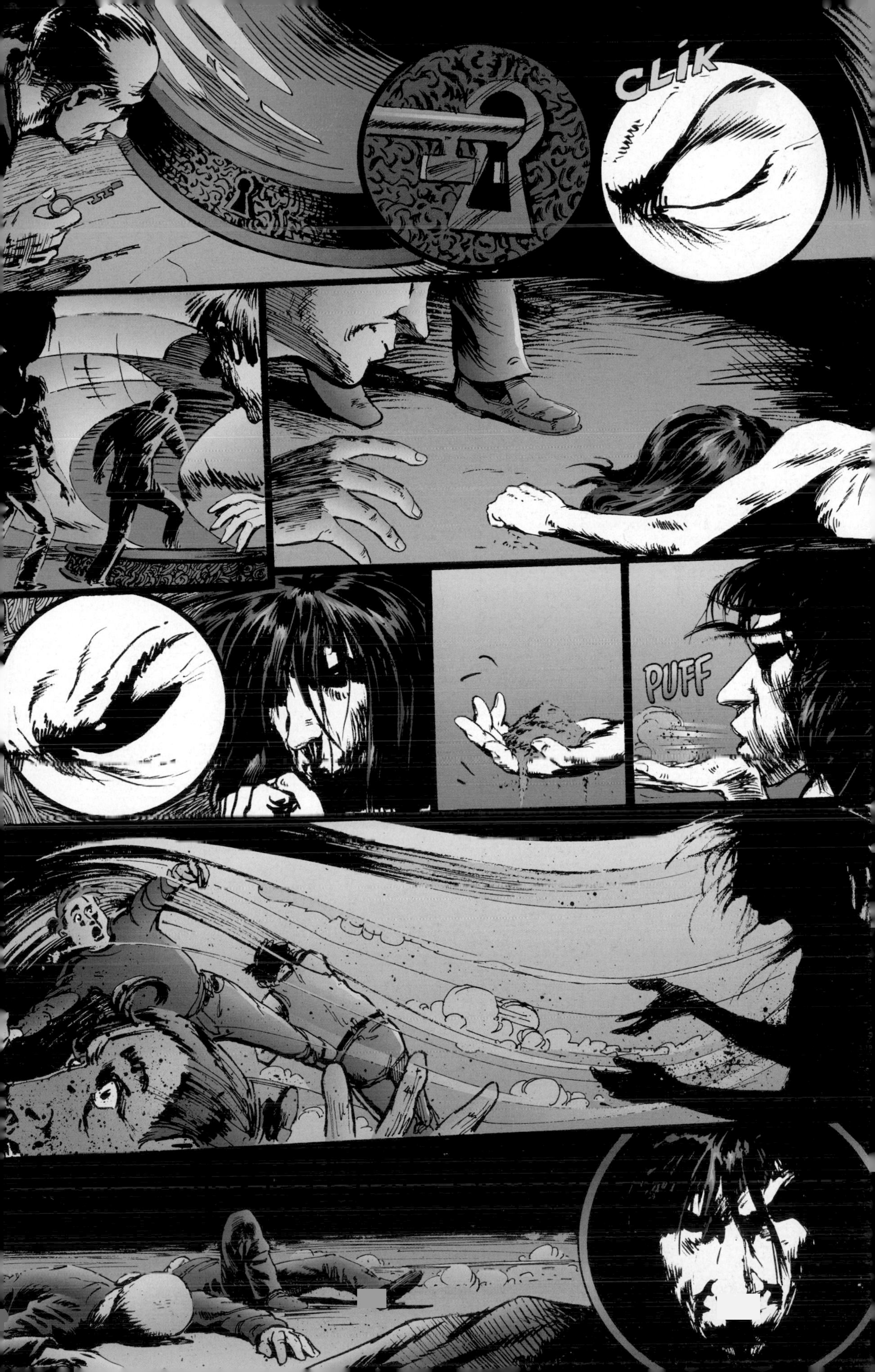
CLIK
PUFF

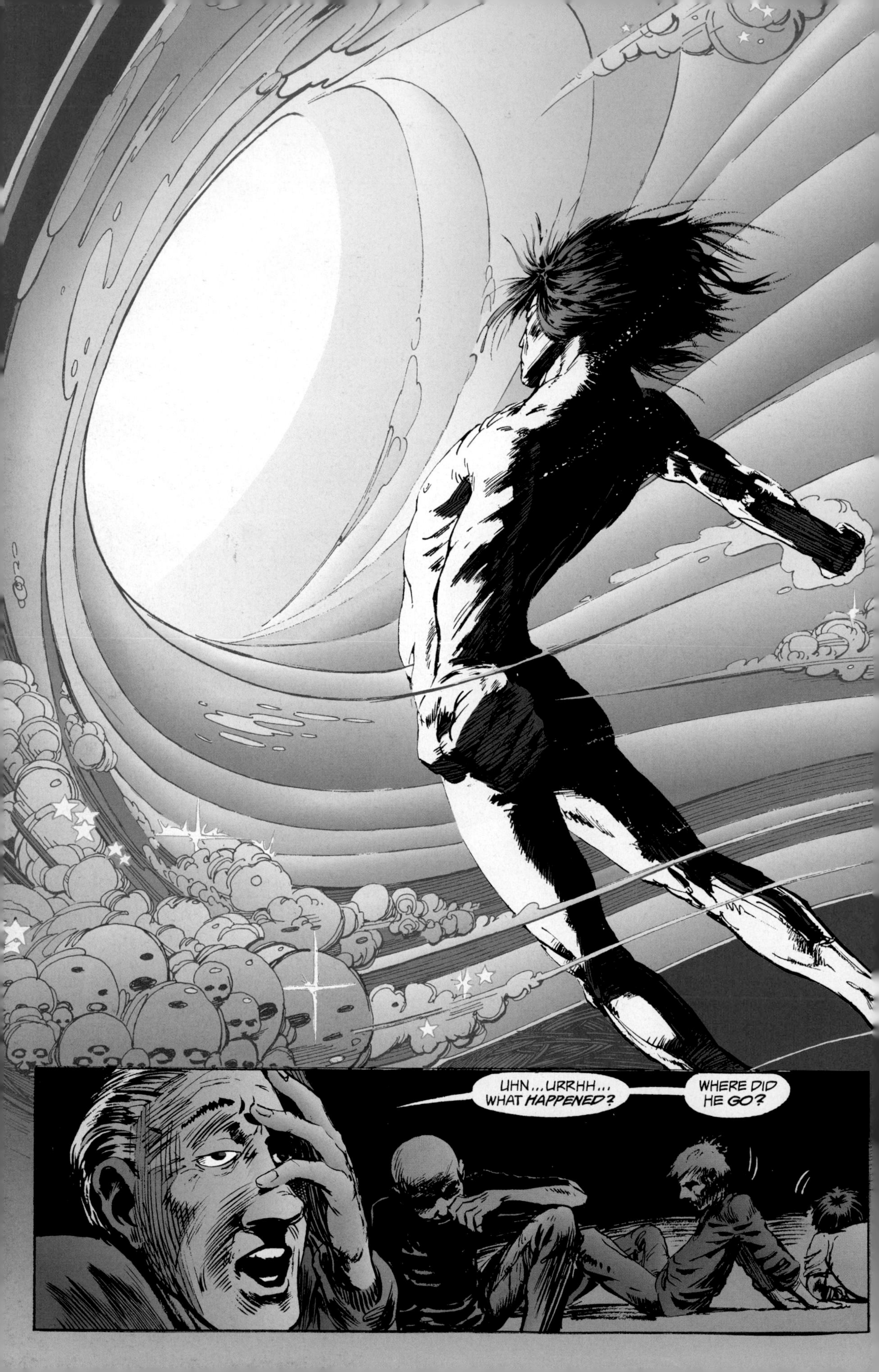
UHN... URRHH... WHAT HAPPENED?
WHERE DID HE GO?

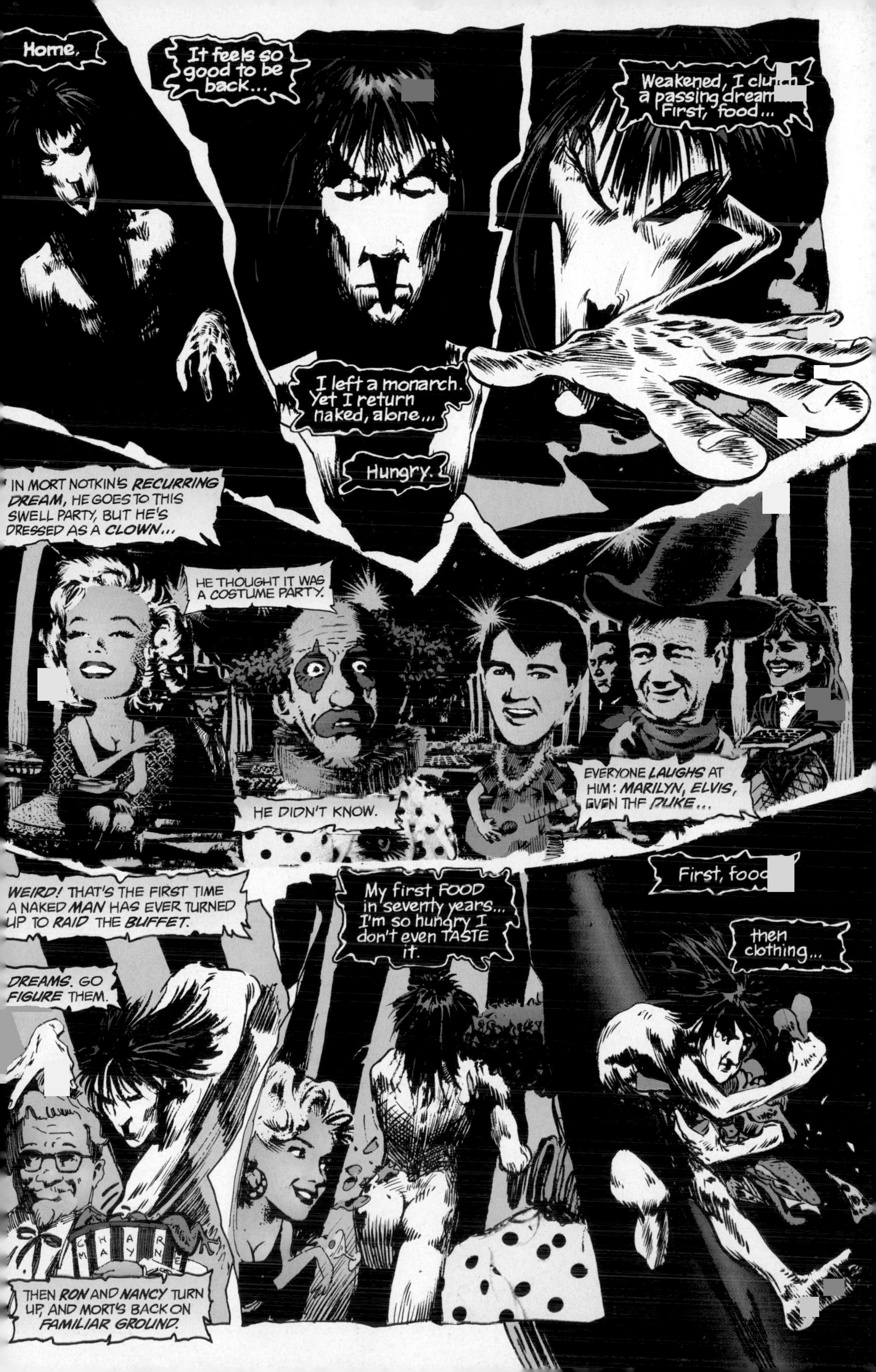

Home,
It feels so good to be back...
I left a monarch. Yet I return naked, alone...
Hungry.
Weakened, I clu ch a passing dream First, food...
IN MORT NOTKIN'S RECURRING DREAM, HE GOES TO THIS SWELL PARTY, BUT HE'S DRESSED AS A CLOWN...
HE THOUGHT IT WAS A COSTUME PARTY.
HE DIDN'T KNOW.
EVERYONE LAUGHS AT HIM: MARILYN, ELVIS, EVEN THE DUKE...
WEIRD! THAT'S THE FIRST TIME A NAKED MAN HAS EVER TURNED UP TO RAID THE BUFFET.
DREAMS. GO FIGURE THEM.
THEN RON AND NANCY TURN UP, AND MORT'S BACK ON FAMILIAR GROUND.
My first FOOD in seventy years... I'm so hungry I don't even TASTE it.
First, foo
then clothing...

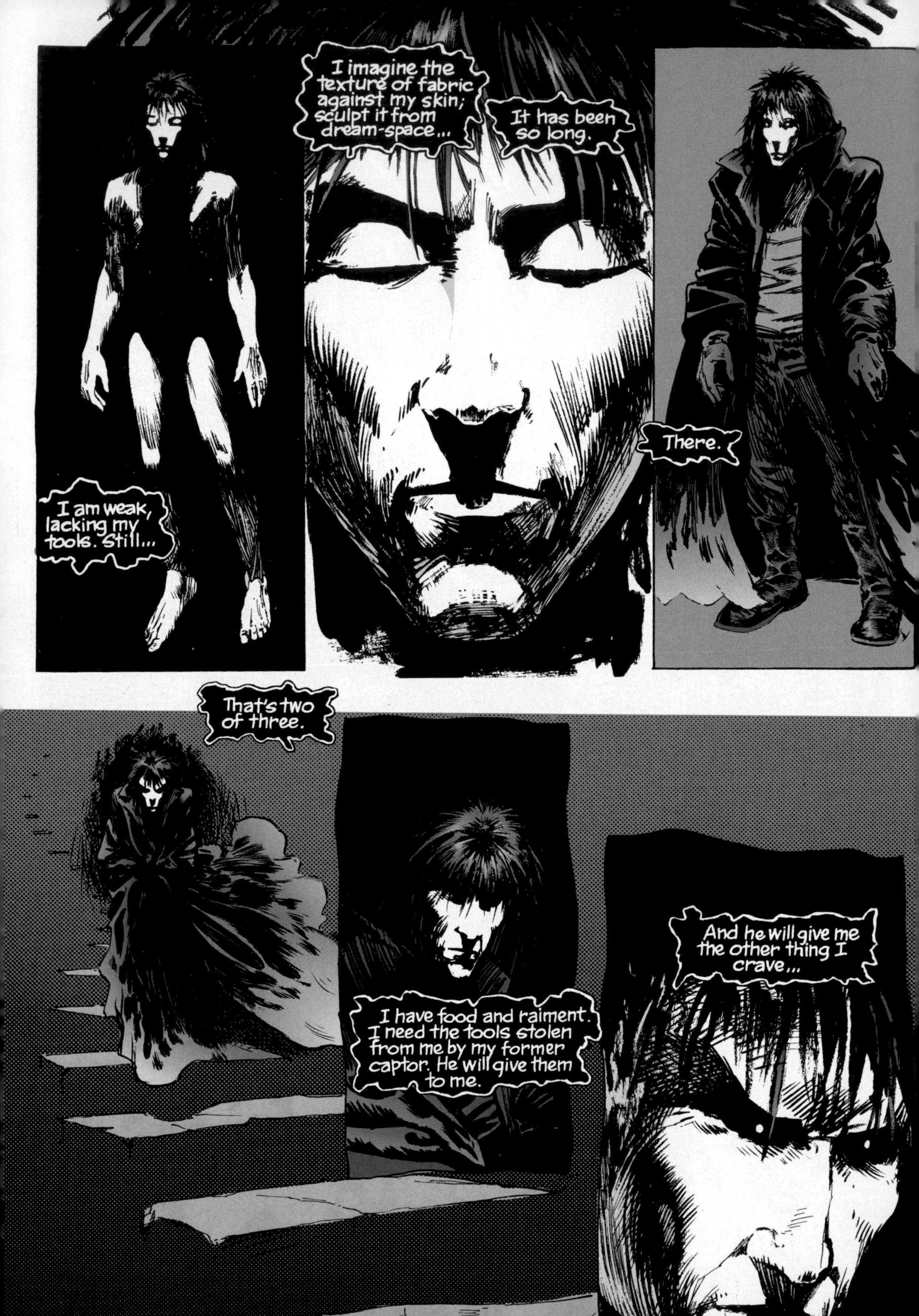
I am weak, lacking my tools. Still...
I imagine the texture of fabric against my skin; sculpt it from dream-space...
It has been so long.
There.
That's two of three.
I have food and raiment. I need the tools stolen from me by my former captor. He will give them to me.
And he will give me the other thing I crave...
REVENGE.

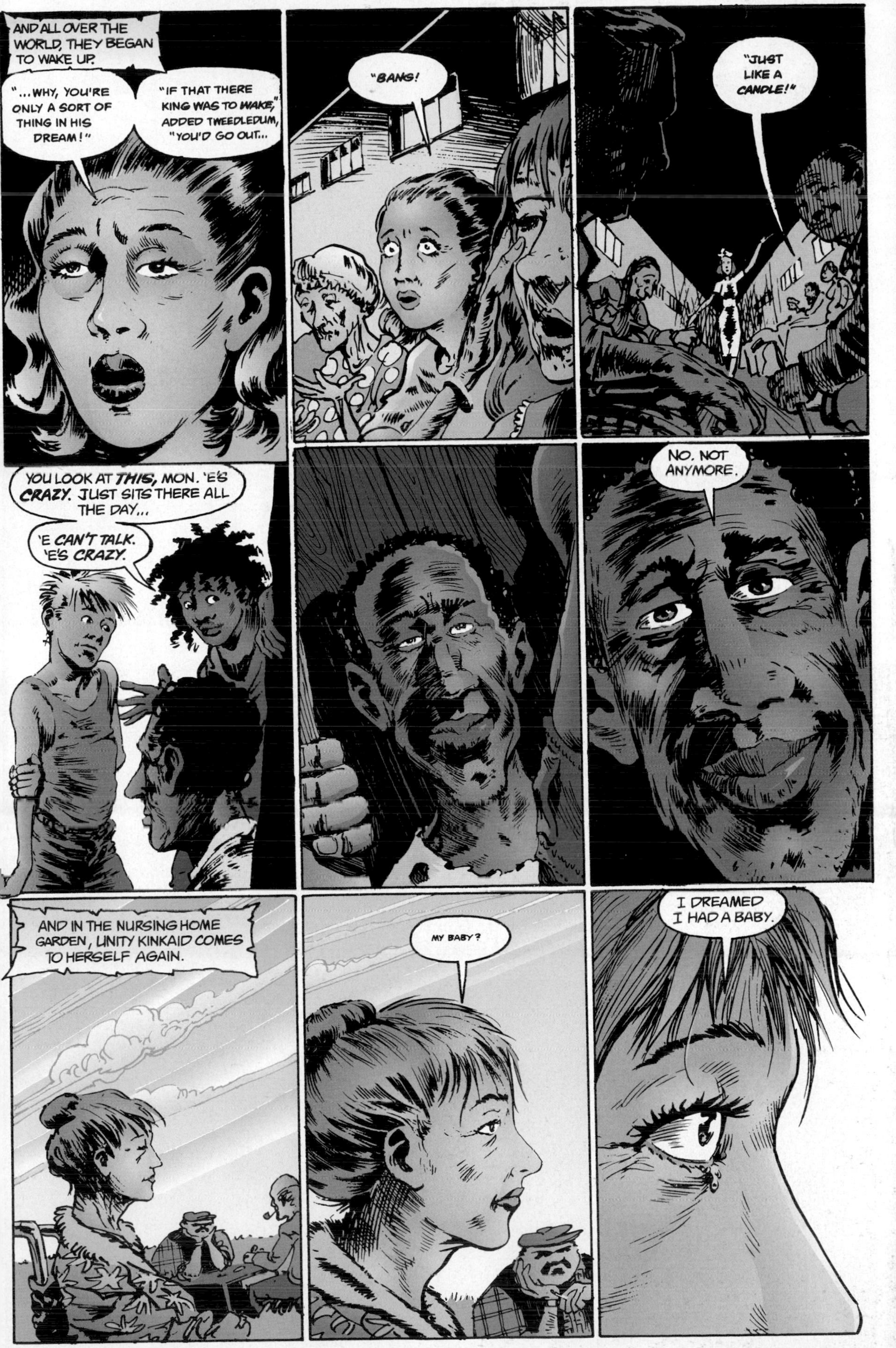

AND ALL OVER THE WORLD, THEY BEGAN TO WAKE UP.
"...WHY, YOU'RE ONLY A SORT OF THING IN HIS DREAM!"
"IF THAT THERE KING WAS TO WAKE," ADDED TWEEDLEDUM, "YOU'D GO OUT...
"BANG!
"JUST LIKE A CANDLE!"
YOU LOOK AT THIS, MON. 'E'S CRAZY. JUST SITS THERE ALL THE DAY...
'E CAN'T TALK. 'E'S CRAZY.
NO. NOT ANYMORE.
AND IN THE NURSING HOME GARDEN, UNITY KINKAID COMES TO HERSELF AGAIN.
MY BABY?
I DREAMED I HAD A BABY.

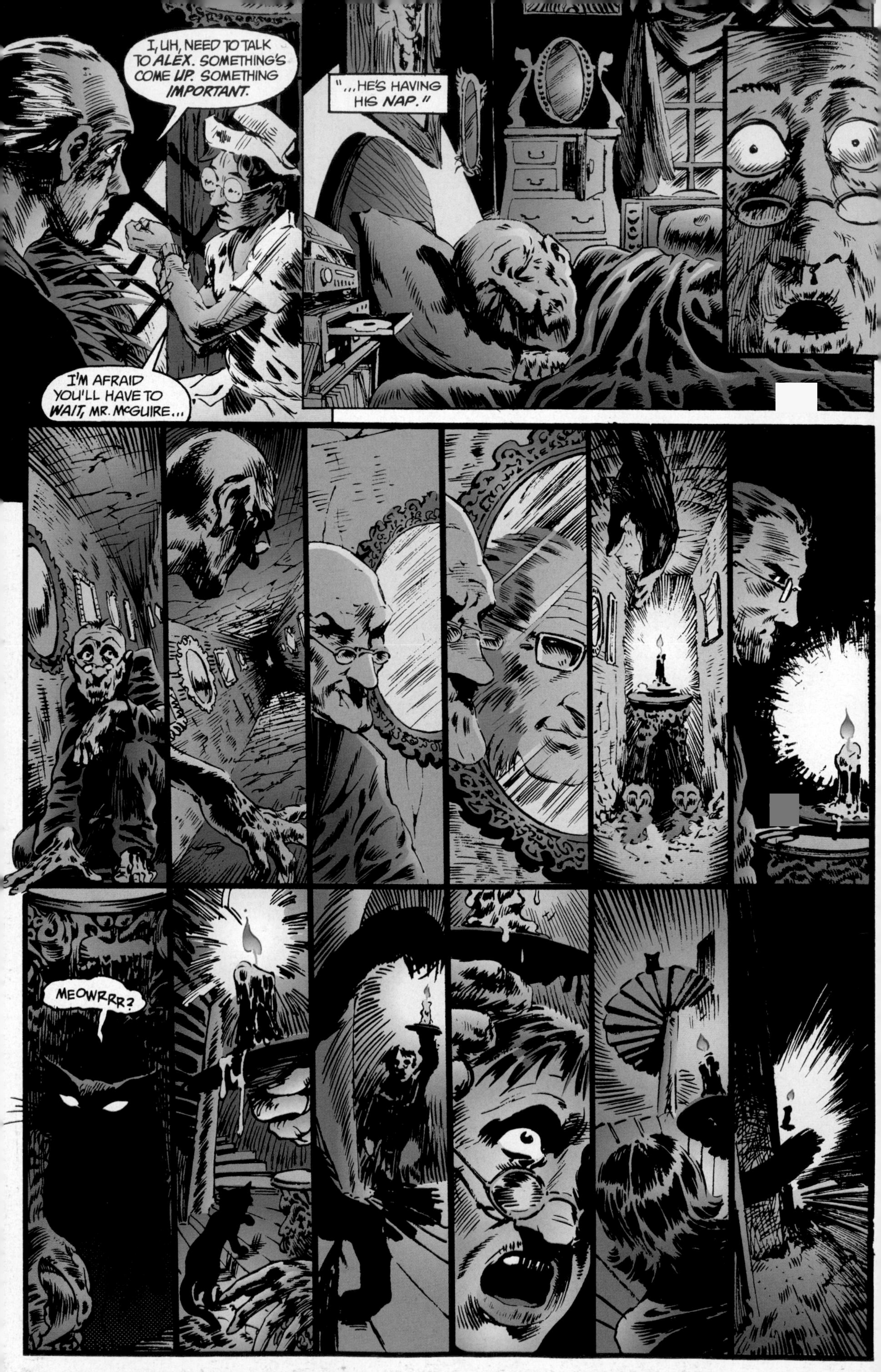
I, UH, NEED TO TALK TO ALEX. SOMETHING'S COME UP. SOMETHING IMPORTANT.
I'M AFRAID YOU'LL HAVE TO WAIT, MR. McGUIRE...
"...HE'S HAVING HIS NAP."
MEOWRRR?

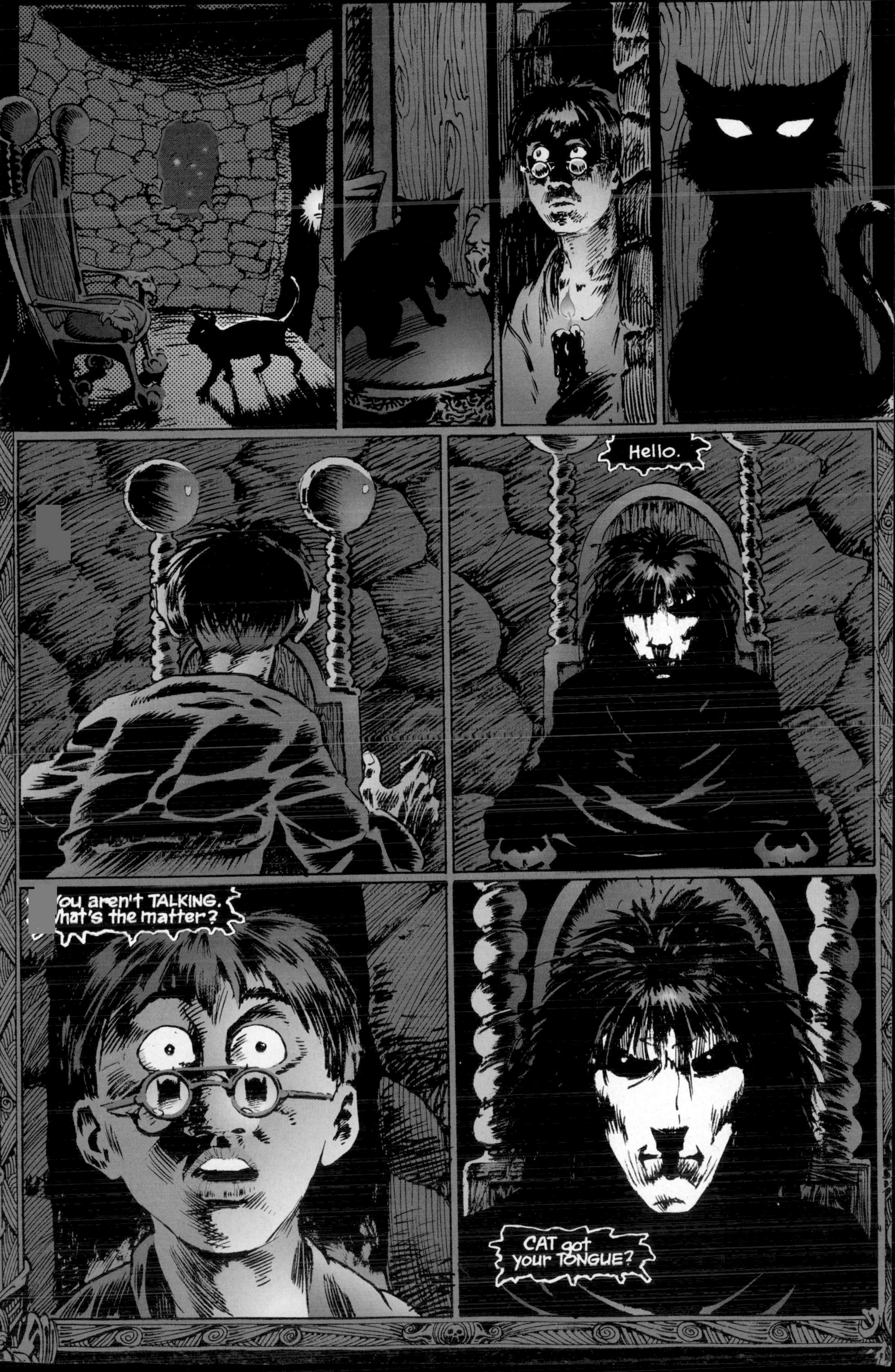
Hello.
You aren't TALKING. What's the matter?
CAT got your TONGUE?

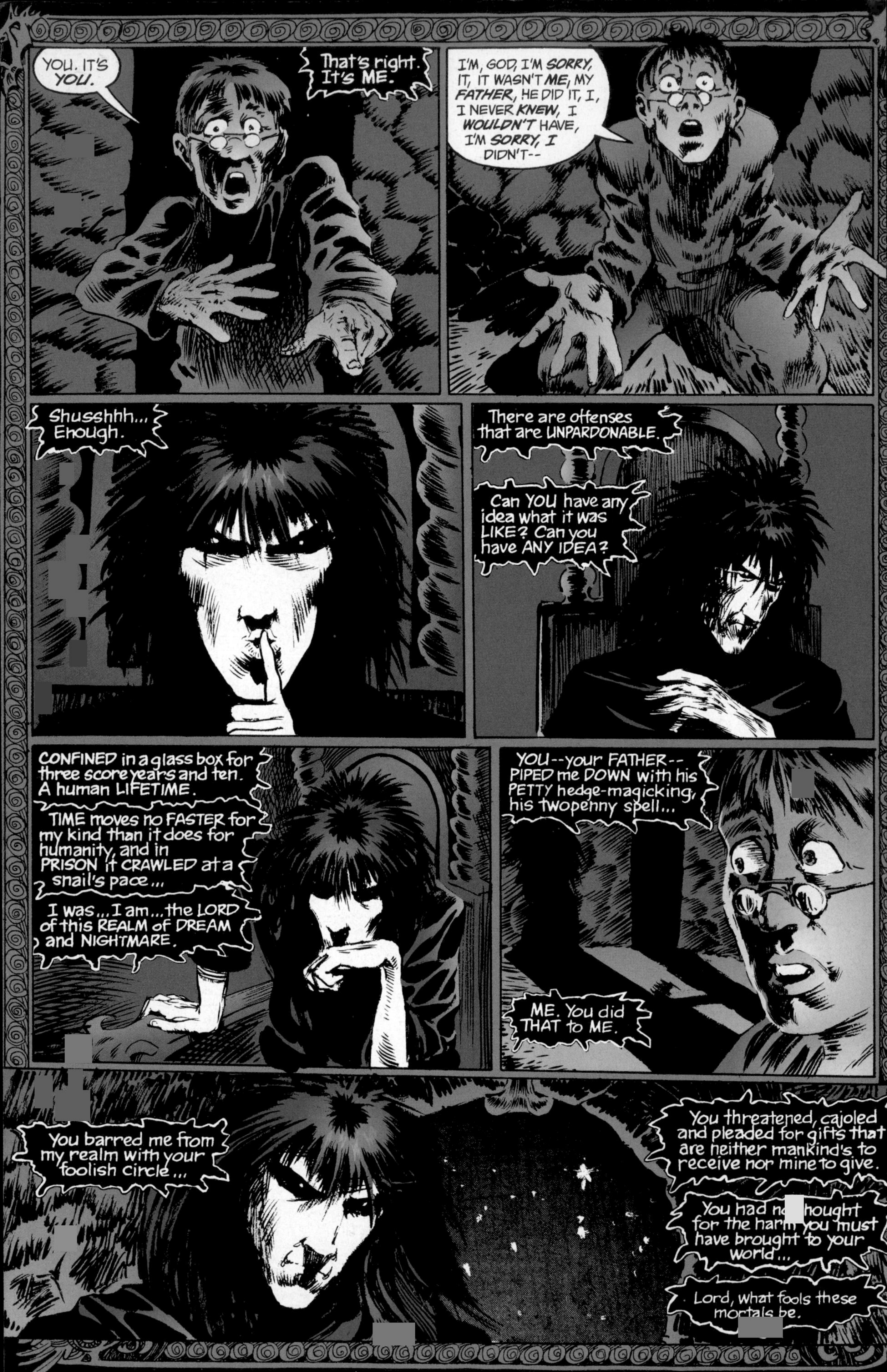
YOU. IT'S YOU.
That's right. It's ME.
I'M, GOD, I'M SORRY, IT, IT WASN'T ME, MY FATHER, HE DID IT, I, I NEVER KNEW, I WOULDN'T HAVE, I'M SORRY, I DIDN'T--
Shusshhh... Enough.
There are offenses that are UNPARDONABLE.
Can YOU have any idea what it was LIKE? Can you have ANY IDEA?
CONFINED in a glass box for three score years and ten. A human LIFETIME.
TIME moves no FASTER for my kind than it does for humanity, and in PRISON it CRAWLED at a snail's pace...
I was... I am... the LORD of this REALM of DREAM and NIGHTMARE.
YOU--your FATHER--PIPED me DOWN with his PETTY hedge-magicking, his twopenny spell...
ME. You did THAT to ME.
You barred me from my realm with your foolish circle...
You threatened, cajoled and pleaded for gifts that are neither mankind's to receive nor mine to give.
You had no thought for the harm you must have brought to your world...
Lord, what fools these mortals be.

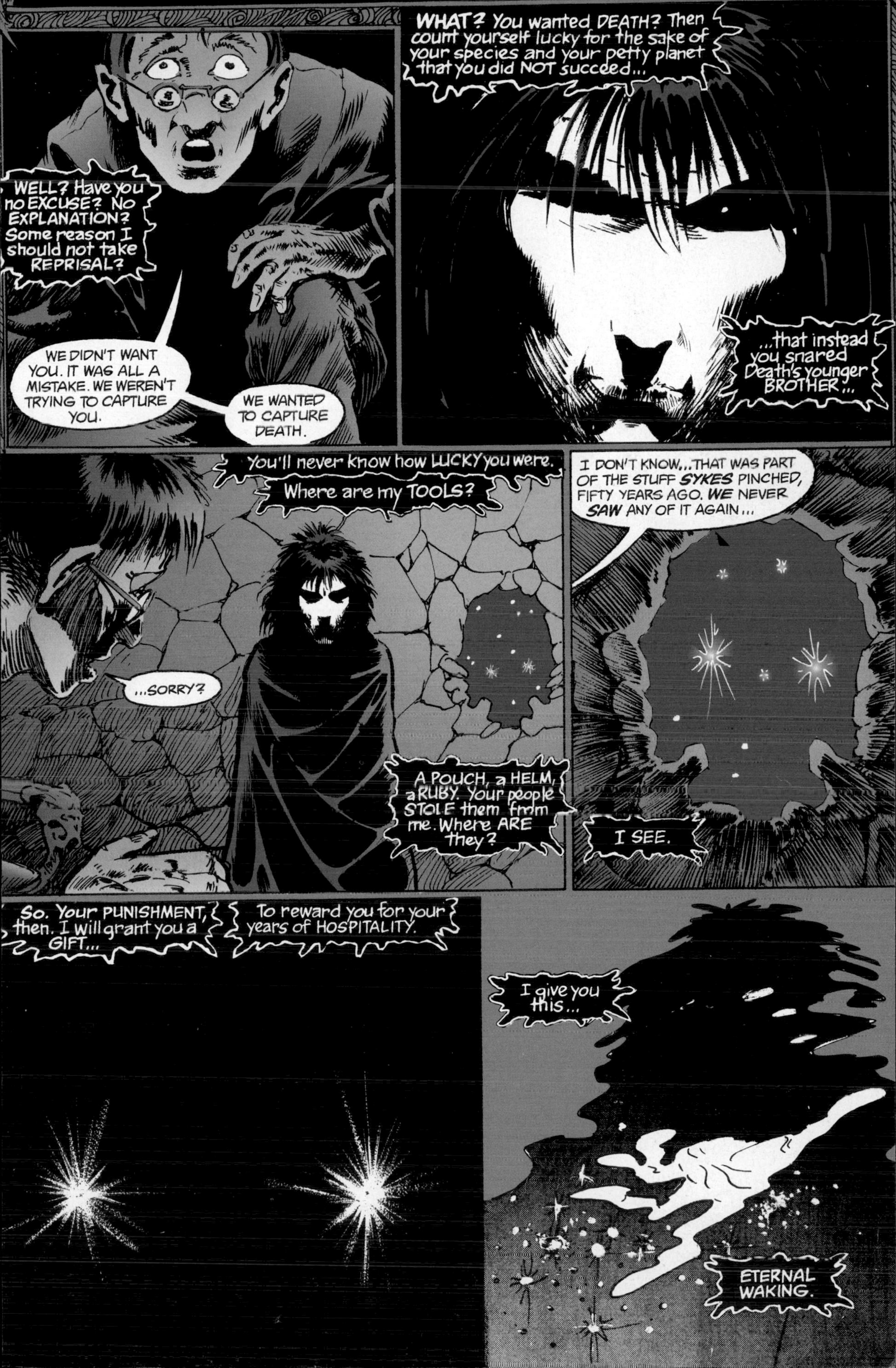
WELL? Have you no EXCUSE? No EXPLANATION? Some reason I should not take REPRISAL?
WE DIDN'T WANT YOU. IT WAS ALL A MISTAKE. WE WEREN'T TRYING TO CAPTURE YOU.
WE WANTED TO CAPTURE DEATH.
WHAT? You wanted DEATH? Then count yourself lucky for the sake of your species and your petty planet that you did NOT succeed...
...that instead you snared Death's younger BROTHER...
You'll never know how LUCKY you were.
Where are my TOOLS?
...SORRY?
A POUCH, a HELM, a RUBY. Your people STOLE them from me. Where ARE they?
I DON'T KNOW...THAT WAS PART OF THE STUFF SYKES PINCHED, FIFTY YEARS AGO. WE NEVER SAW ANY OF IT AGAIN...
I SEE.
So. Your PUNISHMENT, then. I will grant you a GIFT...
To reward you for your years of HOSPITALITY.
I give you this...
ETERNAL WAKING.

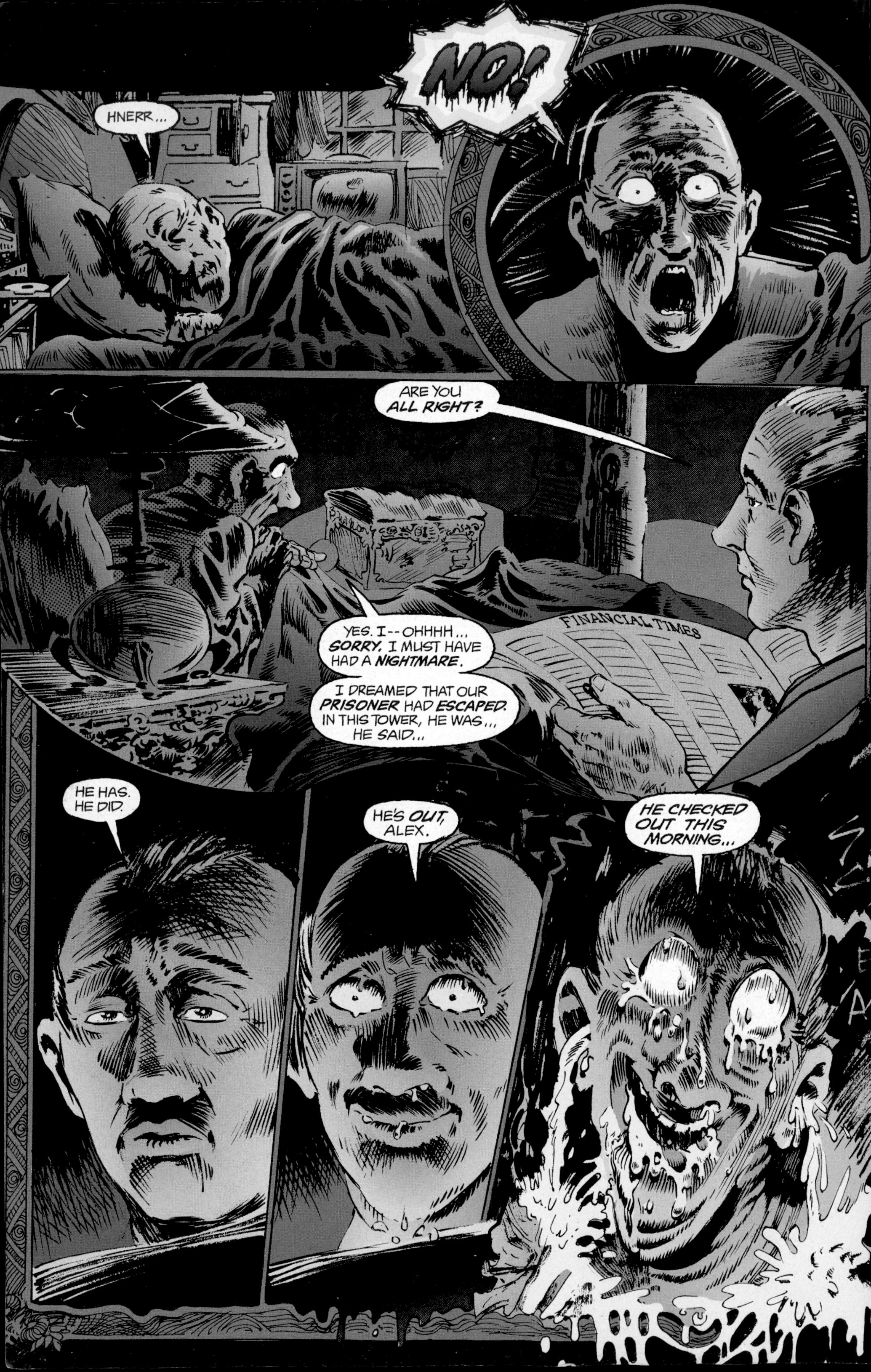
HNERR...
NO!
ARE YOU ALL RIGHT?
FINANCIAL TIMES
YES. I-- OHHHH... SORRY. I MUST HAVE HAD A NIGHTMARE.
I DREAMED THAT OUR PRISONER HAD ESCAPED. IN THIS TOWER, HE WAS... HE SAID...
HE HAS. HE DID.
HE'S OUT, ALEX.
HE CHECKED OUT THIS MORNING...

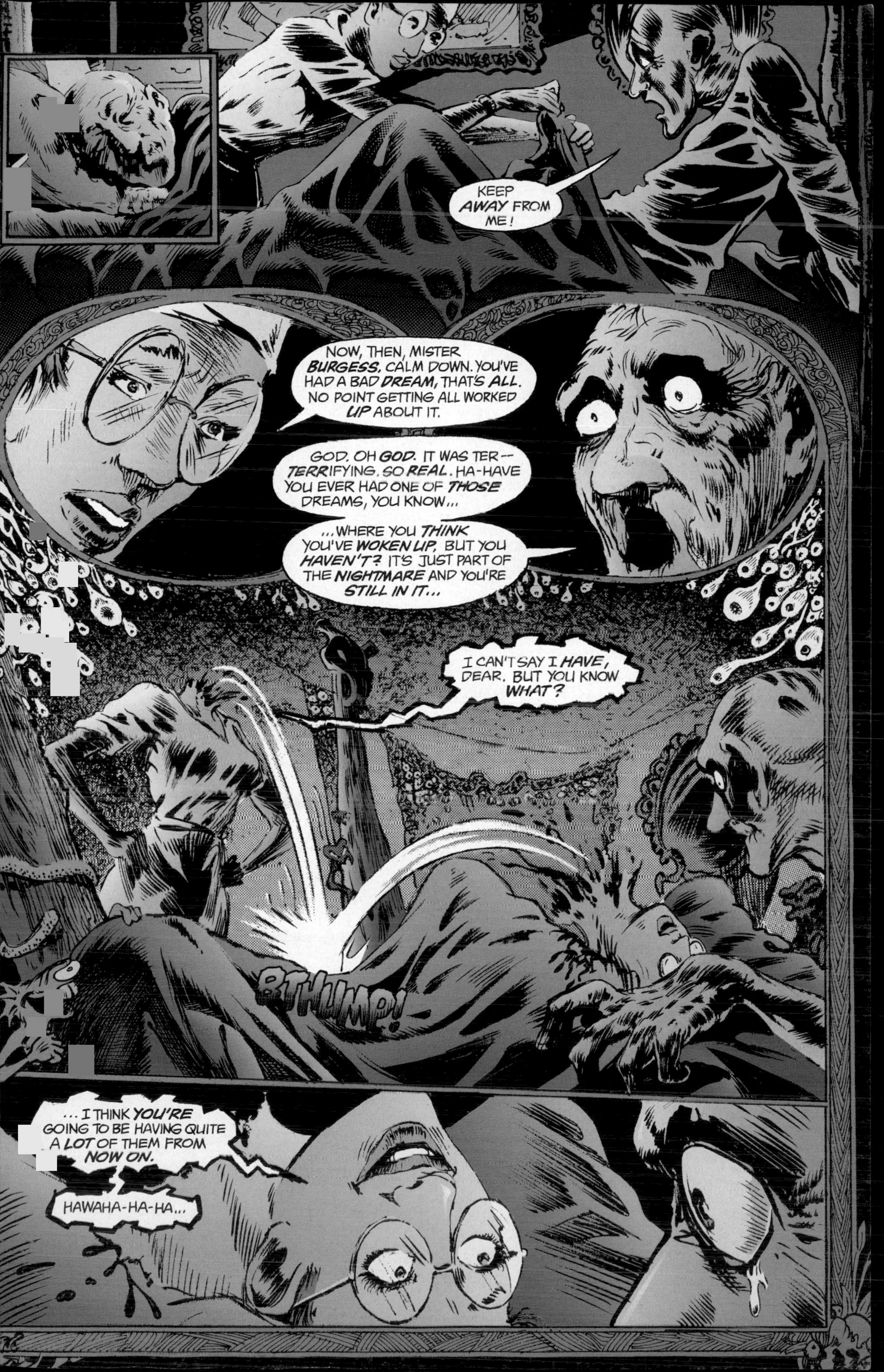
KEEP AWAY FROM ME!
NOW, THEN, MISTER BURGESS. CALM DOWN. YOU'VE HAD A BAD DREAM, THAT'S ALL. NO POINT GETTING ALL WORKED UP ABOUT IT.
GOD. OH GOD. IT WAS TER-- TERRIFYING. SO REAL. HA-HAVE YOU EVER HAD ONE OF THOSE DREAMS, YOU KNOW...
...WHERE YOU THINK YOU'VE WOKEN UP, BUT YOU HAVEN'T? IT'S JUST PART OF THE NIGHTMARE AND YOU'RE STILL IN IT...
I CAN'T SAY I HAVE, DEAR. BUT YOU KNOW WHAT?
BTHUMP!
...I THINK YOU'RE GOING TO BE HAVING QUITE A LOT OF THEM FROM NOW ON.
HAWAHA-HA-HA...

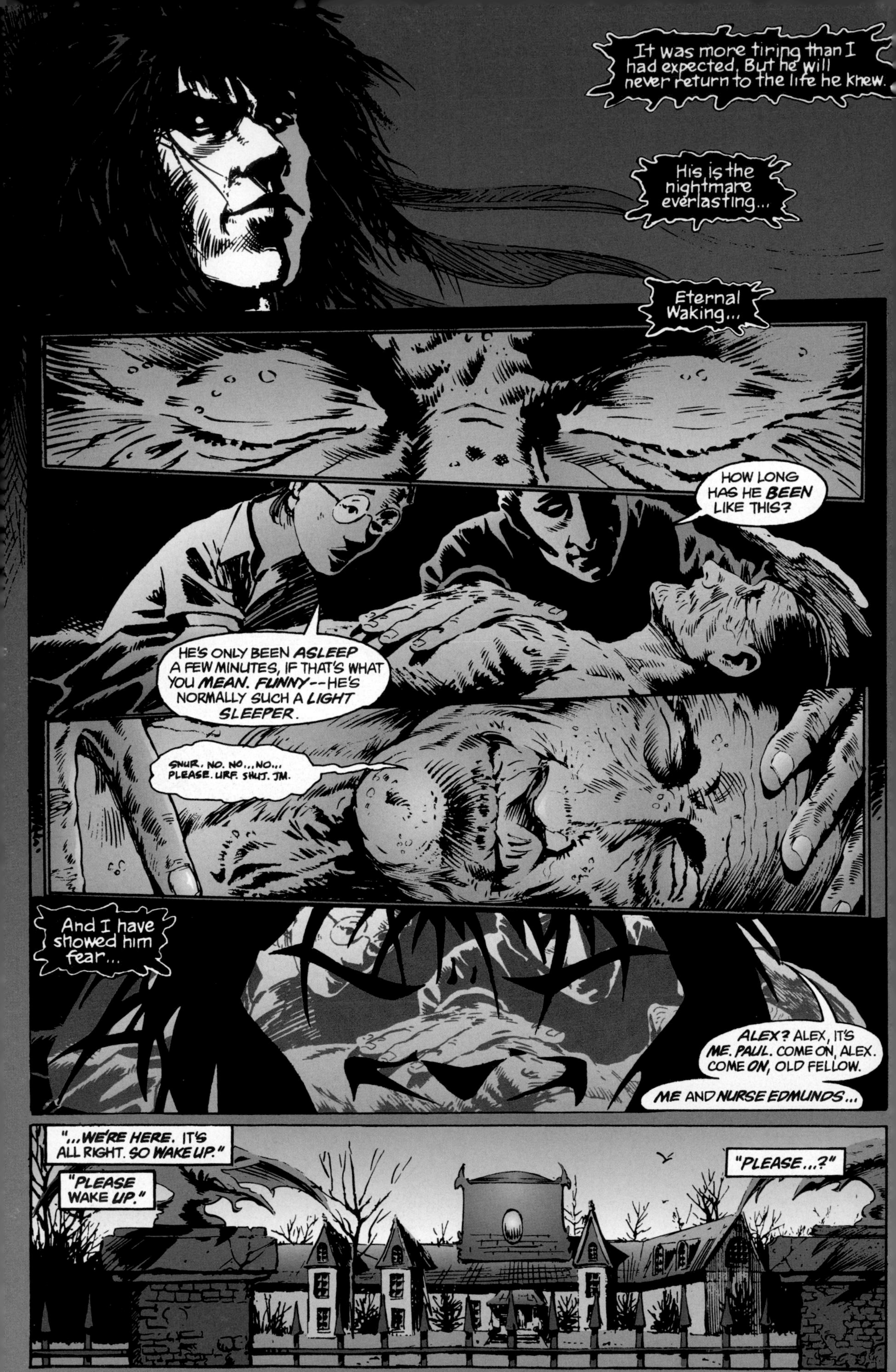
It was more tiring than I had expected. But he will never return to the life he knew.
His is the nightmare everlasting...
Eternal Waking...
HOW LONG HAS HE BEEN LIKE THIS?
HE'S ONLY BEEN ASLEEP A FEW MINUTES, IF THAT'S WHAT YOU MEAN. FUNNY--HE'S NORMALLY SUCH A LIGHT SLEEPER.
SNUR. NO. NO...NO... PLEASE. URF. SHUJ. JM.
And I have showed him fear...
ALEX? ALEX, IT'S ME. PAUL. COME ON, ALEX. COME ON, OLD FELLOW.
ME AND NURSE EDMUNDS...
"...WE'RE HERE. IT'S ALL RIGHT. SO WAKE UP."
"PLEASE WAKE UP."
"PLEASE...?"

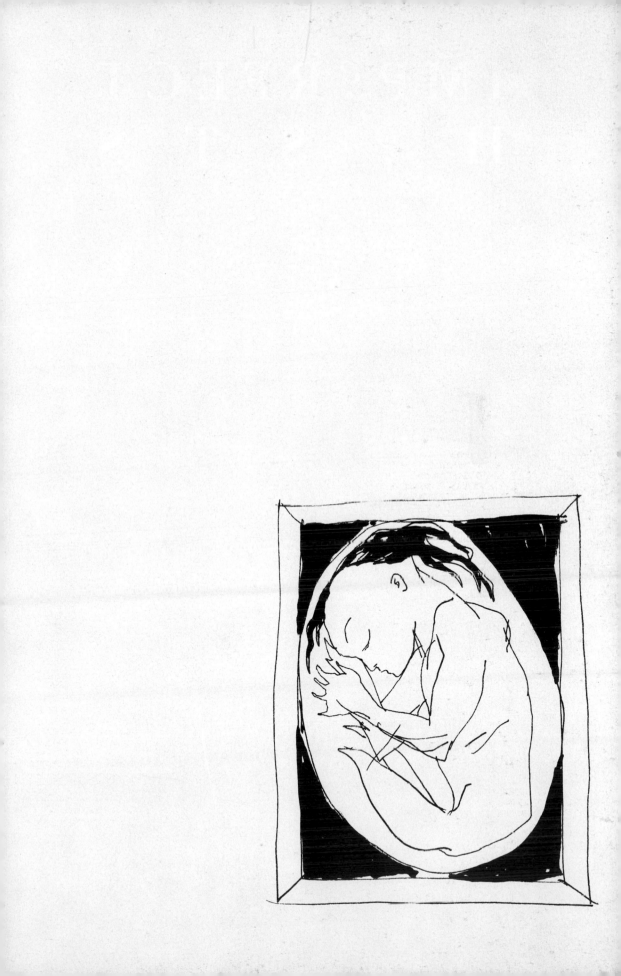

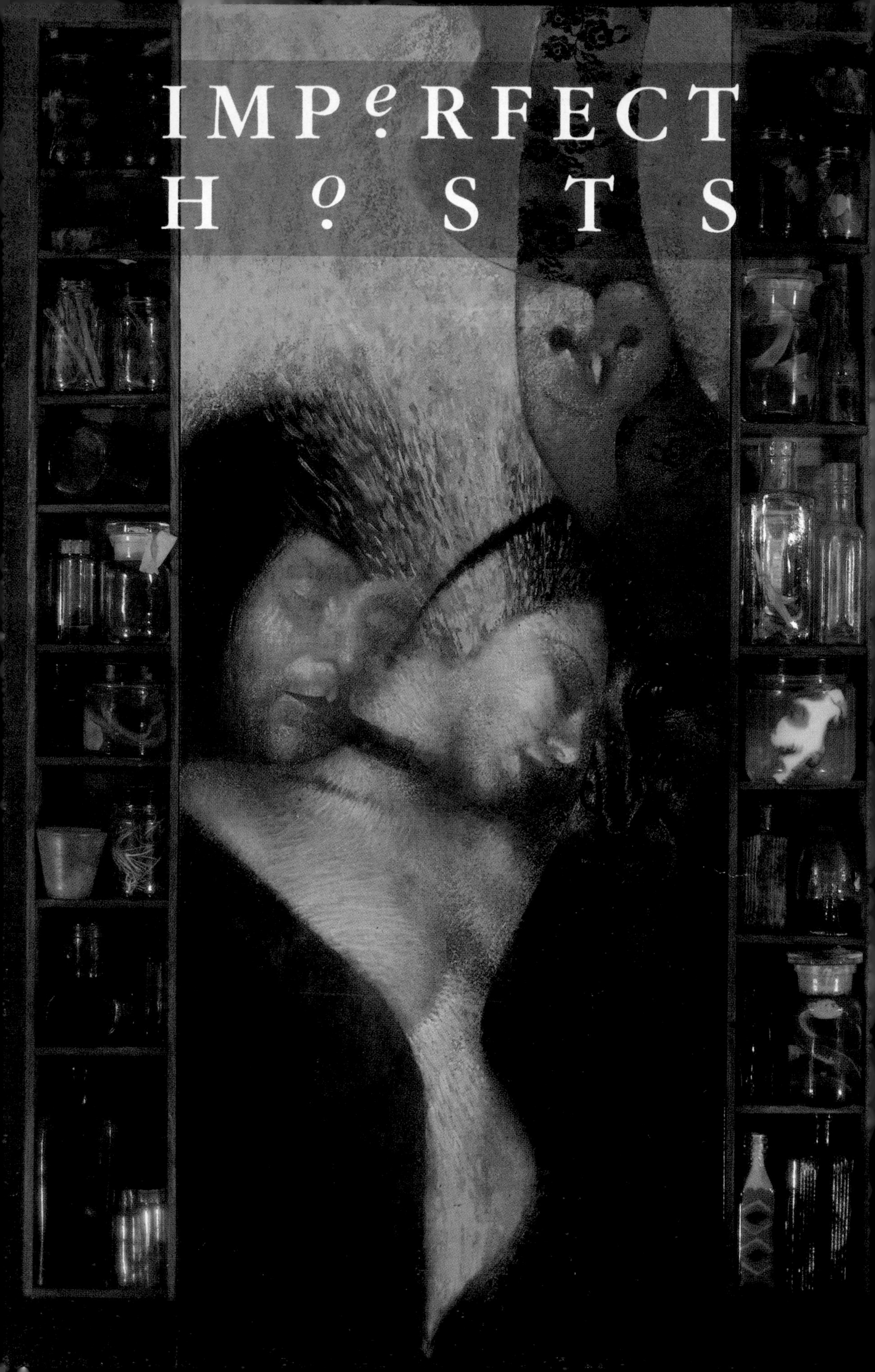
IMPERFECT
HOSTS

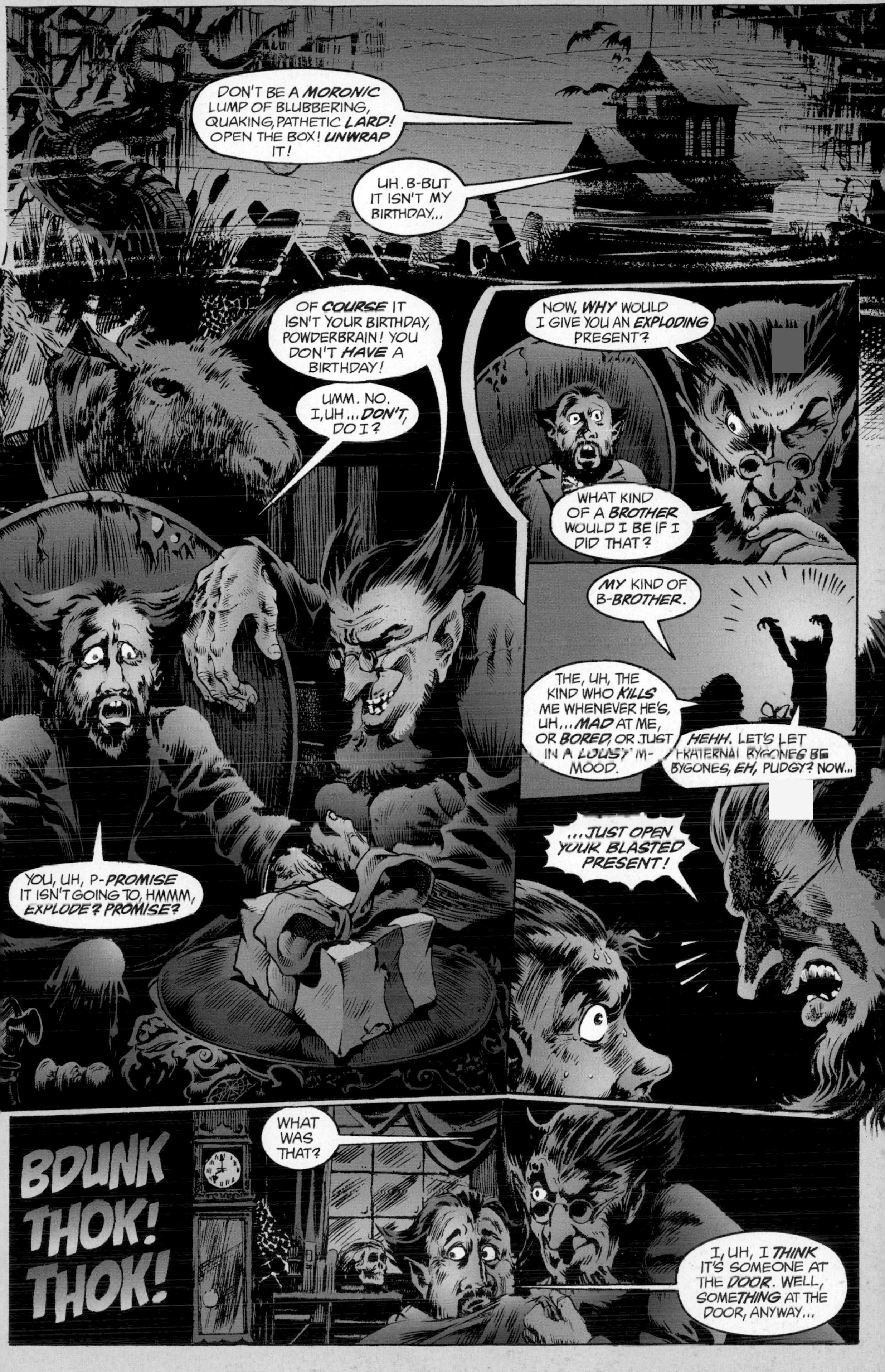
DON'T BE A MORONIC LUMP OF BLUBBERING, QUAKING, PATHETIC LARD! OPEN THE BOX! UNWRAP IT!
UH. B-BUT IT ISN'T MY BIRTHDAY...
OF COURSE IT ISN'T YOUR BIRTHDAY, POWDERBRAIN! YOU DON'T HAVE A BIRTHDAY!
UMM. NO. I, UH ... DON'T, DO I?
YOU, UH, P-PROMISE IT ISN'T GOING TO, HMMM, EXPLODE? PROMISE?
NOW, WHY WOULD I GIVE YOU AN EXPLODING PRESENT?
WHAT KIND OF A BROTHER WOULD I BE IF I DID THAT?
MY KIND OF B-BROTHER.
THE, UH, THE KIND WHO KILLS ME WHENEVER HE'S, UH, ... MAD AT ME, OR BORED, OR JUST IN A LOUSY M- MOOD.
HEHH. LET'S LET FRATERNAL BYGONES BE BYGONES, EH, PUDGY? NOW...
...JUST OPEN YOUR BLASTED PRESENT!
BDUNK
THOK! THOK!
WHAT WAS THAT?
I, UH, I THINK IT'S SOMEONE AT THE DOOR. WELL, SOMETHING AT THE DOOR, ANYWAY...

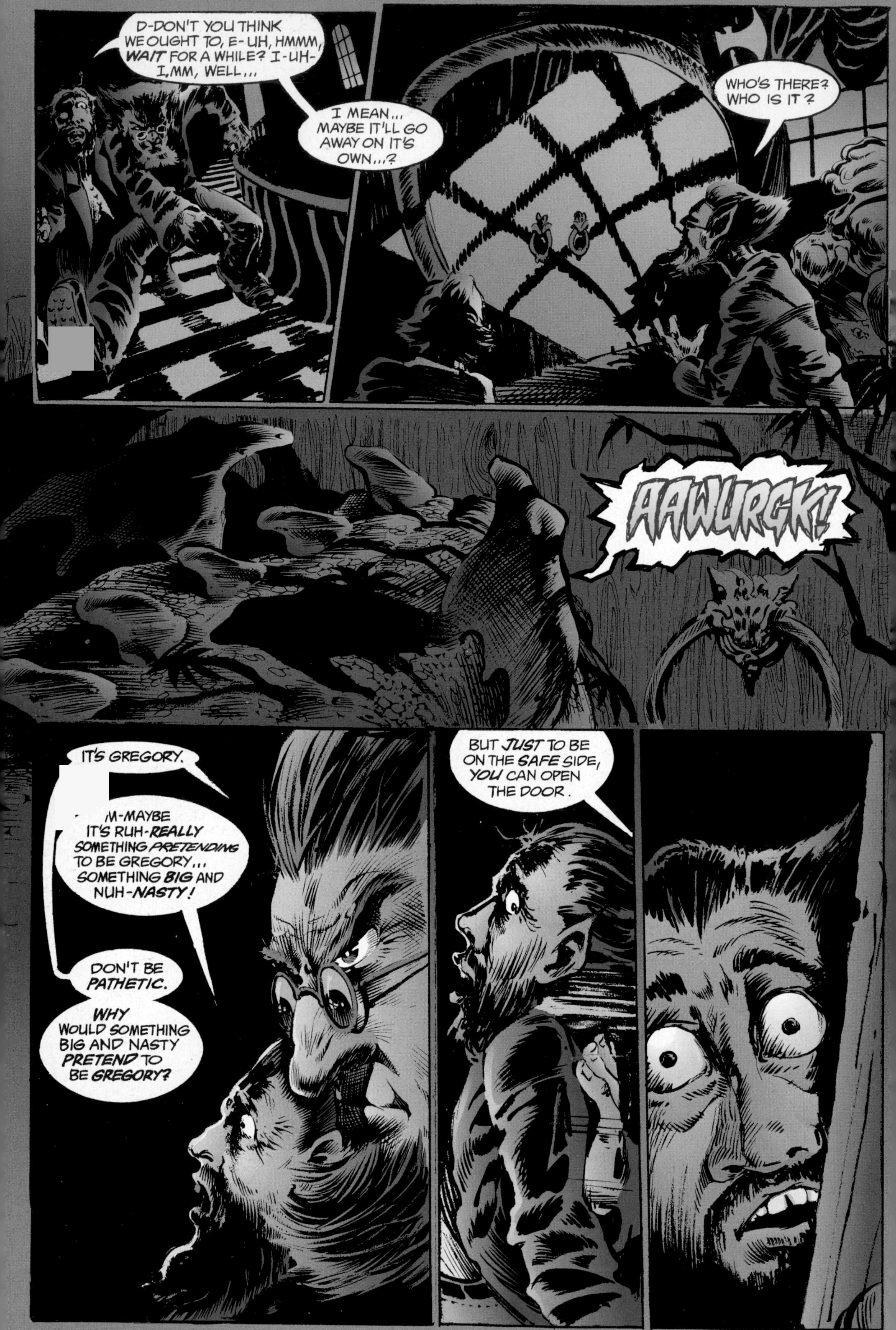
D-DON'T YOU THINK WE OUGHT TO, E-UH, HMMM, WAIT FOR A WHILE? I-UH- I,MM, WELL...
I MEAN... MAYBE IT'LL GO AWAY ON IT'S OWN...?
WHO'S THERE? WHO IS IT?
AAWURGK!
IT'S GREGORY.
M-MAYBE IT'S RUH-REALLY SOMETHING PRETENDING TO BE GREGORY... SOMETHING BIG AND NUH-NASTY!
DON'T BE PATHETIC.
WHY WOULD SOMETHING BIG AND NASTY PRETEND TO BE GREGORY?
BUT JUST TO BE ON THE SAFE SIDE, YOU CAN OPEN THE DOOR.

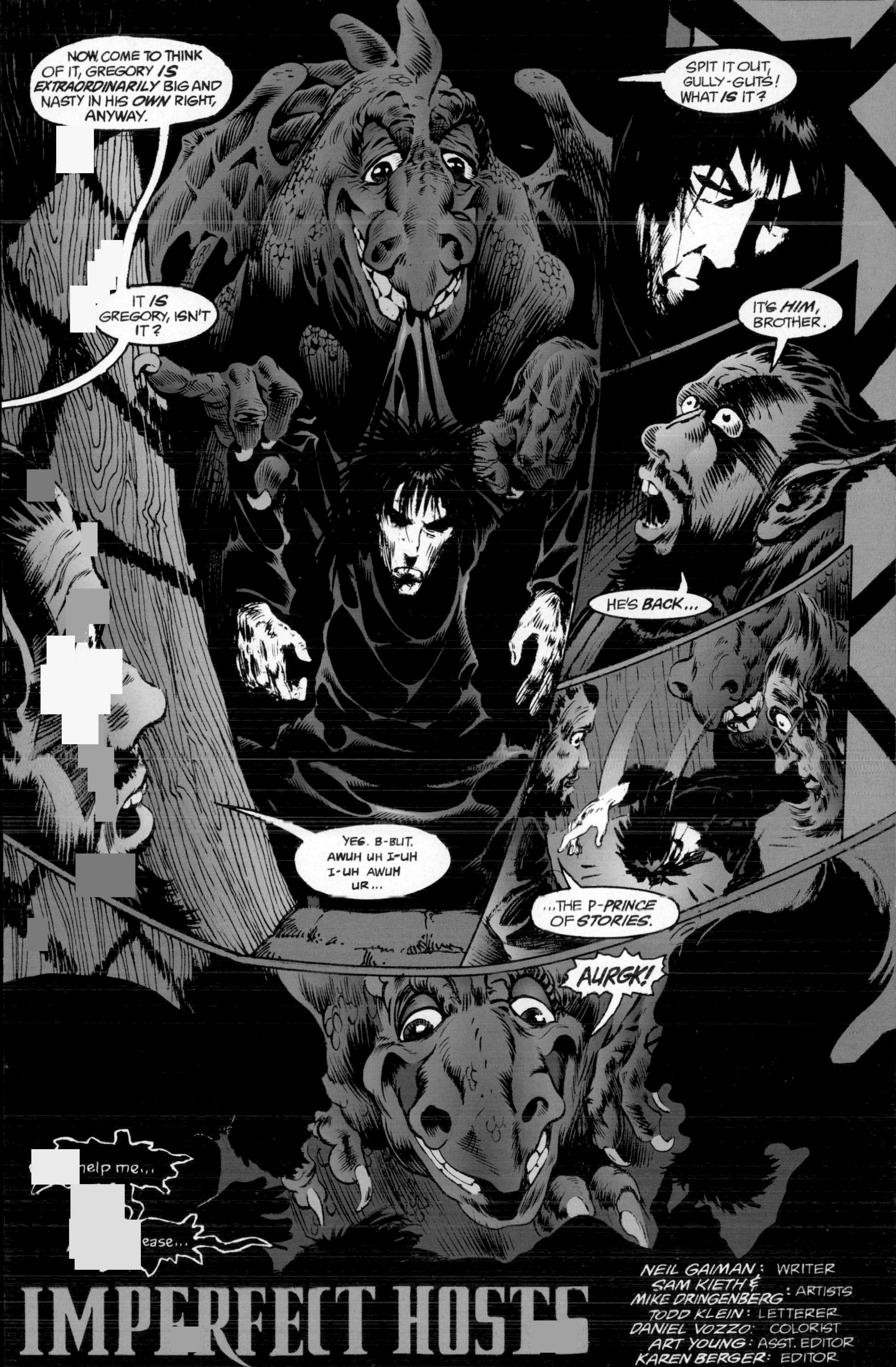
NOW, COME TO THINK OF IT, GREGORY IS EXTRAORDINARILY BIG AND NASTY IN HIS OWN RIGHT, ANYWAY.
IT IS GREGORY, ISN'T IT?
SPIT IT OUT, GULLY-GUTS! WHAT IS IT?
IT'S HIM, BROTHER.
HE'S BACK...
YES. B-BUT. AWUH UH I-UH I-UH AWUH UR...
...THE P-PRINCE OF STORIES.
AURGK!
help me...
ease...
IMPERFECT HOSTS
NEIL GAIMAN: WRITER
SAM KIETH & MIKE DRINGENBERG: ARTISTS
TODD KLEIN: LETTERER
DANIEL VOZZO: COLORIST
ART YOUNG: ASST. EDITOR
KAREN BERGER: EDITOR

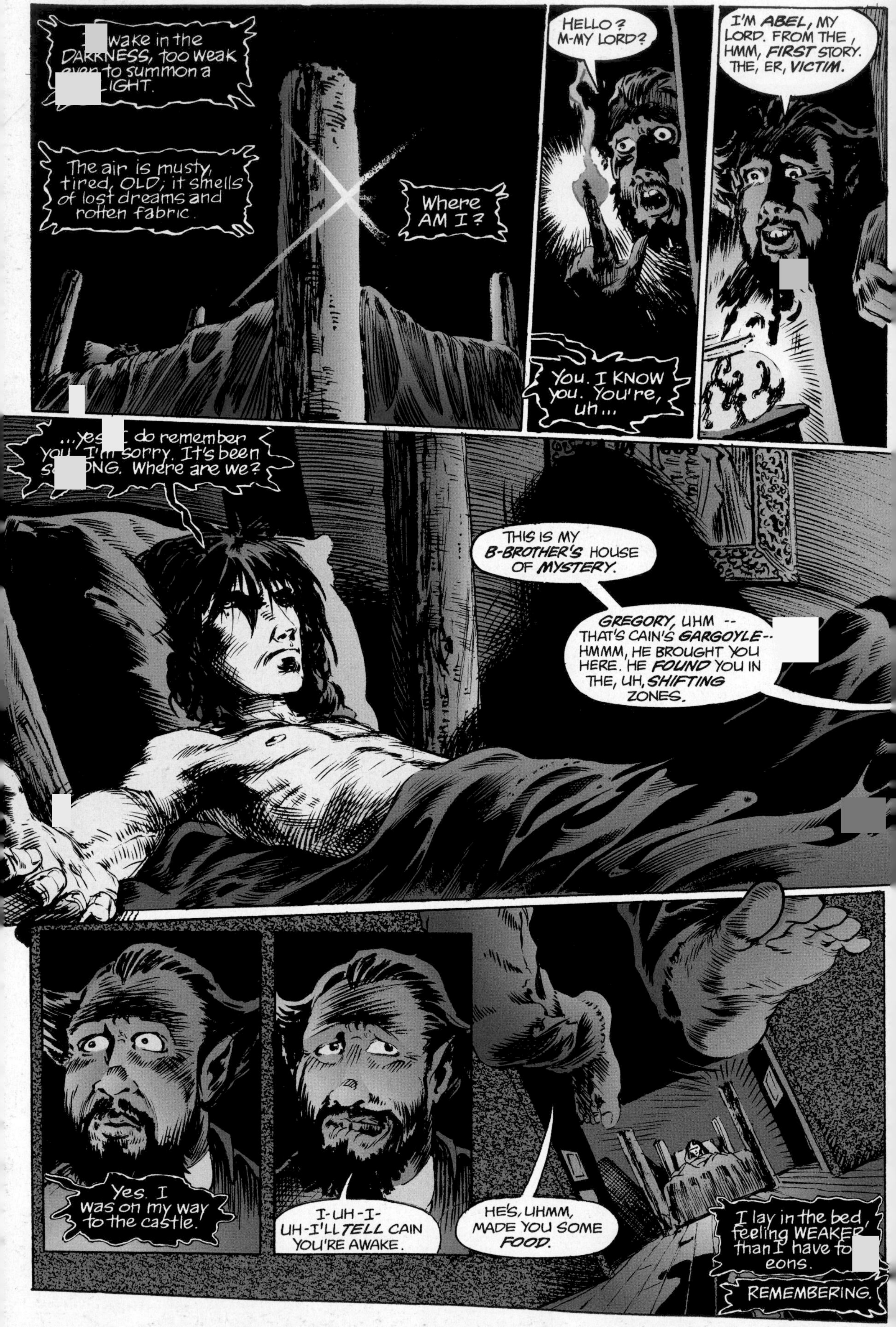
wake in the DARKNESS, too weak even to summon a LIGHT.
The air is musty, tired, OLD; it smells of lost dreams and rotten fabric.
Where AM I?
HELLO? M-MY LORD?
You. I KNOW you. You're, uh...
I'M ABEL, MY LORD. FROM THE, HMM, FIRST STORY. THE, ER, VICTIM.
...yes do remember you. I'm sorry. It's been s ONG. Where are we?
THIS IS MY B-BROTHER'S HOUSE OF MYSTERY.
GREGORY, UHM -- THAT'S CAIN'S GARGOYLE -- HMMM, HE BROUGHT YOU HERE. HE FOUND YOU IN THE, UH, SHIFTING ZONES.
Yes. I was on my way to the castle.
I-UH-I-UH-I'LL TELL CAIN YOU'RE AWAKE.
HE'S, UHMM, MADE YOU SOME FOOD.
I lay in the bed, feeling WEAKER than I have fo eons.
REMEMBERING.

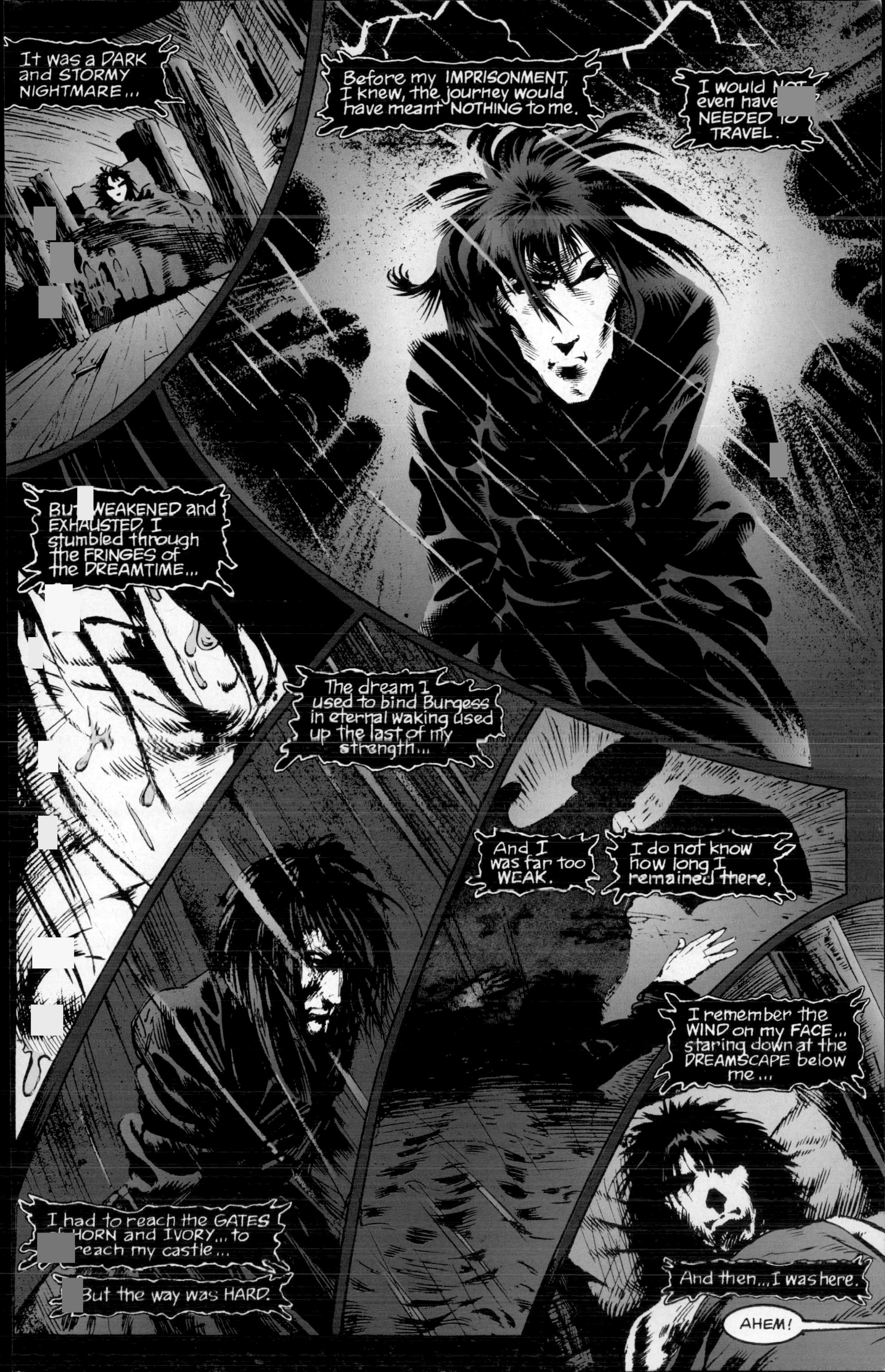

It was a DARK and STORMY NIGHTMARE...
Before my IMPRISONMENT, I knew, the journey would have meant NOTHING to me.
I would NOT even have NEEDED TO TRAVEL.
BUT WEAKENED and EXHAUSTED, I stumbled through the FRINGES of the DREAMTIME...
The dream I used to bind Burgess in eternal waking used up the last of my strength...
And I was far too WEAK.
I do not know how long I remained there.
I had to reach the GATES of HORN and IVORY... to reach my castle...
But the way was HARD.
I remember the WIND on my FACE... staring down at the DREAMSCAPE below me...
And then... I was here.
AHEM!

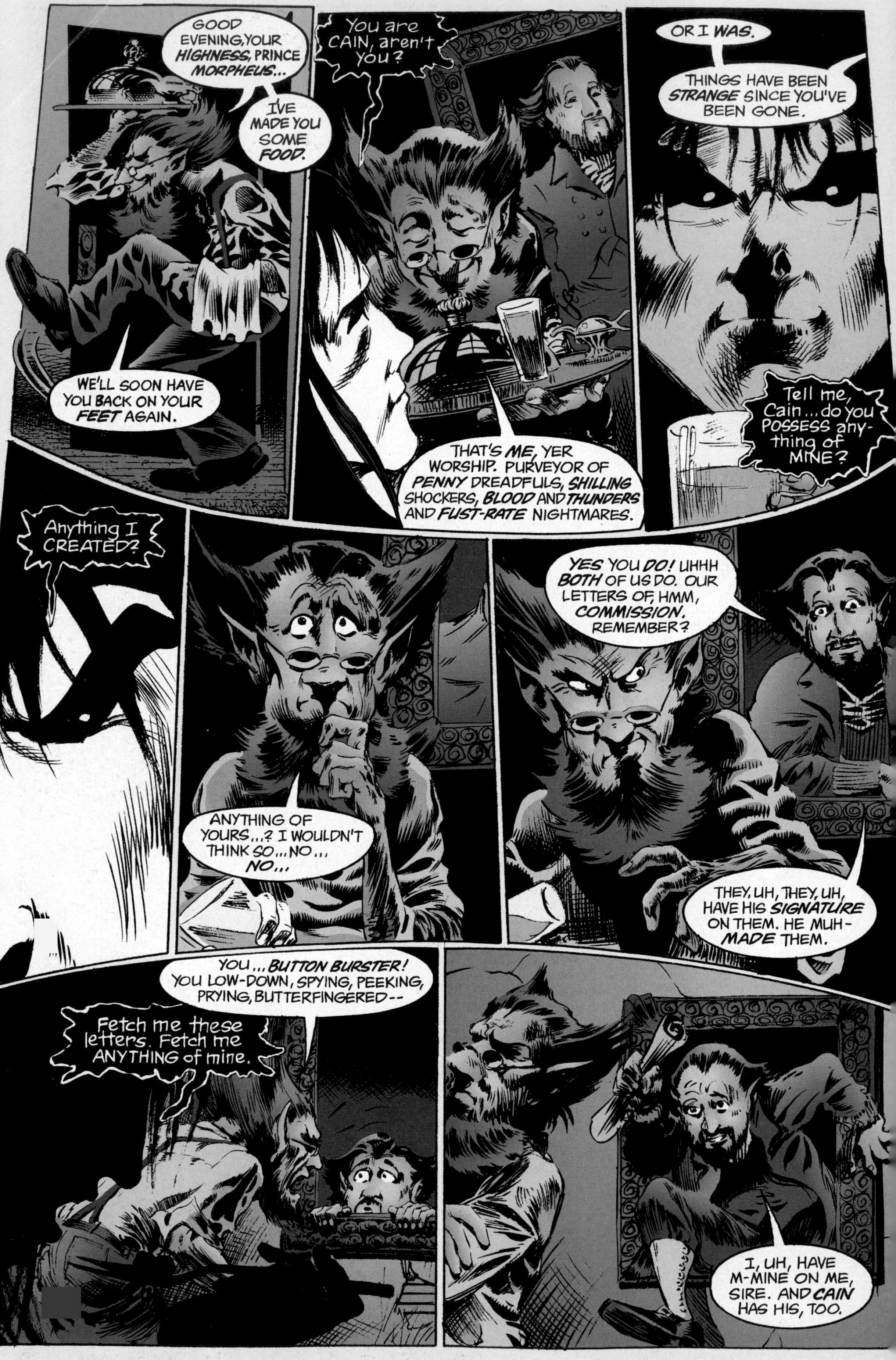
GOOD EVENING, YOUR HIGHNESS, PRINCE MORPHEUS...
I'VE MADE YOU SOME FOOD.
WE'LL SOON HAVE YOU BACK ON YOUR FEET AGAIN.
You are CAIN, aren't you?
THAT'S ME, YER WORSHIP. PURVEYOR OF PENNY DREADFULS, SHILLING SHOCKERS, BLOOD AND THUNDERS AND FUST-RATE NIGHTMARES.
OR I WAS.
THINGS HAVE BEEN STRANGE SINCE YOU'VE BEEN GONE.
Tell me, Cain... do you POSSESS any-thing of MINE?
Anything I CREATED?
ANYTHING OF YOURS...? I WOULDN'T THINK SO... NO... NO...
YES YOU DO! UHHH BOTH OF US DO. OUR LETTERS OF, HMM, COMMISSION. REMEMBER?
THEY, UH, THEY, UH, HAVE HIS SIGNATURE ON THEM. HE MUH-MADE THEM.
Fetch me these letters. Fetch me ANYTHING of mine.
YOU... BUTTON BURSTER! YOU LOW-DOWN, SPYING, PEEKING, PRYING, BUTTERFINGERED--
I, UH, HAVE M-MINE ON ME, SIRE. AND CAIN HAS HIS, TOO.

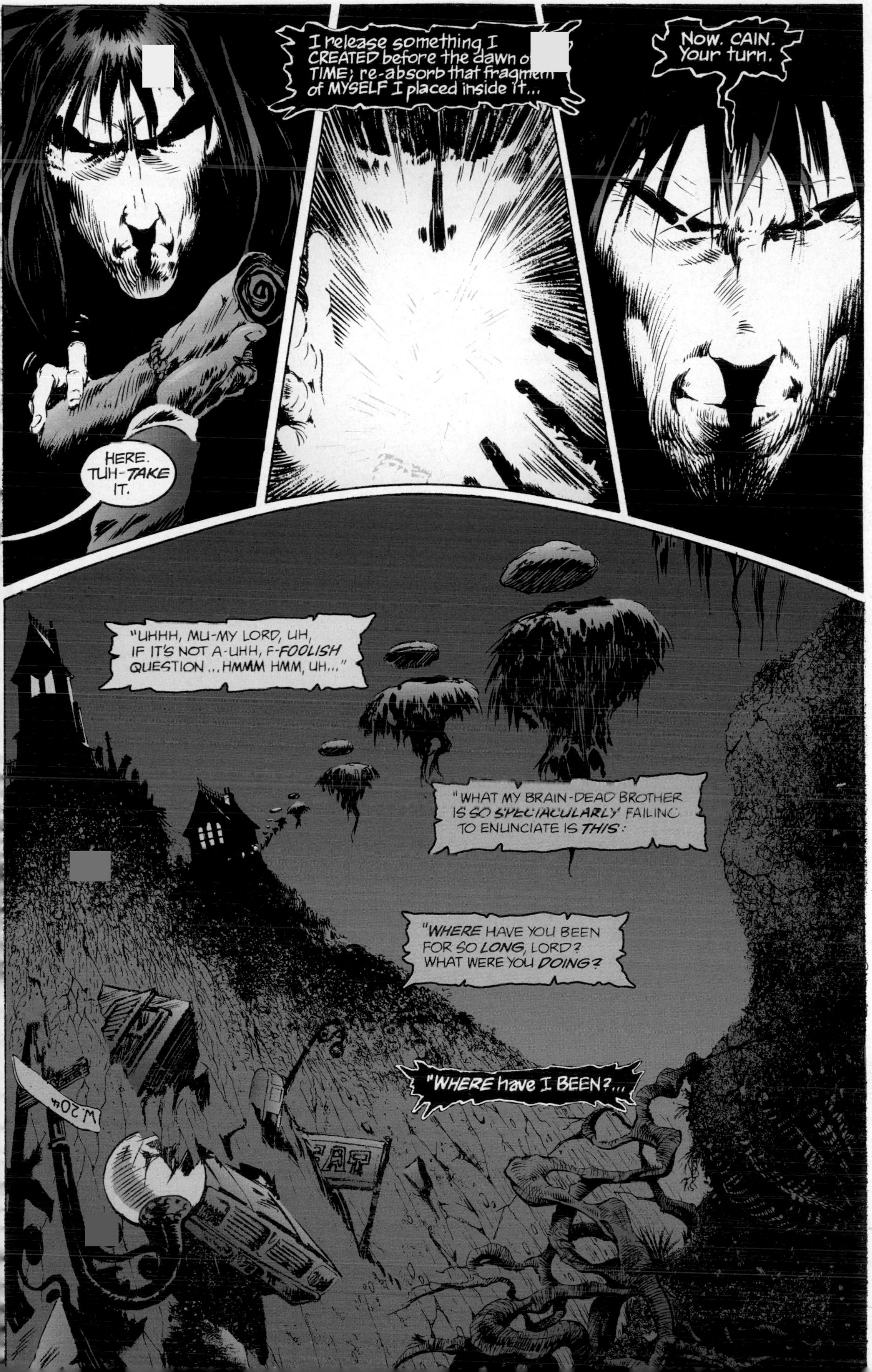
HERE. TUH-TAKE IT.
I release something I CREATED before the dawn o TIME; re-absorb that fragmen of MYSELF I placed inside it...
Now. CAIN. Your turn.
"UHHH, MU-MY LORD, UH, IF IT'S NOT A-UHH, F-FOOLISH QUESTION ... HMMM HMM, UH..."
"WHAT MY BRAIN-DEAD BROTHER IS SO SPECTACULARLY FAILING TO ENUNCIATE IS THIS:
"WHERE HAVE YOU BEEN FOR SO LONG, LORD? WHAT WERE YOU DOING?
"WHERE have I BEEN?...

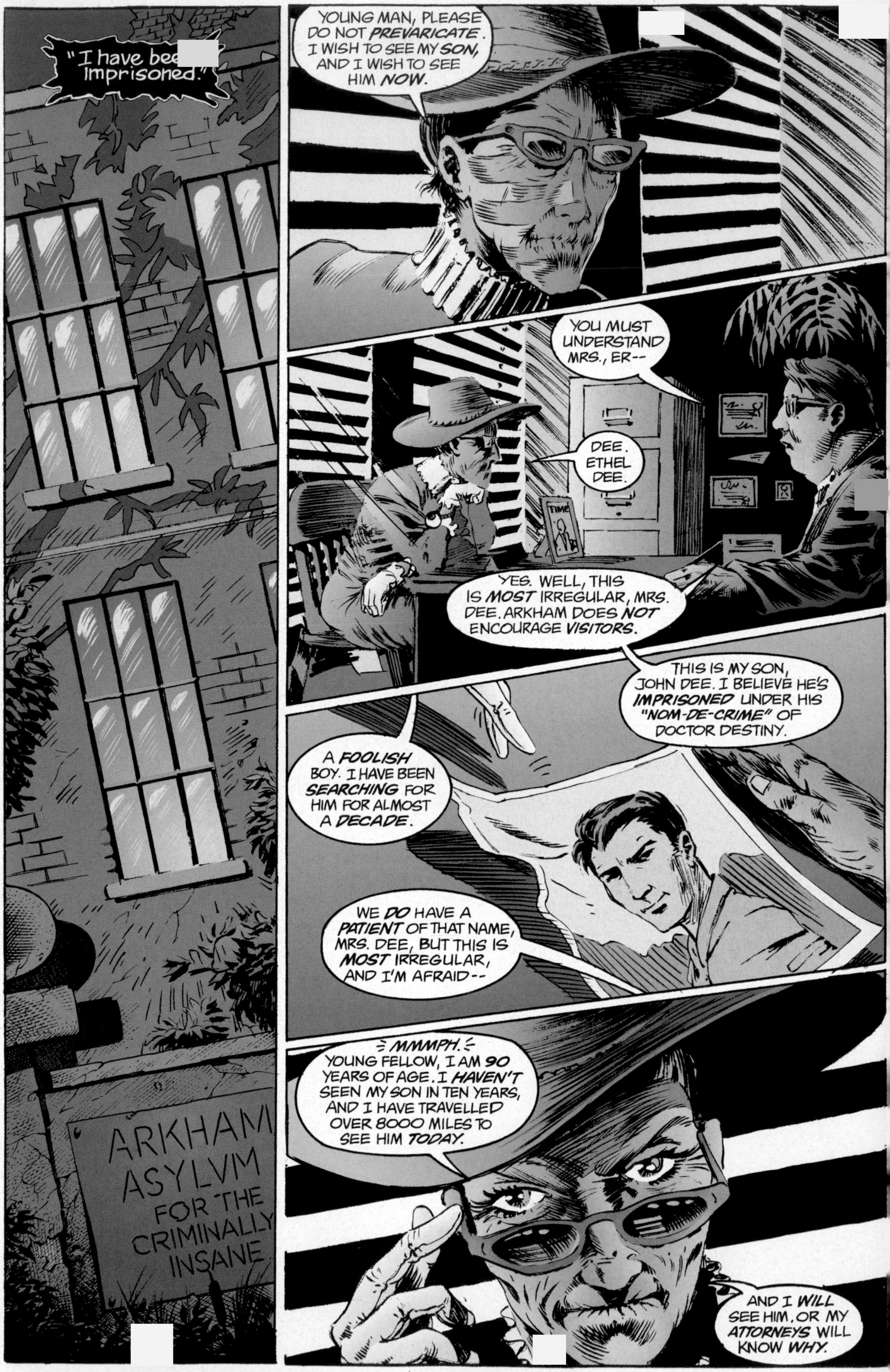
"I have bee
Imprisoned."
ARKHAM ASYLVM FOR THE CRIMINALLY INSANE
YOUNG MAN, PLEASE DO NOT PREVARICATE. I WISH TO SEE MY SON, AND I WISH TO SEE HIM NOW.
YOU MUST UNDERSTAND MRS., ER--
DEE. ETHEL DEE.
TIME
YES. WELL, THIS IS MOST IRREGULAR, MRS. DEE. ARKHAM DOES NOT ENCOURAGE VISITORS.
THIS IS MY SON, JOHN DEE. I BELIEVE HE'S IMPRISONED UNDER HIS "NOM-DE-CRIME" OF DOCTOR DESTINY.
A FOOLISH BOY. I HAVE BEEN SEARCHING FOR HIM FOR ALMOST A DECADE.
WE DO HAVE A PATIENT OF THAT NAME, MRS. DEE, BUT THIS IS MOST IRREGULAR, AND I'M AFRAID--
MMMPH.
YOUNG FELLOW, I AM 90 YEARS OF AGE. I HAVEN'T SEEN MY SON IN TEN YEARS, AND I HAVE TRAVELLED OVER 8000 MILES TO SEE HIM TODAY.
AND I WILL SEE HIM, OR MY ATTORNEYS WILL KNOW WHY.

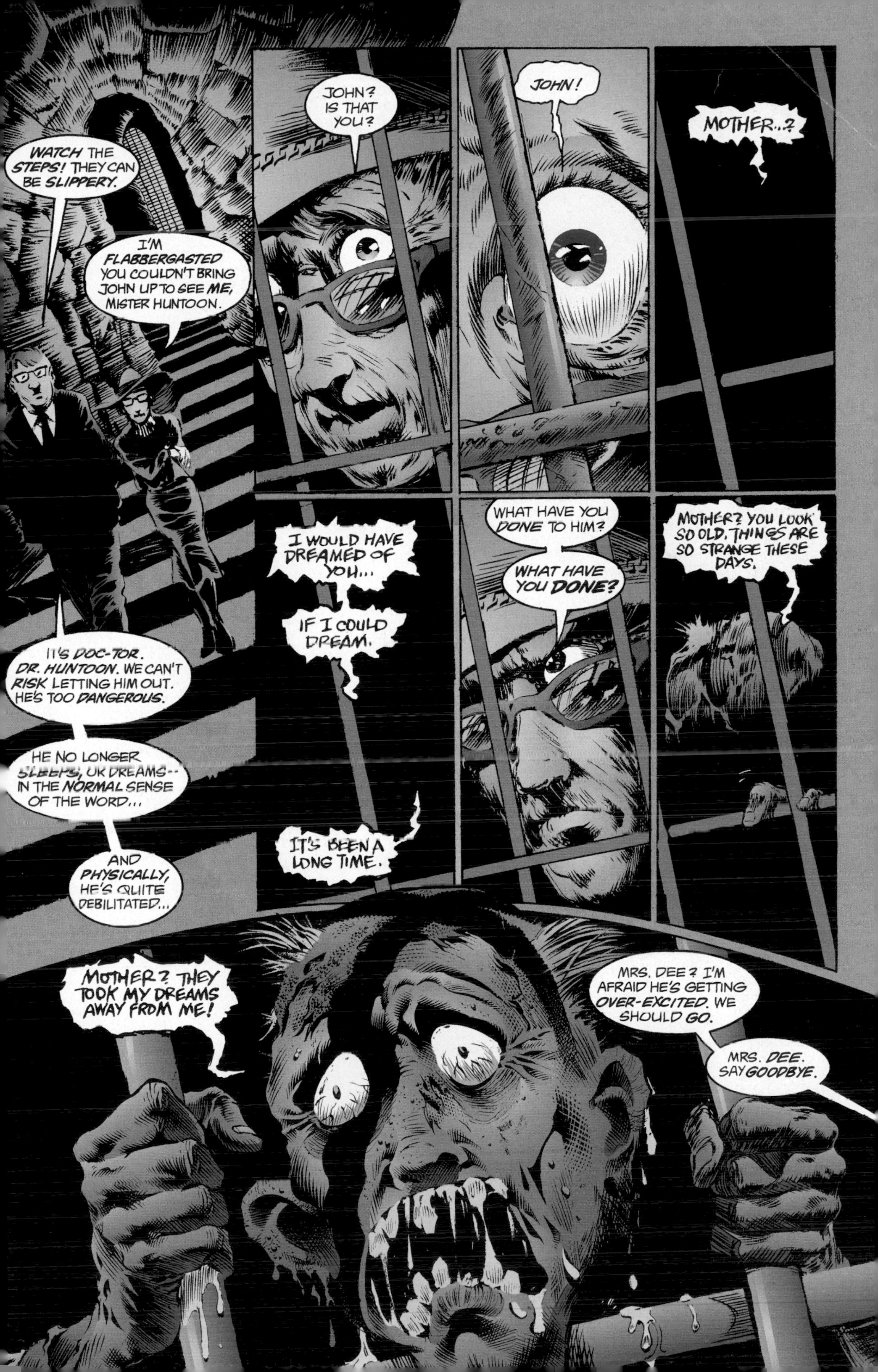

WATCH THE STEPS! THEY CAN BE SLIPPERY.
I'M FLABBERGASTED YOU COULDN'T BRING JOHN UP TO SEE ME, MISTER HUNTOON.
IT'S DOC-TOR. DR. HUNTOON. WE CAN'T RISK LETTING HIM OUT. HE'S TOO DANGEROUS.
HE NO LONGER SLEEPS, OR DREAMS-- IN THE NORMAL SENSE OF THE WORD...
AND PHYSICALLY, HE'S QUITE DEBILITATED...
JOHN? IS THAT YOU?
JOHN!
MOTHER...?
I WOULD HAVE DREAMED OF YOU...
IF I COULD DREAM.
IT'S BEEN A LONG TIME.
WHAT HAVE YOU DONE TO HIM?
WHAT HAVE YOU DONE?
MOTHER? YOU LOOK SO OLD. THINGS ARE SO STRANGE THESE DAYS.
MOTHER? THEY TOOK MY DREAMS AWAY FROM ME!
MRS. DEE? I'M AFRAID HE'S GETTING OVER-EXCITED. WE SHOULD GO.
MRS. DEE. SAY GOODBYE.

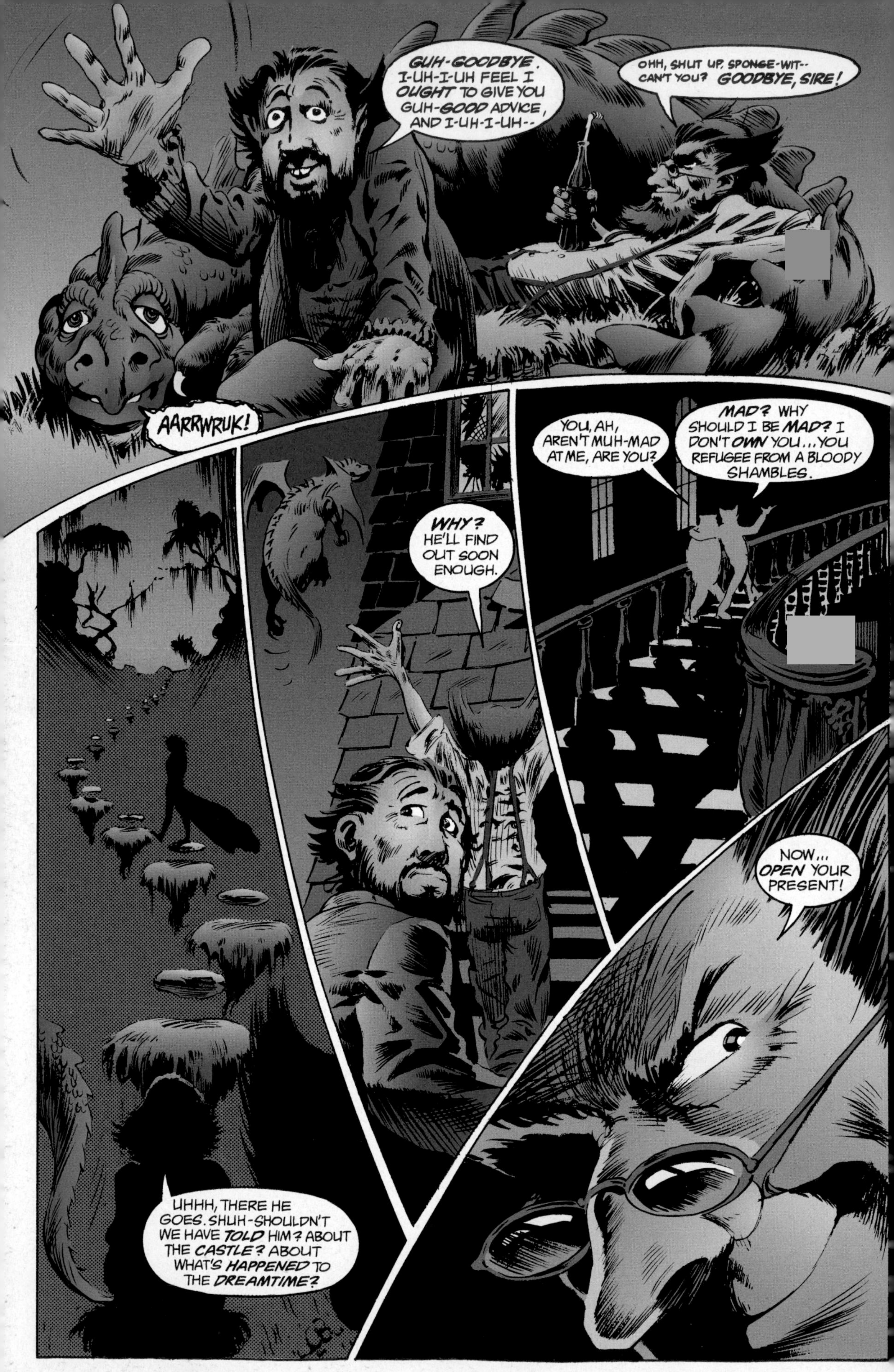
GUH-GOODBYE. I-UH-I-UH FEEL I OUGHT TO GIVE YOU GUH-GOOD ADVICE, AND I-UH-I-UH--
OHH, SHUT UP, SPONGE-WIT-- CAN'T YOU? GOODBYE, SIRE!
AARRWRUK!
UHHH, THERE HE GOES. SHUH-SHOULDN'T WE HAVE TOLD HIM? ABOUT THE CASTLE? ABOUT WHAT'S HAPPENED TO THE DREAMTIME?
WHY? HE'LL FIND OUT SOON ENOUGH.
YOU, AH, AREN'T MUH-MAD AT ME, ARE YOU?
MAD? WHY SHOULD I BE MAD? I DON'T OWN YOU... YOU REFUGEE FROM A BLOODY SHAMBLES.
NOW... OPEN YOUR PRESENT!

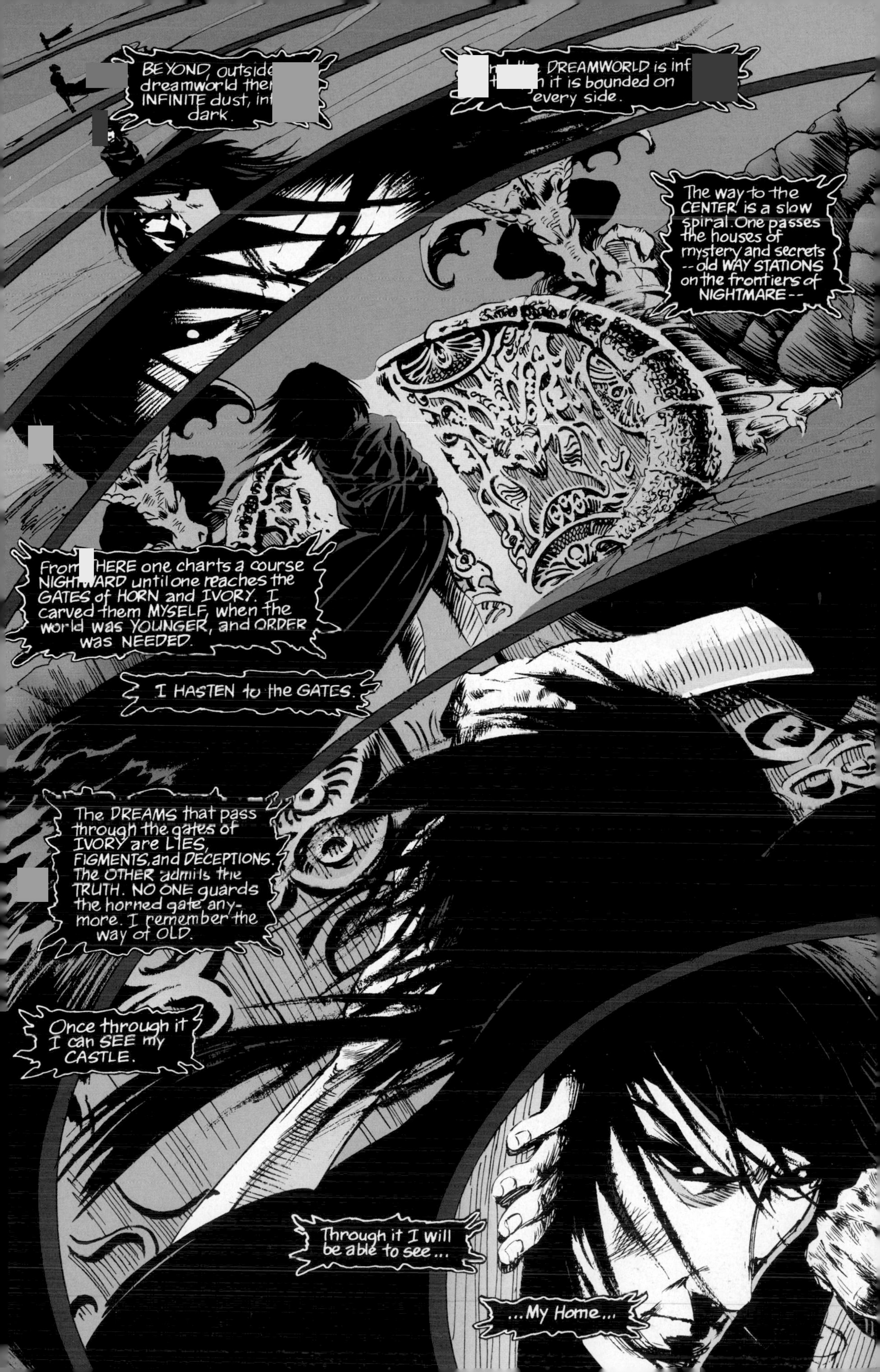
BEYOND, outside[redacted] dreamworld ther[redacted] INFINITE dust, inf[redacted] dark.
[redacted]nd t[redacted]e DREAMWORLD is inf[redacted] t[redacted]h it is bounded on every side.
The way to the CENTER is a slow spiral. One passes the houses of mystery and secrets -- old WAY STATIONS on the frontiers of NIGHTMARE --
From [redacted]HERE one charts a course NIGHTWARD until one reaches the GATES of HORN and IVORY. I carved them MYSELF, when the world was YOUNGER, and ORDER was NEEDED.
I HASTEN to the GATES.
The DREAMS that pass through the gates of IVORY are LIES, FIGMENTS, and DECEPTIONS. The OTHER admits the TRUTH. NO ONE guards the horned gate any-more. I remember the way of OLD.
Once through it I can SEE my CASTLE.
Through it I will be able to see...
...My Home...

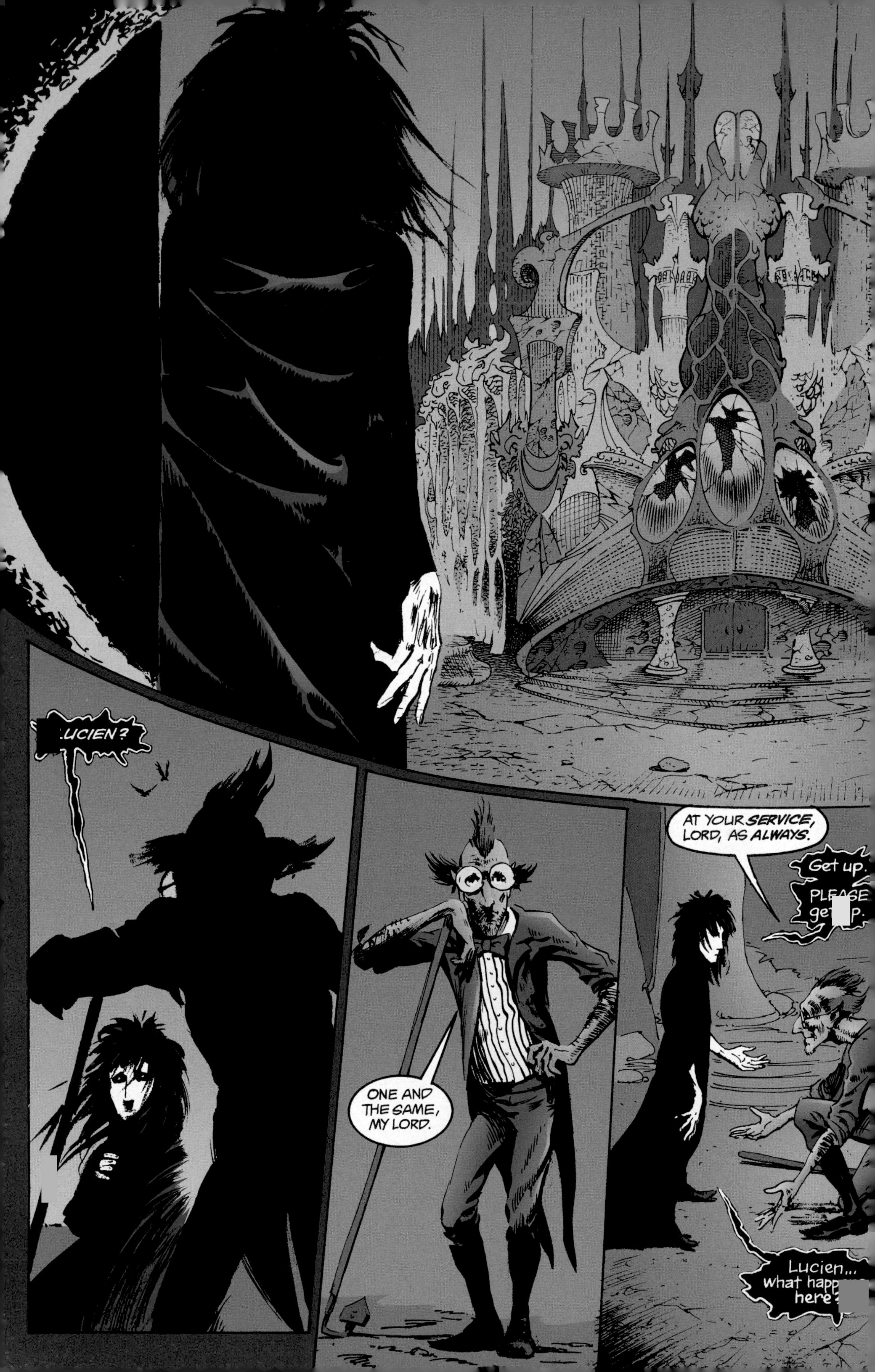
[redacted]UCIEN?
ONE AND THE SAME, MY LORD.
AT YOUR **SERVICE**, LORD, AS **ALWAYS**.
Get up.
PLEASE ge p.
Lucien... what happ
here?

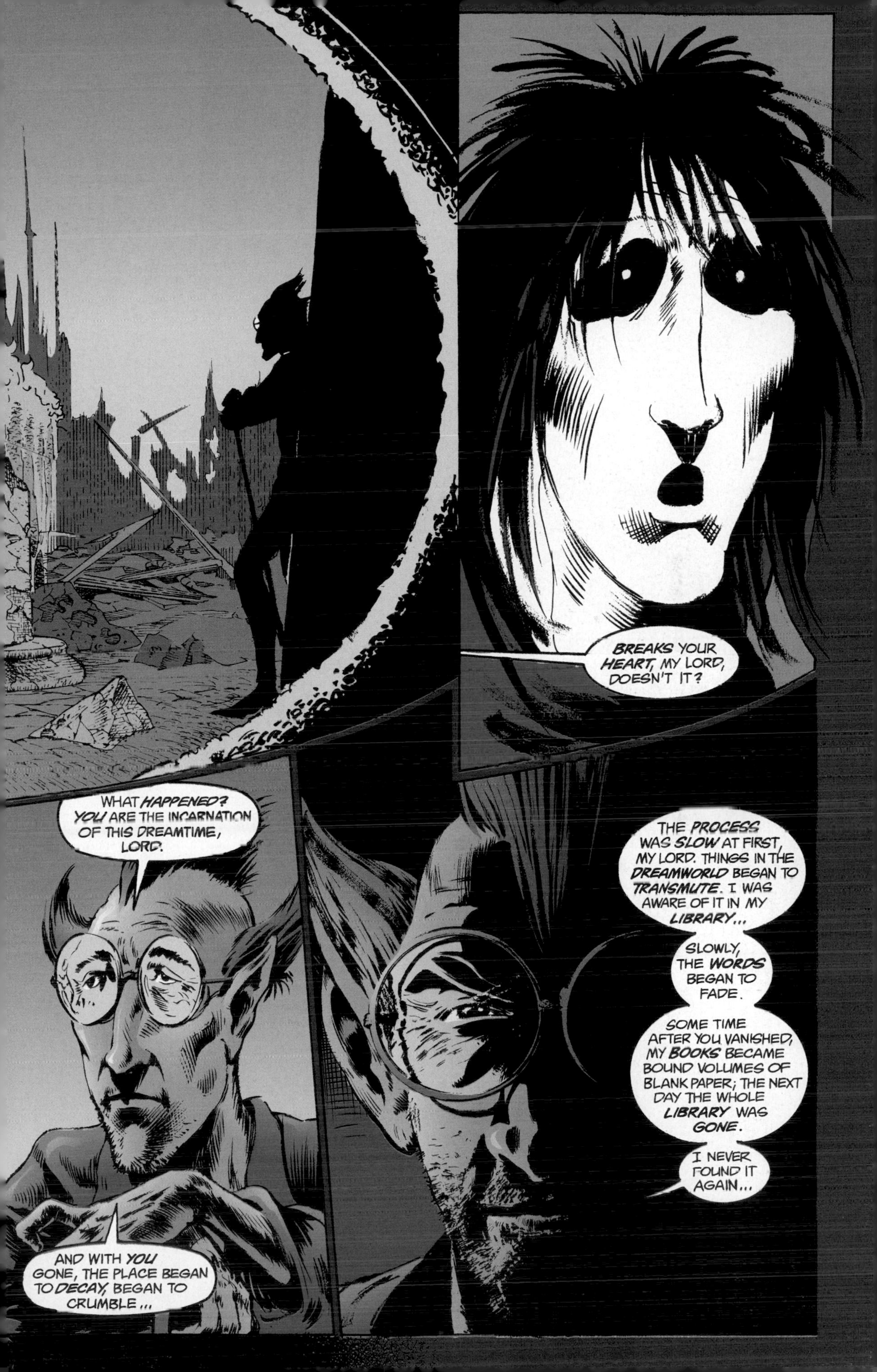
BREAKS YOUR HEART, MY LORD, DOESN'T IT?
WHAT HAPPENED? YOU ARE THE INCARNATION OF THIS DREAMTIME, LORD.
AND WITH YOU GONE, THE PLACE BEGAN TO DECAY, BEGAN TO CRUMBLE...
THE PROCESS WAS SLOW AT FIRST, MY LORD. THINGS IN THE DREAMWORLD BEGAN TO TRANSMUTE. I WAS AWARE OF IT IN MY LIBRARY...
SLOWLY, THE WORDS BEGAN TO FADE.
SOME TIME AFTER YOU VANISHED, MY BOOKS BECAME BOUND VOLUMES OF BLANK PAPER; THE NEXT DAY THE WHOLE LIBRARY WAS GONE.
I NEVER FOUND IT AGAIN...

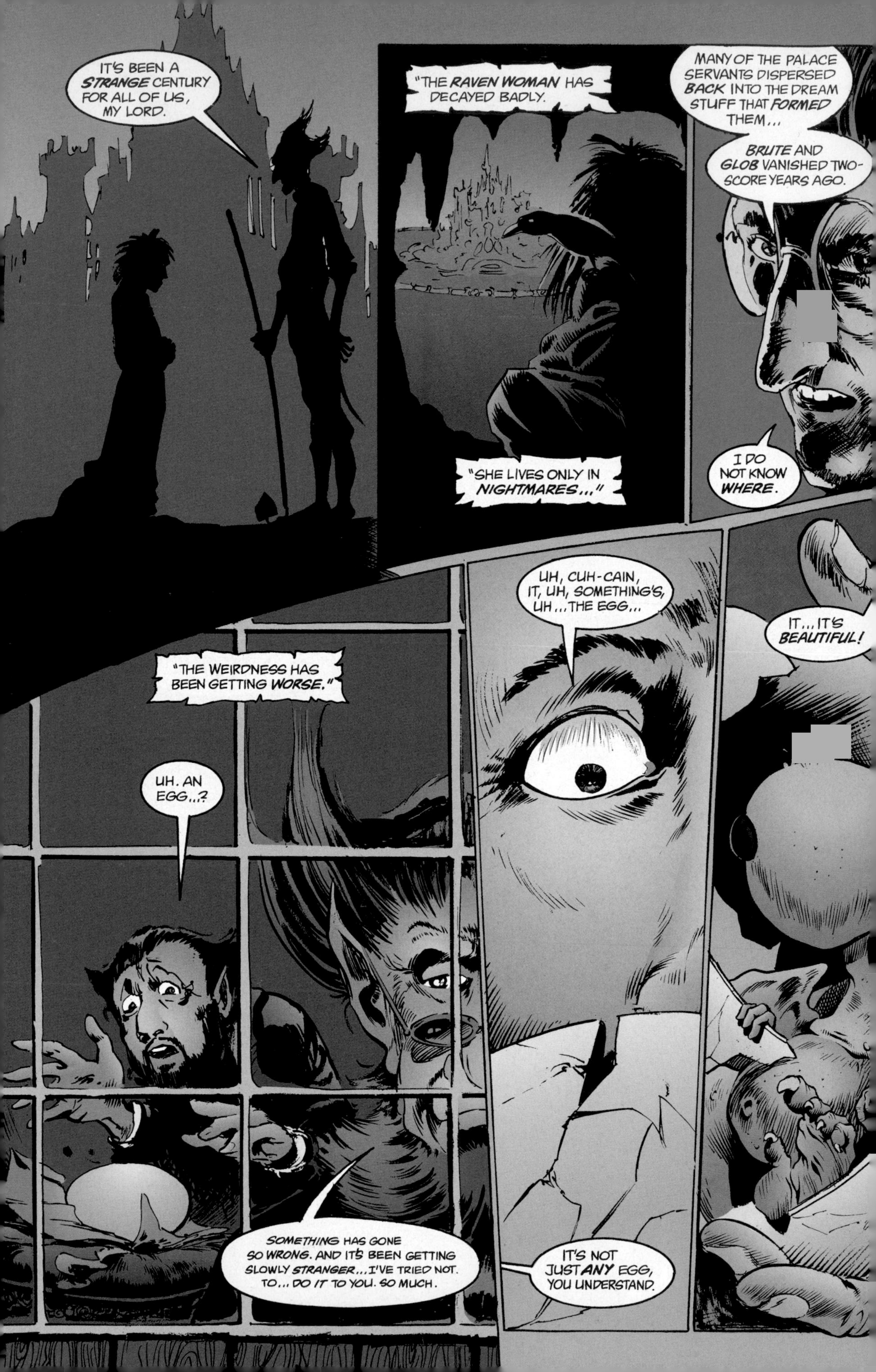
IT'S BEEN A STRANGE CENTURY FOR ALL OF US, MY LORD.
"THE RAVEN WOMAN HAS DECAYED BADLY.
"SHE LIVES ONLY IN NIGHTMARES..."
MANY OF THE PALACE SERVANTS DISPERSED BACK INTO THE DREAM STUFF THAT FORMED THEM...
BRUTE AND GLOB VANISHED TWO-SCORE YEARS AGO.
I DO NOT KNOW WHERE.
"THE WEIRDNESS HAS BEEN GETTING WORSE."
UH. AN EGG...?
SOMETHING HAS GONE SO WRONG. AND IT'S BEEN GETTING SLOWLY STRANGER... I'VE TRIED NOT. TO... DO IT TO YOU. SO MUCH.
UH, CUH-CAIN, IT, UH, SOMETHING'S, UH... THE EGG...
IT'S NOT JUST ANY EGG, YOU UNDERSTAND.
IT... IT'S BEAUTIFUL!

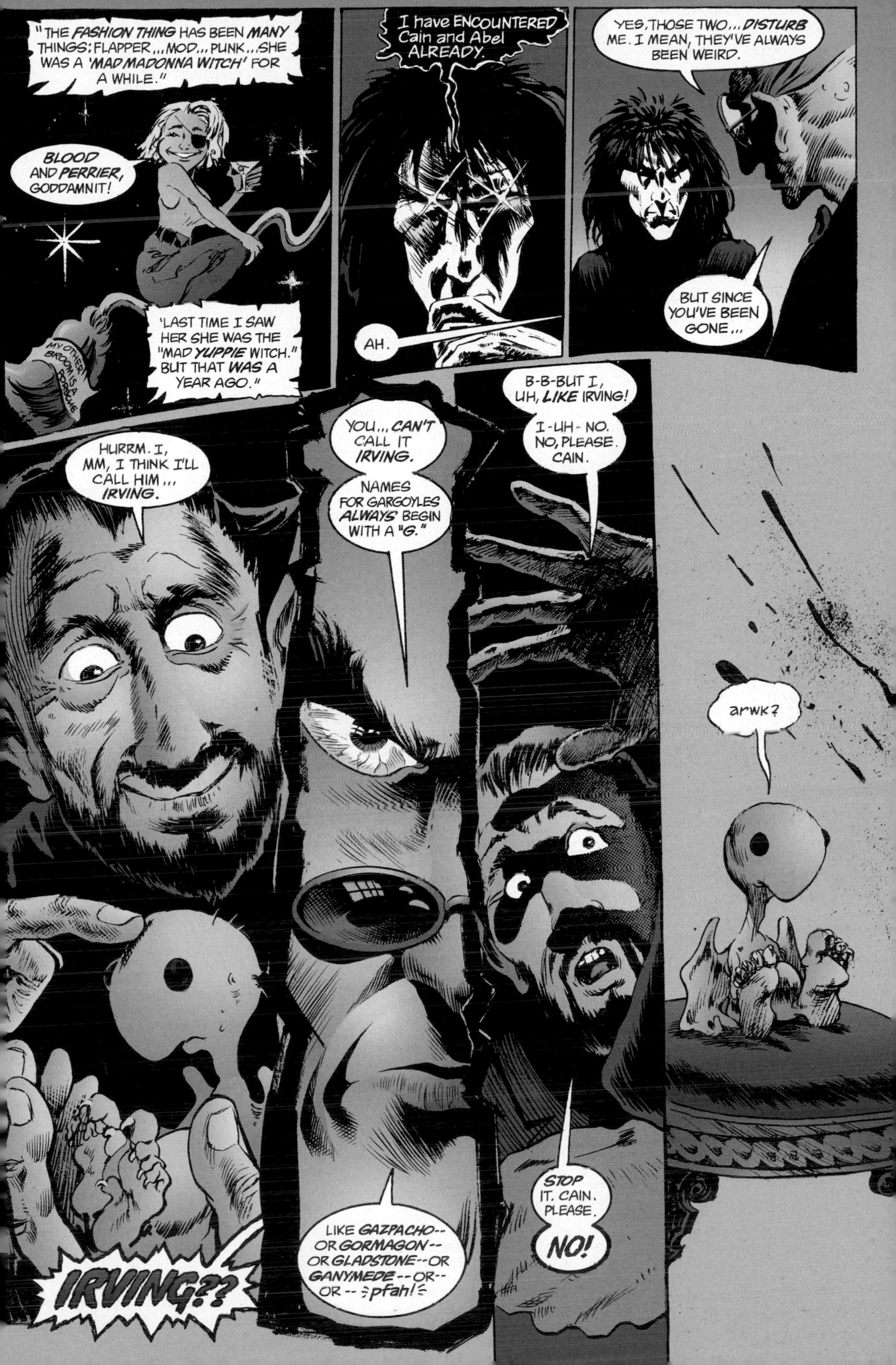
"THE FASHION THING HAS BEEN MANY THINGS: FLAPPER... MOD... PUNK... SHE WAS A 'MAD MADONNA WITCH' FOR A WHILE."
BLOOD AND PERRIER, GODDAMNIT!
MY OTHER BROOM IS A PORSCHE
'LAST TIME I SAW HER SHE WAS THE "MAD YUPPIE WITCH." BUT THAT WAS A YEAR AGO."
I have ENCOUNTERED Cain and Abel ALREADY.
AH.
YES, THOSE TWO... DISTURB ME. I MEAN, THEY'VE ALWAYS BEEN WEIRD.
BUT SINCE YOU'VE BEEN GONE...
HURRM. I, MM, I THINK I'LL CALL HIM... IRVING.
IRVING??
YOU... CAN'T CALL IT IRVING.
NAMES FOR GARGOYLES ALWAYS BEGIN WITH A "G."
LIKE GAZPACHO-- OR GORMAGON-- OR GLADSTONE--OR GANYMEDE--OR-- OR-- pfah!
B-B-BUT I, UH, LIKE IRVING!
I-UH- NO. NO, PLEASE. CAIN.
STOP IT. CAIN. PLEASE.
NO!
arwk?

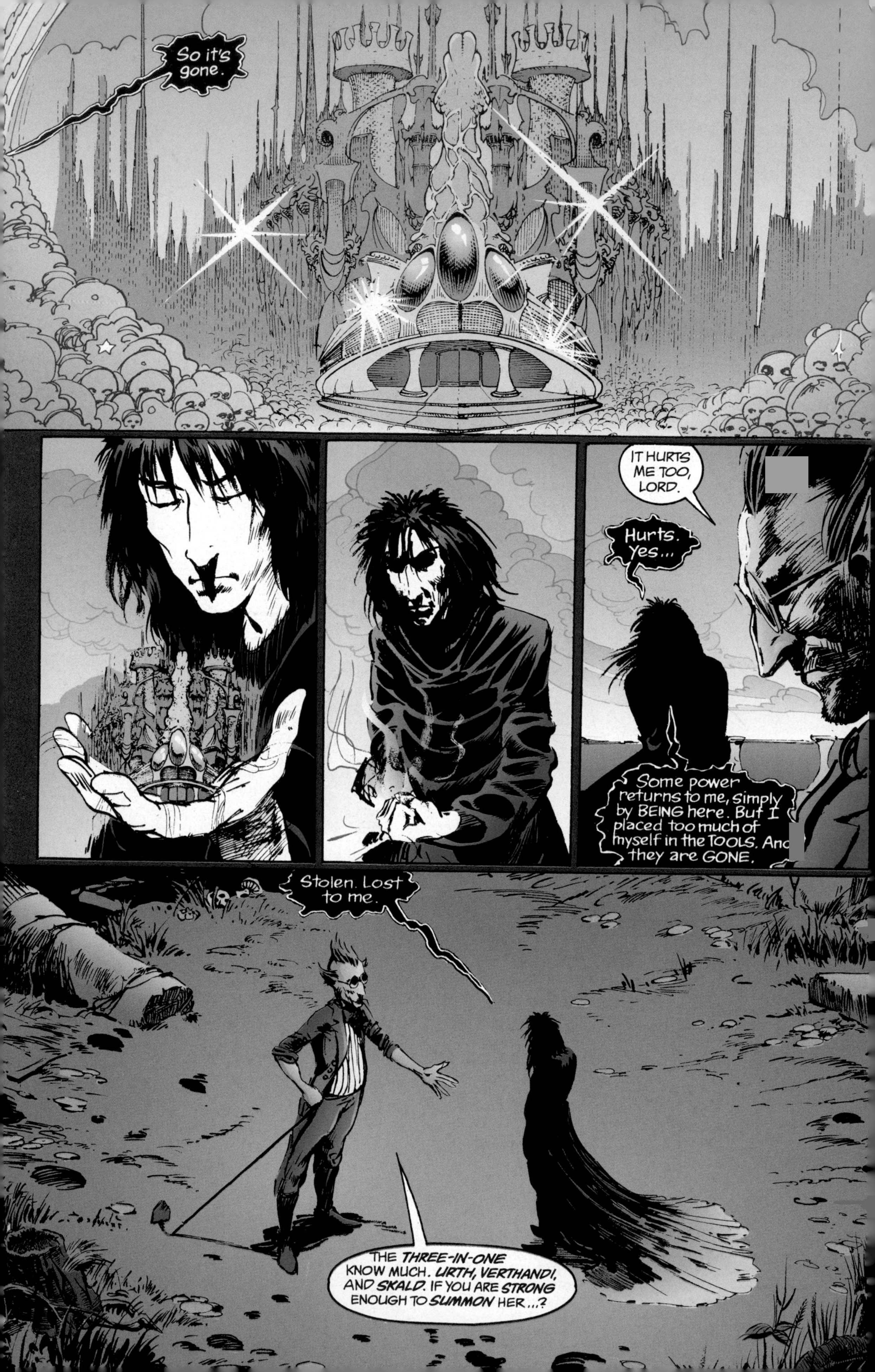
So it's gone.
IT HURTS ME TOO, LORD.
Hurts. Yes...
Some power returns to me, simply by BEING here. But I placed too much of myself in the TOOLS. And they are GONE.
Stolen. Lost to me.
THE *THREE-IN-ONE* KNOW MUCH. *URTH, VERTHANDI,* AND *SKALD.* IF YOU ARE *STRONG* ENOUGH TO *SUMMON* HER...?

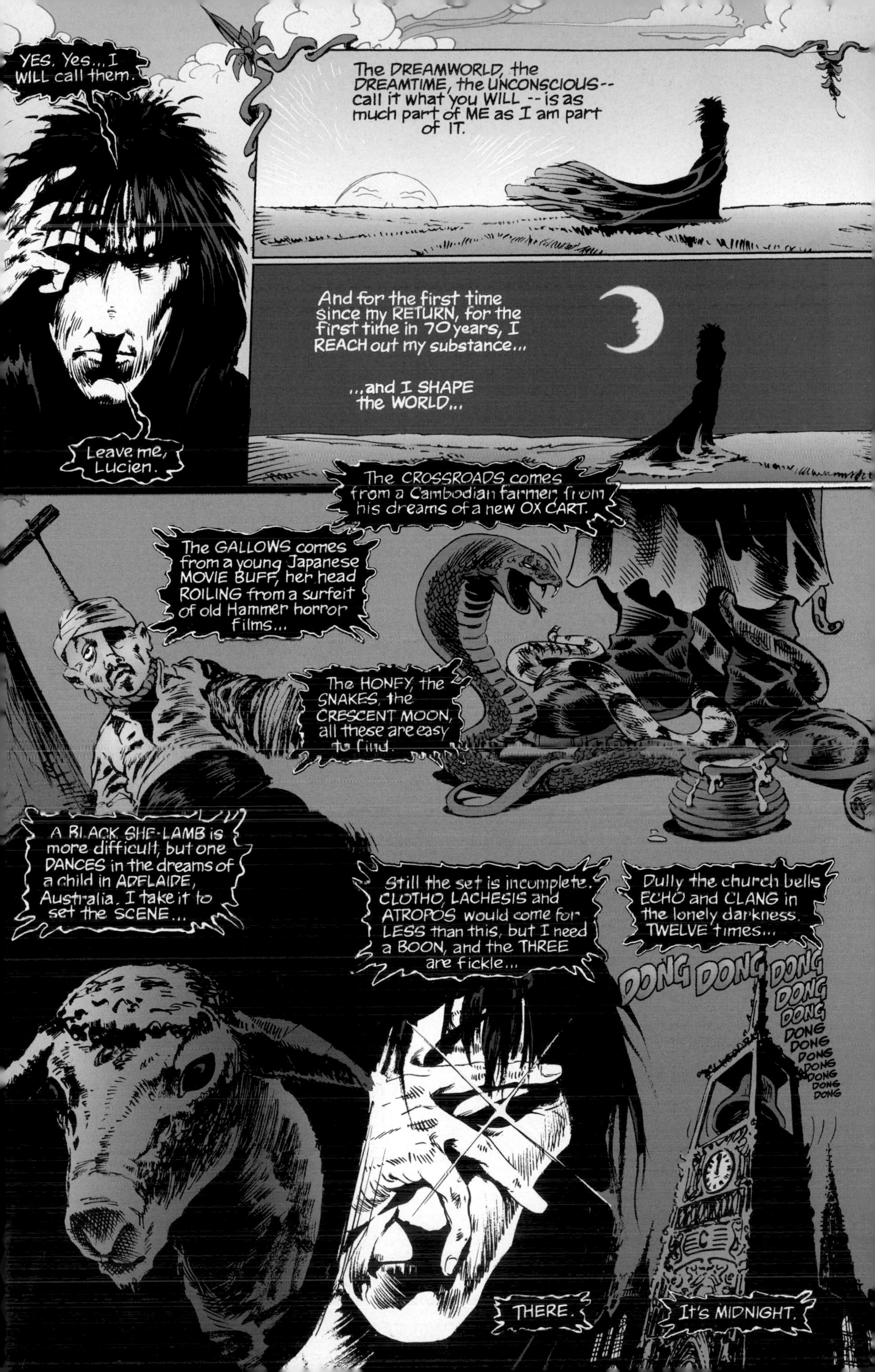
YES. Yes... I WILL call them.
Leave me, Lucien.
The DREAMWORLD, the DREAMTIME, the UNCONSCIOUS-- call it what you WILL --is as much part of ME as I am part of IT.
And for the first time since my RETURN, for the first time in 70 years, I REACH out my substance...
...and I SHAPE the WORLD...
The CROSSROADS comes from a Cambodian farmer, from his dreams of a new OX CART.
The GALLOWS comes from a young Japanese MOVIE BUFF, her head ROILING from a surfeit of old Hammer horror films...
The HONEY, the SNAKES, the CRESCENT MOON, all these are easy to find.
A BLACK SHE-LAMB is more difficult, but one DANCES in the dreams of a child in ADELAIDE, Australia. I take it to set the SCENE...
Still the set is incomplete. CLOTHO, LACHESIS and ATROPOS would come for LESS than this, but I need a BOON, and the THREE are fickle...
Dully the church bells ECHO and CLANG in the lonely darkness. TWELVE times...
DONG DONG DONG DONG DONG DONG DONG DONG DONG DONG DONG DONG
THERE.
It's MIDNIGHT.

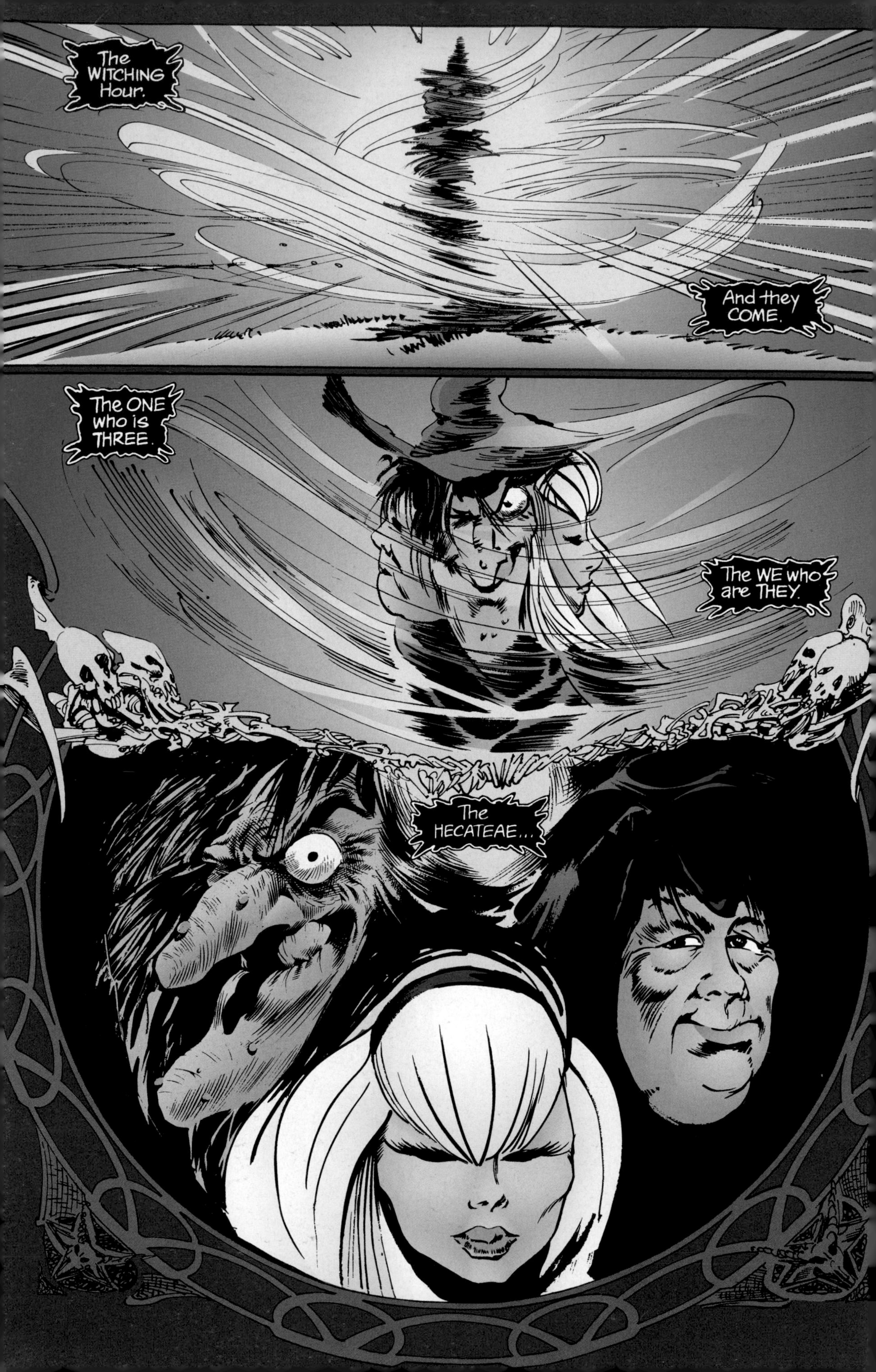
The WITCHING Hour.
And they COME.
The ONE who is THREE.
The WE who are THEY.
The HECATEAE...

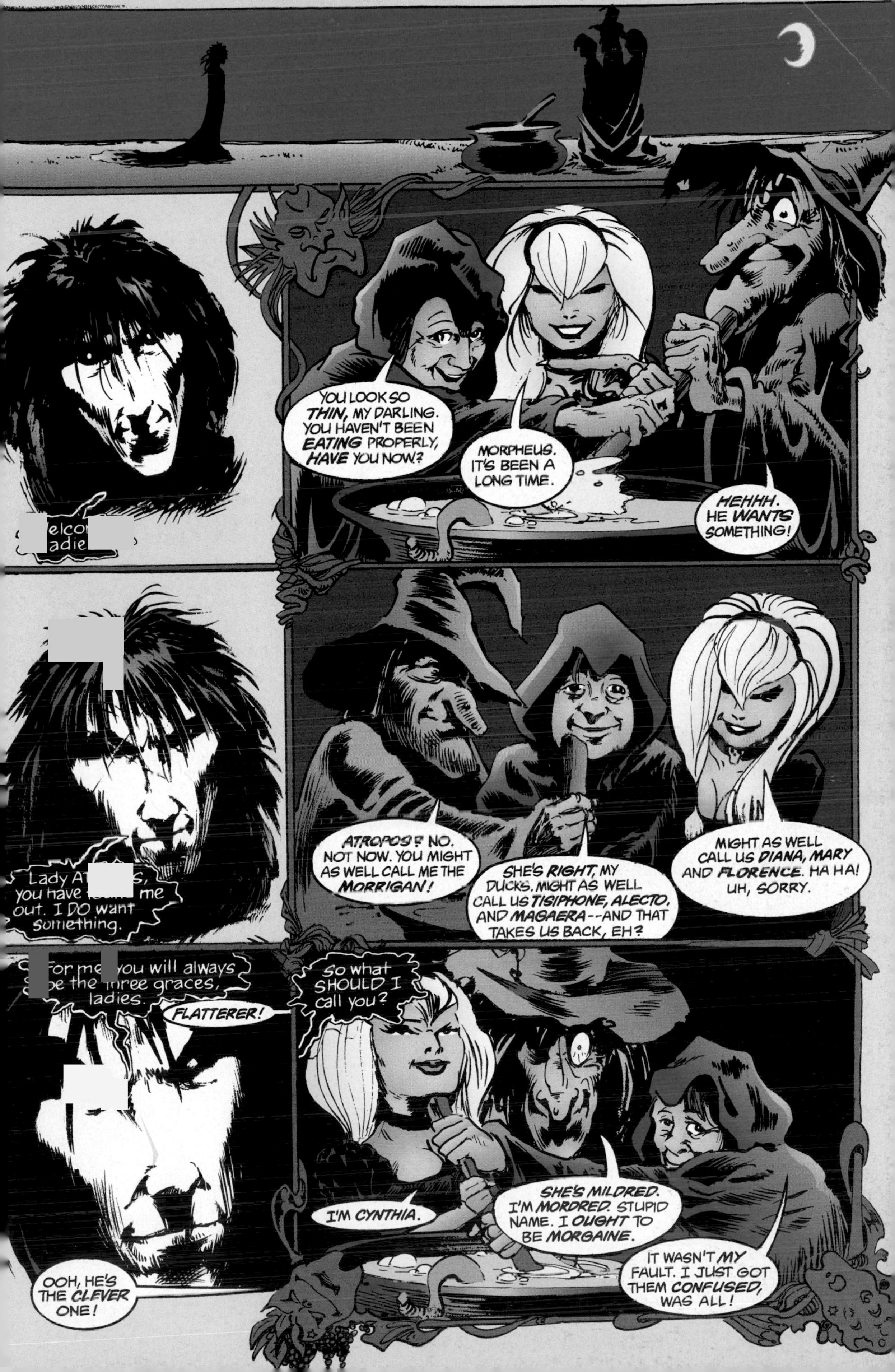
[redacted]elcom[redacted]adie[redacted]
YOU LOOK SO THIN, MY DARLING. YOU HAVEN'T BEEN EATING PROPERLY, HAVE YOU NOW?
MORPHEUS. IT'S BEEN A LONG TIME.
HEHHH. HE WANTS SOMETHING!
Lady AT[redacted]s, you have [redacted] me out. I DO want something.
ATROPOS? NO. NOT NOW. YOU MIGHT AS WELL CALL ME THE MORRIGAN!
SHE'S RIGHT, MY DUCKS. MIGHT AS WELL CALL US TISIPHONE, ALECTO, AND MAGAERA--AND THAT TAKES US BACK, EH?
MIGHT AS WELL CALL US DIANA, MARY AND FLORENCE. HA HA! UH, SORRY.
[redacted]For me[redacted]you will always [redacted]be the [redacted]hree graces, ladies.
FLATTERER!
So what SHOULD I call you?
I'M CYNTHIA.
SHE'S MILDRED. I'M MORDRED. STUPID NAME. I OUGHT TO BE MORGAINE.
OOH, HE'S THE CLEVER ONE!
IT WASN'T MY FAULT. I JUST GOT THEM CONFUSED, WAS ALL!

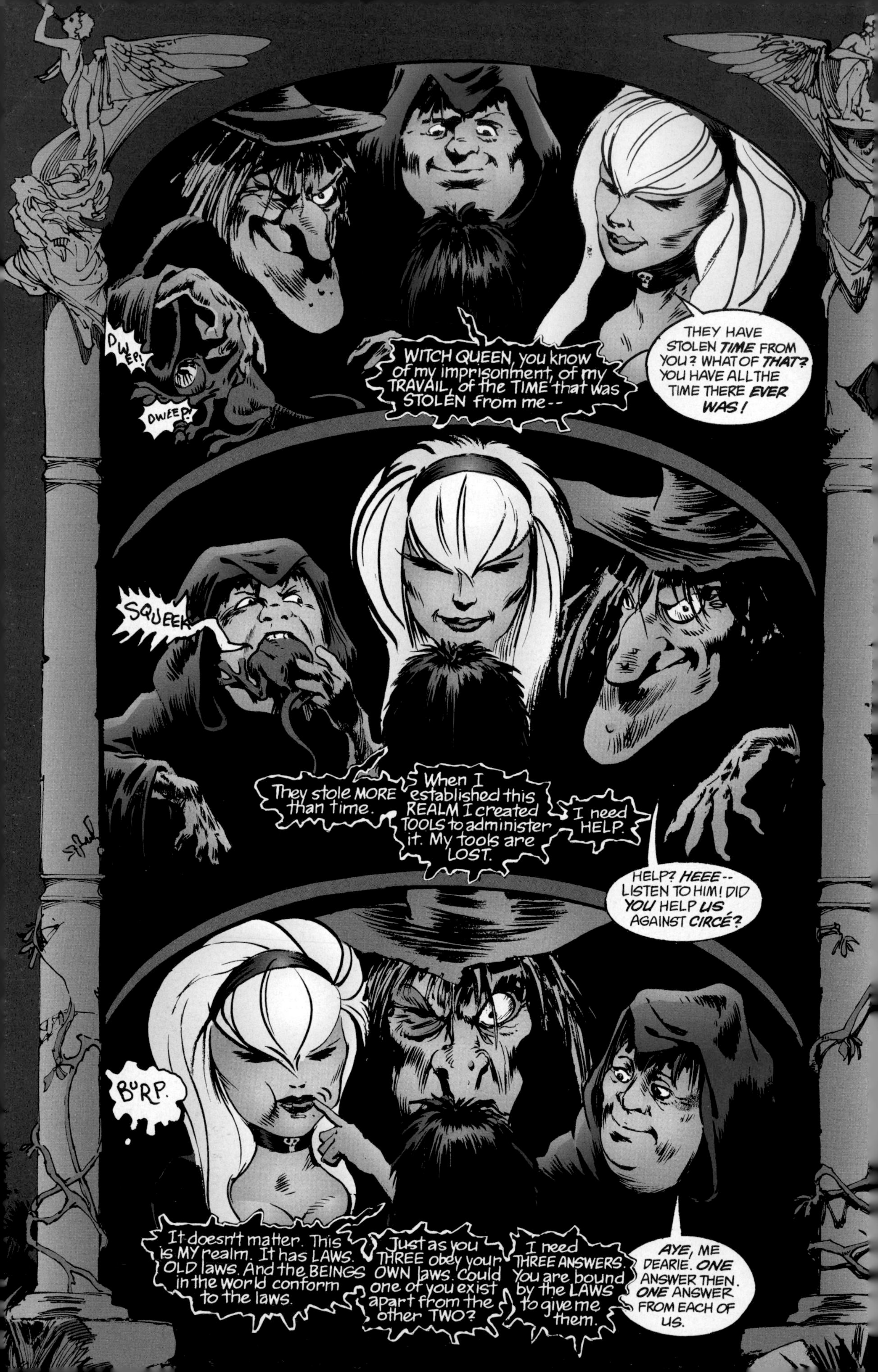
DWEEP!
DWEEP!
WITCH QUEEN, you know of my imprisonment, of my TRAVAIL, of the TIME that was STOLEN from me--
THEY HAVE STOLEN TIME FROM YOU? WHAT OF THAT? YOU HAVE ALL THE TIME THERE EVER WAS!
SQUEEK
They stole MORE than time.
When I established this REALM I created TOOLS to administer it. My tools are LOST.
I need HELP.
HELP? HEEE-- LISTEN TO HIM! DID YOU HELP US AGAINST CIRCÉ?
BURP.
It doesn't matter. This is MY realm. It has LAWS. OLD laws. And the BEINGS in the world conform to the laws.
Just as you THREE obey your OWN laws. Could one of you exist apart from the other TWO?
I need THREE ANSWERS. You are bound by the LAWS to give me them.
AYE, ME DEARIE. ONE ANSWER THEN. ONE ANSWER FROM EACH OF US.

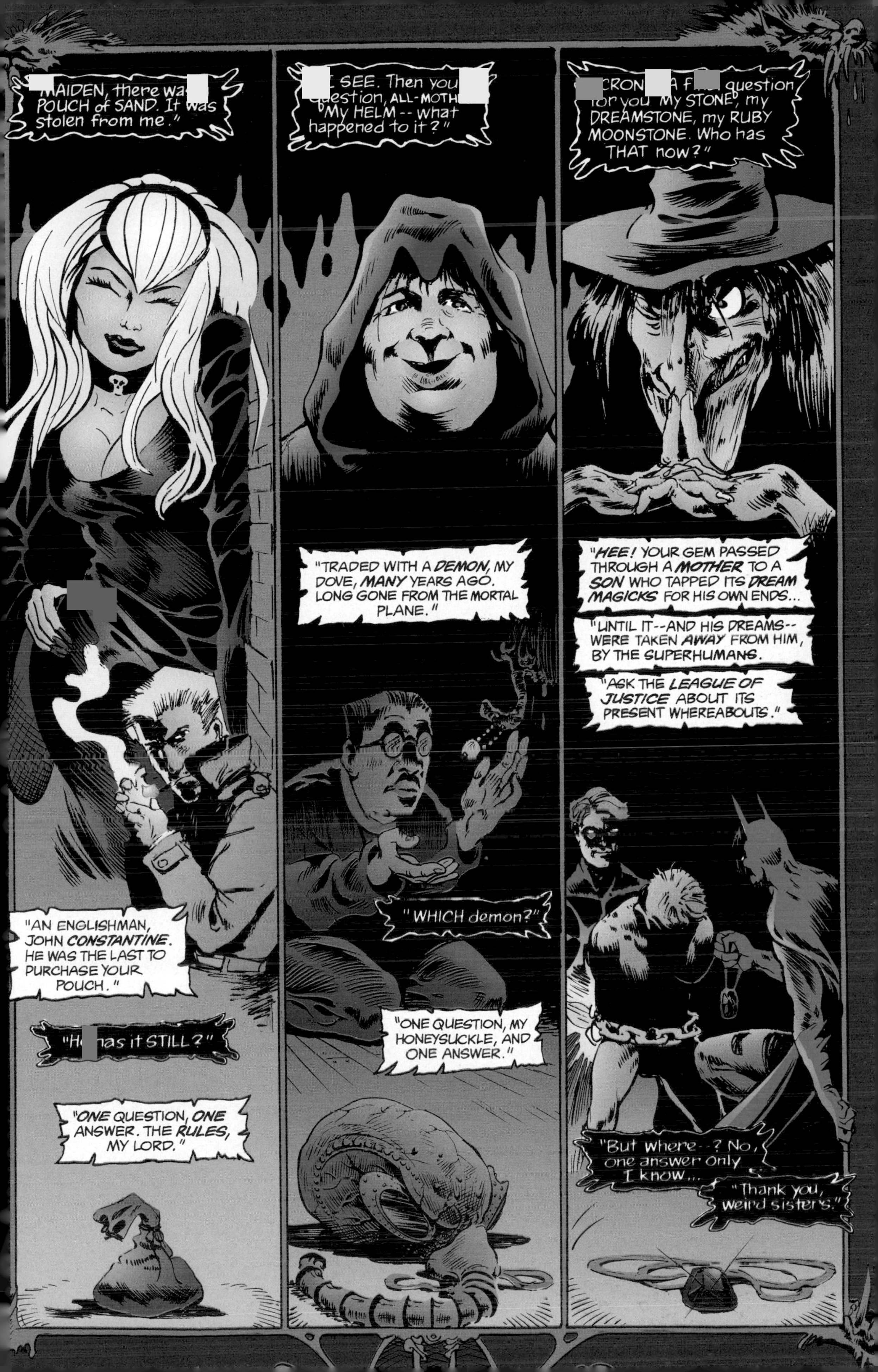

"MAIDEN, there wa POUCH of SAND. It was stolen from me."
"AN ENGLISHMAN, JOHN CONSTANTINE. HE WAS THE LAST TO PURCHASE YOUR POUCH."
"H as it STILL?"
"ONE QUESTION, ONE ANSWER. THE RULES, MY LORD."
" SEE. Then you uestion, ALL-MOTH "My HELM -- what happened to it?"
"TRADED WITH A DEMON, MY DOVE, MANY YEARS AGO. LONG GONE FROM THE MORTAL PLANE."
"WHICH demon?"
"ONE QUESTION, MY HONEYSUCKLE, AND ONE ANSWER."
CRON A f question for you My STONE, my DREAMSTONE, my RUBY MOONSTONE. Who has THAT now?"
"HEE! YOUR GEM PASSED THROUGH A MOTHER TO A SON WHO TAPPED ITS DREAM MAGICKS FOR HIS OWN ENDS...
"UNTIL IT--AND HIS DREAMS--WERE TAKEN AWAY FROM HIM, BY THE SUPERHUMANS.
"ASK THE LEAGUE OF JUSTICE ABOUT ITS PRESENT WHEREABOUTS."
"But where--? No, one answer only I know...
"Thank you, weird sisters."

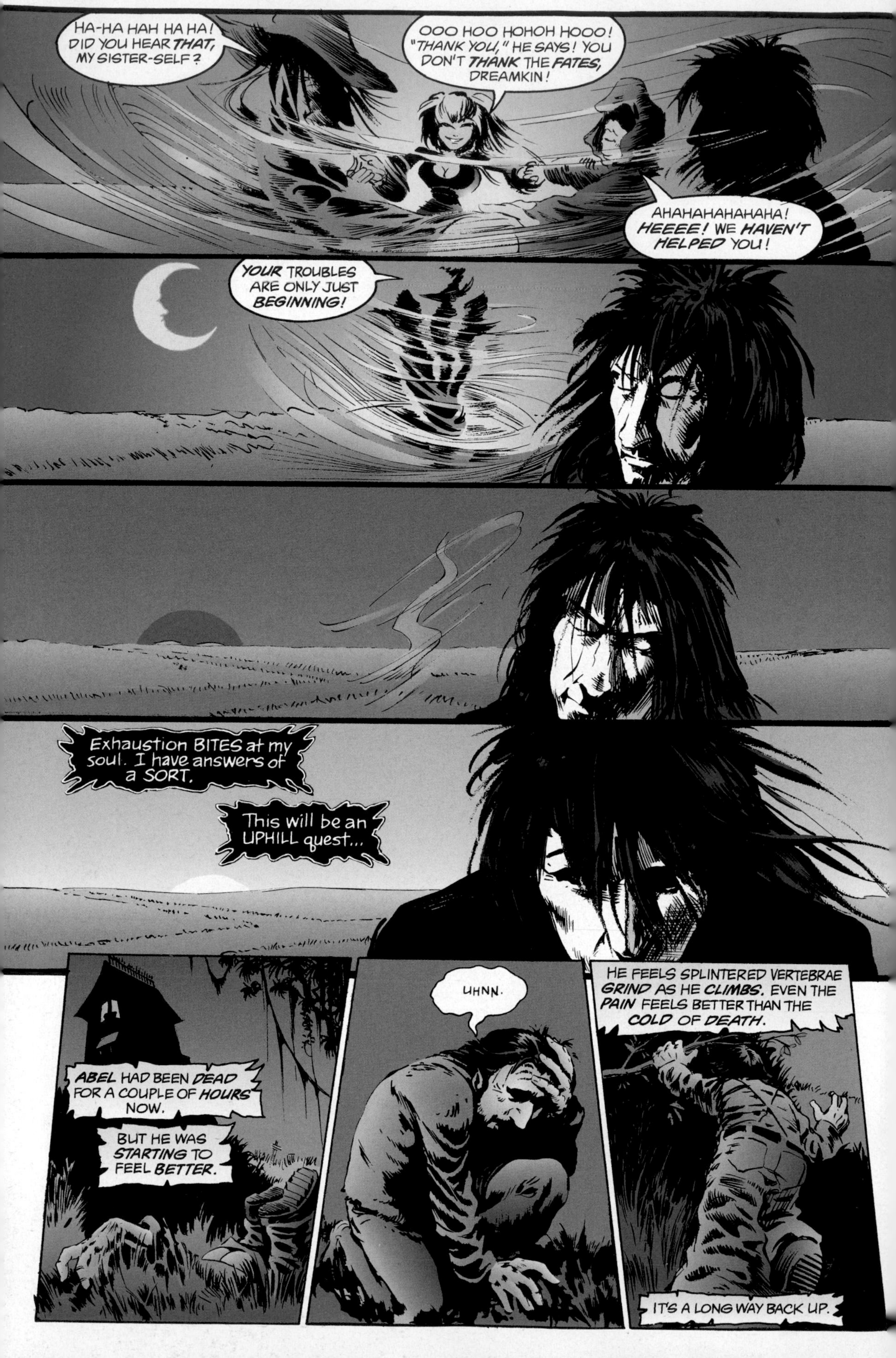
HA-HA HAH HA HA! DID YOU HEAR THAT, MY SISTER-SELF?
OOO HOO HOHOH HOOO! "THANK YOU," HE SAYS! YOU DON'T THANK THE FATES, DREAMKIN!
AHAHAHAHAHAHA! HEEEE! WE HAVEN'T HELPED YOU!
YOUR TROUBLES ARE ONLY JUST BEGINNING!
Exhaustion BITES at my soul. I have answers of a SORT.
This will be an UPHILL quest...
ABEL HAD BEEN DEAD FOR A COUPLE OF HOURS NOW.
BUT HE WAS STARTING TO FEEL BETTER.
UHNN.
HE FEELS SPLINTERED VERTEBRAE GRIND AS HE CLIMBS. EVEN THE PAIN FEELS BETTER THAN THE COLD OF DEATH.
IT'S A LONG WAY BACK UP.

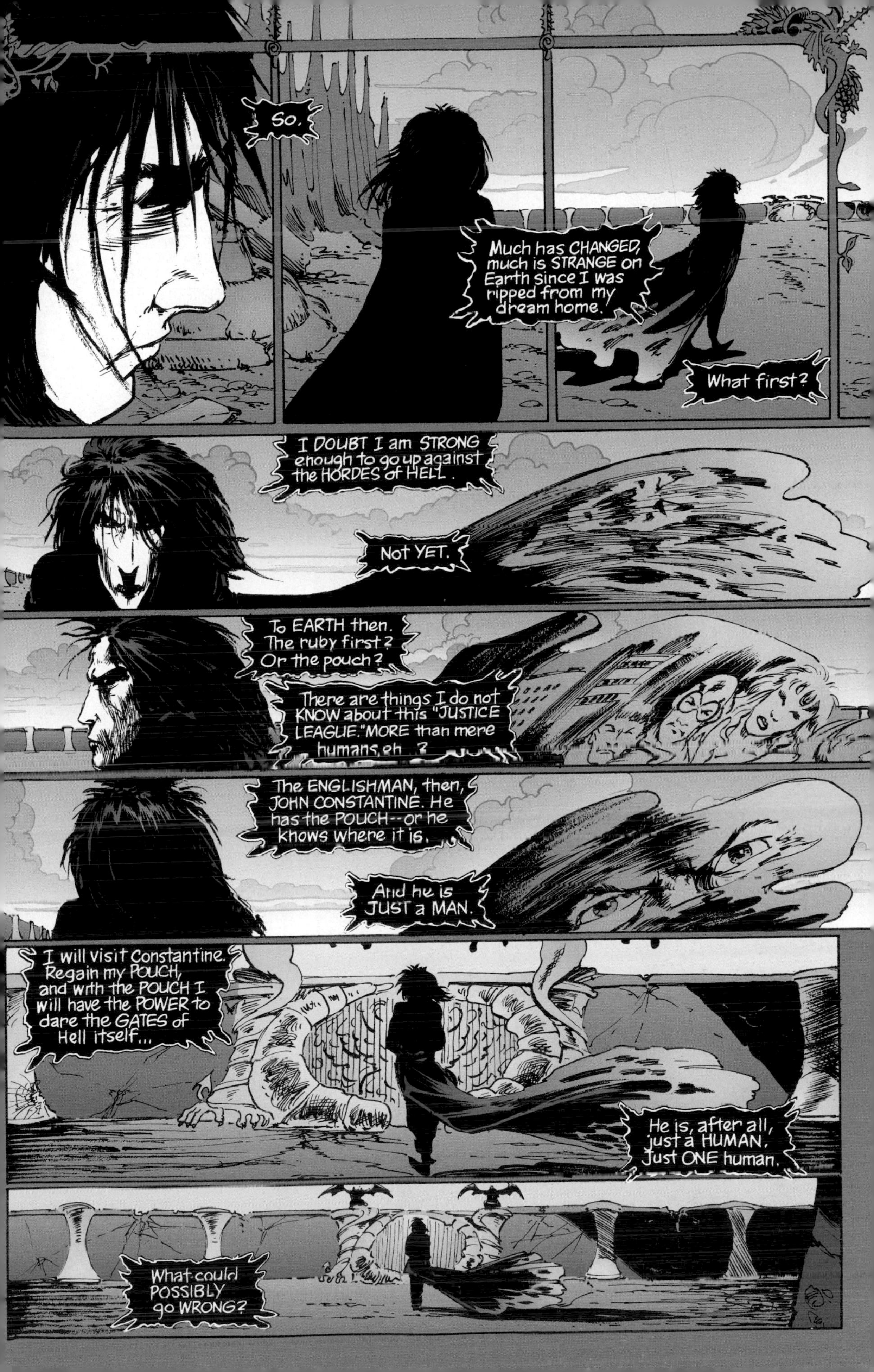
So.
Much has CHANGED, much is STRANGE on Earth since I was ripped from my dream home.
What first?
I DOUBT I am STRONG enough to go up against the HORDES of HELL.
Not YET.
To EARTH then. The ruby first? Or the pouch?
There are things I do not KNOW about this "JUSTICE LEAGUE." MORE than mere humans, eh...?
The ENGLISHMAN, then, JOHN CONSTANTINE. He has the POUCH--or he knows where it is.
And he is JUST a MAN.
I will visit Constantine. Regain my POUCH, and with the POUCH I will have the POWER to dare the GATES of Hell itself...
He is, after all, just a HUMAN. Just ONE human.
What could POSSIBLY go WRONG?

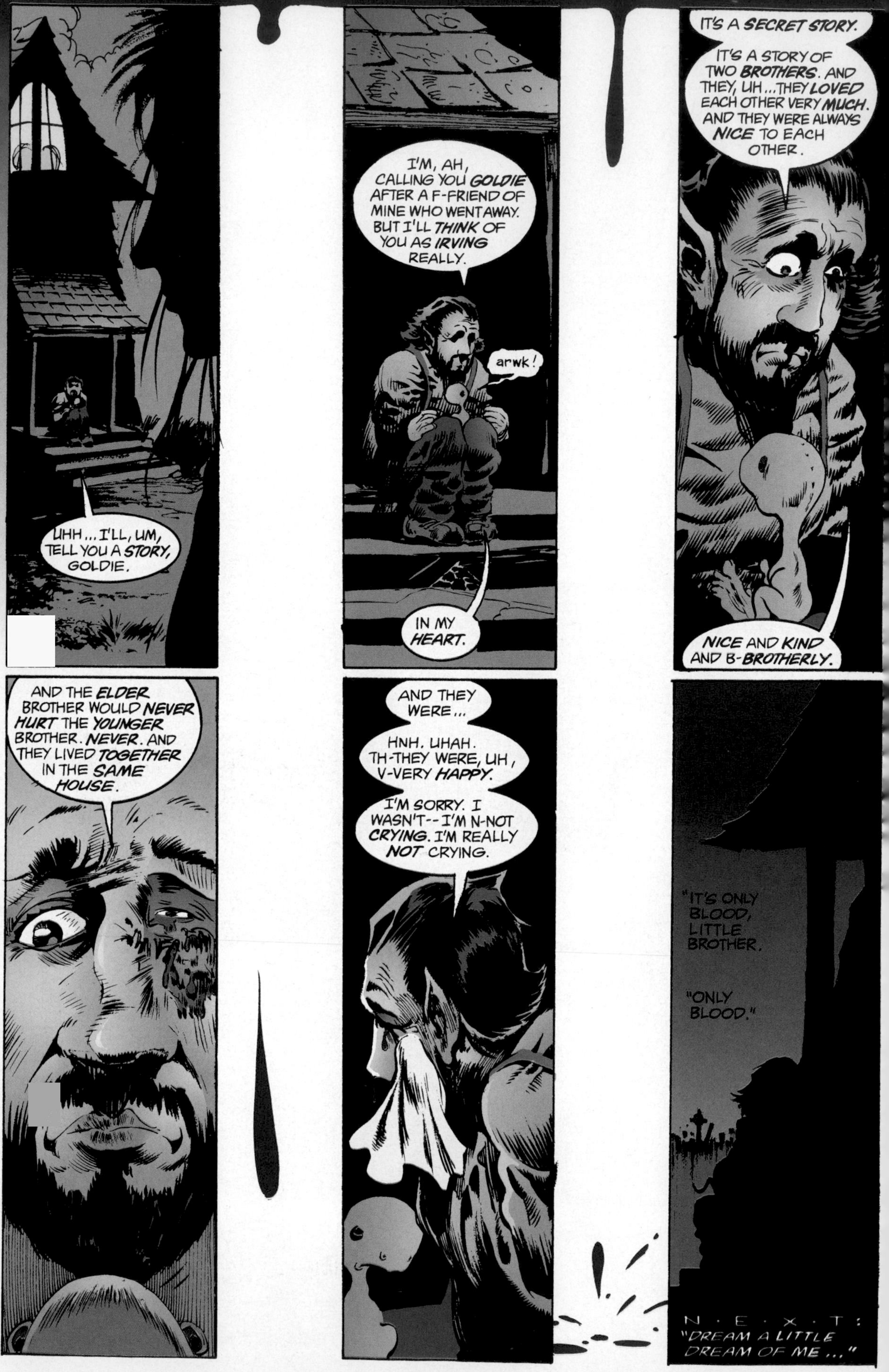
UHH... I'LL, UM, TELL YOU A STORY, GOLDIE.
I'M, AH, CALLING YOU GOLDIE AFTER A F-FRIEND OF MINE WHO WENT AWAY. BUT I'LL THINK OF YOU AS IRVING REALLY.
arwk!
IN MY HEART.
IT'S A SECRET STORY.
IT'S A STORY OF TWO BROTHERS. AND THEY, UH... THEY LOVED EACH OTHER VERY MUCH. AND THEY WERE ALWAYS NICE TO EACH OTHER.
NICE AND KIND AND B-BROTHERLY.
AND THE ELDER BROTHER WOULD NEVER HURT THE YOUNGER BROTHER. NEVER. AND THEY LIVED TOGETHER IN THE SAME HOUSE.
AND THEY WERE...
HNH. UHAH. TH-THEY WERE, UH, V-VERY HAPPY.
I'M SORRY. I WASN'T-- I'M N-NOT CRYING. I'M REALLY NOT CRYING.
"IT'S ONLY BLOOD, LITTLE BROTHER.
"ONLY BLOOD."
N·E·X·T: "DREAM A LITTLE DREAM OF ME..."

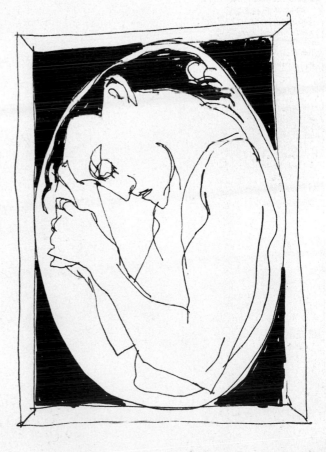

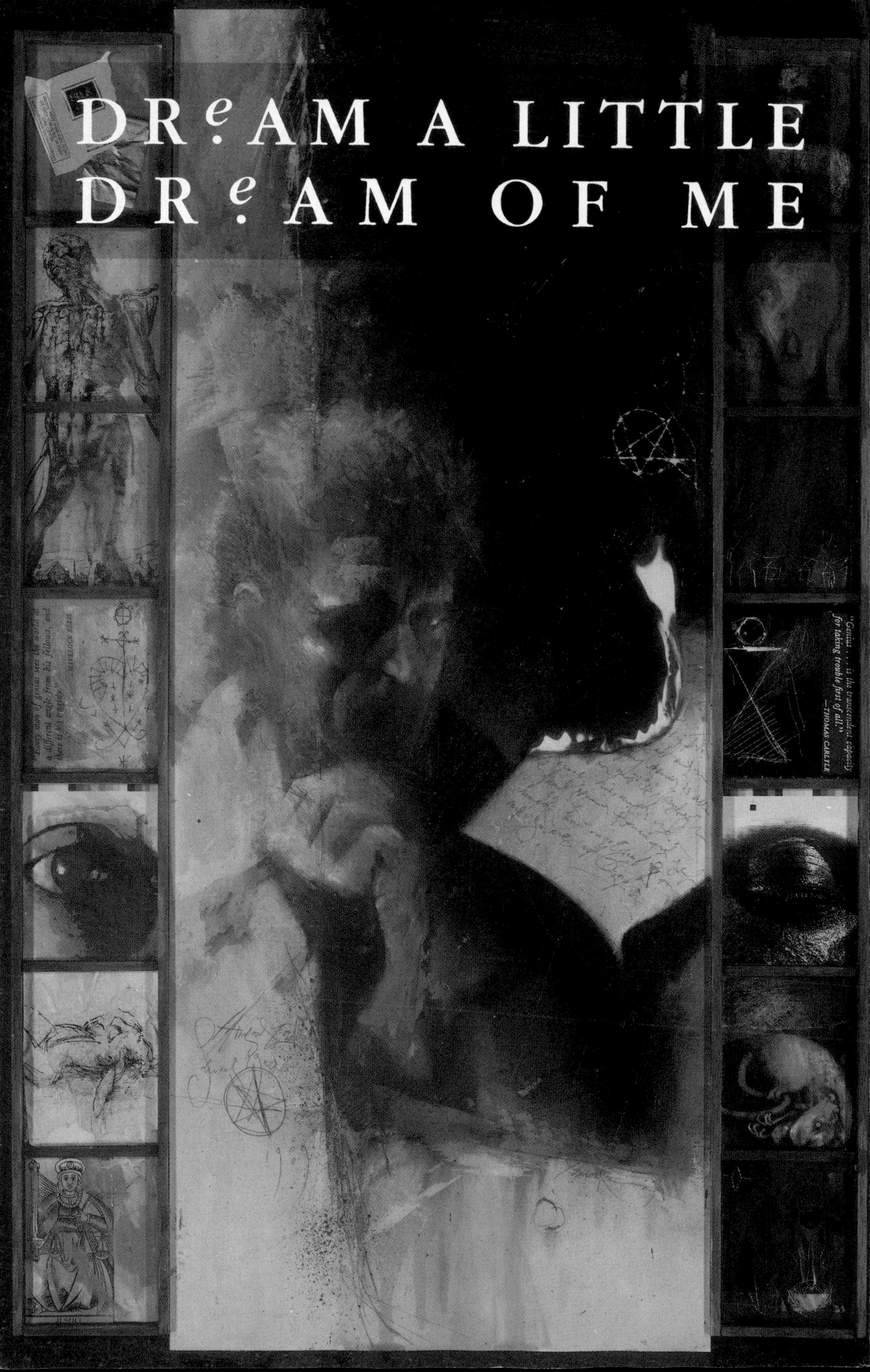
DREAM A LITTLE
DREAM OF ME
"Genius . . . is the transcendent capacity for taking trouble first of all."
—THOMAS CARLYLE

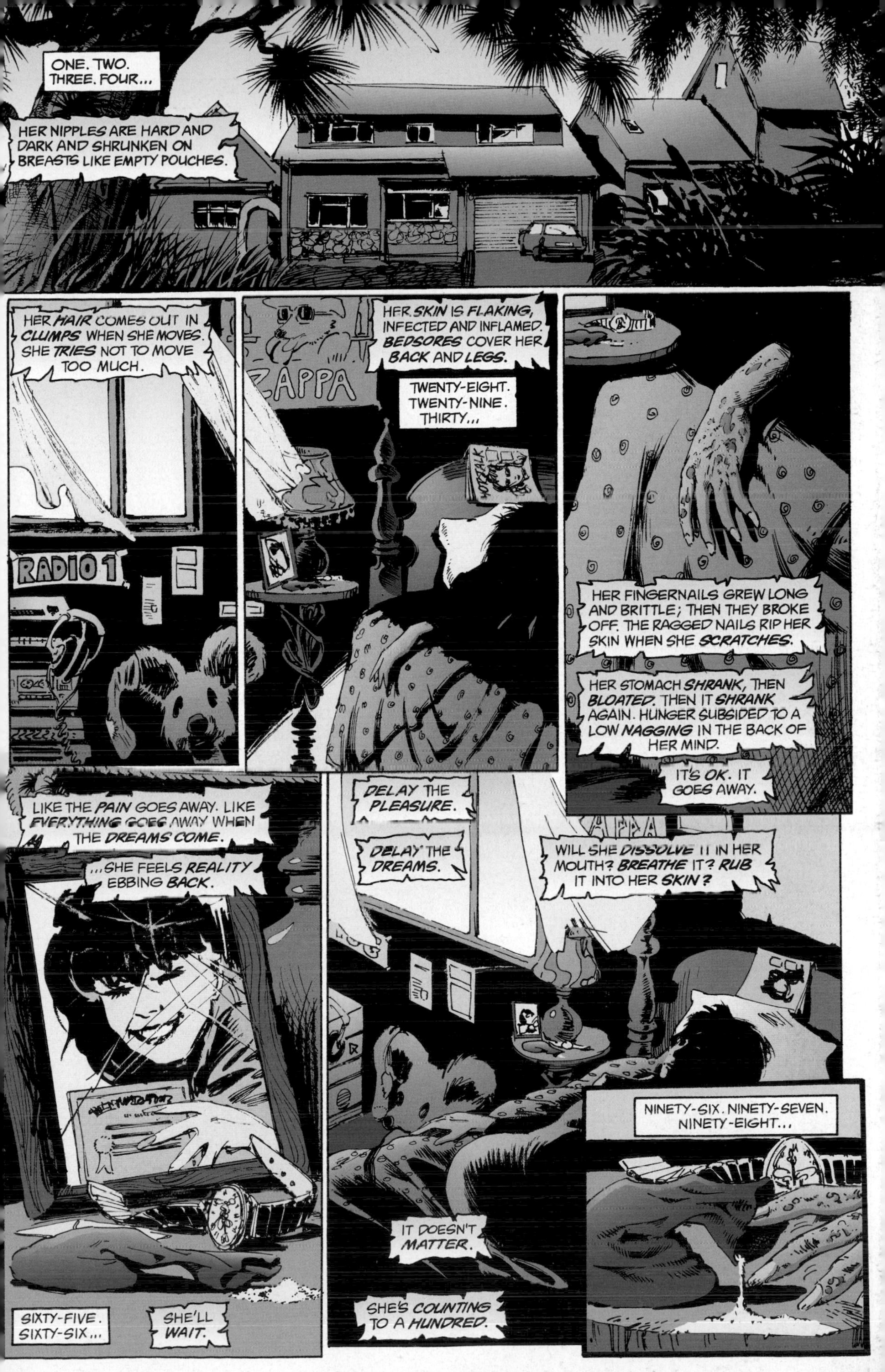

ONE. TWO. THREE. FOUR...
HER NIPPLES ARE HARD AND DARK AND SHRUNKEN ON BREASTS LIKE EMPTY POUCHES.
HER HAIR COMES OUT IN CLUMPS WHEN SHE MOVES. SHE TRIES NOT TO MOVE TOO MUCH.
RADIO 1
HER SKIN IS FLAKING, INFECTED AND INFLAMED. BEDSORES COVER HER BACK AND LEGS.
ZAPPA
TWENTY-EIGHT. TWENTY-NINE. THIRTY...
HER FINGERNAILS GREW LONG AND BRITTLE; THEN THEY BROKE OFF. THE RAGGED NAILS RIP HER SKIN WHEN SHE SCRATCHES.
HER STOMACH SHRANK, THEN BLOATED. THEN IT SHRANK AGAIN. HUNGER SUBSIDED TO A LOW NAGGING IN THE BACK OF HER MIND.
IT'S OK. IT GOES AWAY.
LIKE THE PAIN GOES AWAY. LIKE EVERYTHING GOES AWAY WHEN THE DREAMS COME.
...SHE FEELS REALITY EBBING BACK.
SIXTY-FIVE. SIXTY-SIX...
SHE'LL WAIT.
DELAY THE PLEASURE.
DELAY THE DREAMS.
WILL SHE DISSOLVE IT IN HER MOUTH? BREATHE IT? RUB IT INTO HER SKIN?
IT DOESN'T MATTER.
SHE'S COUNTING TO A HUNDRED.
NINETY-SIX. NINETY-SEVEN. NINETY-EIGHT...

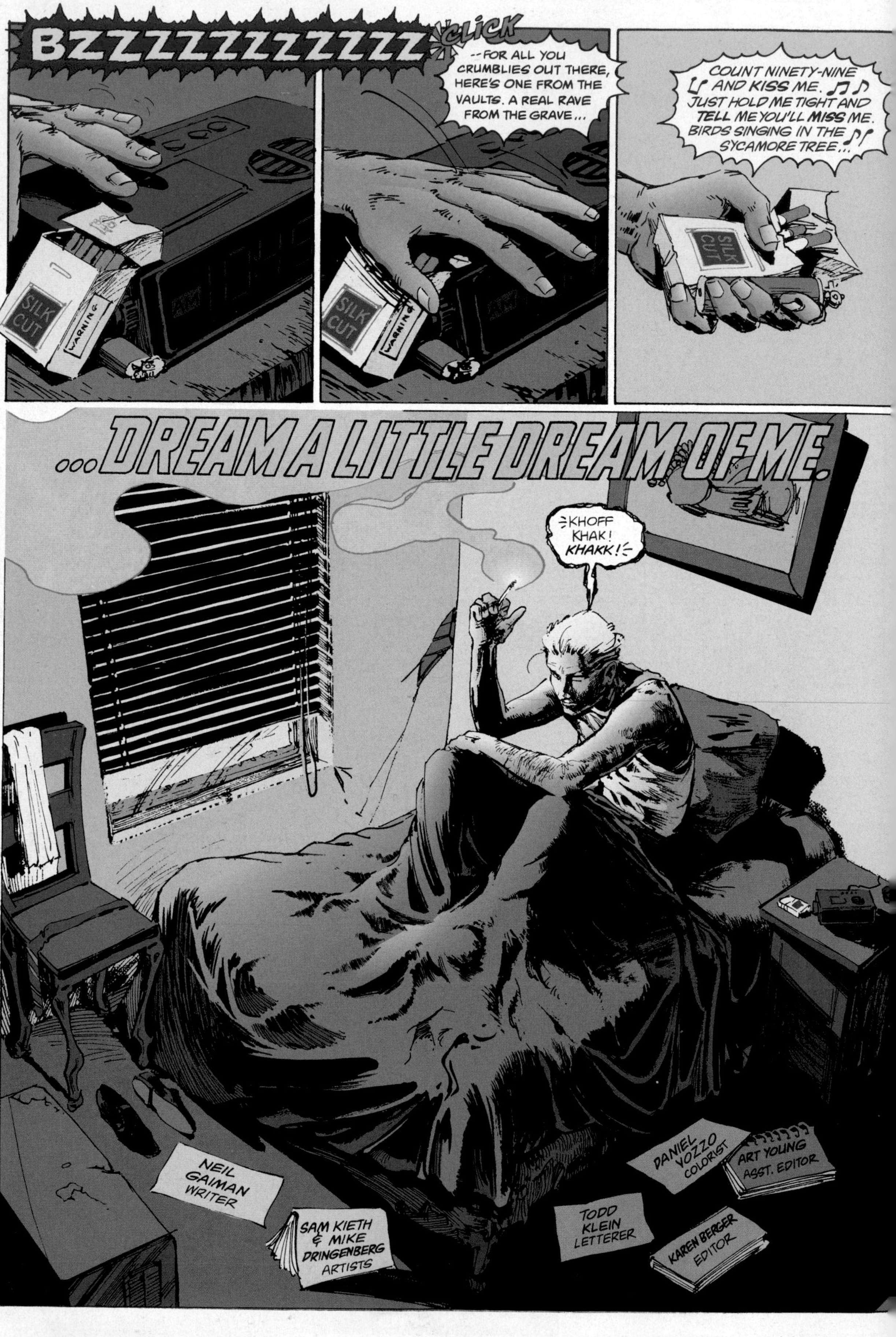
BZZZZZZZZZZZZ
CLICK
--FOR ALL YOU CRUMBLIES OUT THERE, HERE'S ONE FROM THE VAULTS. A REAL RAVE FROM THE GRAVE...
SILK CUT
WARNING
COUNT NINETY-NINE AND KISS ME. JUST HOLD ME TIGHT AND TELL ME YOU'LL MISS ME. BIRDS SINGING IN THE SYCAMORE TREE...
SILK CUT
...DREAM A LITTLE DREAM OF ME.
KHOFF KHAK! KHAKK!
NEIL GAIMAN WRITER
SAM KIETH & MIKE DRINGENBERG ARTISTS
DANIEL VOZZO COLORIST
TODD KLEIN LETTERER
ART YOUNG ASST. EDITOR
KAREN BERGER EDITOR

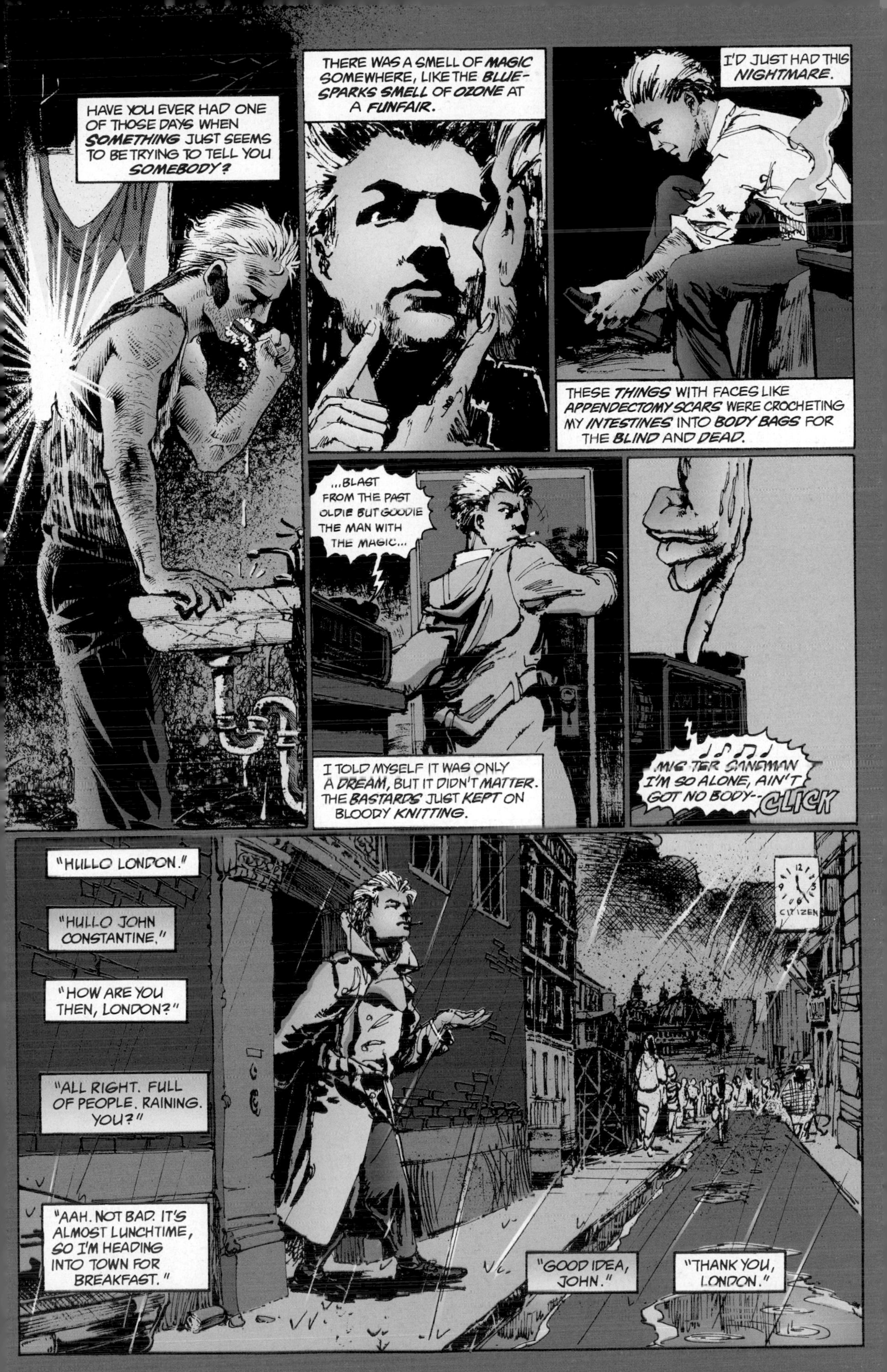

HAVE YOU EVER HAD ONE OF THOSE DAYS WHEN SOMETHING JUST SEEMS TO BE TRYING TO TELL YOU SOMEBODY?
THERE WAS A SMELL OF MAGIC SOMEWHERE, LIKE THE BLUE-SPARKS SMELL OF OZONE AT A FUNFAIR.
I'D JUST HAD THIS NIGHTMARE.
THESE THINGS WITH FACES LIKE APPENDECTOMY SCARS WERE CROCHETING MY INTESTINES INTO BODY BAGS FOR THE BLIND AND DEAD.
...BLAST FROM THE PAST OLDIE BUT GOODIE THE MAN WITH THE MAGIC...
I TOLD MYSELF IT WAS ONLY A DREAM, BUT IT DIDN'T MATTER. THE BASTARDS JUST KEPT ON BLOODY KNITTING.
MIS-TER SANDMAN I'M SO ALONE, AIN'T GOT NO BODY--
CLICK
"HULLO LONDON."
"HULLO JOHN CONSTANTINE."
"HOW ARE YOU THEN, LONDON?"
"ALL RIGHT. FULL OF PEOPLE. RAINING. YOU?"
"AAH. NOT BAD. IT'S ALMOST LUNCHTIME, SO I'M HEADING INTO TOWN FOR BREAKFAST."
"GOOD IDEA, JOHN."
"THANK YOU, LONDON."
CITIZEN

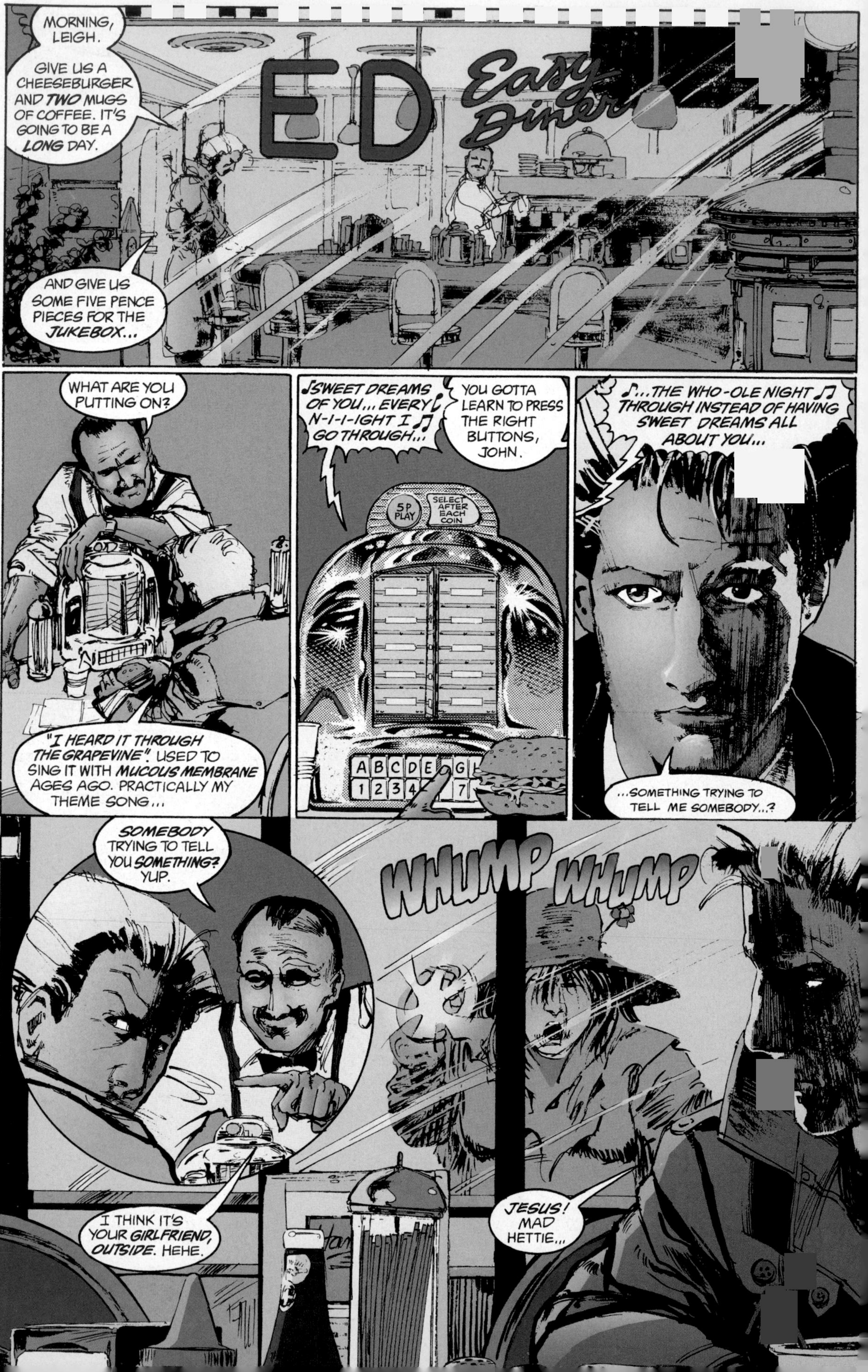
MORNING, LEIGH.
GIVE US A CHEESEBURGER AND TWO MUGS OF COFFEE. IT'S GOING TO BE A LONG DAY.
ED Easy Diner
AND GIVE US SOME FIVE PENCE PIECES FOR THE JUKEBOX...
WHAT ARE YOU PUTTING ON?
"I HEARD IT THROUGH THE GRAPEVINE". USED TO SING IT WITH MUCOUS MEMBRANE AGES AGO. PRACTICALLY MY THEME SONG...
♪SWEET DREAMS OF YOU... EVERY N-I-I-IGHT I GO THROUGH...♪
YOU GOTTA LEARN TO PRESS THE RIGHT BUTTONS, JOHN.
5P PLAY
SELECT AFTER EACH COIN
♪...THE WHO-OLE NIGHT THROUGH INSTEAD OF HAVING SWEET DREAMS ALL ABOUT YOU...♪
...SOMETHING TRYING TO TELL ME SOMEBODY...?
SOMEBODY TRYING TO TELL YOU SOMETHING? YUP.
I THINK IT'S YOUR GIRLFRIEND, OUTSIDE. HEHE.
WHUMP WHUMP
JESUS! MAD HETTIE...

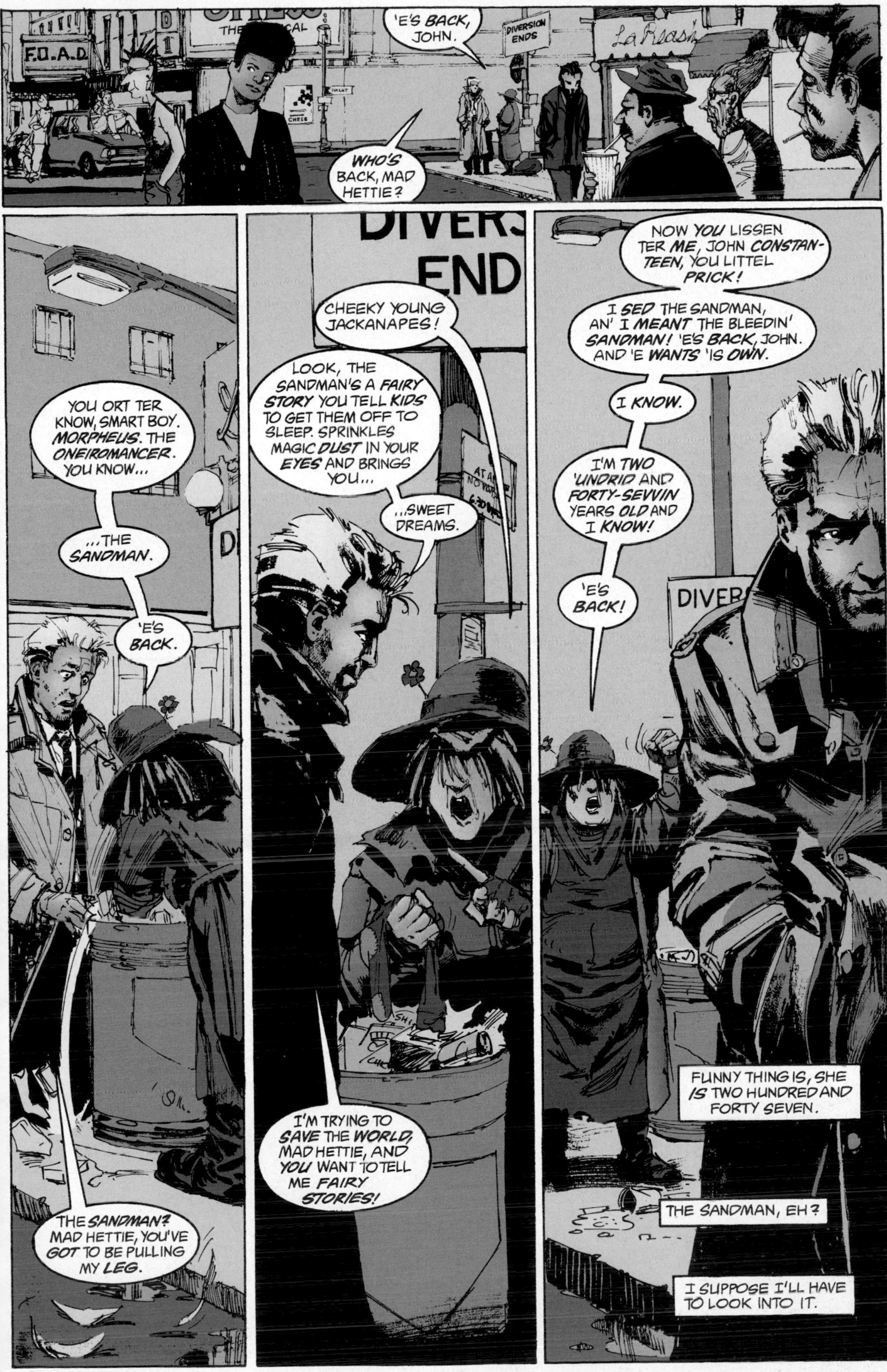
F.O.A.D
DIVERSION ENDS
'E'S BACK, JOHN.
WHO'S BACK, MAD HETTIE?
YOU ORT TER KNOW, SMART BOY. MORPHEUS. THE ONEIROMANCER. YOU KNOW...
...THE SANDMAN.
'E'S BACK.
THE SANDMAN? MAD HETTIE, YOU'VE GOT TO BE PULLING MY LEG.
DIVERS END
CHEEKY YOUNG JACKANAPES!
LOOK, THE SANDMAN'S A FAIRY STORY YOU TELL KIDS TO GET THEM OFF TO SLEEP. SPRINKLES MAGIC DUST IN YOUR EYES AND BRINGS YOU...
...SWEET DREAMS.
I'M TRYING TO SAVE THE WORLD, MAD HETTIE, AND YOU WANT TO TELL ME FAIRY STORIES!
NOW YOU LISSEN TER ME, JOHN CONSTAN-TEEN, YOU LITTEL PRICK!
I SED THE SANDMAN, AN' I MEANT THE BLEEDIN' SANDMAN! 'E'S BACK, JOHN. AND 'E WANTS 'IS OWN.
I KNOW.
I'M TWO 'UNDRID AND FORTY-SEVVIN YEARS OLD AND I KNOW!
'E'S BACK!
FUNNY THING IS, SHE IS TWO HUNDRED AND FORTY SEVEN.
THE SANDMAN, EH?
I SUPPOSE I'LL HAVE TO LOOK INTO IT.

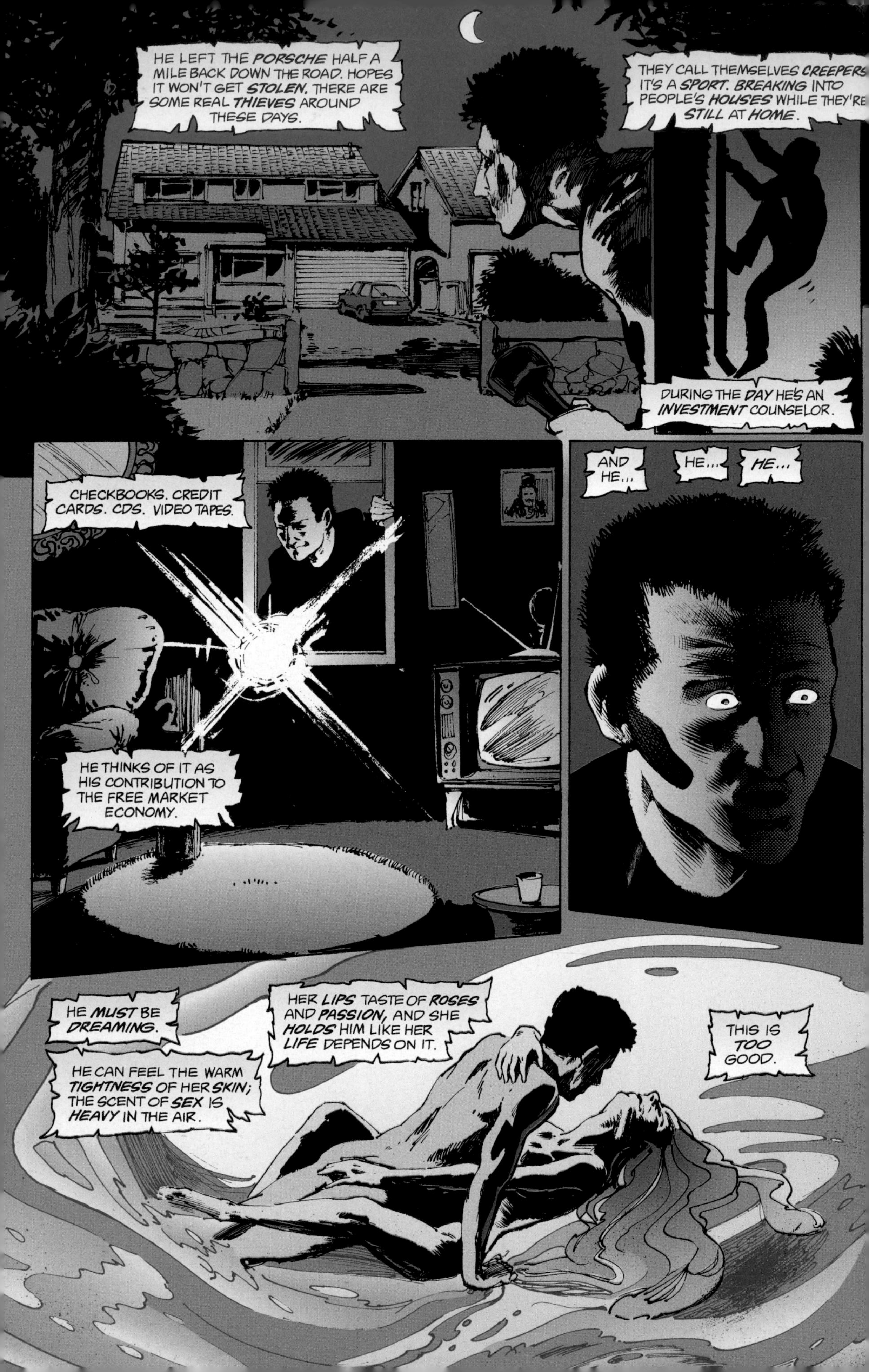
HE LEFT THE PORSCHE HALF A MILE BACK DOWN THE ROAD. HOPES IT WON'T GET STOLEN. THERE ARE SOME REAL THIEVES AROUND THESE DAYS.
THEY CALL THEMSELVES CREEPERS. IT'S A SPORT. BREAKING INTO PEOPLE'S HOUSES WHILE THEY'RE STILL AT HOME.
DURING THE DAY HE'S AN INVESTMENT COUNSELOR.
CHECKBOOKS. CREDIT CARDS. CDS. VIDEO TAPES.
HE THINKS OF IT AS HIS CONTRIBUTION TO THE FREE MARKET ECONOMY.
AND HE...
HE...
HE...
HE MUST BE DREAMING.
HE CAN FEEL THE WARM TIGHTNESS OF HER SKIN; THE SCENT OF SEX IS HEAVY IN THE AIR.
HER LIPS TASTE OF ROSES AND PASSION, AND SHE HOLDS HIM LIKE HER LIFE DEPENDS ON IT.
THIS IS TOO GOOD.

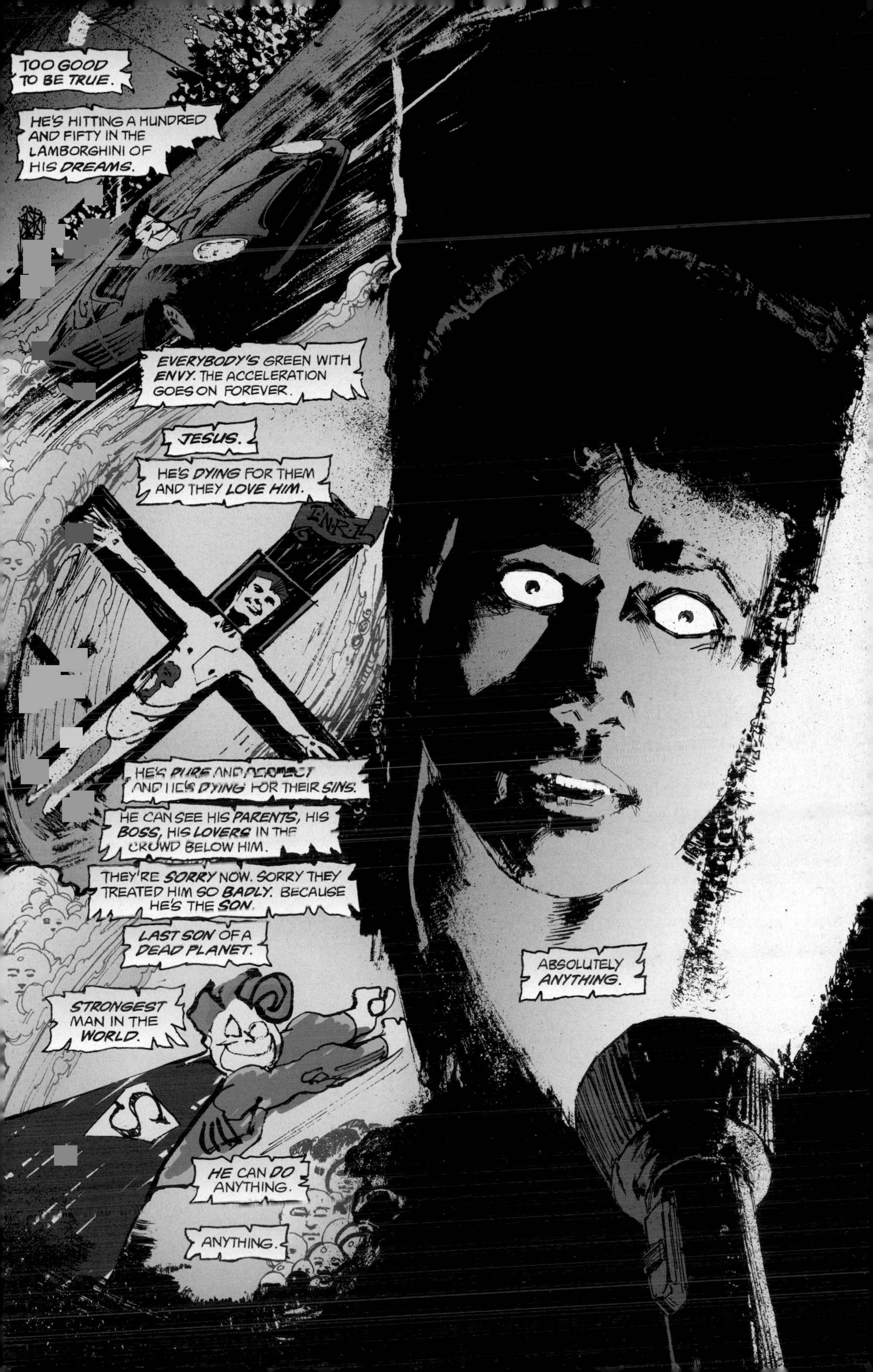
TOO GOOD TO BE TRUE.
HE'S HITTING A HUNDRED AND FIFTY IN THE LAMBORGHINI OF HIS DREAMS.
EVERYBODY'S GREEN WITH ENVY. THE ACCELERATION GOES ON FOREVER.
JESUS.
HE'S DYING FOR THEM AND THEY LOVE HIM.
I.N.R.I.
HE'S PURE AND PERFECT AND HE'S DYING FOR THEIR SINS.
HE CAN SEE HIS PARENTS, HIS BOSS, HIS LOVERS IN THE CROWD BELOW HIM.
THEY'RE SORRY NOW. SORRY THEY TREATED HIM SO BADLY. BECAUSE HE'S THE SON.
LAST SON OF A DEAD PLANET.
STRONGEST MAN IN THE WORLD.
HE CAN DO ANYTHING.
ANYTHING.
ABSOLUTELY ANYTHING.

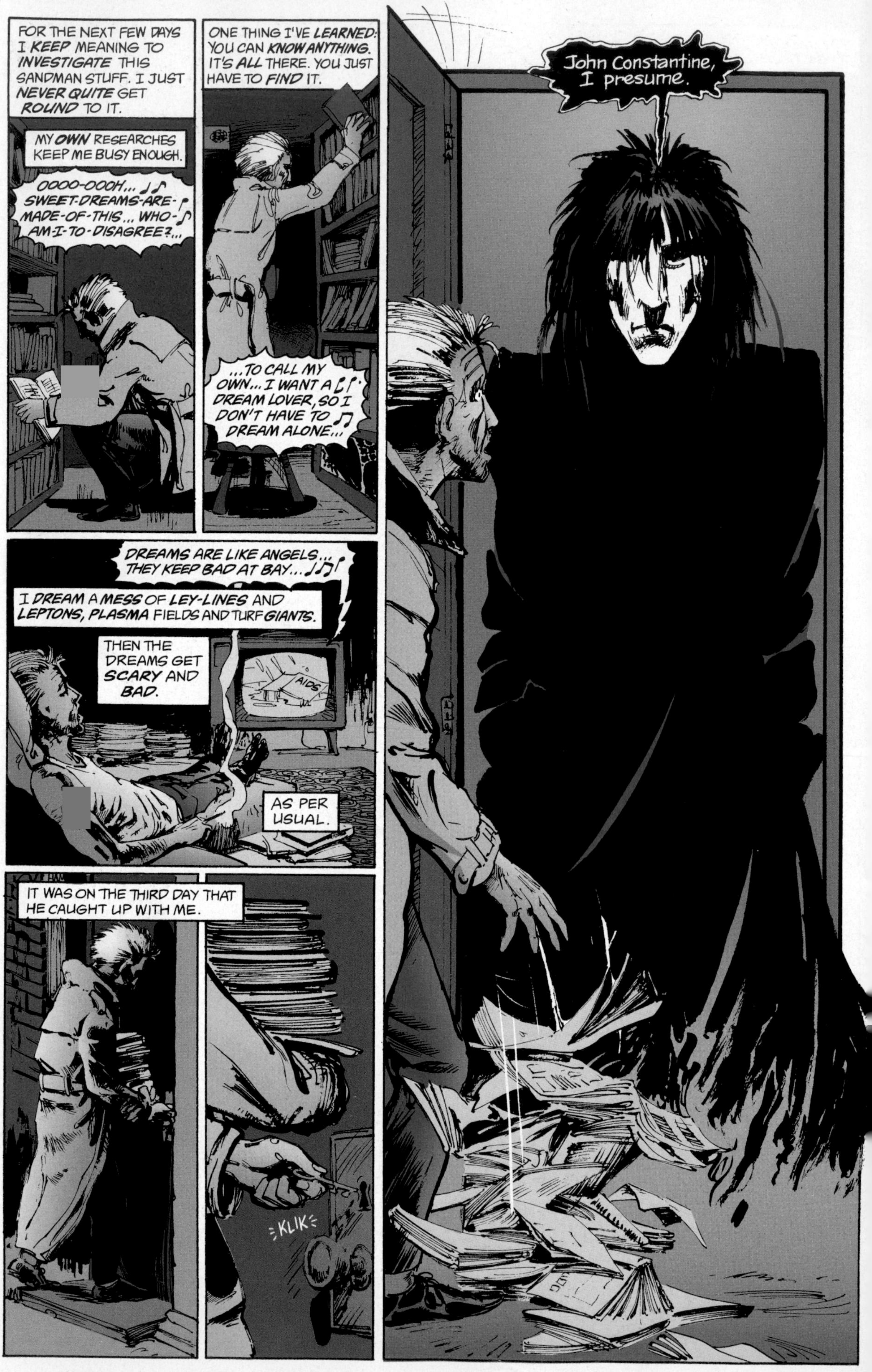
FOR THE NEXT FEW DAYS I KEEP MEANING TO INVESTIGATE THIS SANDMAN STUFF. I JUST NEVER QUITE GET ROUND TO IT.
MY OWN RESEARCHES KEEP ME BUSY ENOUGH.
OOOO-OOOH... SWEET-DREAMS-ARE-MADE-OF-THIS... WHO-AM-I-TO-DISAGREE?...
ONE THING I'VE LEARNED: YOU CAN KNOW ANYTHING. IT'S ALL THERE. YOU JUST HAVE TO FIND IT.
...TO CALL MY OWN... I WANT A DREAM LOVER, SO I DON'T HAVE TO DREAM ALONE...
DREAMS ARE LIKE ANGELS... THEY KEEP BAD AT BAY...
I DREAM A MESS OF LEY-LINES AND LEPTONS, PLASMA FIELDS AND TURF GIANTS.
THEN THE DREAMS GET SCARY AND BAD.
AIDS
AS PER USUAL.
IT WAS ON THE THIRD DAY THAT HE CAUGHT UP WITH ME.
KLIK
John Constantine, I presume.

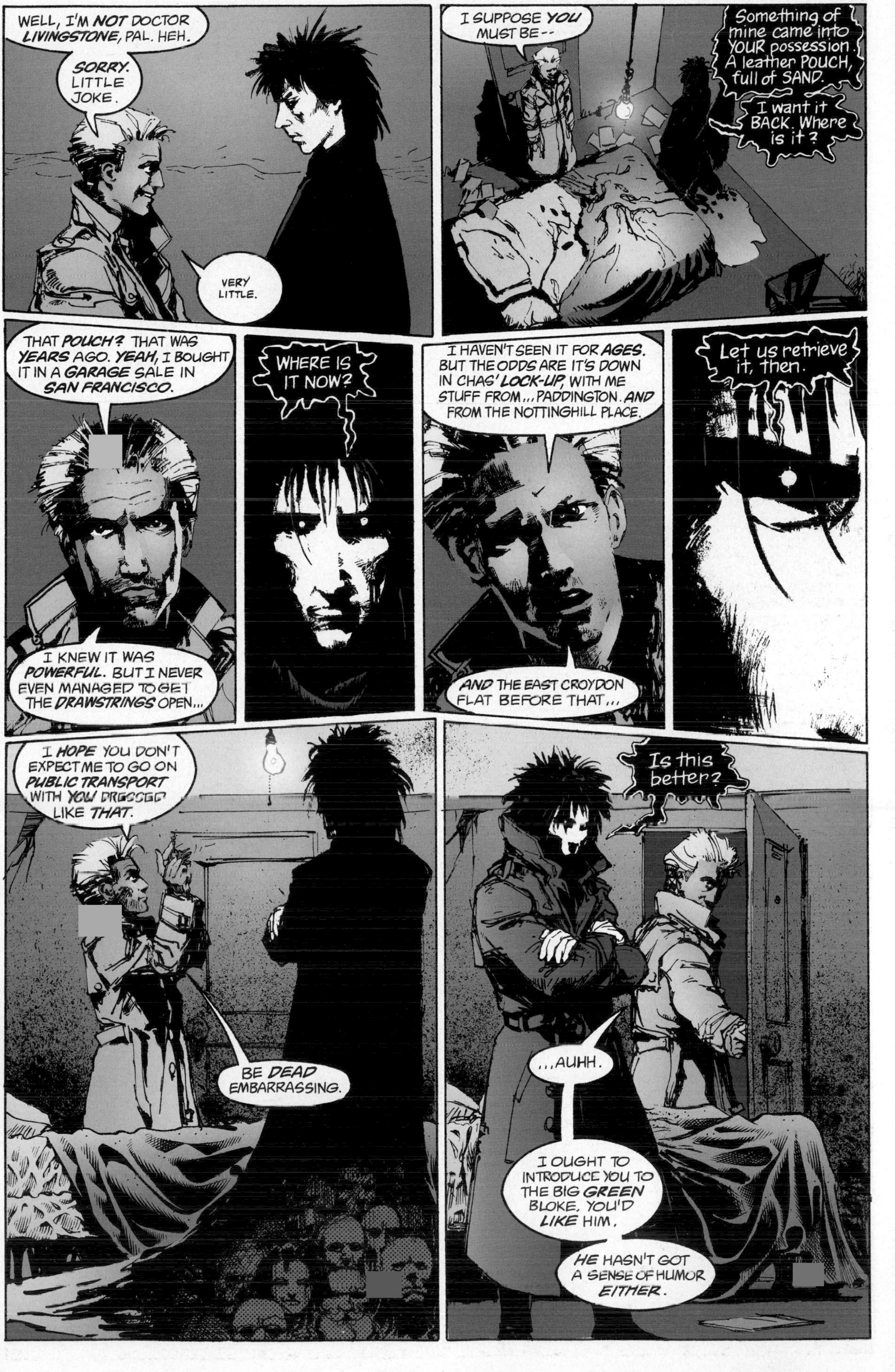
WELL, I'M NOT DOCTOR LIVINGSTONE, PAL. HEH.
SORRY. LITTLE JOKE.
VERY LITTLE.
I SUPPOSE YOU MUST BE--
Something of mine came into YOUR possession. A leather POUCH, full of SAND.
I want it BACK. Where is it?
THAT POUCH? THAT WAS YEARS AGO. YEAH, I BOUGHT IT IN A GARAGE SALE IN SAN FRANCISCO.
I KNEW IT WAS POWERFUL. BUT I NEVER EVEN MANAGED TO GET THE DRAWSTRINGS OPEN...
WHERE IS IT NOW?
I HAVEN'T SEEN IT FOR AGES. BUT THE ODDS ARE IT'S DOWN IN CHAS' LOCK-UP, WITH ME STUFF FROM... PADDINGTON. AND FROM THE NOTTINGHILL PLACE.
AND THE EAST CROYDON FLAT BEFORE THAT...
Let us retrieve it, then.
I HOPE YOU DON'T EXPECT ME TO GO ON PUBLIC TRANSPORT WITH YOU DRESSED LIKE THAT.
BE DEAD EMBARRASSING.
Is this better?
...AUHH.
I OUGHT TO INTRODUCE YOU TO THE BIG GREEN BLOKE. YOU'D LIKE HIM.
HE HASN'T GOT A SENSE OF HUMOR EITHER.

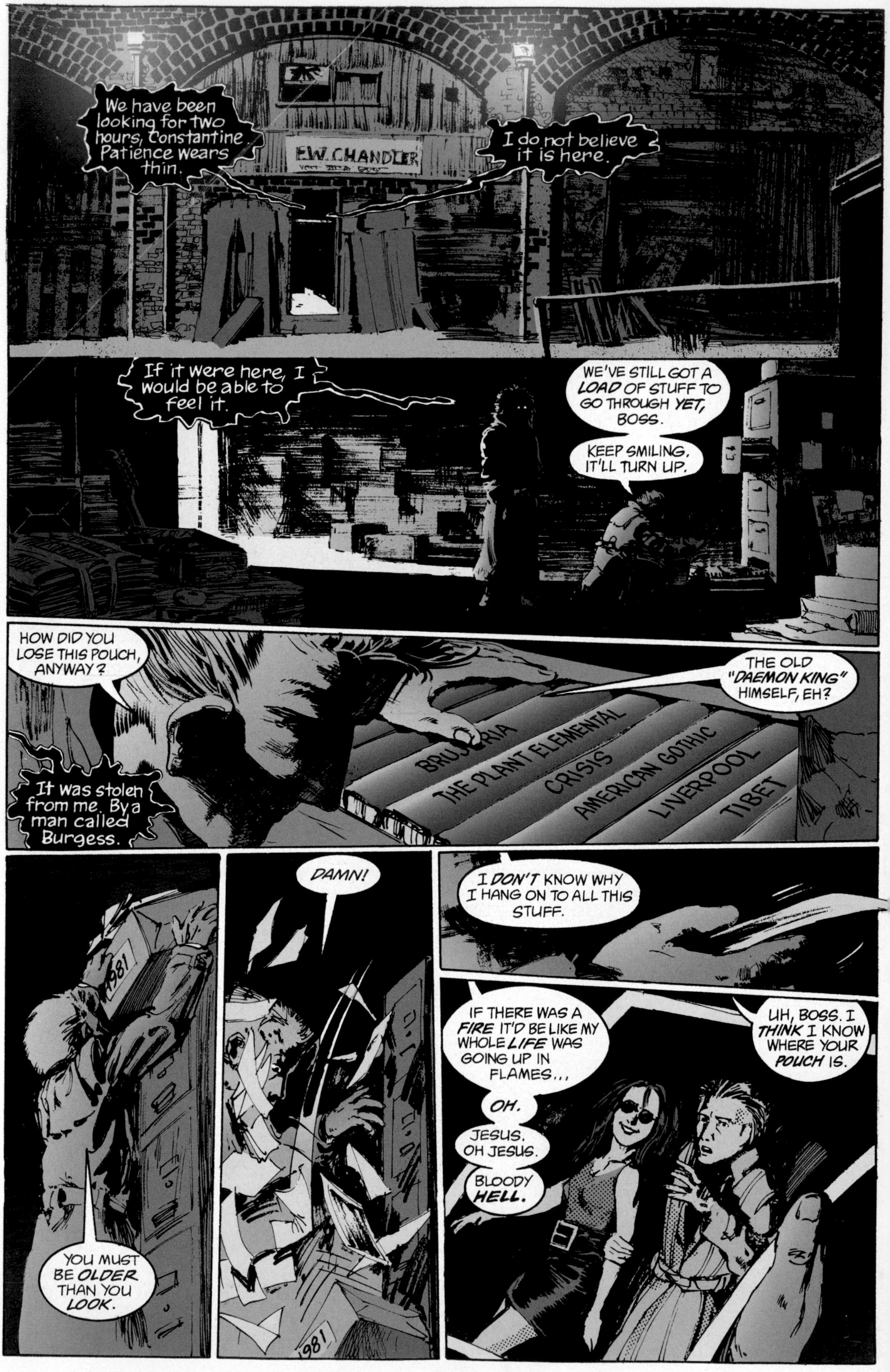

We have been looking for two hours, Constantine. Patience wears thin.
E.W. CHANDLER
I do not believe it is here.
If it were here, I would be able to feel it.
WE'VE STILL GOT A LOAD OF STUFF TO GO THROUGH YET, BOSS.
KEEP SMILING. IT'LL TURN UP.
HOW DID YOU LOSE THIS POUCH, ANYWAY?
THE OLD "DAEMON KING" HIMSELF, EH?
It was stolen from me. By a man called Burgess.
BRUJERIA
THE PLANT ELEMENTAL
CRISIS
AMERICAN GOTHIC
LIVERPOOL
TIBET
1981
YOU MUST BE OLDER THAN YOU LOOK.
DAMN!
1981
I DON'T KNOW WHY I HANG ON TO ALL THIS STUFF.
IF THERE WAS A FIRE IT'D BE LIKE MY WHOLE LIFE WAS GOING UP IN FLAMES...
OH.
JESUS. OH JESUS.
BLOODY HELL.
UH, BOSS. I THINK I KNOW WHERE YOUR POUCH IS.

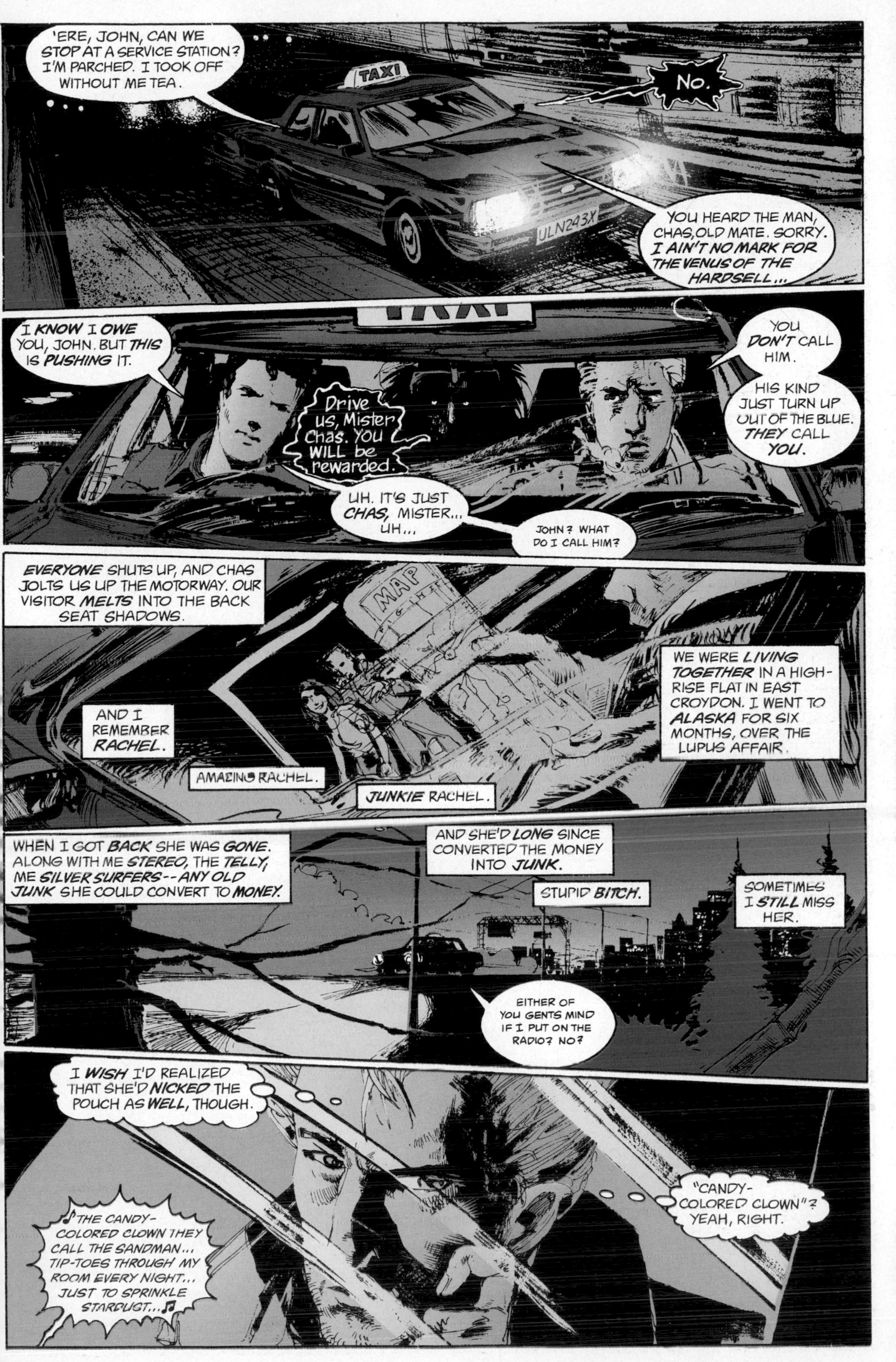
'ERE, JOHN, CAN WE STOP AT A SERVICE STATION? I'M PARCHED. I TOOK OFF WITHOUT ME TEA.
TAXI
No.
ULN243X
YOU HEARD THE MAN, CHAS, OLD MATE. SORRY. I AIN'T NO MARK FOR THE VENUS OF THE HARDSELL...
I KNOW I OWE YOU, JOHN. BUT THIS IS PUSHING IT.
Drive us, Mister Chas. You WILL be rewarded.
UH. IT'S JUST CHAS, MISTER... UH...
JOHN? WHAT DO I CALL HIM?
YOU DON'T CALL HIM.
HIS KIND JUST TURN UP OUT OF THE BLUE. THEY CALL YOU.
EVERYONE SHUTS UP, AND CHAS JOLTS US UP THE MOTORWAY. OUR VISITOR MELTS INTO THE BACK SEAT SHADOWS.
MAP
AND I REMEMBER RACHEL.
AMAZING RACHEL.
JUNKIE RACHEL.
WE WERE LIVING TOGETHER IN A HIGH-RISE FLAT IN EAST CROYDON. I WENT TO ALASKA FOR SIX MONTHS, OVER THE LUPUS AFFAIR.
WHEN I GOT BACK SHE WAS GONE. ALONG WITH ME STEREO, THE TELLY, ME SILVER SURFERS--ANY OLD JUNK SHE COULD CONVERT TO MONEY.
AND SHE'D LONG SINCE CONVERTED THE MONEY INTO JUNK.
STUPID BITCH.
SOMETIMES I STILL MISS HER.
EITHER OF YOU GENTS MIND IF I PUT ON THE RADIO? NO?
I WISH I'D REALIZED THAT SHE'D NICKED THE POUCH AS WELL, THOUGH.
♪THE CANDY-COLORED CLOWN THEY CALL THE SANDMAN... TIP-TOES THROUGH MY ROOM EVERY NIGHT... JUST TO SPRINKLE STARDUST...♫
"CANDY-COLORED CLOWN"? YEAH, RIGHT.

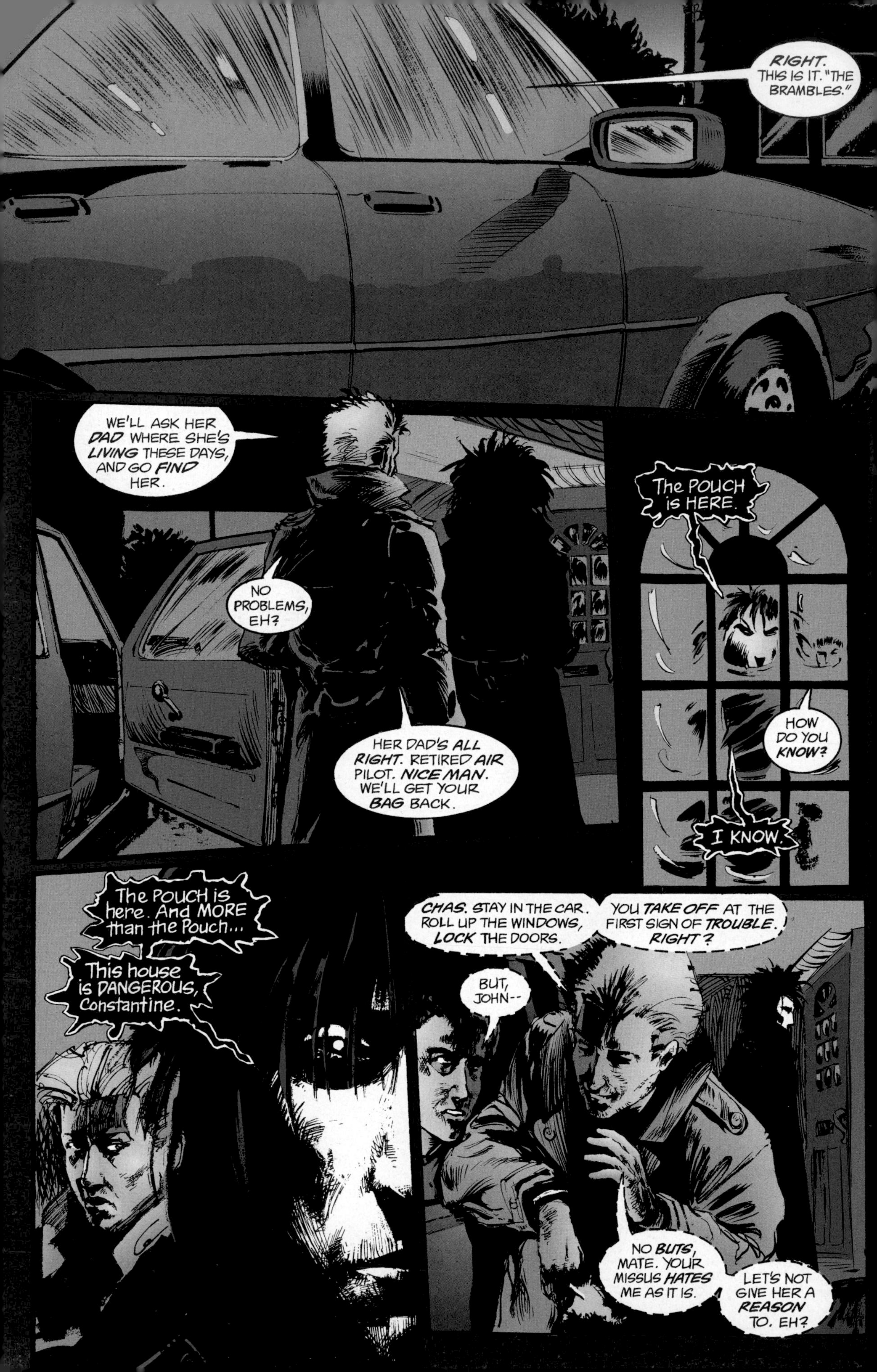
RIGHT. THIS IS IT. "THE BRAMBLES."
WE'LL ASK HER DAD WHERE SHE'S LIVING THESE DAYS, AND GO FIND HER.
NO PROBLEMS, EH?
HER DAD'S ALL RIGHT. RETIRED AIR PILOT. NICE MAN. WE'LL GET YOUR BAG BACK.
The POUCH is HERE.
HOW DO YOU KNOW?
I KNOW.
The POUCH is here. And MORE than the Pouch...
This house is DANGEROUS, Constantine.
CHAS. STAY IN THE CAR. ROLL UP THE WINDOWS, LOCK THE DOORS.
YOU TAKE OFF AT THE FIRST SIGN OF TROUBLE. RIGHT?
BUT, JOHN--
NO BUTS, MATE. YOUR MISSUS HATES ME AS IT IS.
LET'S NOT GIVE HER A REASON TO. EH?

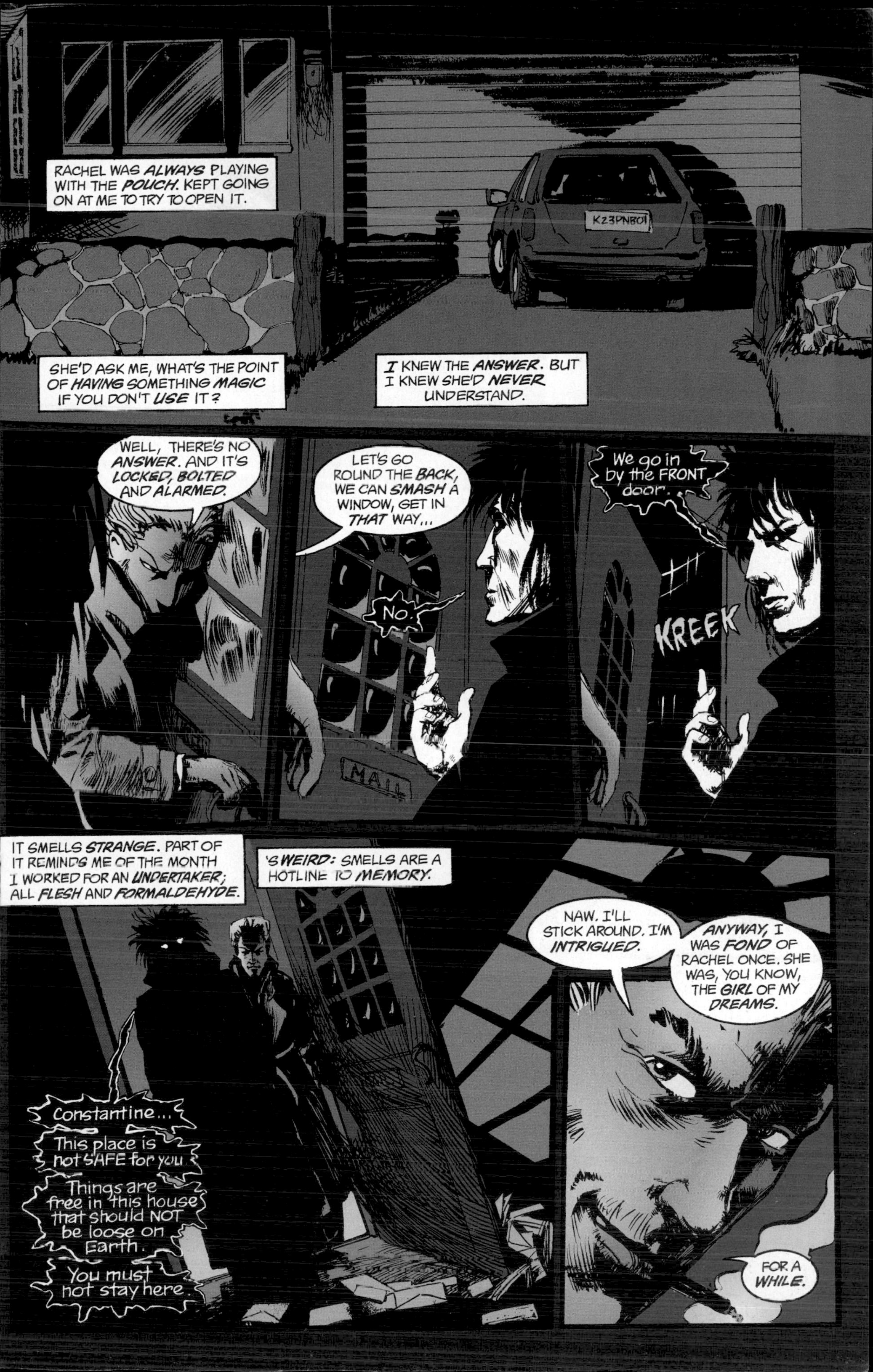
RACHEL WAS ALWAYS PLAYING WITH THE POUCH. KEPT GOING ON AT ME TO TRY TO OPEN IT.
K23PNB01
SHE'D ASK ME, WHAT'S THE POINT OF HAVING SOMETHING MAGIC IF YOU DON'T USE IT?
I KNEW THE ANSWER. BUT I KNEW SHE'D NEVER UNDERSTAND.
WELL, THERE'S NO ANSWER. AND IT'S LOCKED, BOLTED AND ALARMED.
LET'S GO ROUND THE BACK, WE CAN SMASH A WINDOW, GET IN THAT WAY...
NO.
MAIL
We go in by the FRONT door.
KREEK
IT SMELLS STRANGE. PART OF IT REMINDS ME OF THE MONTH I WORKED FOR AN UNDERTAKER; ALL FLESH AND FORMALDEHYDE.
'S WEIRD: SMELLS ARE A HOTLINE TO MEMORY.
Constantine...
This place is not SAFE for you
Things are free in this house that should NOT be loose on Earth.
You must not stay here.
NAW. I'LL STICK AROUND. I'M INTRIGUED.
ANYWAY, I WAS FOND OF RACHEL ONCE. SHE WAS, YOU KNOW, THE GIRL OF MY DREAMS.
FOR A WHILE.

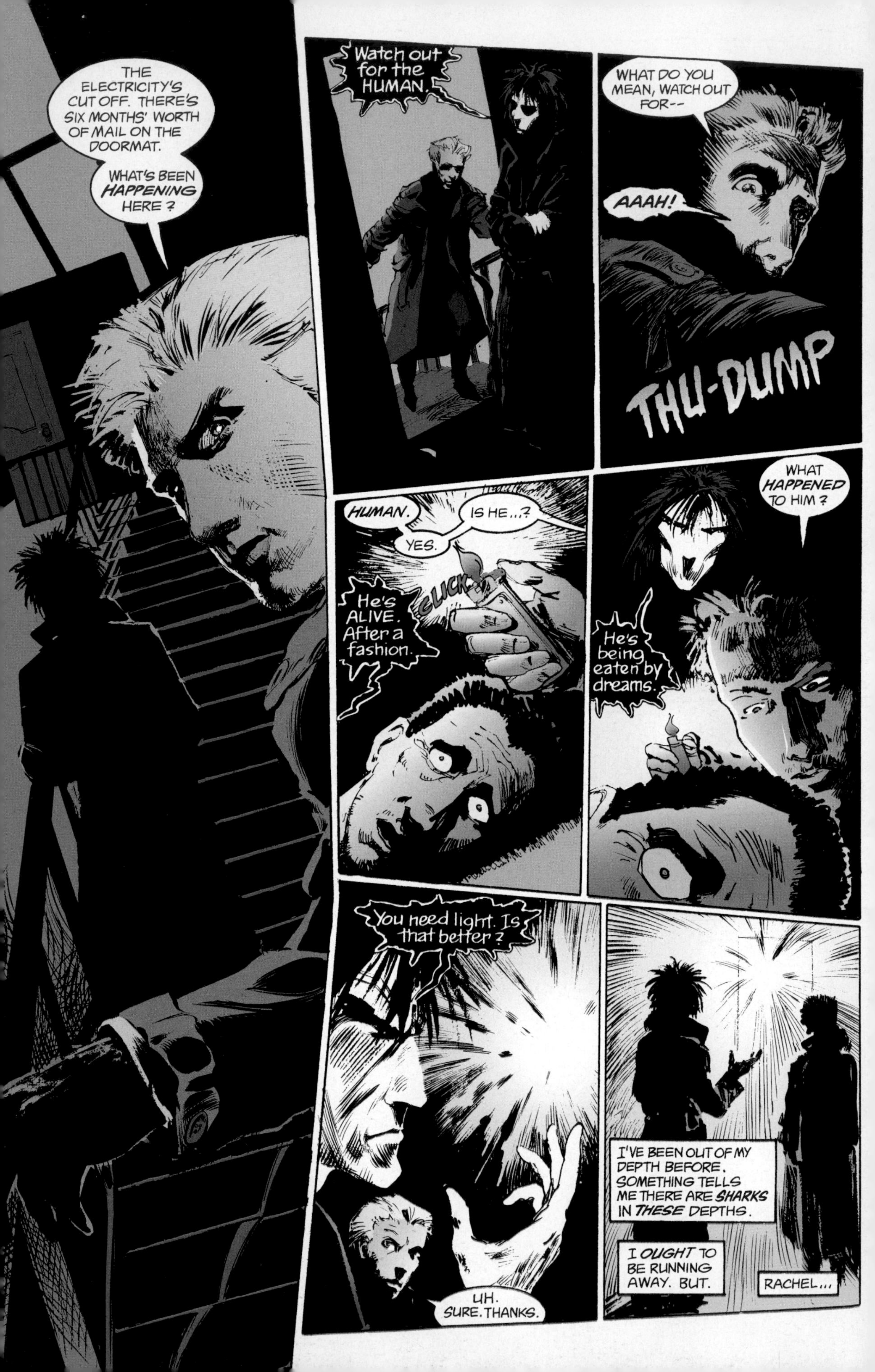
THE ELECTRICITY'S CUT OFF. THERE'S SIX MONTHS' WORTH OF MAIL ON THE DOORMAT.
WHAT'S BEEN *HAPPENING* HERE?
Watch out for the HUMAN.
WHAT DO YOU MEAN, WATCH OUT FOR--
AAAH!
THU-DUMP
HUMAN.
IS HE...?
YES.
CLICK
He's ALIVE. After a fashion.
WHAT *HAPPENED* TO HIM?
He's being eaten by dreams.
You need light. Is that better?
UH. SURE. THANKS.
I'VE BEEN OUT OF MY DEPTH BEFORE. SOMETHING TELLS ME THERE ARE *SHARKS* IN *THESE* DEPTHS.
I *OUGHT* TO BE RUNNING AWAY. BUT.
RACHEL...

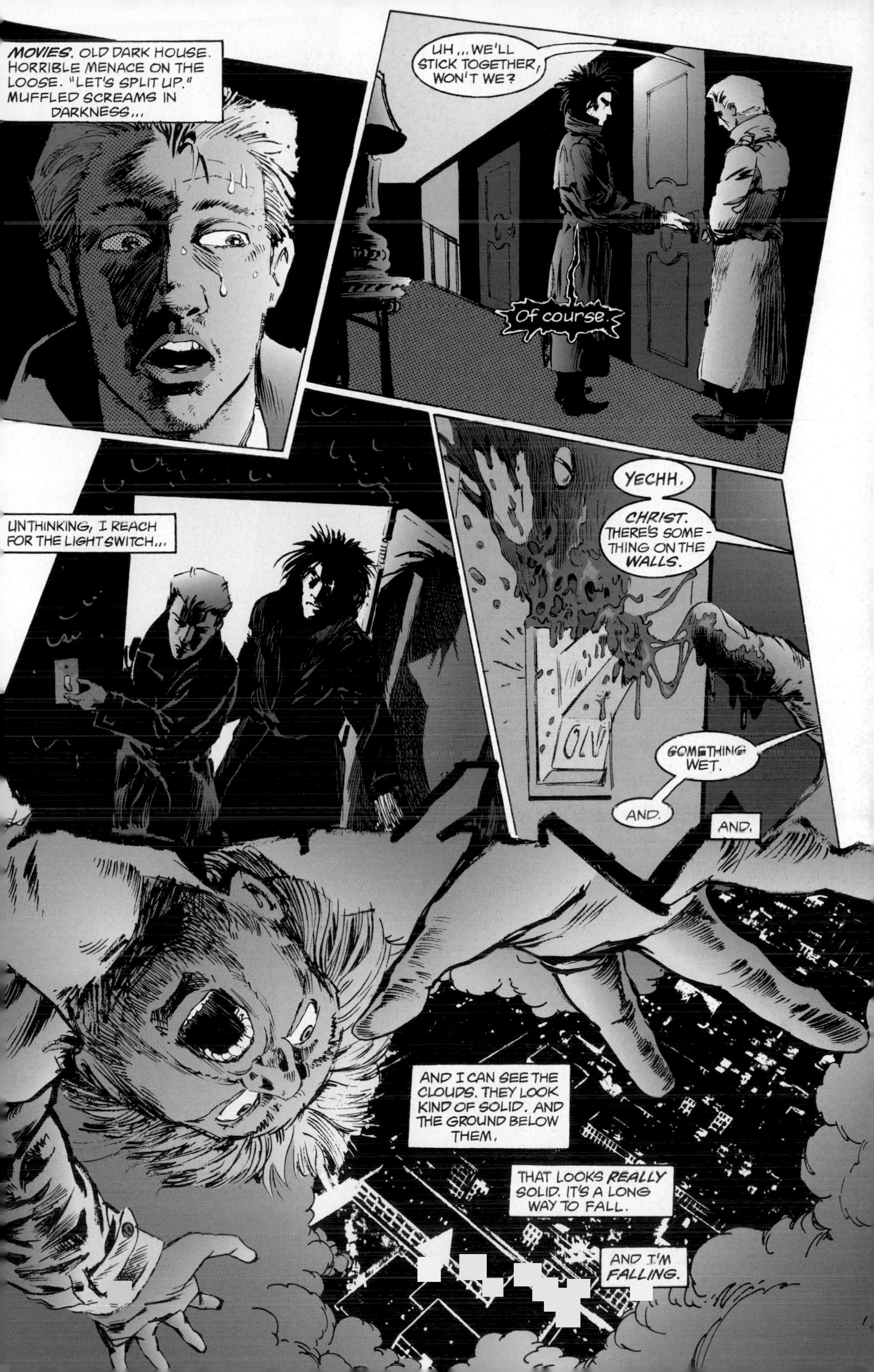
MOVIES. OLD DARK HOUSE. HORRIBLE MENACE ON THE LOOSE. "LET'S SPLIT UP." MUFFLED SCREAMS IN DARKNESS...
UH... WE'LL STICK TOGETHER, WON'T WE?
Of course.
UNTHINKING, I REACH FOR THE LIGHTSWITCH...
YECHH.
CHRIST. THERE'S SOME-THING ON THE WALLS.
SOMETHING WET.
AND.
AND.
AND I CAN SEE THE CLOUDS. THEY LOOK KIND OF SOLID. AND THE GROUND BELOW THEM.
THAT LOOKS REALLY SOLID. IT'S A LONG WAY TO FALL.
AND I'M FALLING.

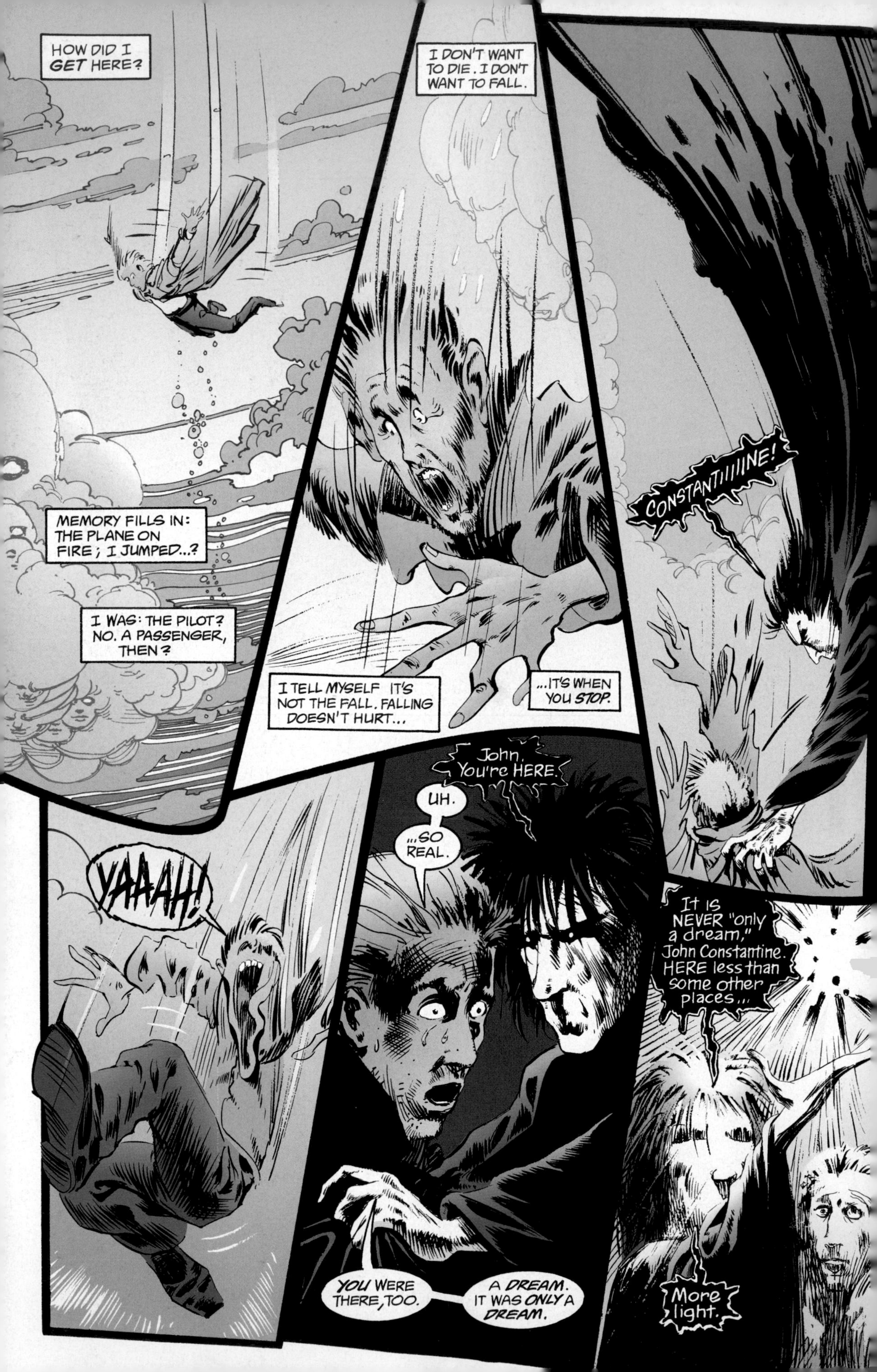
HOW DID I GET HERE?
MEMORY FILLS IN: THE PLANE ON FIRE; I JUMPED...?
I WAS: THE PILOT? NO. A PASSENGER, THEN?
I DON'T WANT TO DIE. I DON'T WANT TO FALL.
I TELL MYSELF IT'S NOT THE FALL. FALLING DOESN'T HURT...
...IT'S WHEN YOU STOP.
CONSTANTIIIIIINE!
YAAAH!
John. You're HERE.
UH.
...SO REAL.
YOU WERE THERE, TOO.
A DREAM. IT WAS ONLY A DREAM.
It is NEVER "only a dream," John Constantine. HERE less than some other places...
More light.

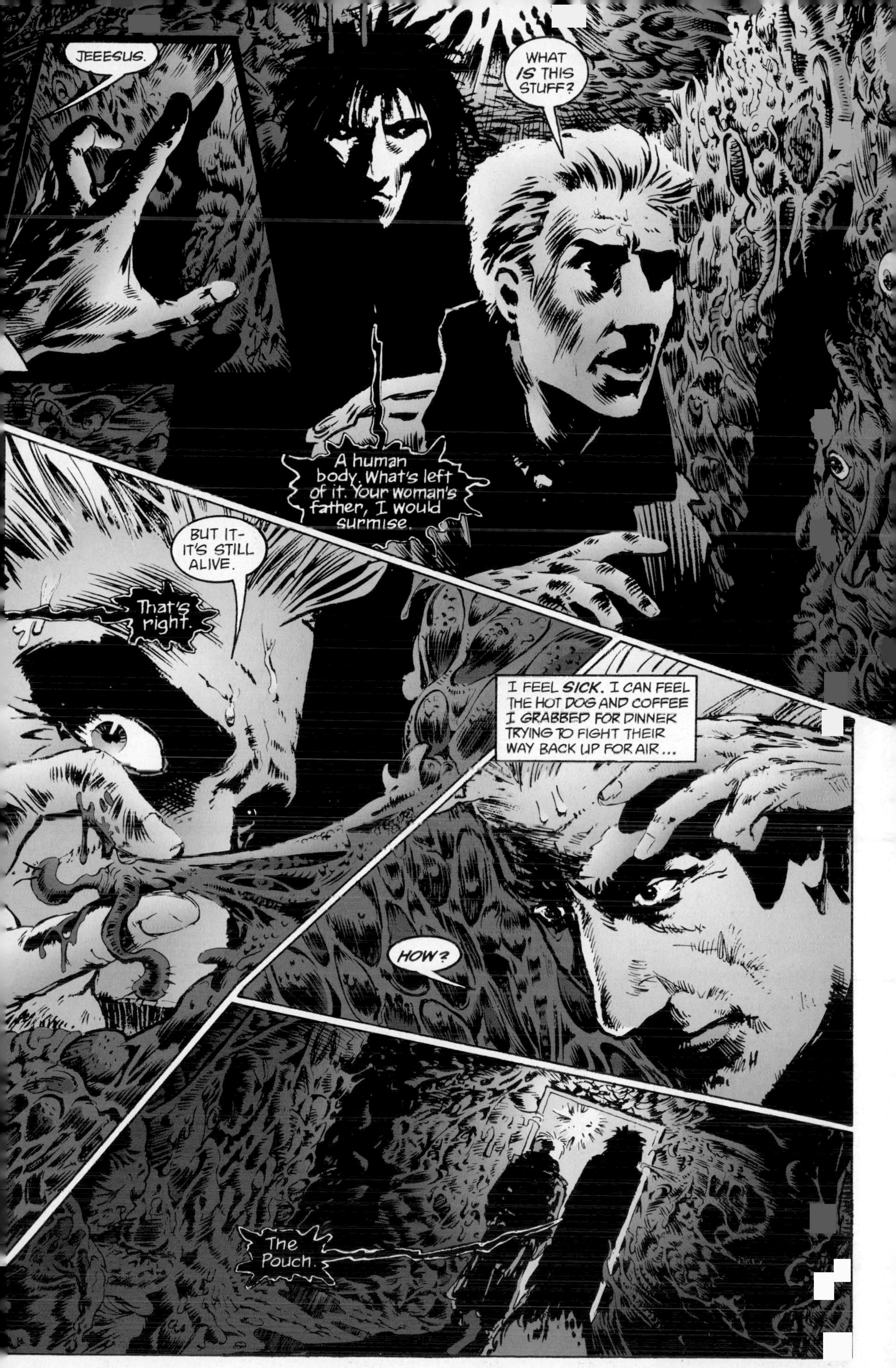
JEEESUS.
WHAT IS THIS STUFF?
A human body. What's left of it. Your woman's father, I would surmise.
BUT IT-IT'S STILL ALIVE.
That's right.
I FEEL SICK. I CAN FEEL THE HOT DOG AND COFFEE I GRABBED FOR DINNER TRYING TO FIGHT THEIR WAY BACK UP FOR AIR...
HOW?
The Pouch.

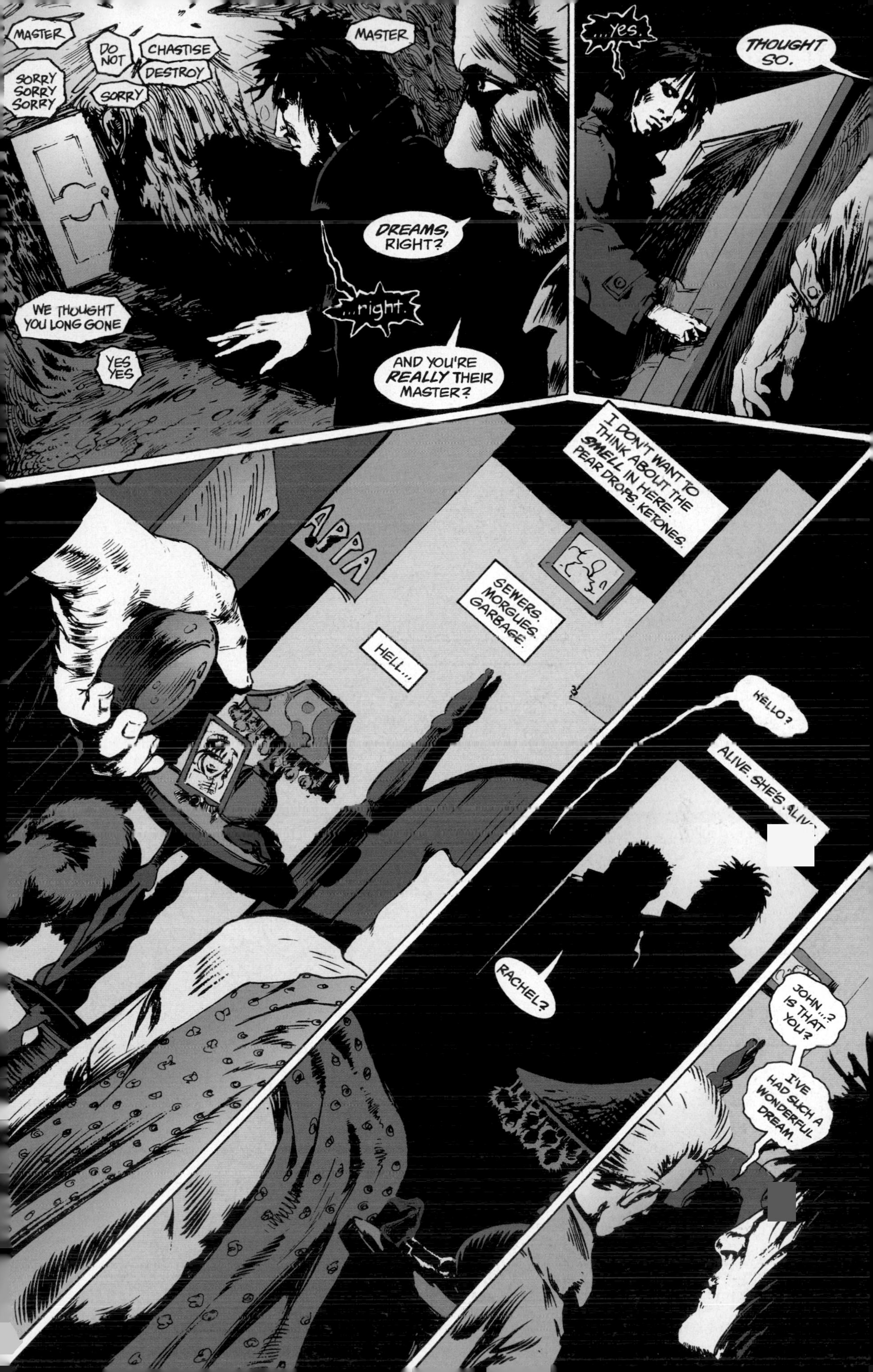
MASTER
SORRY SORRY SORRY
DO NOT
CHASTISE
DESTROY
SORRY
MASTER
DREAMS, RIGHT?
...right.
WE THOUGHT YOU LONG GONE
YES YES
AND YOU'RE REALLY THEIR MASTER?
...yes.
THOUGHT SO.
I DON'T WANT TO THINK ABOUT THE SMELL IN HERE. PEAR DROPS. KETONES.
SEWERS. MORGUES. GARBAGE.
HELL...
HELLO?
ALIVE. SHE'S ALIV
RACHEL?
JOHN...? IS THAT YOU?
I'VE HAD SUCH A WONDERFUL DREAM.

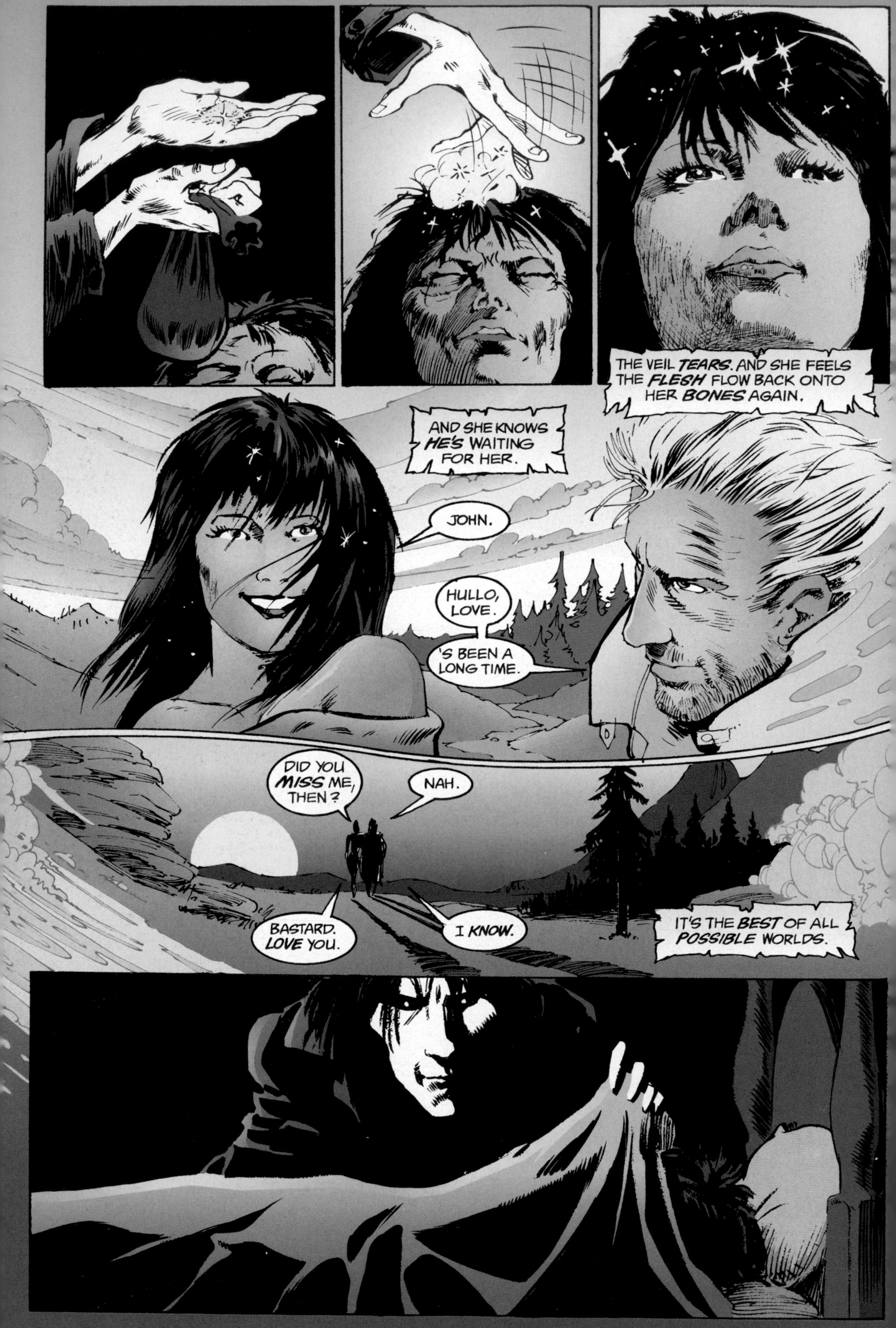
THE VEIL TEARS. AND SHE FEELS THE FLESH FLOW BACK ONTO HER BONES AGAIN.
AND SHE KNOWS HE'S WAITING FOR HER.
JOHN.
HULLO, LOVE.
'S BEEN A LONG TIME.
DID YOU MISS ME, THEN?
NAH.
BASTARD. LOVE YOU.
I KNOW.
IT'S THE BEST OF ALL POSSIBLE WORLDS.

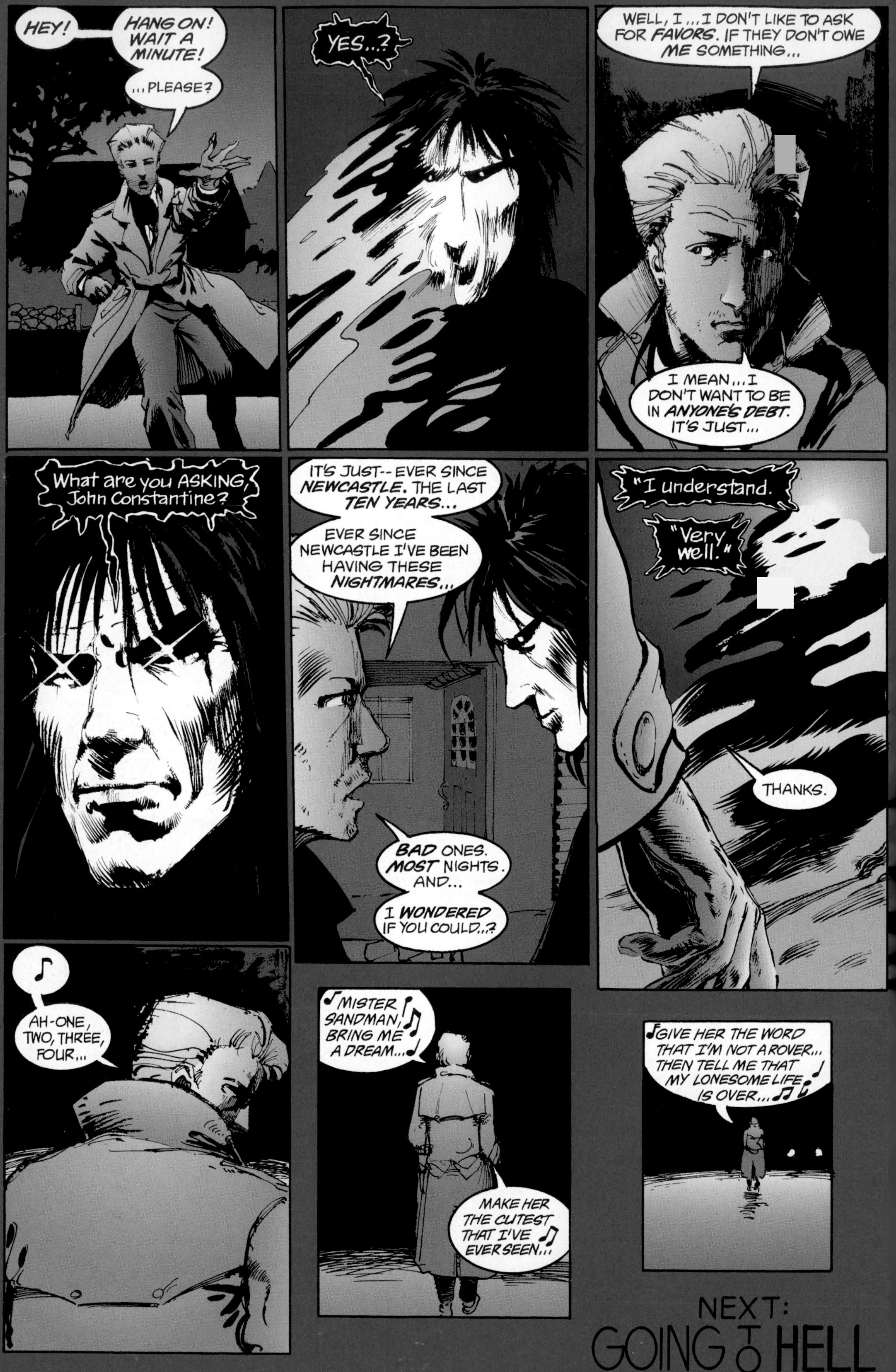
HEY!
HANG ON! WAIT A MINUTE!
...PLEASE?
YES...?
WELL, I... I DON'T LIKE TO ASK FOR FAVORS. IF THEY DON'T OWE ME SOMETHING...
I MEAN... I DON'T WANT TO BE IN ANYONE'S DEBT. IT'S JUST...
What are you ASKING, John Constantine?
IT'S JUST-- EVER SINCE NEWCASTLE. THE LAST TEN YEARS...
EVER SINCE NEWCASTLE I'VE BEEN HAVING THESE NIGHTMARES...
BAD ONES. MOST NIGHTS. AND...
I WONDERED IF YOU COULD...?
"I understand.
"Very well."
THANKS.
♪
AH-ONE, TWO, THREE, FOUR...
♪MISTER SANDMAN, ♪BRING ME A DREAM...♪
MAKE HER THE CUTEST THAT I'VE EVER SEEN...♪
♪GIVE HER THE WORD THAT I'M NOT A ROVER... THEN TELL ME THAT MY LONESOME LIFE IS OVER...♫
NEXT:
GOING TO HELL

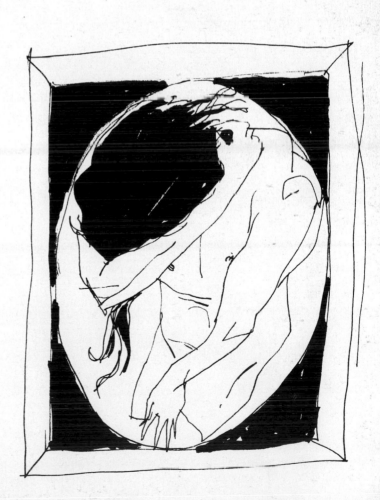

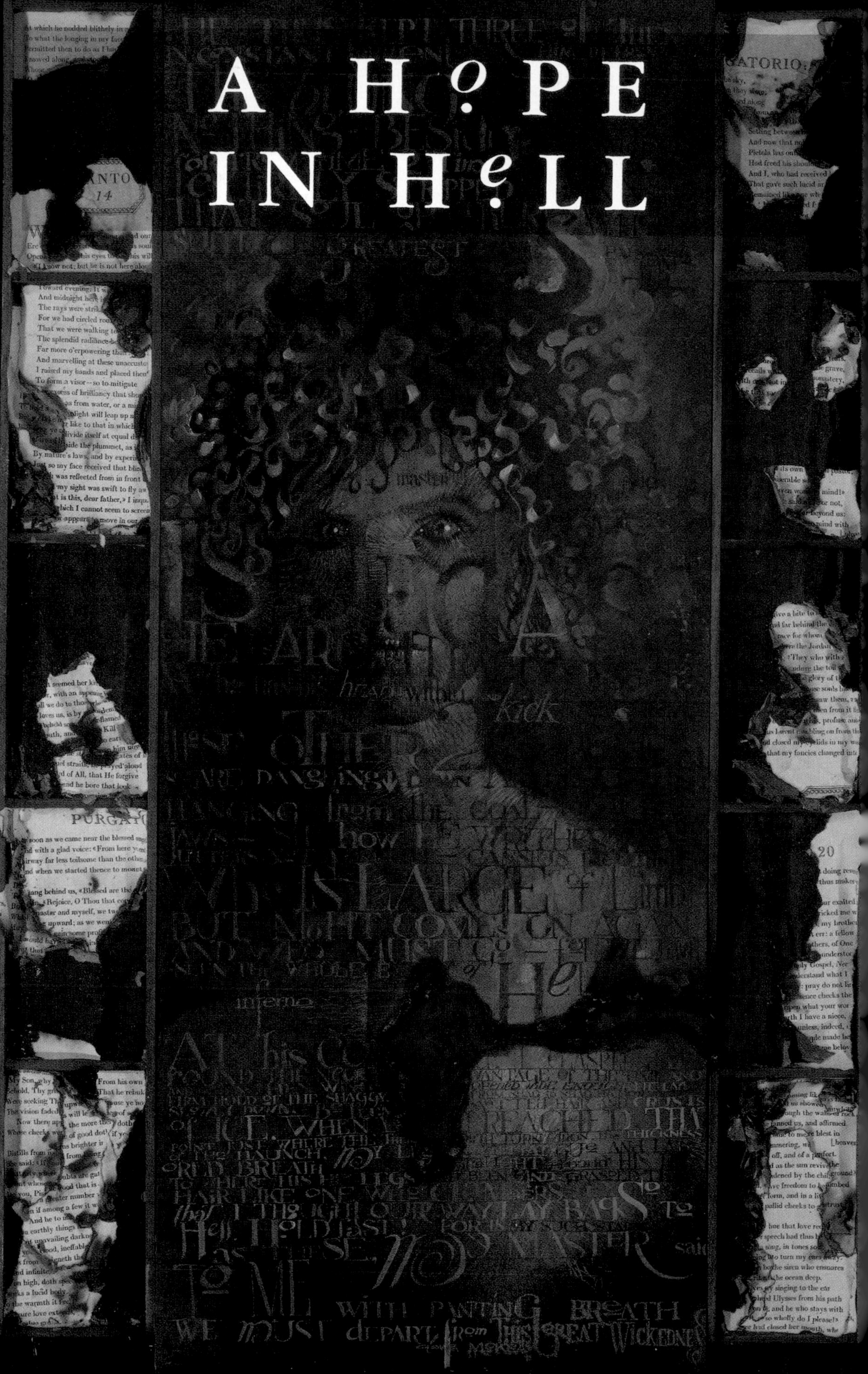
A HOPE
IN HELL

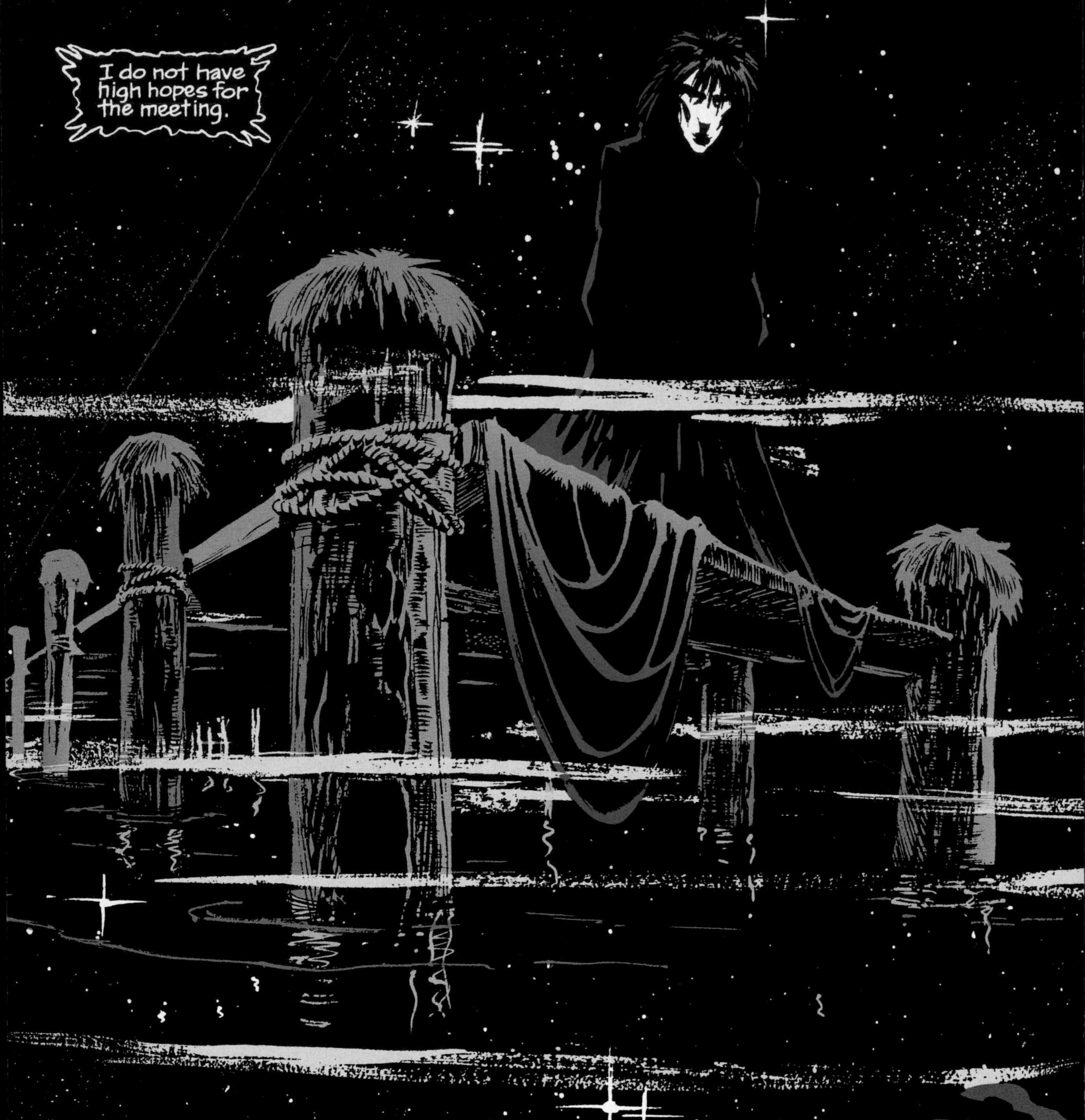
I do not have high hopes for the meeting.
A HOPE IN HE
NEIL GAIMAN WRITER
SAM KIETH & MIKE DRINGENBERG ARTISTS
DANIEL VOZZO COLORIST
TODD KLEIN LETTERER
ART YOUNG ASST. EDITOR
KAREN BERGER EDITOR

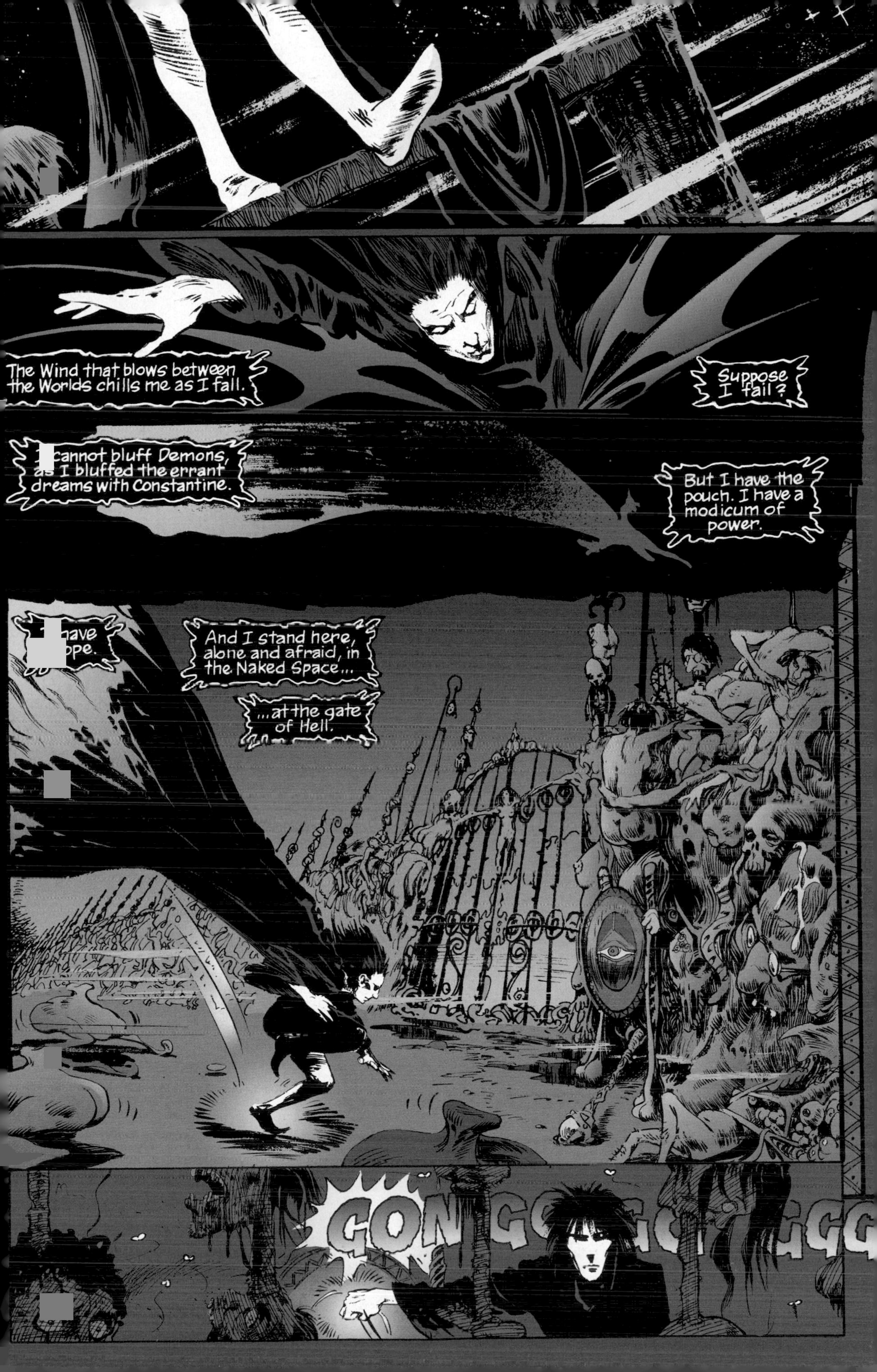

The Wind that blows between the Worlds chills me as I fall.
Suppose I fail?
I cannot bluff Demons, as I bluffed the errant dreams with Constantine.
But I have the pouch. I have a modicum of power.
I have hope.
And I stand here, alone and afraid, in the Naked Space...
...at the gate of Hell.
GON

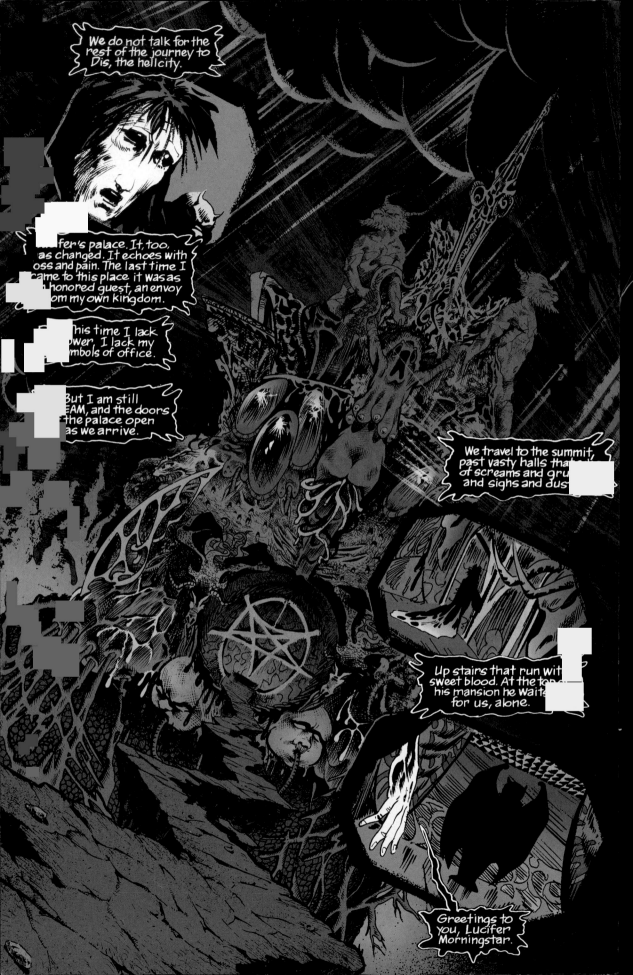

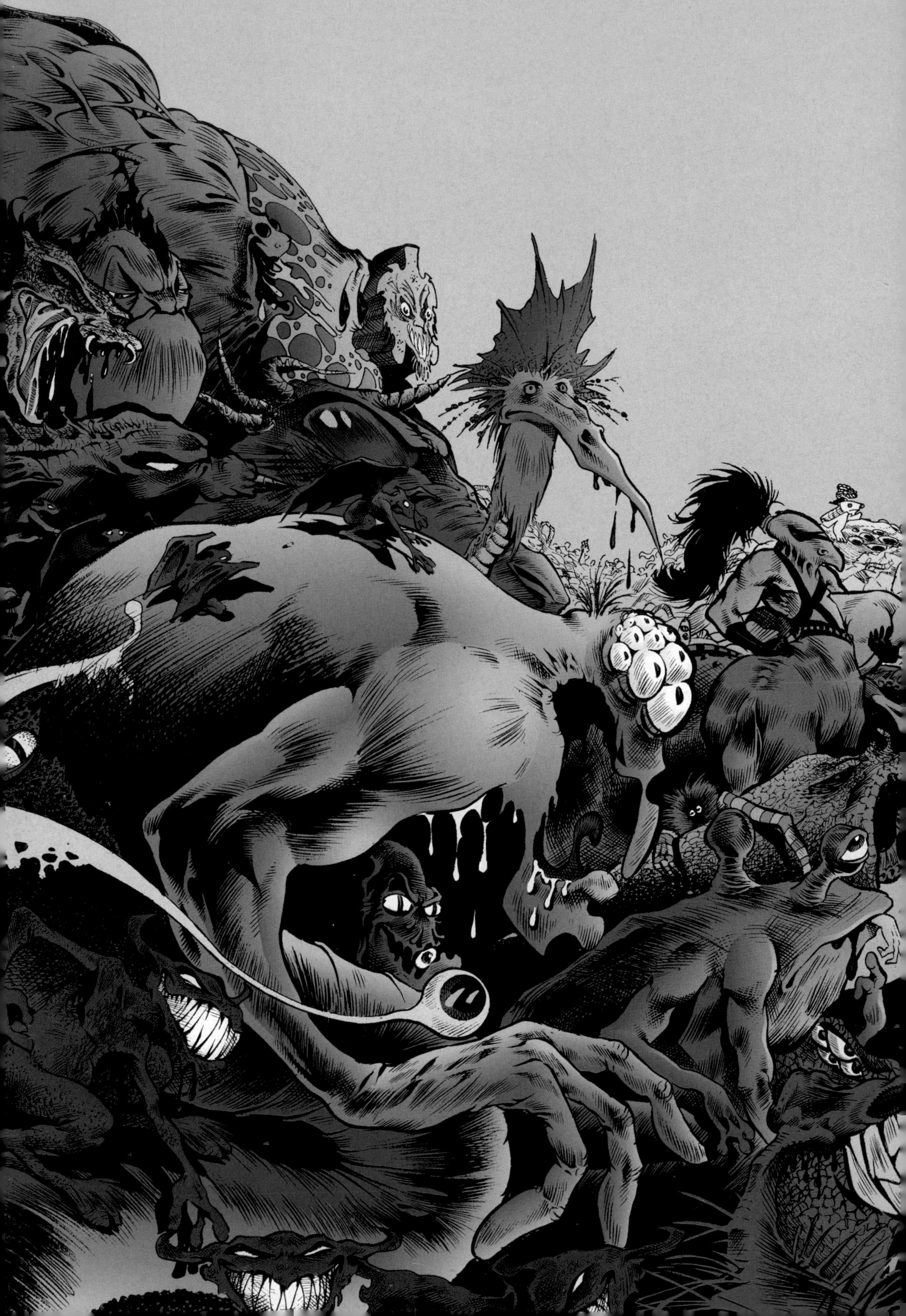

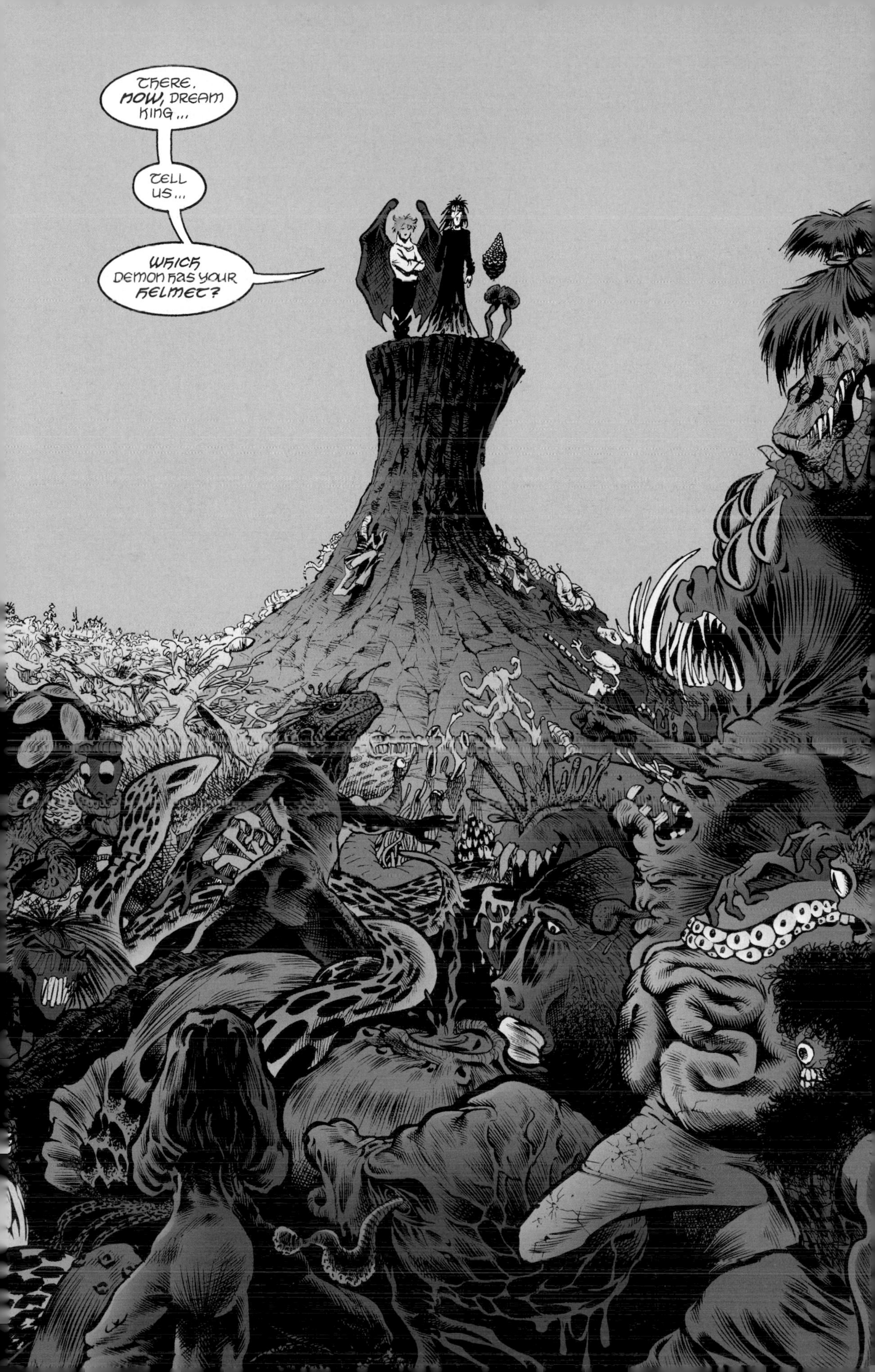
THERE. NOW, DREAM KING...
TELL US...
WHICH DEMON HAS YOUR HELMET?

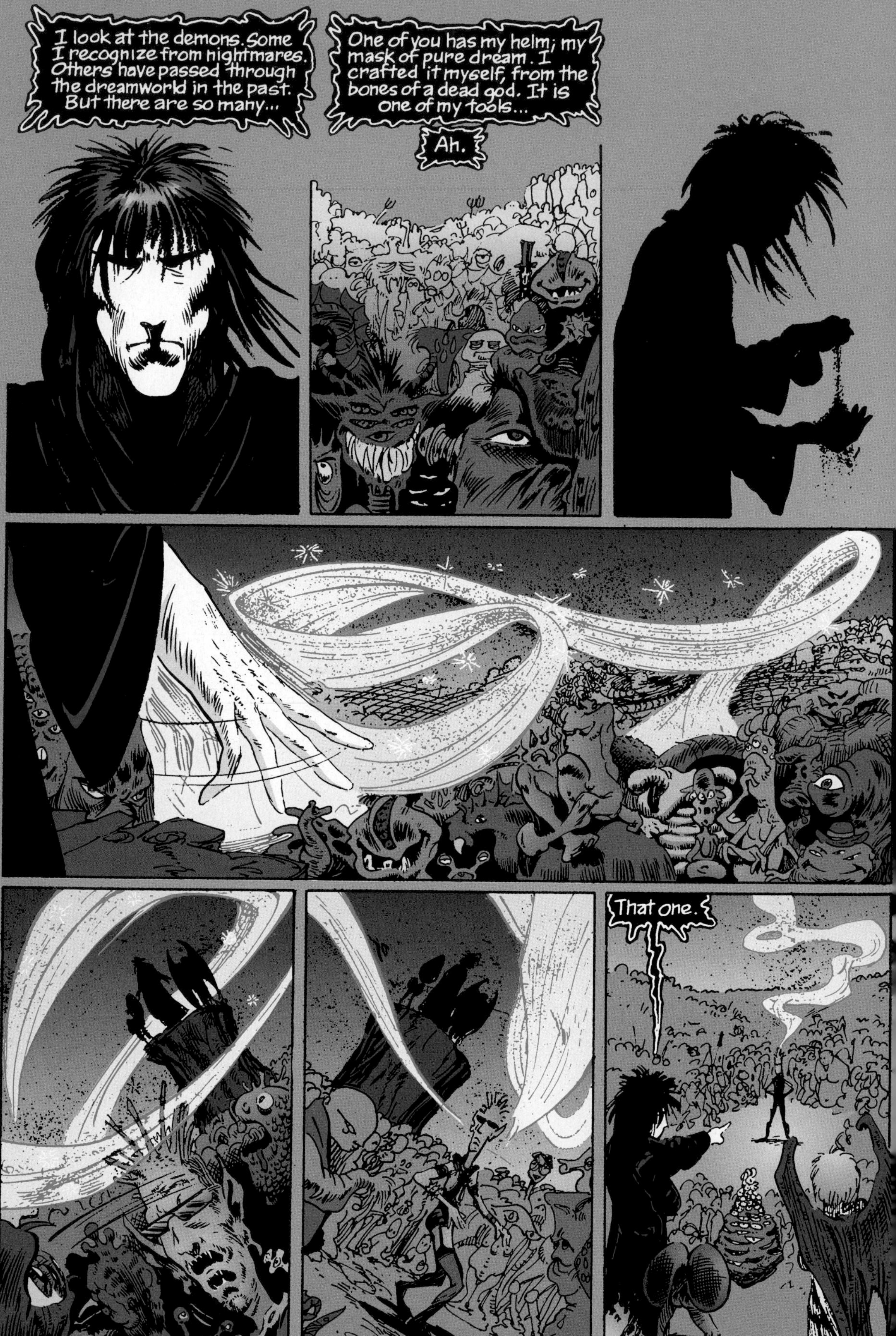
I look at the demons. Some I recognize from nightmares. Others have passed through the dreamworld in the past. But there are so many...
One of you has my helm; my mask of pure dream. I crafted it myself, from the bones of a dead god. It is one of my tools...
Ah.
That one.

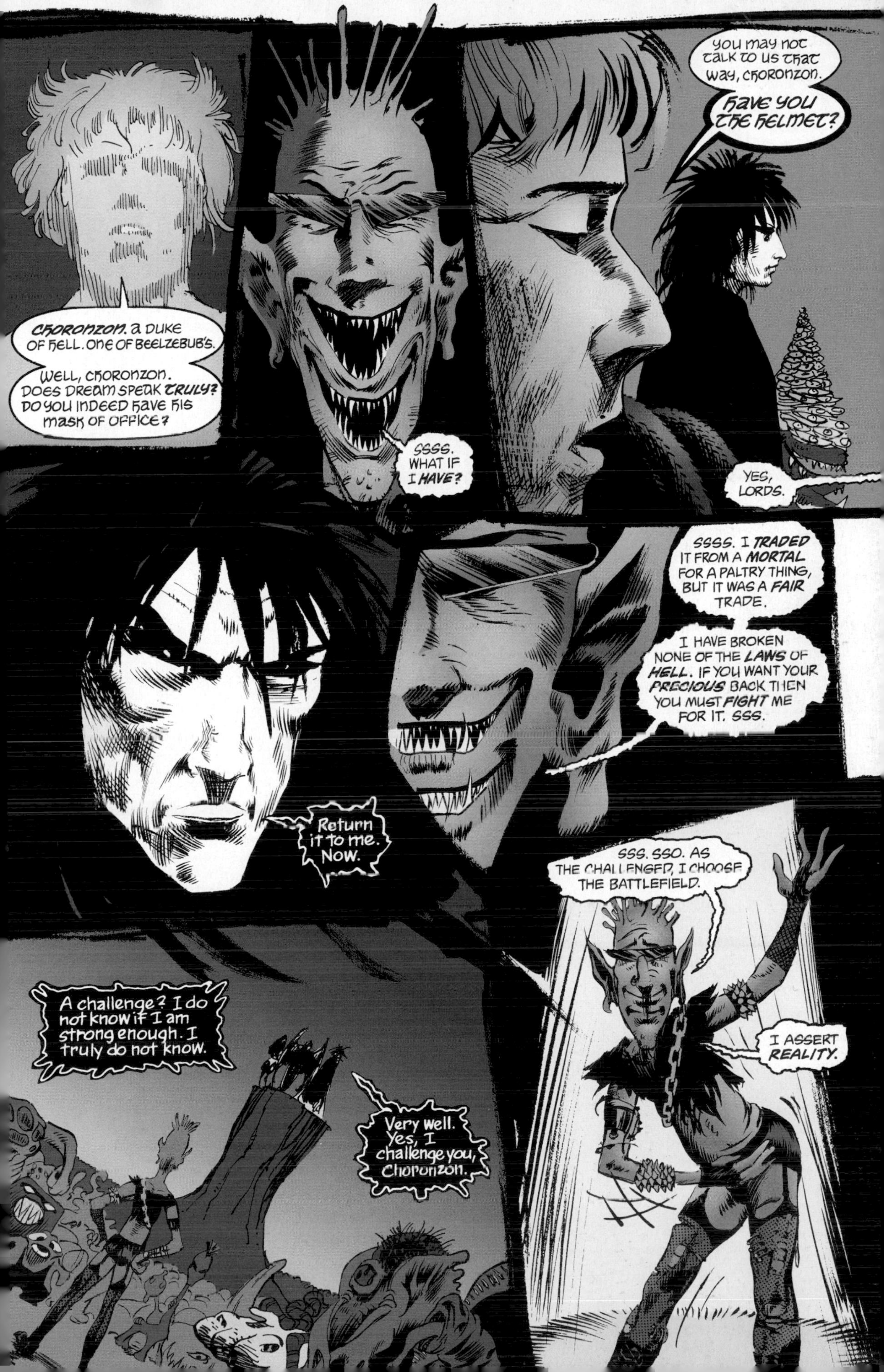

CHORONZON. A DUKE OF HELL. ONE OF BEELZEBUB'S.
WELL, CHORONZON. DOES DREAM SPEAK TRULY? DO YOU INDEED HAVE HIS MASK OF OFFICE?
SSSS. WHAT IF I HAVE?
YOU MAY NOT TALK TO US THAT WAY, CHORONZON.
HAVE YOU THE HELMET?
YES, LORDS.
Return it to me. Now.
SSSS. I TRADED IT FROM A MORTAL FOR A PALTRY THING, BUT IT WAS A FAIR TRADE.
I HAVE BROKEN NONE OF THE LAWS OF HELL. IF YOU WANT YOUR PRECIOUS BACK THEN YOU MUST FIGHT ME FOR IT. SSS.
A challenge? I do not know if I am strong enough. I truly do not know.
Very well. Yes, I challenge you, Choronzon.
SSS. SSO. AS THE CHALLENGED, I CHOOSE THE BATTLEFIELD.
I ASSERT REALITY.

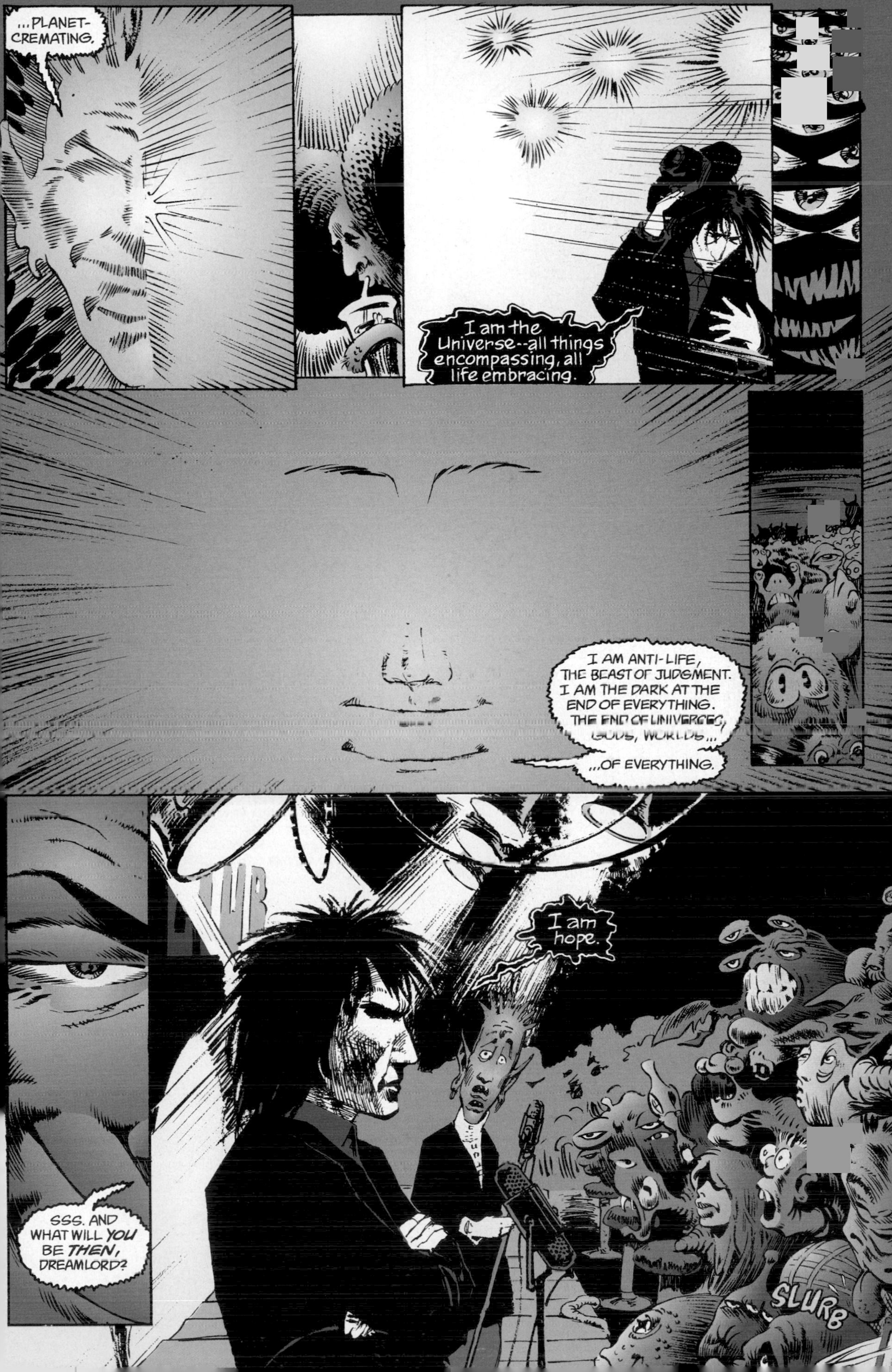
...PLANET-CREMATING.
I am the Universe--all things encompassing, all life embracing.
I AM ANTI-LIFE, THE BEAST OF JUDGMENT. I AM THE DARK AT THE END OF EVERYTHING. THE END OF UNIVERSES, GODS, WORLDS...
...OF EVERYTHING.
SSS. AND WHAT WILL *YOU* BE *THEN*, DREAMLORD?
I am hope.
SLURB

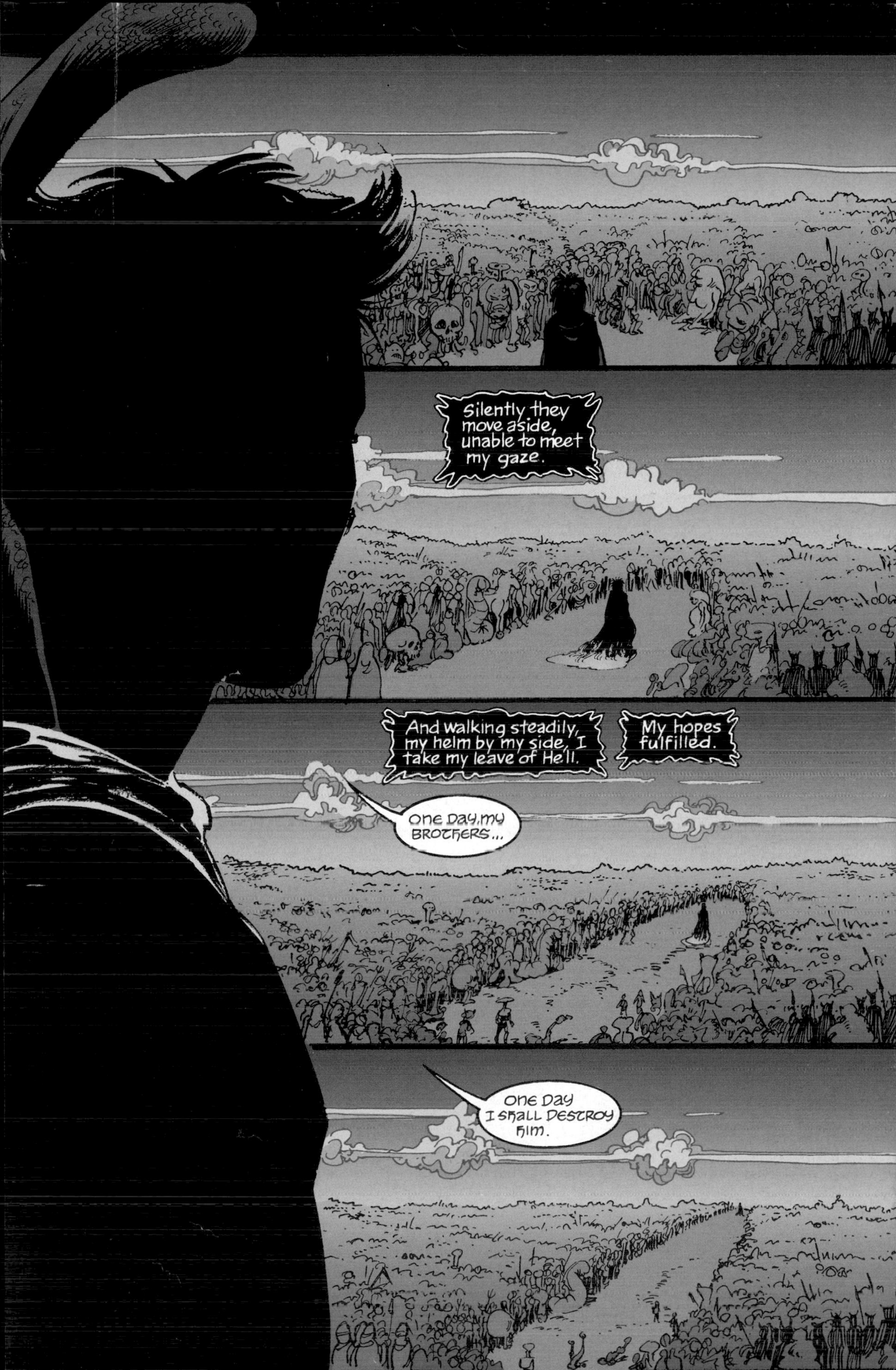

Silently they move aside, unable to meet my gaze.
And walking steadily, my helm by my side, I take my leave of Hell.
My hopes fulfilled.
ONE DAY, MY BROTHERS...
ONE DAY I SHALL DESTROY HIM.

EPILOGUE

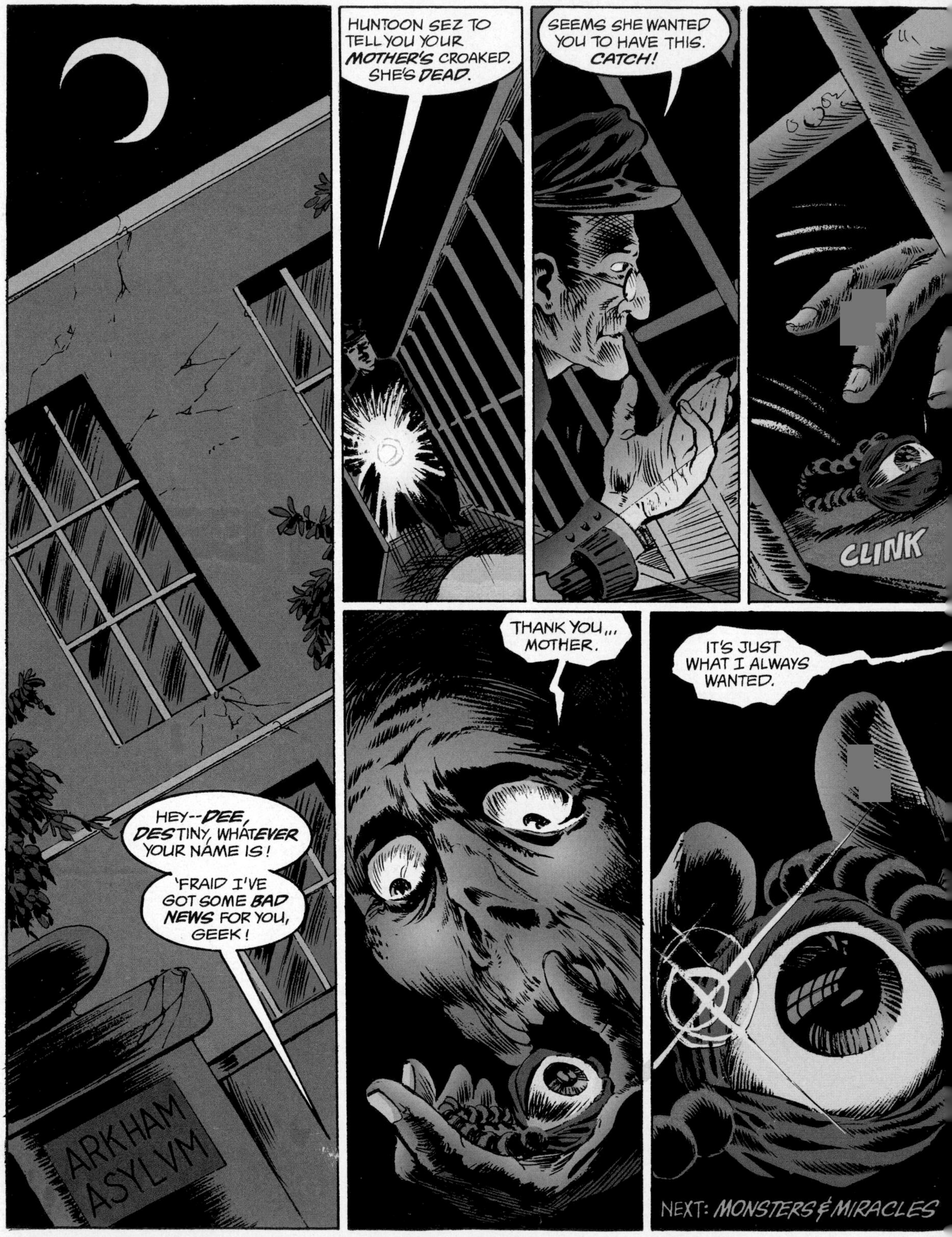
HEY--*DEE, DES*TINY, WHAT*EVER* YOUR NAME IS!
'FRAID I'VE GOT SOME ***BAD NEWS*** FOR YOU, GEEK!
ARKHAM ASYLUM
HUNTOON SEZ TO TELL YOU YOUR ***MOTHER'S*** CROAKED. SHE'S ***DEAD***.
SEEMS SHE WANTED YOU TO HAVE THIS. *CATCH!*
CLINK
THANK YOU... MOTHER.
IT'S JUST WHAT I ALWAYS WANTED.
NEXT: *MONSTERS & MIRACLES*

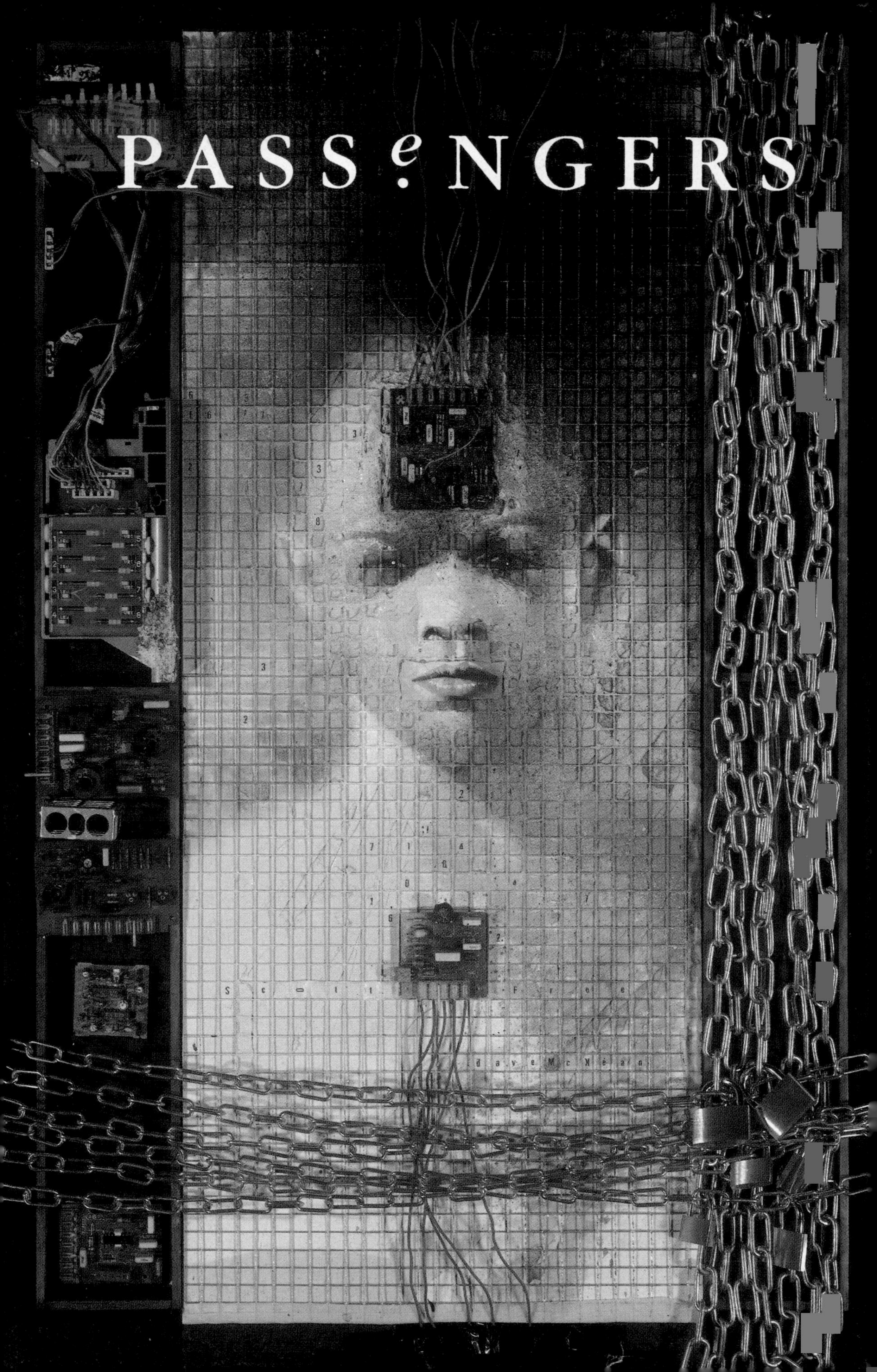
PASSeNGERS
Scott Free
dave McKean

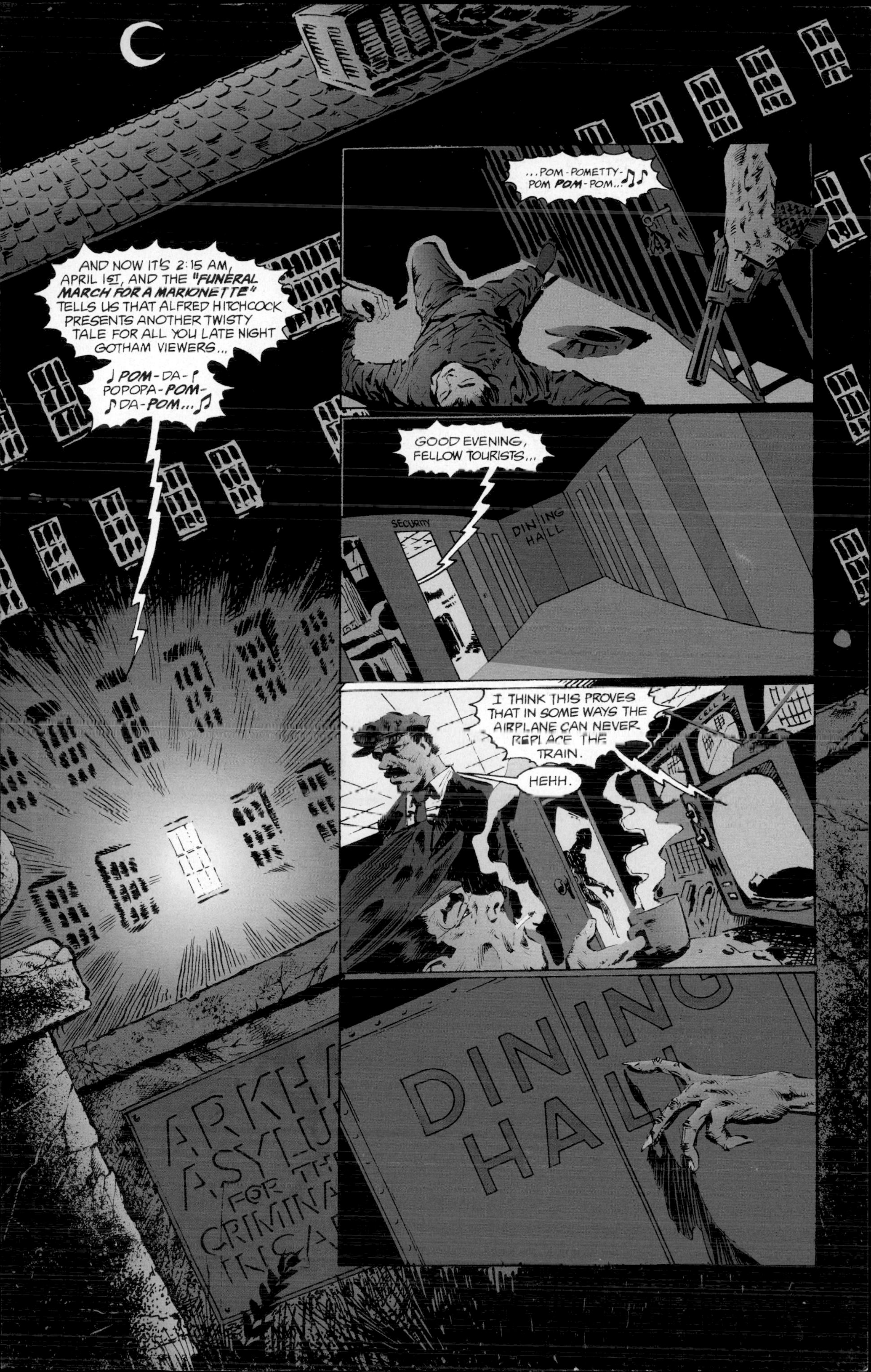
AND NOW IT'S 2:15 AM, APRIL 1ST, AND THE "FUNERAL MARCH FOR A MARIONETTE" TELLS US THAT ALFRED HITCHCOCK PRESENTS ANOTHER TWISTY TALE FOR ALL YOU LATE NIGHT GOTHAM VIEWERS...
♪ POM-DA-♪ POPOPA-POM-♪ DA-POM...♫
...POM-POMETTY-POM POM-POM...♫♪
GOOD EVENING, FELLOW TOURISTS...
SECURITY
DINING HALL
I THINK THIS PROVES THAT IN SOME WAYS THE AIRPLANE CAN NEVER REPLACE THE TRAIN.
HEHH.
CELL 2
DINING HALL

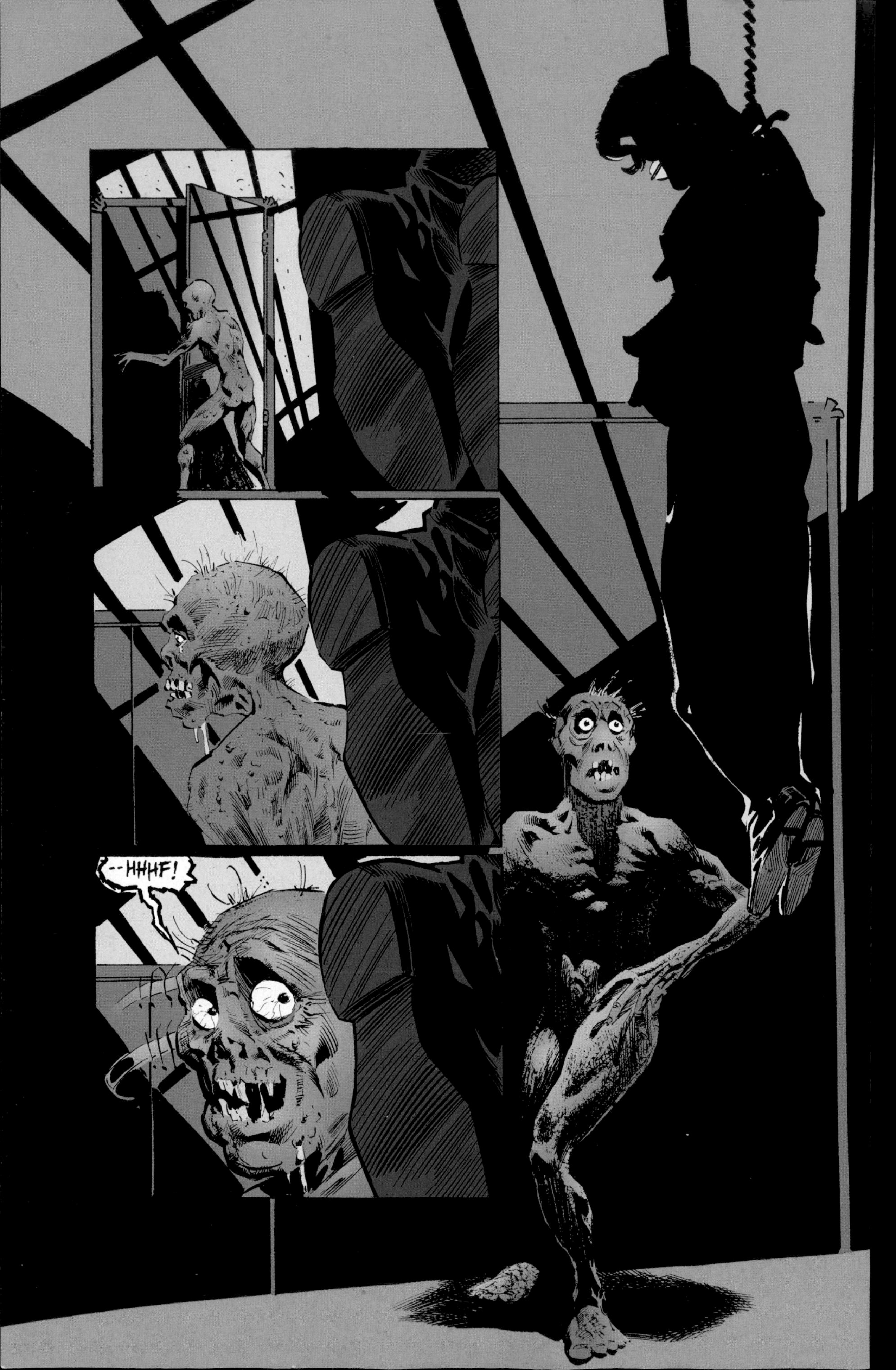
--HHHF!

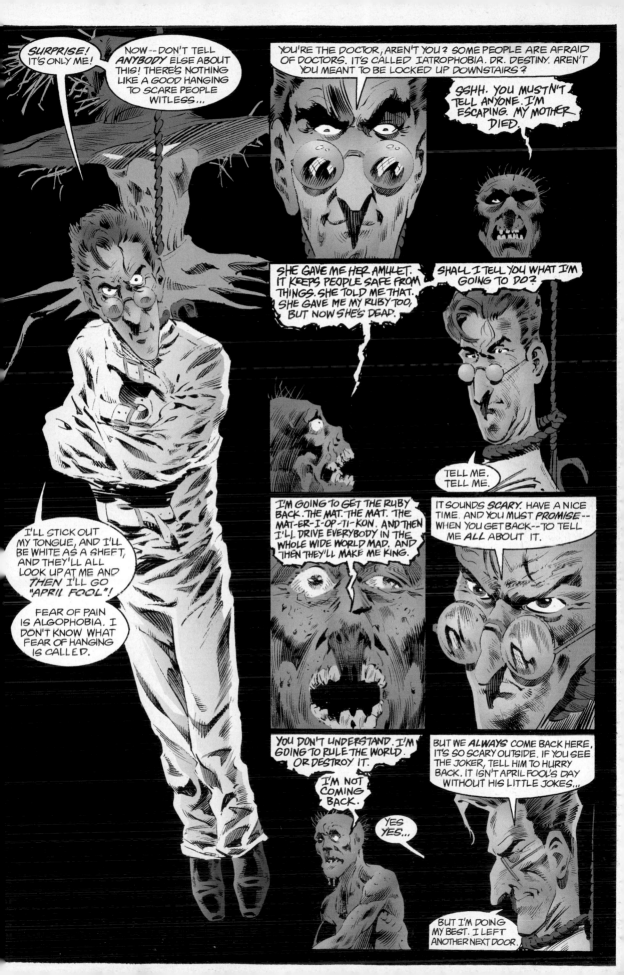

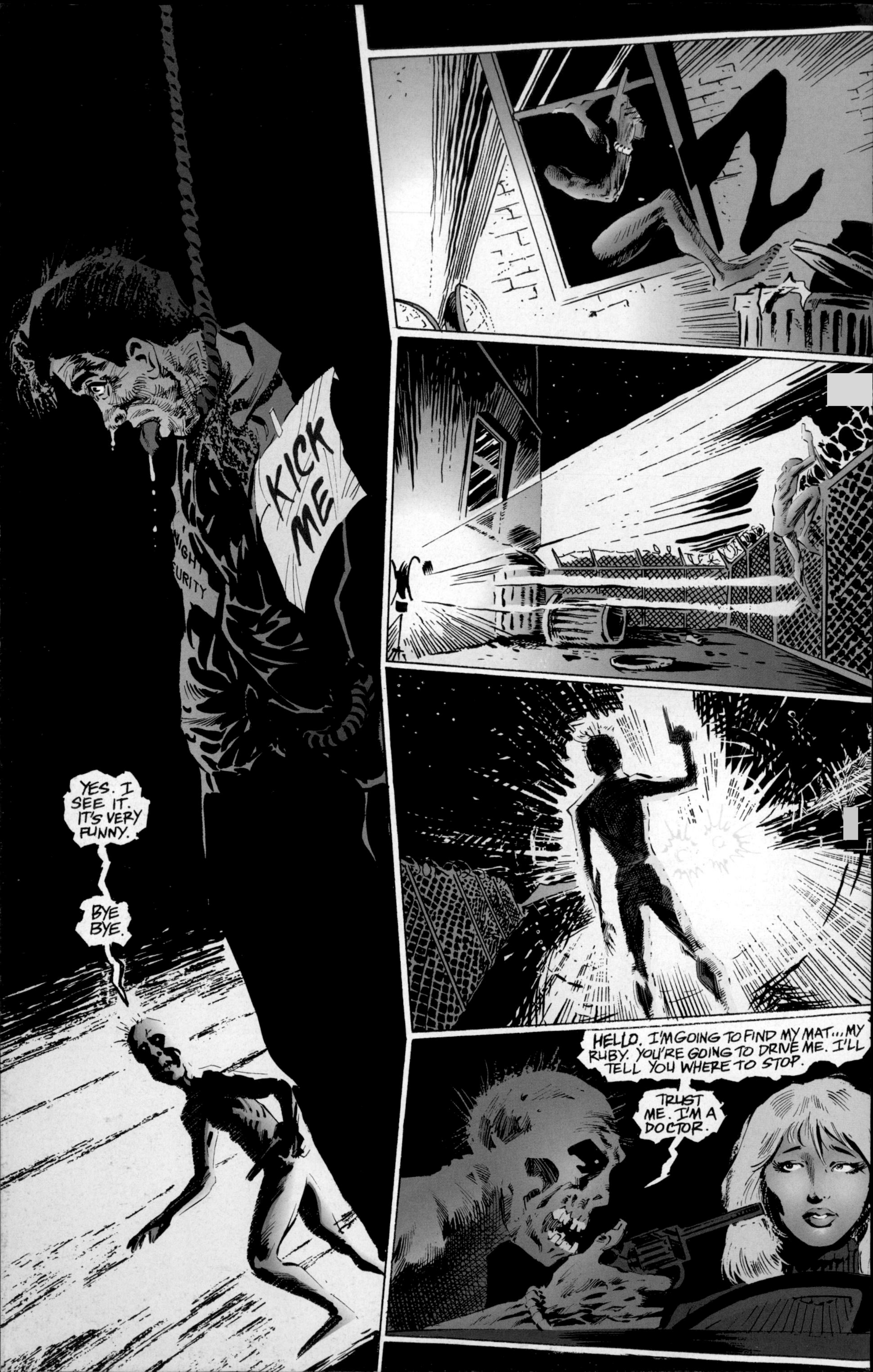
KICK ME
YES. I SEE IT. IT'S VERY FUNNY.
BYE BYE.
HELLO. I'M GOING TO FIND MY MAT... MY RUBY. YOU'RE GOING TO DRIVE ME. I'LL TELL YOU WHERE TO STOP.
TRUST ME. I'M A DOCTOR.

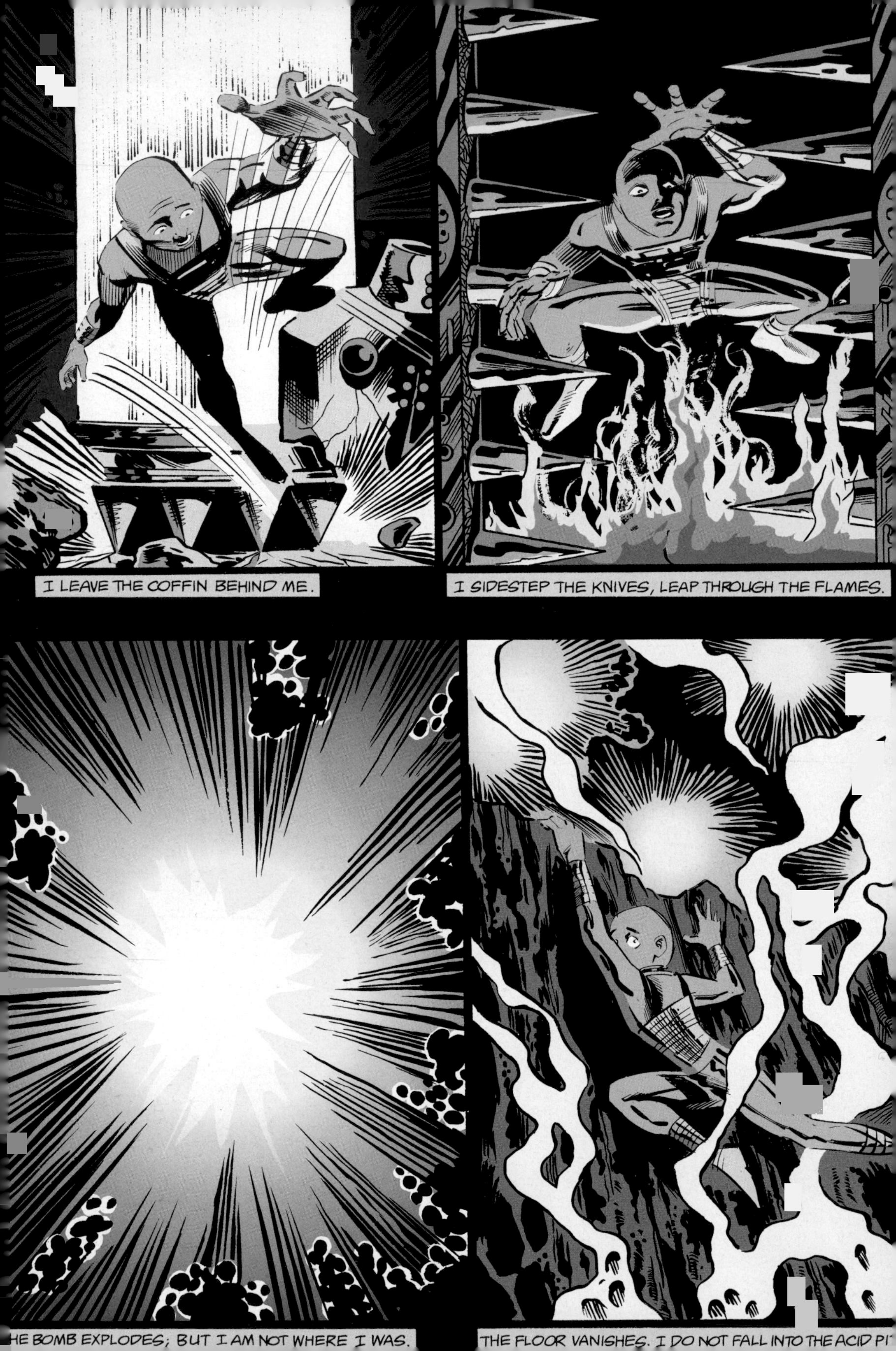
I LEAVE THE COFFIN BEHIND ME.
I SIDESTEP THE KNIVES, LEAP THROUGH THE FLAMES.
HE BOMB EXPLODES; BUT I AM NOT WHERE I WAS.
THE FLOOR VANISHES. I DO NOT FALL INTO THE ACID PI

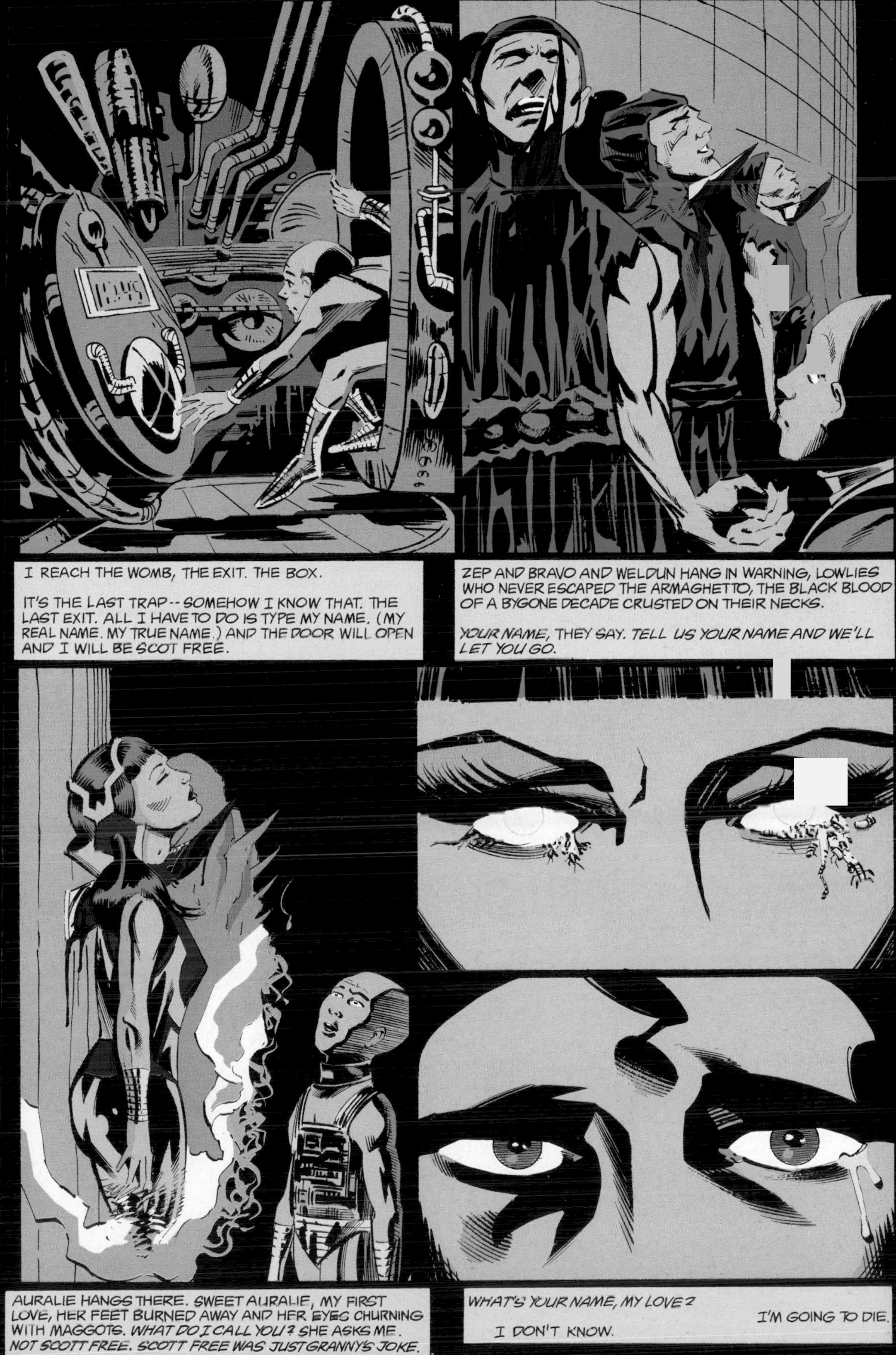
I REACH THE WOMB, THE EXIT. THE BOX.
IT'S THE LAST TRAP-- SOMEHOW I KNOW THAT. THE LAST EXIT. ALL I HAVE TO DO IS TYPE MY NAME. (MY REAL NAME. MY TRUE NAME.) AND THE DOOR WILL OPEN AND I WILL BE SCOT FREE.
ZEP AND BRAVO AND WELDUN HANG IN WARNING, LOWLIES WHO NEVER ESCAPED THE ARMAGHETTO, THE BLACK BLOOD OF A BYGONE DECADE CRUSTED ON THEIR NECKS.
YOUR NAME, THEY SAY. *TELL US YOUR NAME AND WE'LL LET YOU GO.*
AURALIE HANGS THERE. SWEET AURALIE, MY FIRST LOVE, HER FEET BURNED AWAY AND HER EYES CHURNING WITH MAGGOTS. *WHAT DO I CALL YOU?* SHE ASKS ME. *NOT SCOTT FREE. SCOTT FREE WAS JUST GRANNY'S JOKE.*
WHAT'S YOUR NAME, MY LOVE?
I'M GOING TO DIE.
I DON'T KNOW.

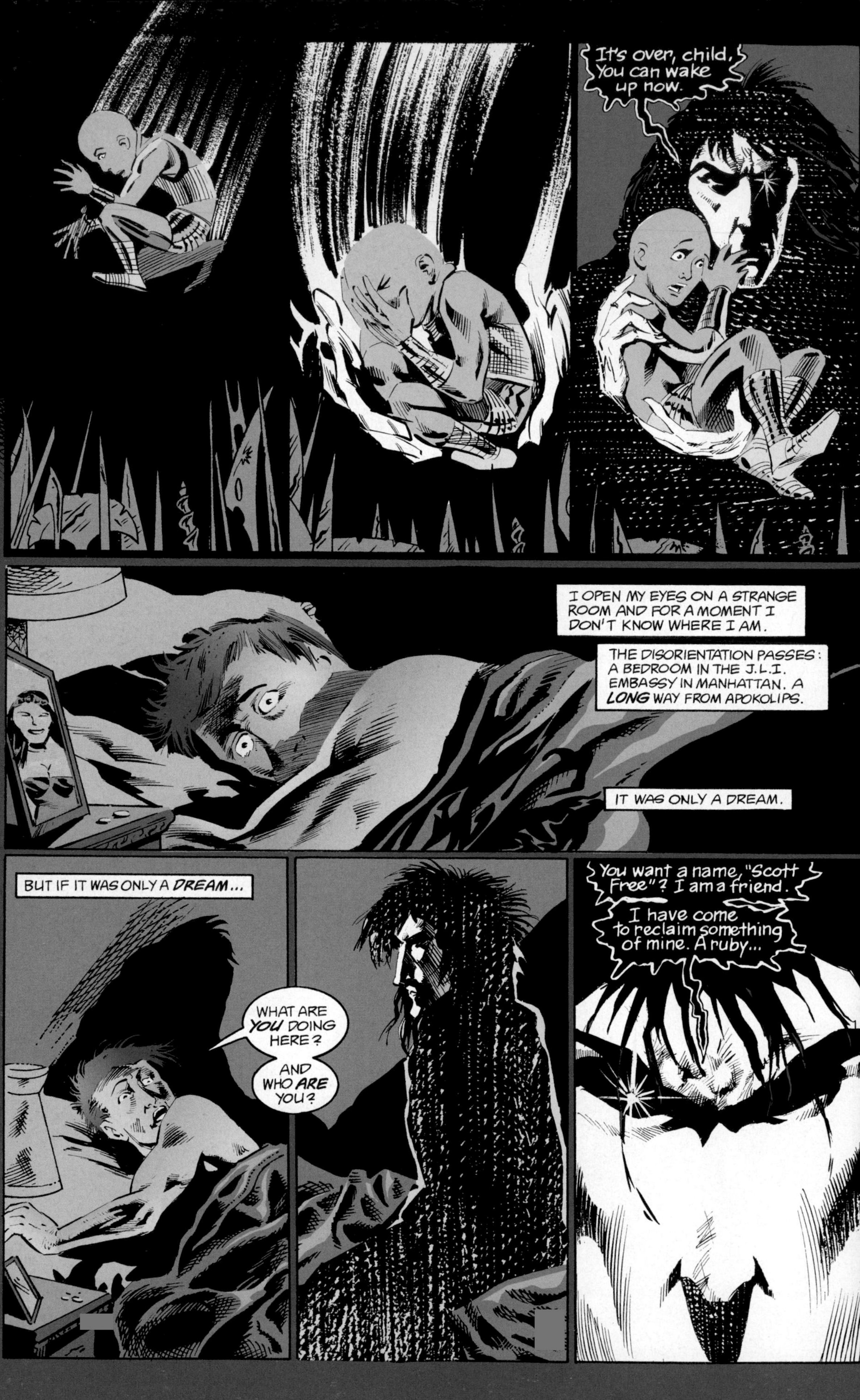
It's over, child, You can wake up now.
I OPEN MY EYES ON A STRANGE ROOM AND FOR A MOMENT I DON'T KNOW WHERE I AM.
THE DISORIENTATION PASSES: A BEDROOM IN THE J.L.I. EMBASSY IN MANHATTAN. A LONG WAY FROM APOKOLIPS.
IT WAS ONLY A DREAM.
BUT IF IT WAS ONLY A DREAM...
WHAT ARE YOU DOING HERE?
AND WHO ARE YOU?
You want a name, "Scott Free"? I am a friend.
I have come to reclaim something of mine. A ruby...

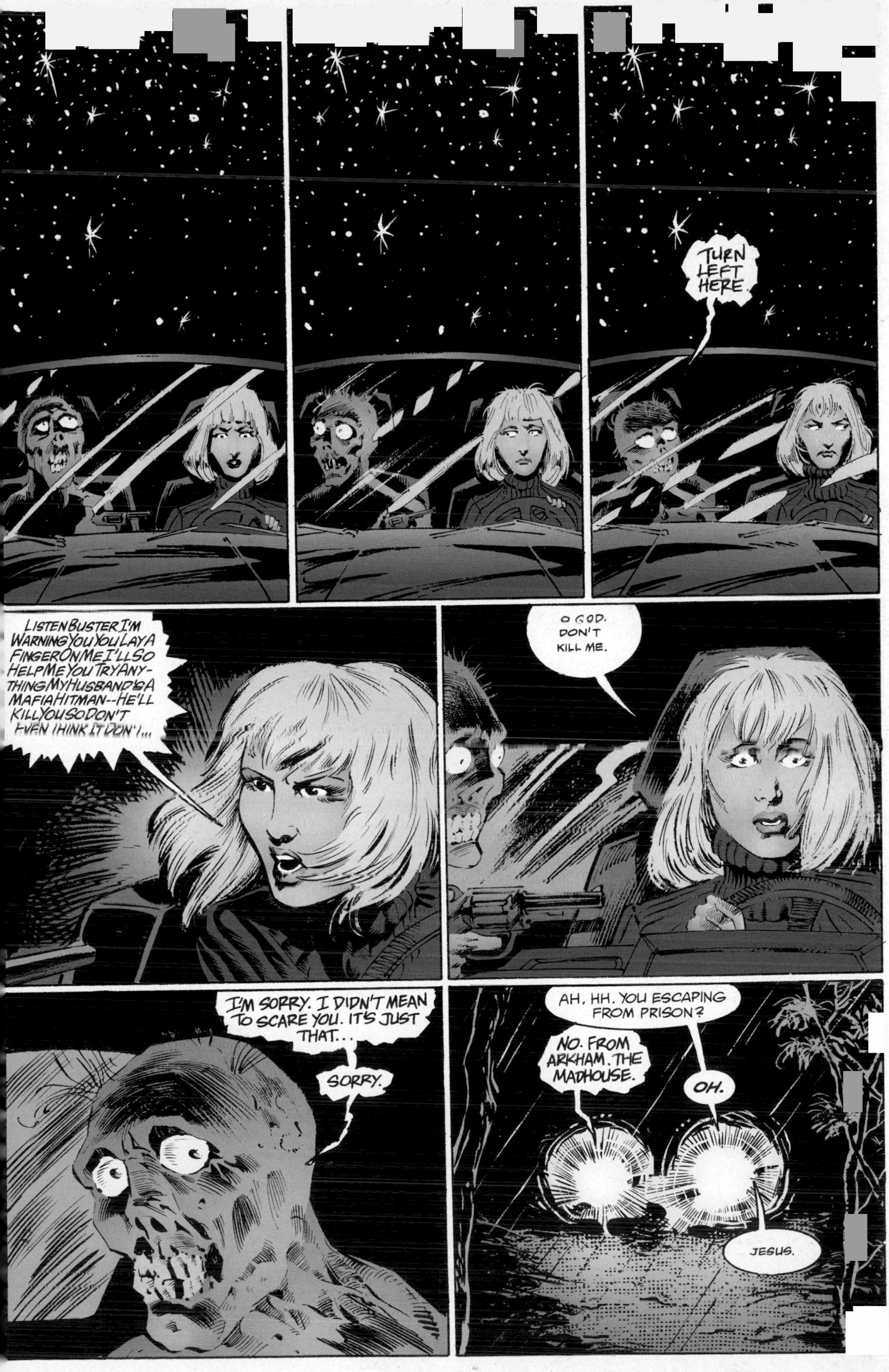
TURN LEFT HERE.
LISTEN BUSTER I'M WARNING YOU YOU LAY A FINGER ON ME I'LL SO HELP ME YOU TRY ANY-THING MY HUSBAND'S A MAFIA HITMAN--HE'LL KILL YOU SO DON'T EVEN THINK IT DON'T...
O GOD. DON'T KILL ME.
I'M SORRY. I DIDN'T MEAN TO SCARE YOU. IT'S JUST THAT...
SORRY.
AH, HH, YOU ESCAPING FROM PRISON?
NO. FROM ARKHAM. THE MADHOUSE.
OH.
JESUS.

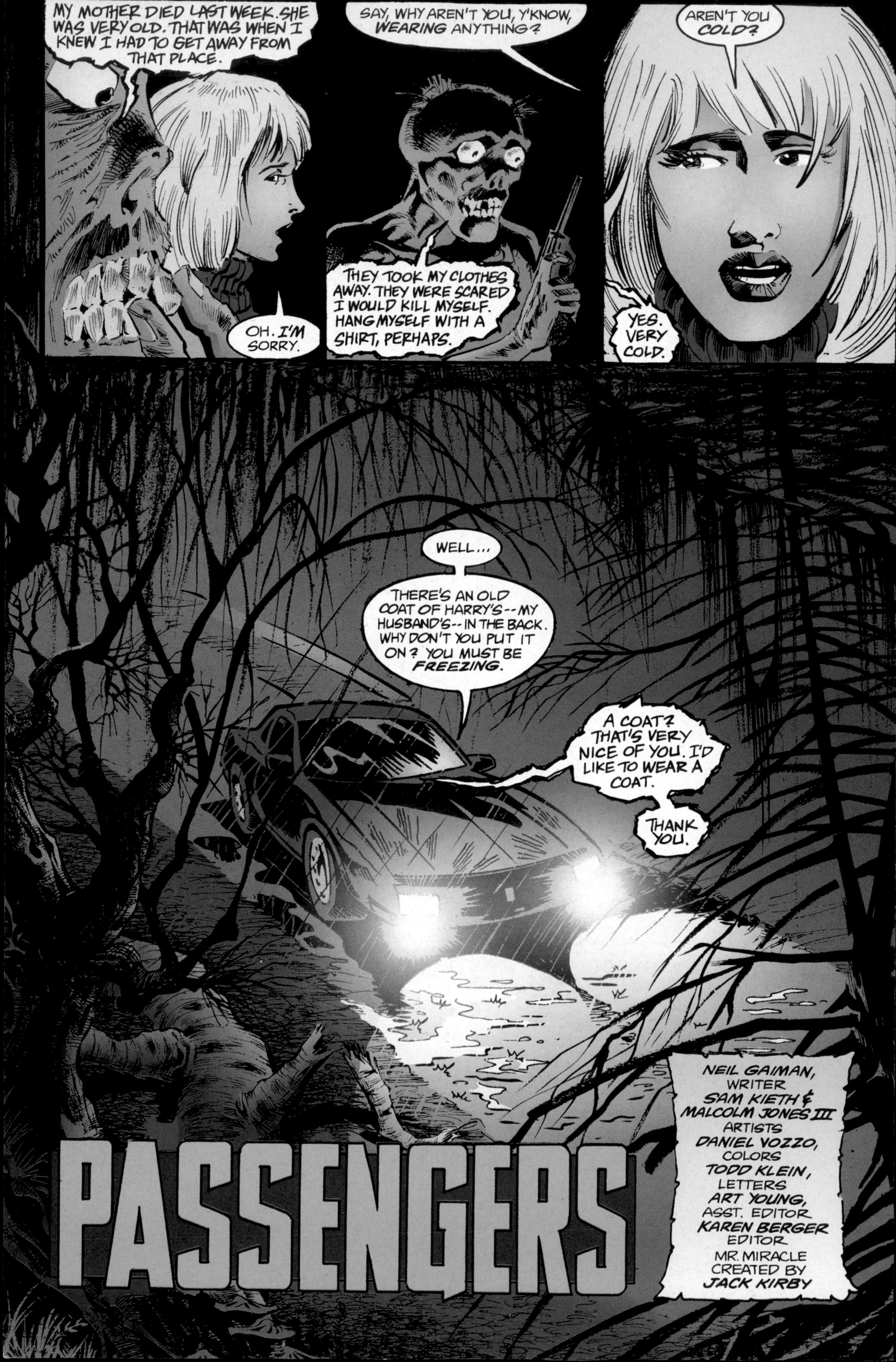
MY MOTHER DIED LAST WEEK. SHE WAS VERY OLD. THAT WAS WHEN I KNEW I HAD TO GET AWAY FROM THAT PLACE.
OH. I'M SORRY.
SAY, WHY AREN'T YOU, Y'KNOW, WEARING ANYTHING?
THEY TOOK MY CLOTHES AWAY. THEY WERE SCARED I WOULD KILL MYSELF. HANG MYSELF WITH A SHIRT, PERHAPS.
AREN'T YOU COLD?
YES. VERY COLD.
WELL...
THERE'S AN OLD COAT OF HARRY'S--MY HUSBAND'S--IN THE BACK. WHY DON'T YOU PUT IT ON? YOU MUST BE FREEZING.
A COAT? THAT'S VERY NICE OF YOU. I'D LIKE TO WEAR A COAT.
THANK YOU.
PASSENGERS
NEIL GAIMAN, WRITER
SAM KIETH & MALCOLM JONES III ARTISTS
DANIEL VOZZO, COLORS
TODD KLEIN, LETTERS
ART YOUNG, ASST. EDITOR
KAREN BERGER EDITOR
MR. MIRACLE CREATED BY JACK KIRBY

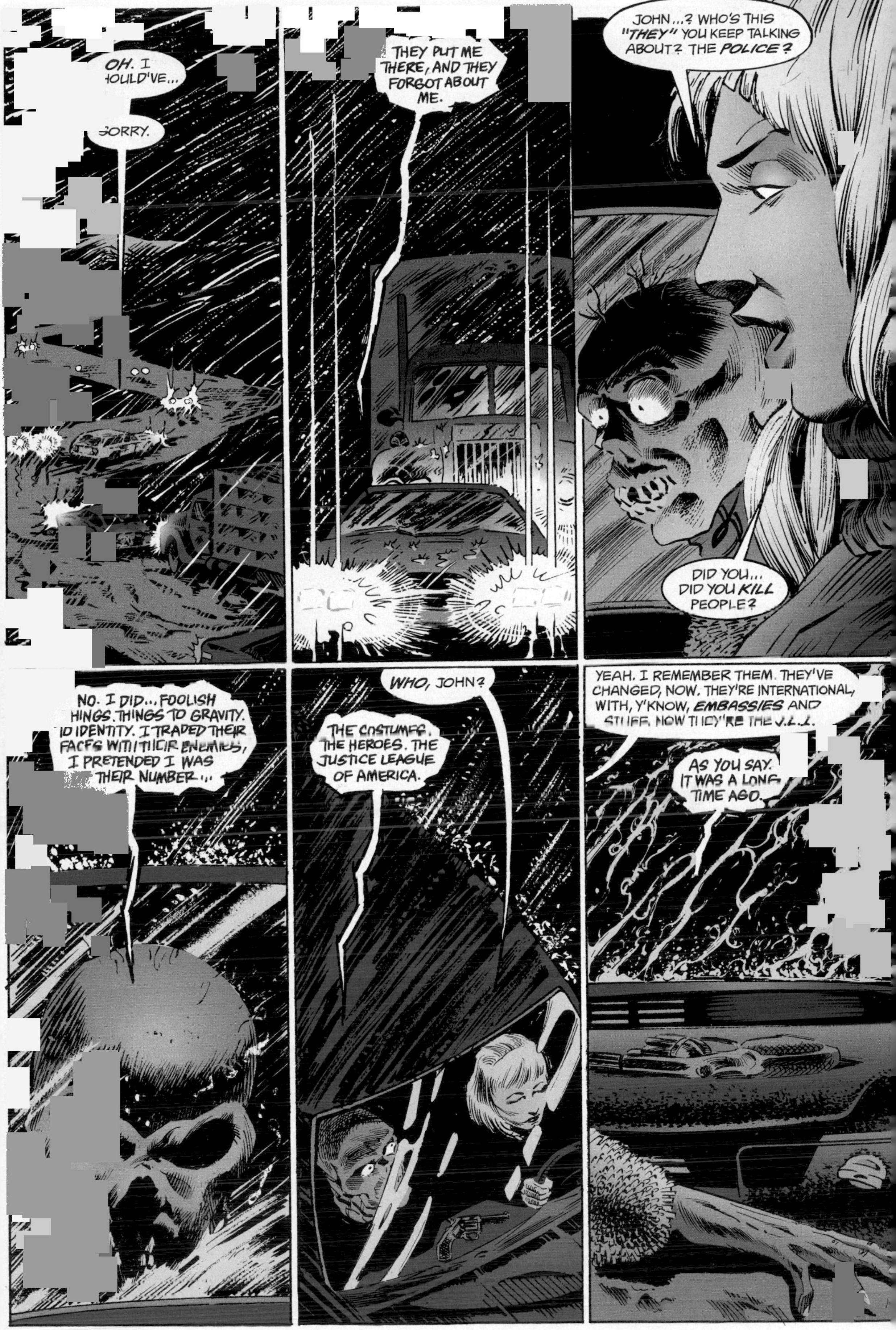
OH. I
HOULD'VE...
SORRY.
THEY PUT ME THERE, AND THEY FORGOT ABOUT ME.
JOHN...? WHO'S THIS "THEY" YOU KEEP TALKING ABOUT? THE POLICE?
DID YOU... DID YOU KILL PEOPLE?
NO. I DID... FOOLISH HINGS. THINGS TO GRAVITY. ID IDENTITY. I TRADED THEIR FACES WITH THEIR ENEMIES, I PRETENDED I WAS THEIR NUMBER...
WHO, JOHN?
THE COSTUMES. THE HEROES. THE JUSTICE LEAGUE OF AMERICA.
YEAH. I REMEMBER THEM. THEY'VE CHANGED, NOW. THEY'RE INTERNATIONAL, WITH, Y'KNOW, EMBASSIES AND STUFF. NOW THEY'RE THE J.L.I.
AS YOU SAY. IT WAS A LONG TIME AGO.

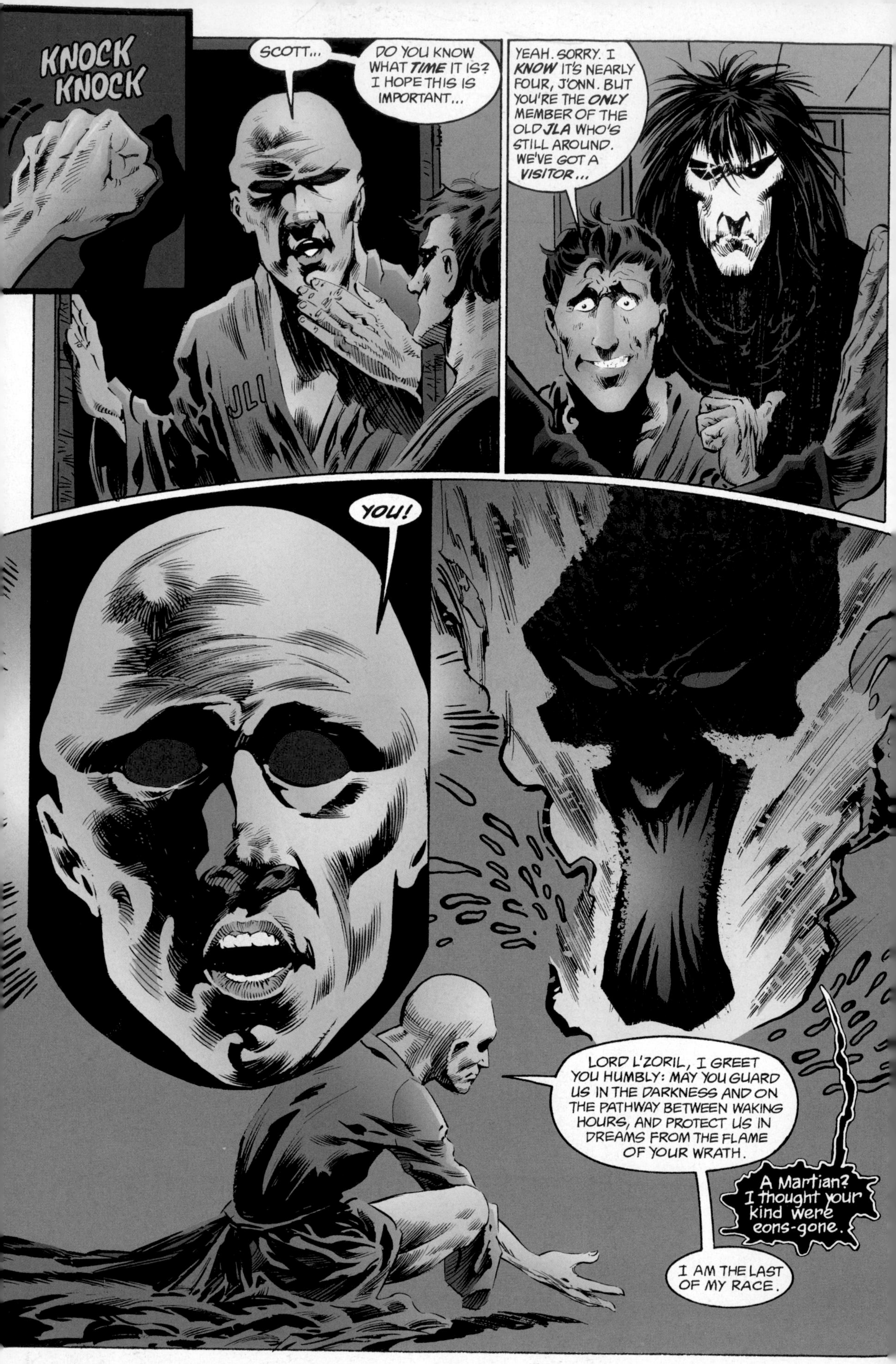
KNOCK KNOCK
SCOTT...
DO YOU KNOW WHAT TIME IT IS? I HOPE THIS IS IMPORTANT...
JLI
YEAH. SORRY. I KNOW IT'S NEARLY FOUR, J'ONN. BUT YOU'RE THE ONLY MEMBER OF THE OLD JLA WHO'S STILL AROUND. WE'VE GOT A VISITOR...
YOU!
LORD L'ZORIL, I GREET YOU HUMBLY: MAY YOU GUARD US IN THE DARKNESS AND ON THE PATHWAY BETWEEN WAKING HOURS, AND PROTECT US IN DREAMS FROM THE FLAME OF YOUR WRATH.
A Martian? I thought your kind were eons-gone.
I AM THE LAST OF MY RACE.

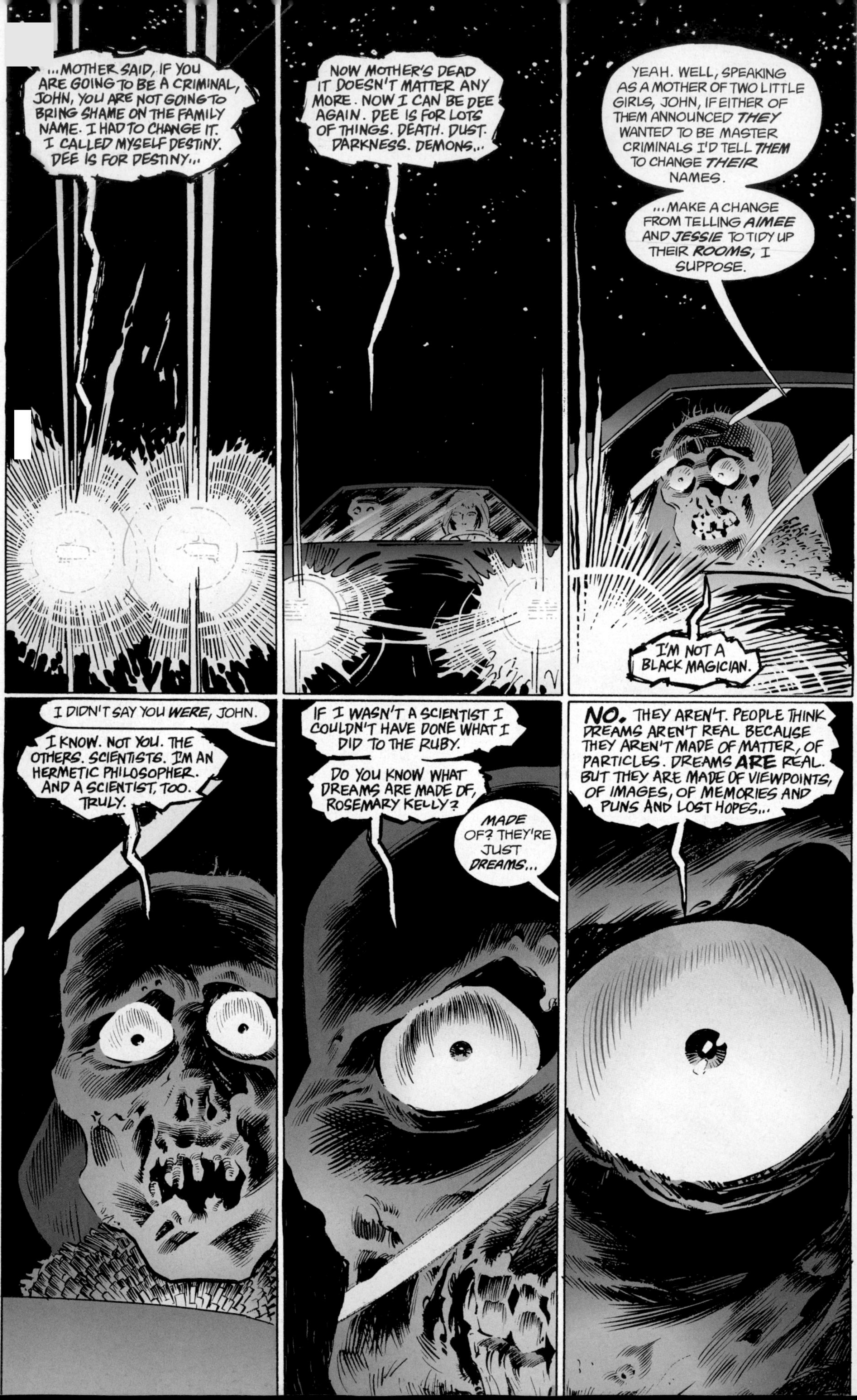
...MOTHER SAID, IF YOU ARE GOING TO BE A CRIMINAL, JOHN, YOU ARE NOT GOING TO BRING SHAME ON THE FAMILY NAME. I HAD TO CHANGE IT. I CALLED MYSELF DESTINY. DEE IS FOR DESTINY...
NOW MOTHER'S DEAD IT DOESN'T MATTER ANY MORE. NOW I CAN BE DEE AGAIN. DEE IS FOR LOTS OF THINGS. DEATH. DUST. DARKNESS. DEMONS...
YEAH. WELL, SPEAKING AS A MOTHER OF TWO LITTLE GIRLS, JOHN, IF EITHER OF THEM ANNOUNCED *THEY* WANTED TO BE MASTER CRIMINALS I'D TELL *THEM* TO CHANGE *THEIR* NAMES.
...MAKE A CHANGE FROM TELLING *AIMEE* AND *JESSIE* TO TIDY UP THEIR *ROOMS*, I SUPPOSE.
I'M NOT A BLACK MAGICIAN.
I DIDN'T SAY YOU *WERE*, JOHN.
I KNOW. NOT YOU. THE OTHERS. SCIENTISTS. I'M AN HERMETIC PHILOSOPHER. AND A SCIENTIST, TOO. TRULY.
IF I WASN'T A SCIENTIST I COULDN'T HAVE DONE WHAT I DID TO THE RUBY.
DO YOU KNOW WHAT DREAMS ARE MADE OF, ROSEMARY KELLY?
MADE OF? THEY'RE JUST *DREAMS*...
NO. THEY AREN'T. PEOPLE THINK DREAMS AREN'T REAL BECAUSE THEY AREN'T MADE OF MATTER, OF PARTICLES. DREAMS **ARE** REAL. BUT THEY ARE MADE OF VIEWPOINTS, OF IMAGES, OF MEMORIES AND PUNS AND LOST HOPES...

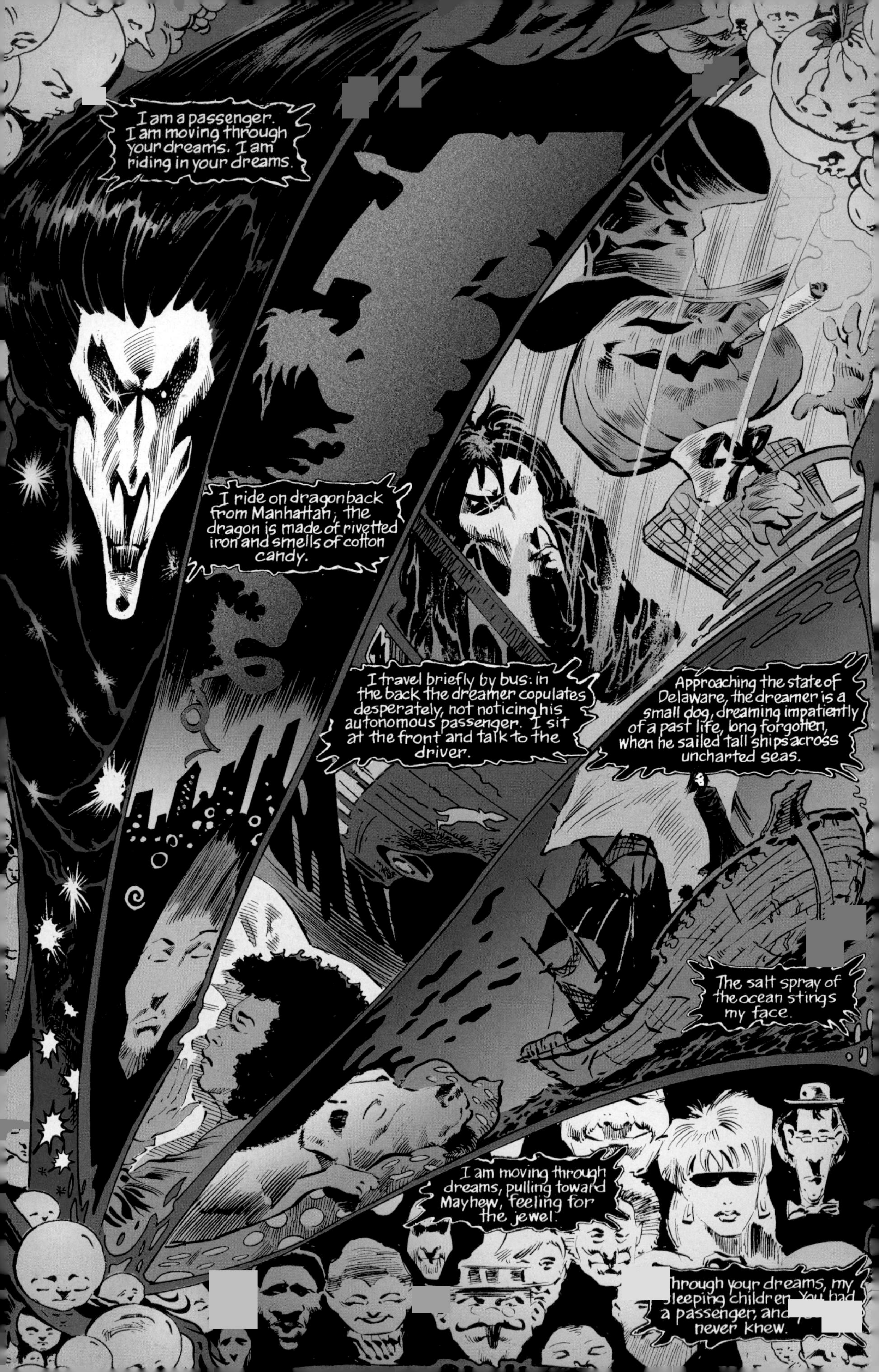
I am a passenger. I am moving through your dreams. I am riding in your dreams.
I ride on dragonback from Manhattan; the dragon is made of rivetted iron and smells of cotton candy.
I travel briefly by bus: in the back the dreamer copulates desperately, not noticing his autonomous passenger. I sit at the front and talk to the driver.
Approaching the state of Delaware, the dreamer is a small dog, dreaming impatiently of a past life, long forgotten, when he sailed tall ships across uncharted seas.
The salt spray of the ocean stings my face.
I am moving through dreams, pulling toward Mayhew, feeling for the jewel.
hrough your dreams, my leeping children. You had a passenger, and never knew.

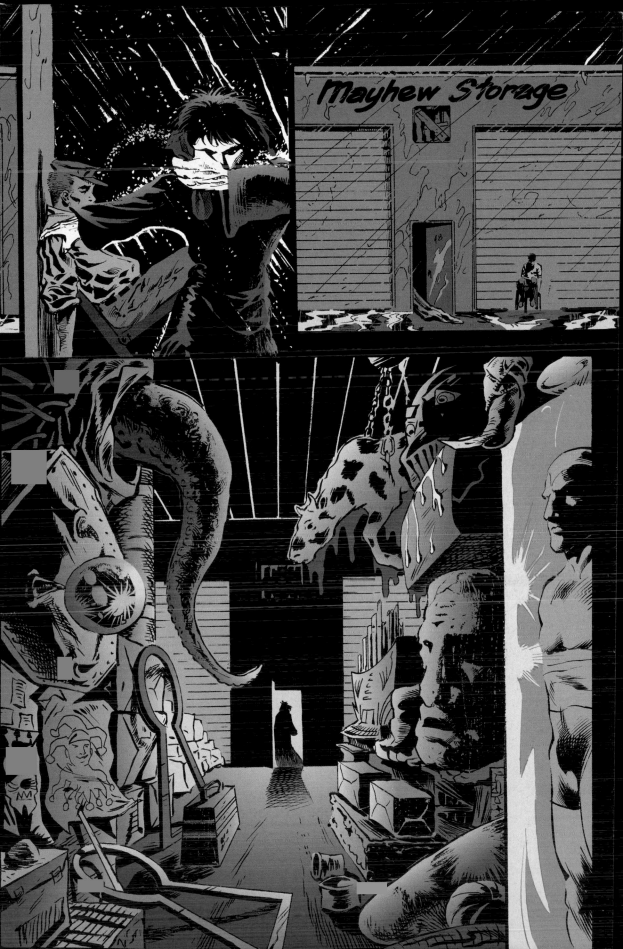

Mayhew Storage

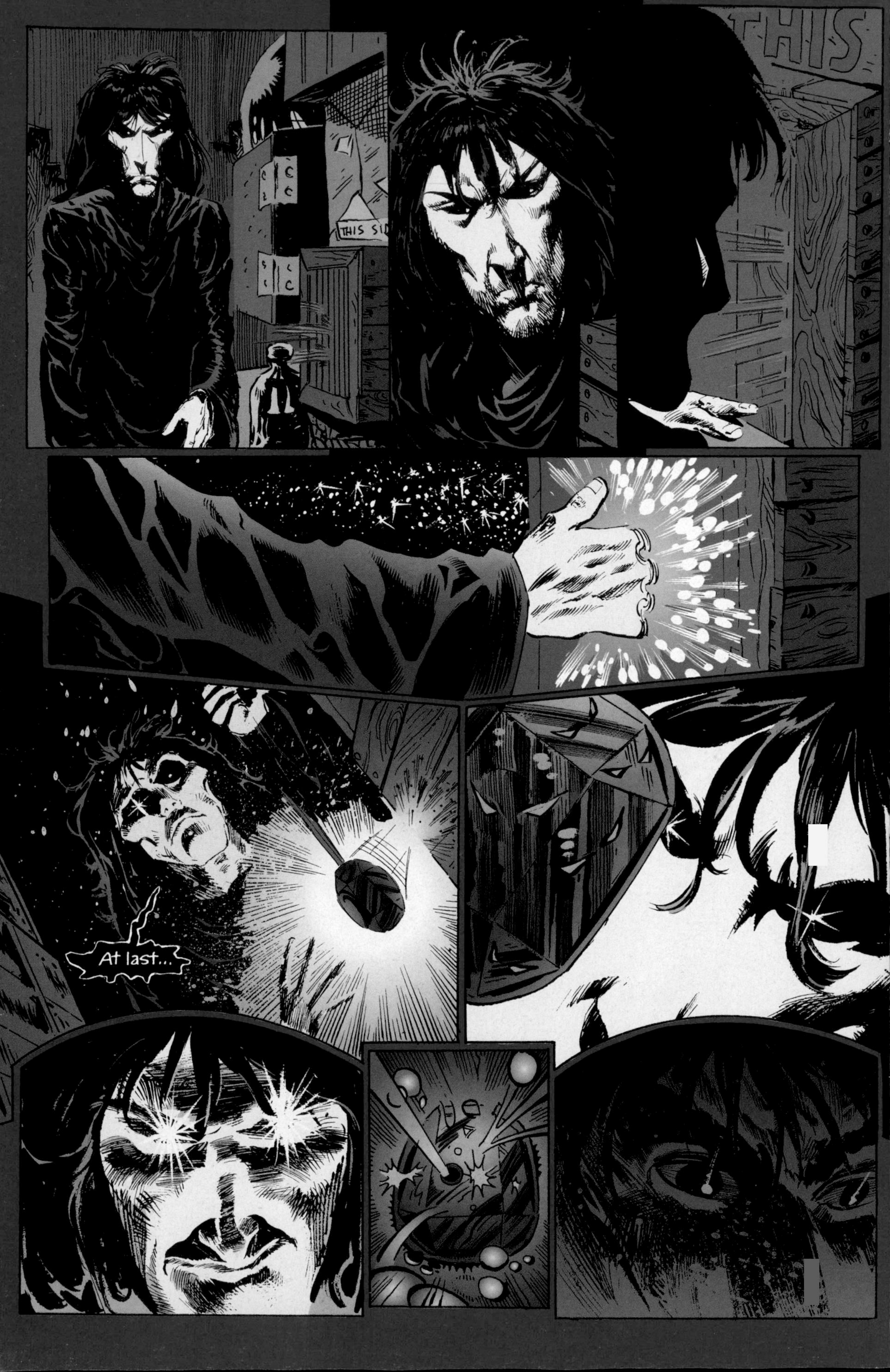
THIS
THIS SI
At last...

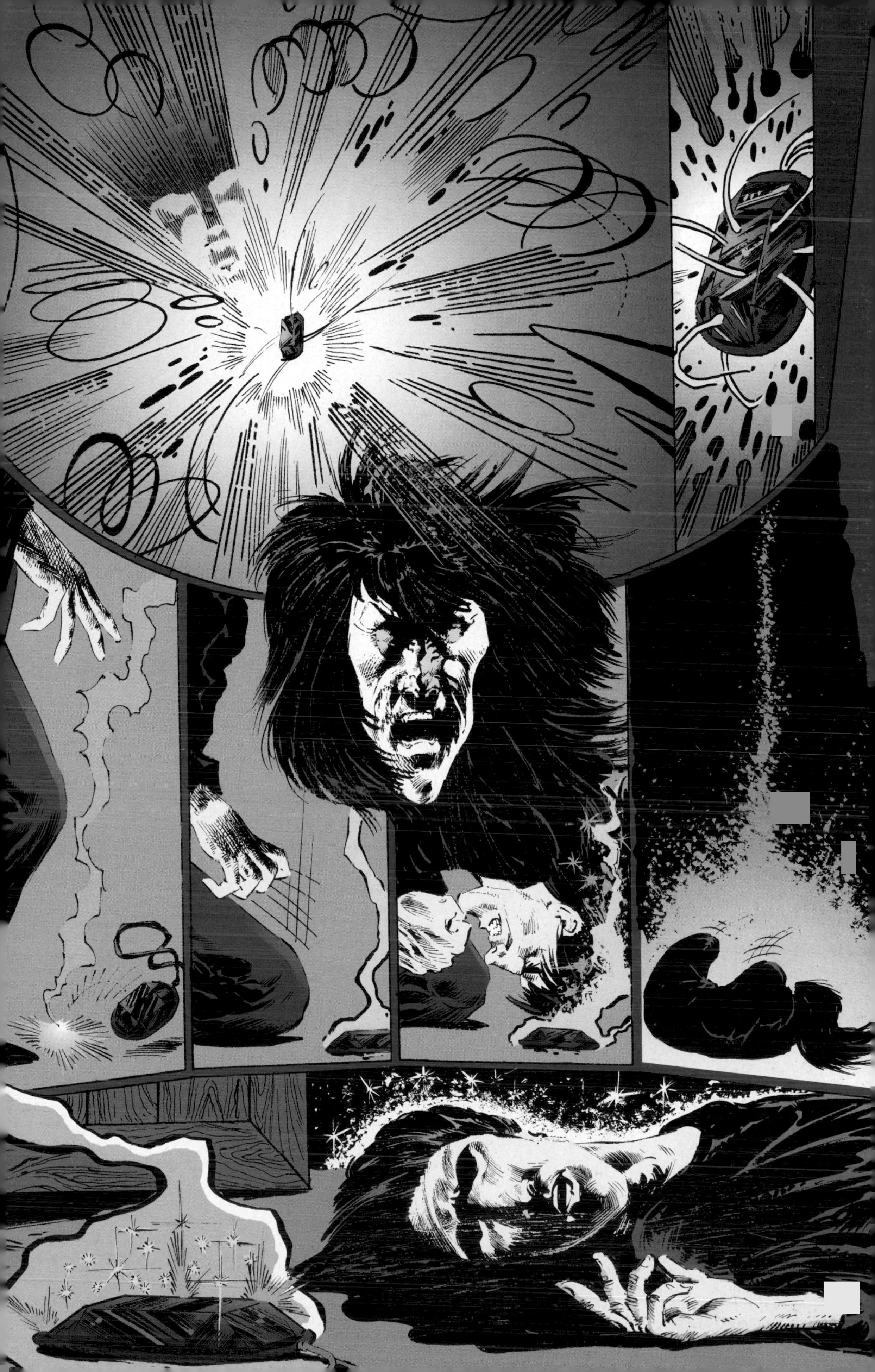

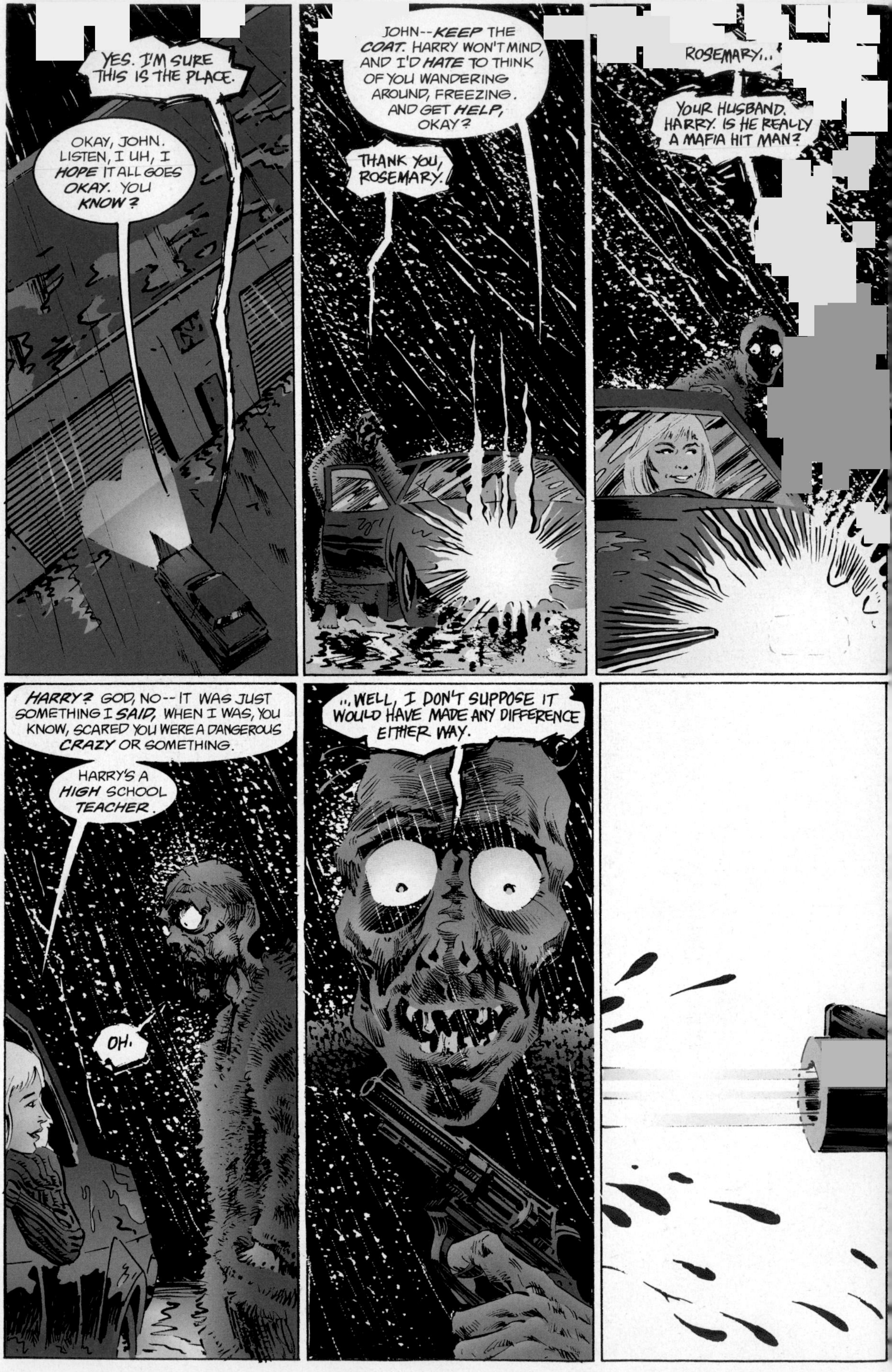
YES. I'M SURE THIS IS THE PLACE.
OKAY, JOHN. LISTEN, I UH, I HOPE IT ALL GOES OKAY. YOU KNOW?
JOHN--KEEP THE COAT. HARRY WON'T MIND, AND I'D HATE TO THINK OF YOU WANDERING AROUND, FREEZING. AND GET HELP, OKAY?
THANK YOU, ROSEMARY.
ROSEMARY...
YOUR HUSBAND. HARRY. IS HE REALLY A MAFIA HIT MAN?
HARRY? GOD, NO--IT WAS JUST SOMETHING I SAID, WHEN I WAS, YOU KNOW, SCARED YOU WERE A DANGEROUS CRAZY OR SOMETHING.
HARRY'S A HIGH SCHOOL TEACHER.
OH.
...WELL, I DON'T SUPPOSE IT WOULD HAVE MADE ANY DIFFERENCE EITHER WAY.

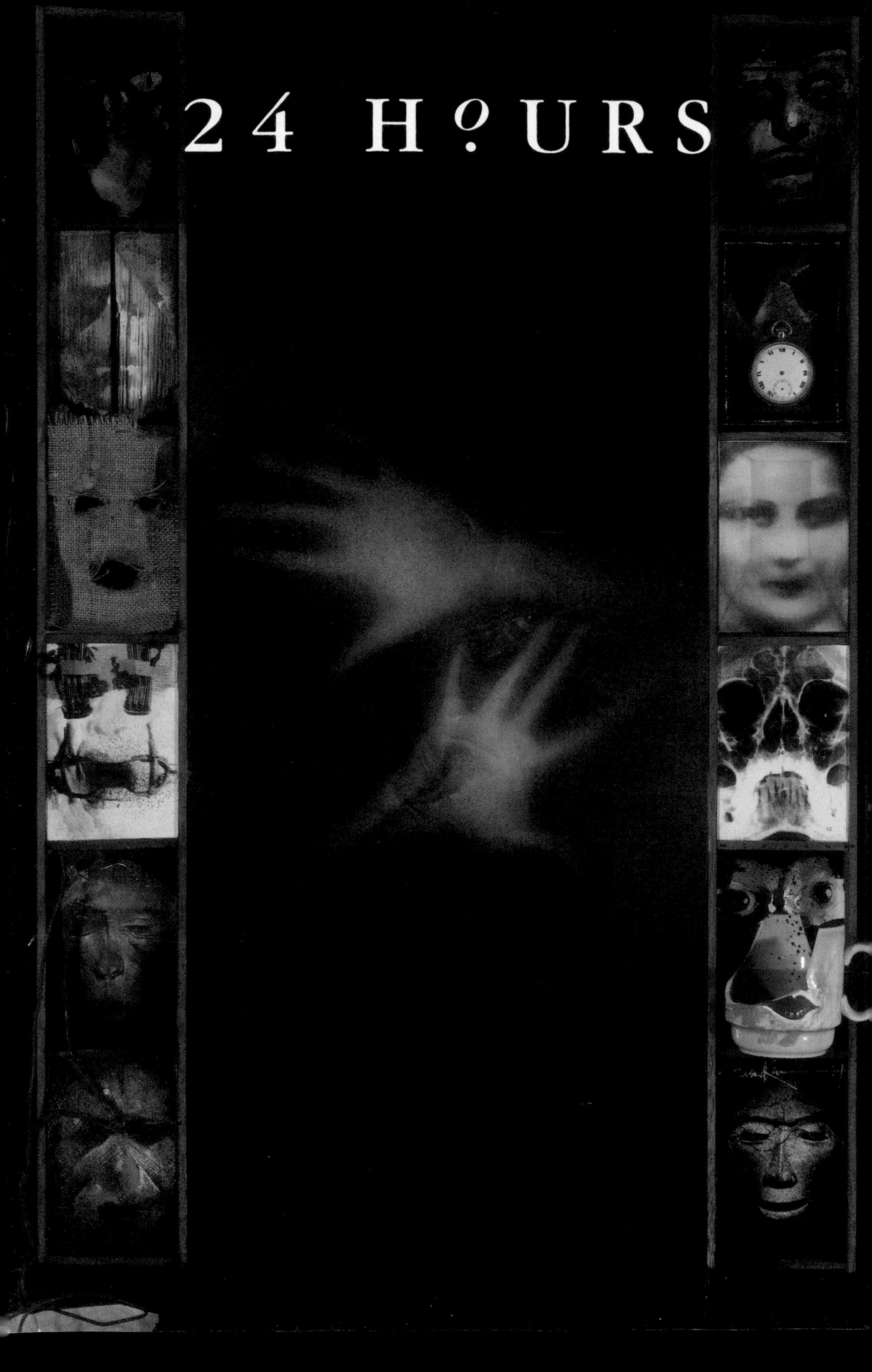
24 HOURS

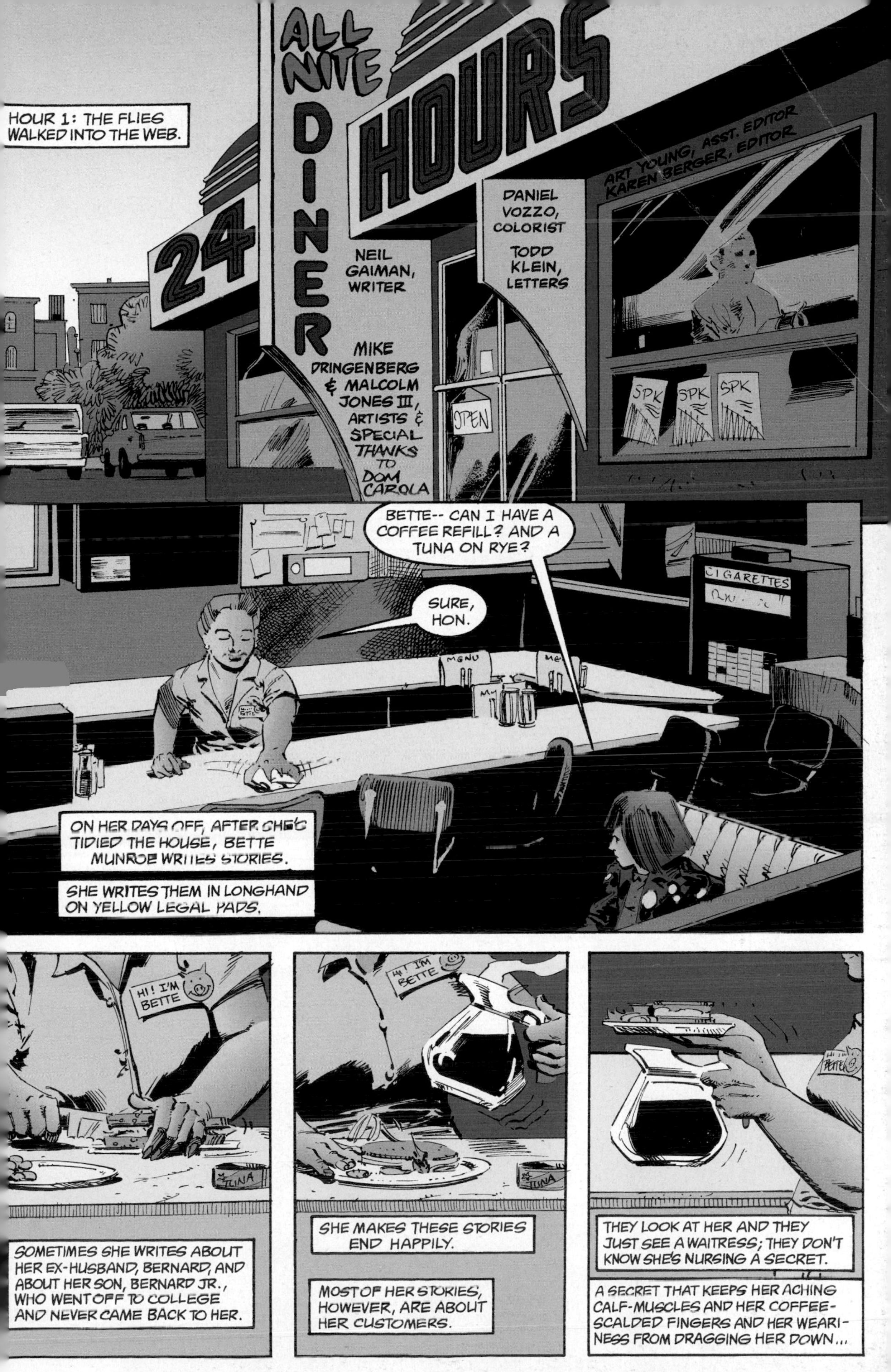
ALL NITE
24
DINER
HOURS
HOUR 1: THE FLIES WALKED INTO THE WEB.
ART YOUNG, ASST. EDITOR
KAREN BERGER, EDITOR
DANIEL VOZZO, COLORIST
TODD KLEIN, LETTERS
NEIL GAIMAN, WRITER
MIKE DRINGENBERG & MALCOLM JONES III, ARTISTS & SPECIAL THANKS TO DOM CAROLA
OPEN
SPK
SPK
SPK
BETTE-- CAN I HAVE A COFFEE REFILL? AND A TUNA ON RYE?
SURE, HON.
CIGARETTES
MENU
ON HER DAYS OFF, AFTER SHE'S TIDIED THE HOUSE, BETTE MUNROE WRITES STORIES.
SHE WRITES THEM IN LONGHAND ON YELLOW LEGAL PADS.
HI! I'M BETTE
TUNA
SOMETIMES SHE WRITES ABOUT HER EX-HUSBAND, BERNARD, AND ABOUT HER SON, BERNARD JR., WHO WENT OFF TO COLLEGE AND NEVER CAME BACK TO HER.
HI! I'M BETTE
TUNA
SHE MAKES THESE STORIES END HAPPILY.
MOST OF HER STORIES, HOWEVER, ARE ABOUT HER CUSTOMERS.
THEY LOOK AT HER AND THEY JUST SEE A WAITRESS; THEY DON'T KNOW SHE'S NURSING A SECRET.
A SECRET THAT KEEPS HER ACHING CALF-MUSCLES AND HER COFFEE-SCALDED FINGERS AND HER WEARINESS FROM DRAGGING HER DOWN...

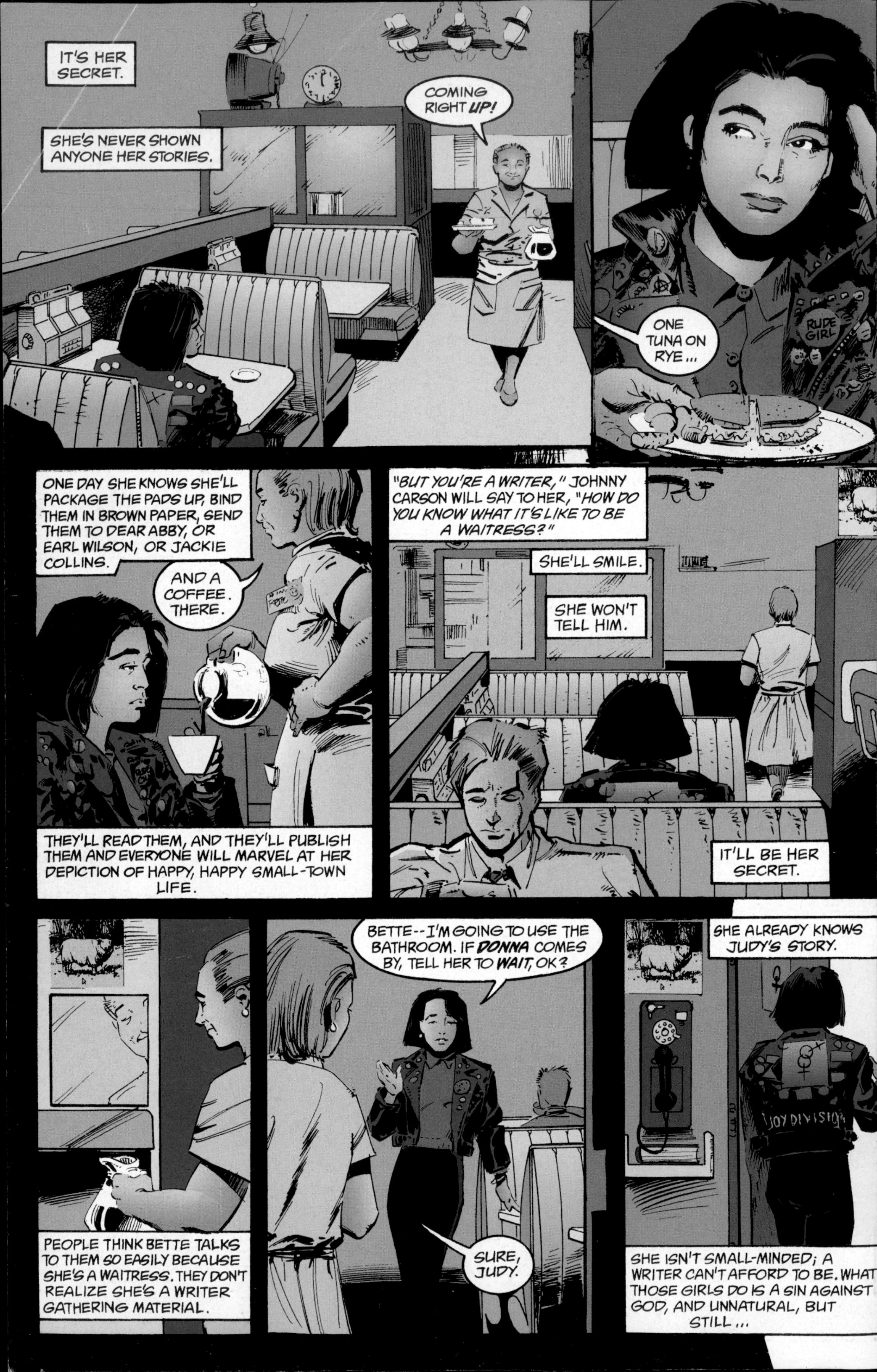
IT'S HER SECRET.
SHE'S NEVER SHOWN ANYONE HER STORIES.
COMING RIGHT UP!
ONE TUNA ON RYE...
RUDE GIRL
ONE DAY SHE KNOWS SHE'LL PACKAGE THE PADS UP, BIND THEM IN BROWN PAPER, SEND THEM TO DEAR ABBY, OR EARL WILSON, OR JACKIE COLLINS.
AND A COFFEE. THERE.
THEY'LL READ THEM, AND THEY'LL PUBLISH THEM AND EVERYONE WILL MARVEL AT HER DEPICTION OF HAPPY, HAPPY SMALL-TOWN LIFE.
"BUT YOU'RE A WRITER," JOHNNY CARSON WILL SAY TO HER, "HOW DO YOU KNOW WHAT IT'S LIKE TO BE A WAITRESS?"
SHE'LL SMILE.
SHE WON'T TELL HIM.
IT'LL BE HER SECRET.
PEOPLE THINK BETTE TALKS TO THEM SO EASILY BECAUSE SHE'S A WAITRESS. THEY DON'T REALIZE SHE'S A WRITER GATHERING MATERIAL.
BETTE--I'M GOING TO USE THE BATHROOM. IF DONNA COMES BY, TELL HER TO WAIT, OK?
SURE, JUDY.
SHE ALREADY KNOWS JUDY'S STORY.
JOY DIVISION
SHE ISN'T SMALL-MINDED; A WRITER CAN'T AFFORD TO BE. WHAT THOSE GIRLS DO IS A SIN AGAINST GOD, AND UNNATURAL, BUT STILL...

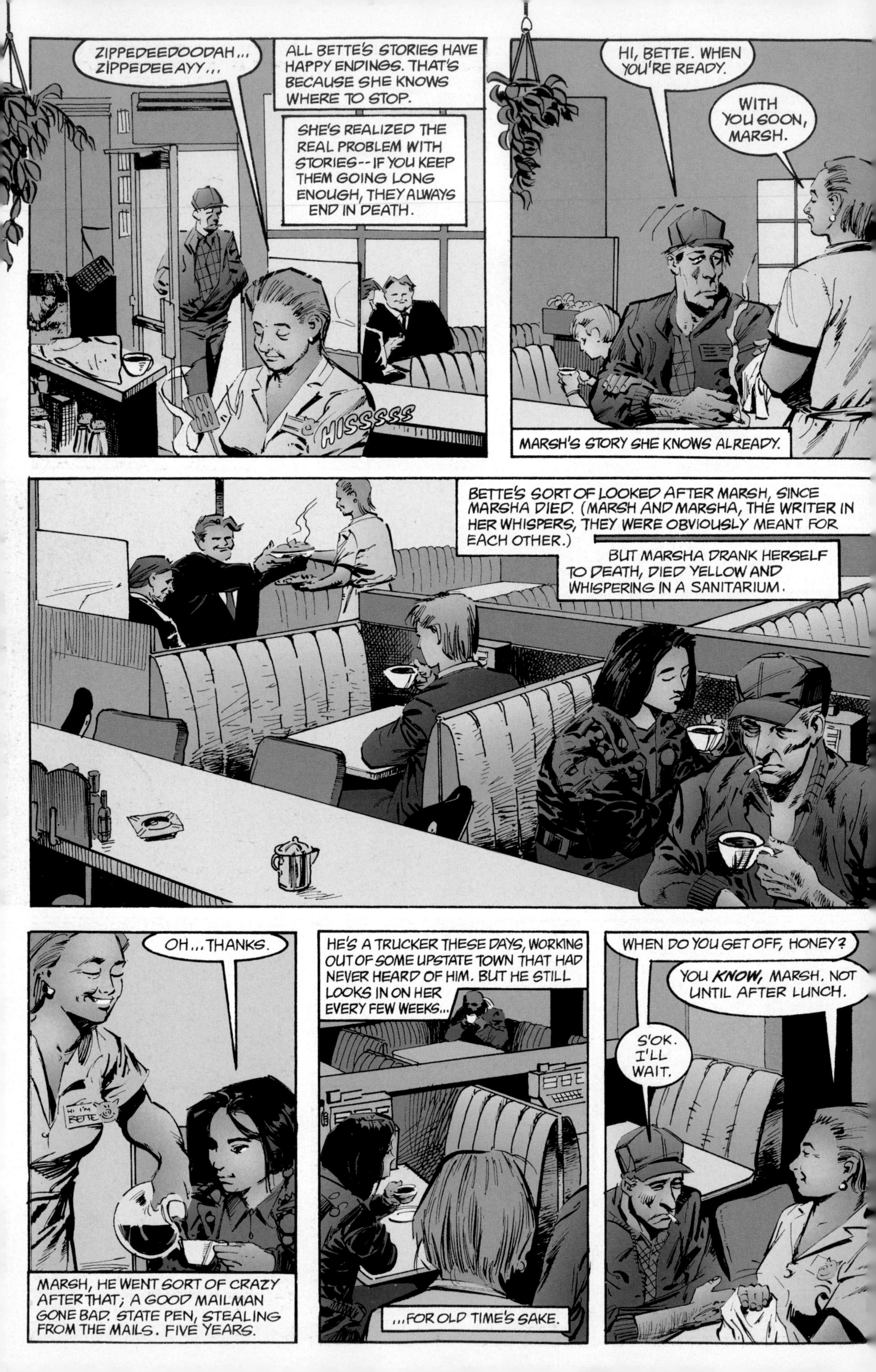
ZIPPEDEEDOODAH... ZIPPEDEEAYY...
ALL BETTE'S STORIES HAVE HAPPY ENDINGS. THAT'S BECAUSE SHE KNOWS WHERE TO STOP.
SHE'S REALIZED THE REAL PROBLEM WITH STORIES--IF YOU KEEP THEM GOING LONG ENOUGH, THEY ALWAYS END IN DEATH.
HISSSSS
HI, BETTE. WHEN YOU'RE READY.
WITH YOU SOON, MARSH.
MARSH'S STORY SHE KNOWS ALREADY.
BETTE'S SORT OF LOOKED AFTER MARSH, SINCE MARSHA DIED. (MARSH AND MARSHA, THE WRITER IN HER WHISPERS, THEY WERE OBVIOUSLY MEANT FOR EACH OTHER.)
BUT MARSHA DRANK HERSELF TO DEATH, DIED YELLOW AND WHISPERING IN A SANITARIUM.
OH... THANKS.
HI I'M BETTE
MARSH, HE WENT SORT OF CRAZY AFTER THAT; A GOOD MAILMAN GONE BAD. STATE PEN, STEALING FROM THE MAILS. FIVE YEARS.
HE'S A TRUCKER THESE DAYS, WORKING OUT OF SOME UPSTATE TOWN THAT HAD NEVER HEARD OF HIM. BUT HE STILL LOOKS IN ON HER EVERY FEW WEEKS...
...FOR OLD TIME'S SAKE.
WHEN DO YOU GET OFF, HONEY?
YOU KNOW, MARSH. NOT UNTIL AFTER LUNCH.
S'OK. I'LL WAIT.

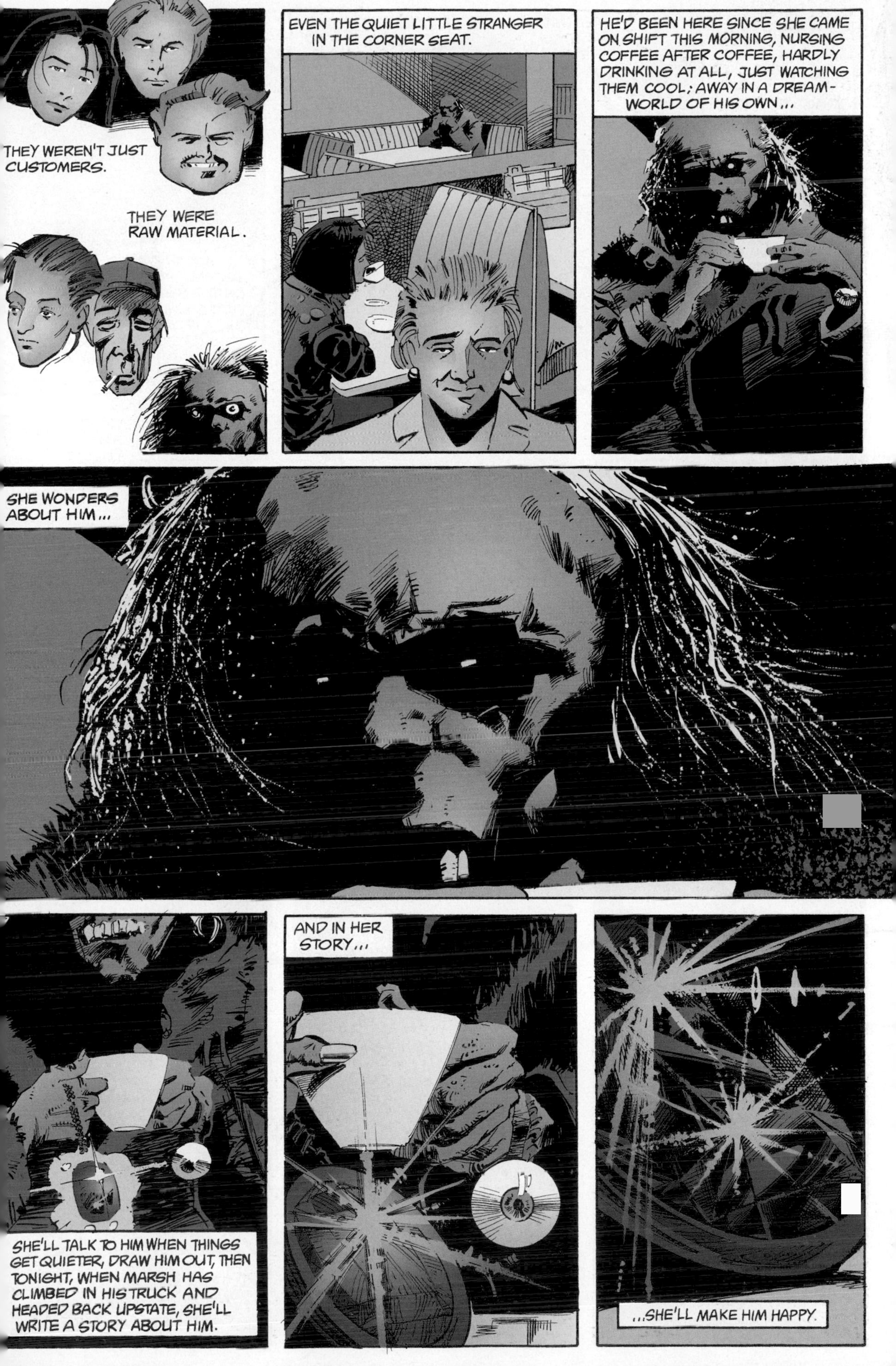
THEY WEREN'T JUST CUSTOMERS.
THEY WERE RAW MATERIAL.
EVEN THE QUIET LITTLE STRANGER IN THE CORNER SEAT.
HE'D BEEN HERE SINCE SHE CAME ON SHIFT THIS MORNING, NURSING COFFEE AFTER COFFEE, HARDLY DRINKING AT ALL, JUST WATCHING THEM COOL; AWAY IN A DREAM-WORLD OF HIS OWN...
SHE WONDERS ABOUT HIM...
SHE'LL TALK TO HIM WHEN THINGS GET QUIETER, DRAW HIM OUT, THEN TONIGHT, WHEN MARSH HAS CLIMBED IN HIS TRUCK AND HEADED BACK UPSTATE, SHE'LL WRITE A STORY ABOUT HIM.
AND IN HER STORY...
...SHE'LL MAKE HIM HAPPY.

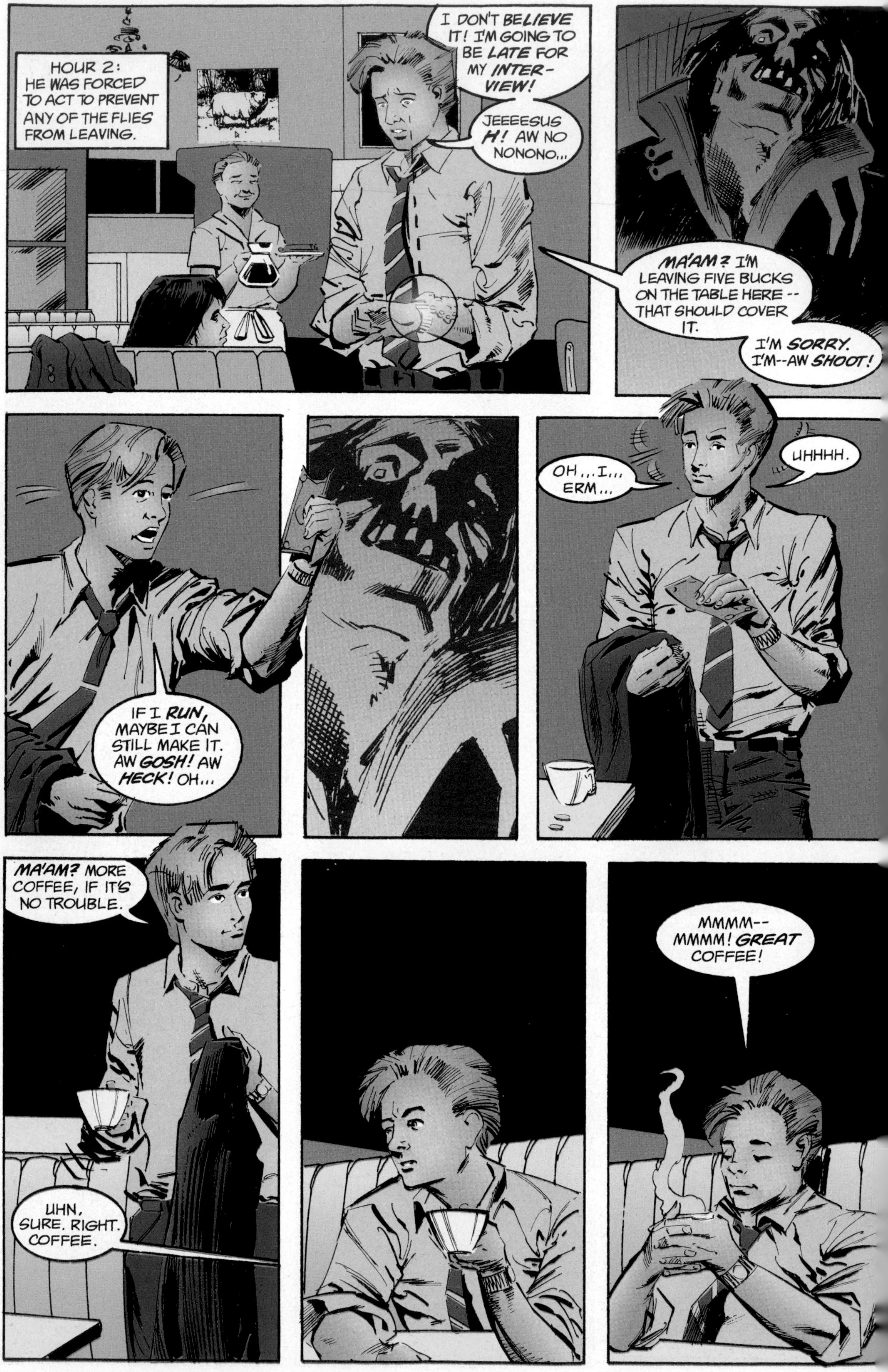

HOUR 2: HE WAS FORCED TO ACT TO PREVENT ANY OF THE FLIES FROM LEAVING.
I DON'T BELIEVE IT! I'M GOING TO BE LATE FOR MY INTER-VIEW!
JEEEESUS H! AW NO NONONO...
MA'AM? I'M LEAVING FIVE BUCKS ON THE TABLE HERE -- THAT SHOULD COVER IT.
I'M SORRY. I'M--AW SHOOT!
IF I RUN, MAYBE I CAN STILL MAKE IT. AW GOSH! AW HECK! OH...
OH... I... ERM...
UHHHH.
MA'AM? MORE COFFEE, IF IT'S NO TROUBLE.
UHN, SURE. RIGHT. COFFEE.
MMMM--MMMM! GREAT COFFEE!

HOUR 3: AFTERNOON SOAP OPERA

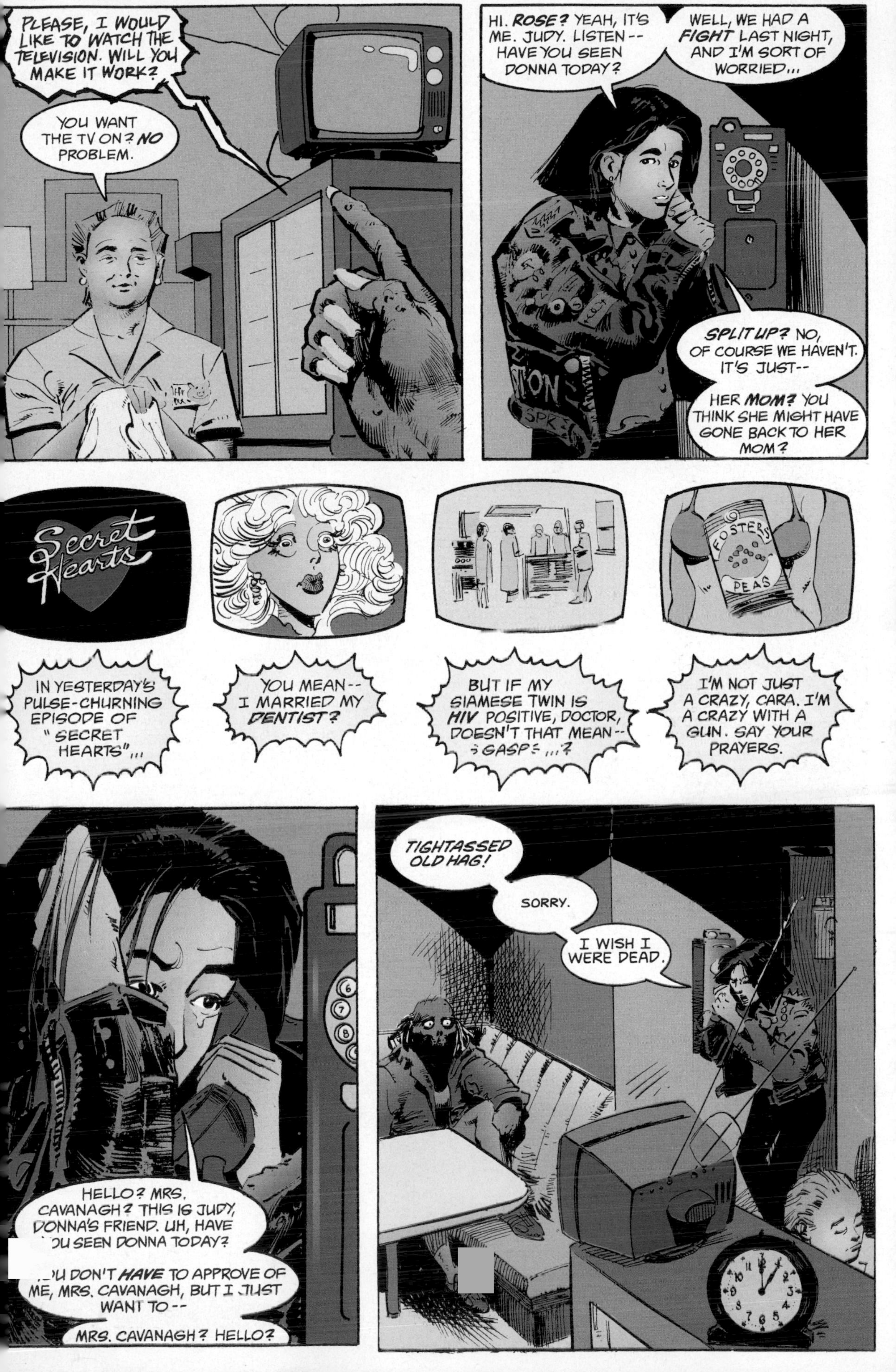

PLEASE, I WOULD LIKE TO WATCH THE TELEVISION. WILL YOU MAKE IT WORK?
YOU WANT THE TV ON? NO PROBLEM.
HI. ROSE? YEAH, IT'S ME. JUDY. LISTEN -- HAVE YOU SEEN DONNA TODAY?
WELL, WE HAD A FIGHT LAST NIGHT, AND I'M SORT OF WORRIED...
SPLIT UP? NO, OF COURSE WE HAVEN'T. IT'S JUST--
HER MOM? YOU THINK SHE MIGHT HAVE GONE BACK TO HER MOM?
Secret Hearts
FOSTERS PEAS
IN YESTERDAY'S PULSE-CHURNING EPISODE OF "SECRET HEARTS"...
YOU MEAN -- I MARRIED MY DENTIST?
BUT IF MY SIAMESE TWIN IS HIV POSITIVE, DOCTOR, DOESN'T THAT MEAN -- :GASP: ...?
I'M NOT JUST A CRAZY, CARA. I'M A CRAZY WITH A GUN. SAY YOUR PRAYERS.
HELLO? MRS. CAVANAGH? THIS IS JUDY, DONNA'S FRIEND. UH, HAVE ...OU SEEN DONNA TODAY?
...OU DON'T HAVE TO APPROVE OF ME, MRS. CAVANAGH, BUT I JUST WANT TO --
MRS. CAVANAGH? HELLO?
TIGHTASSED OLD HAG!
SORRY.
I WISH I WERE DEAD.

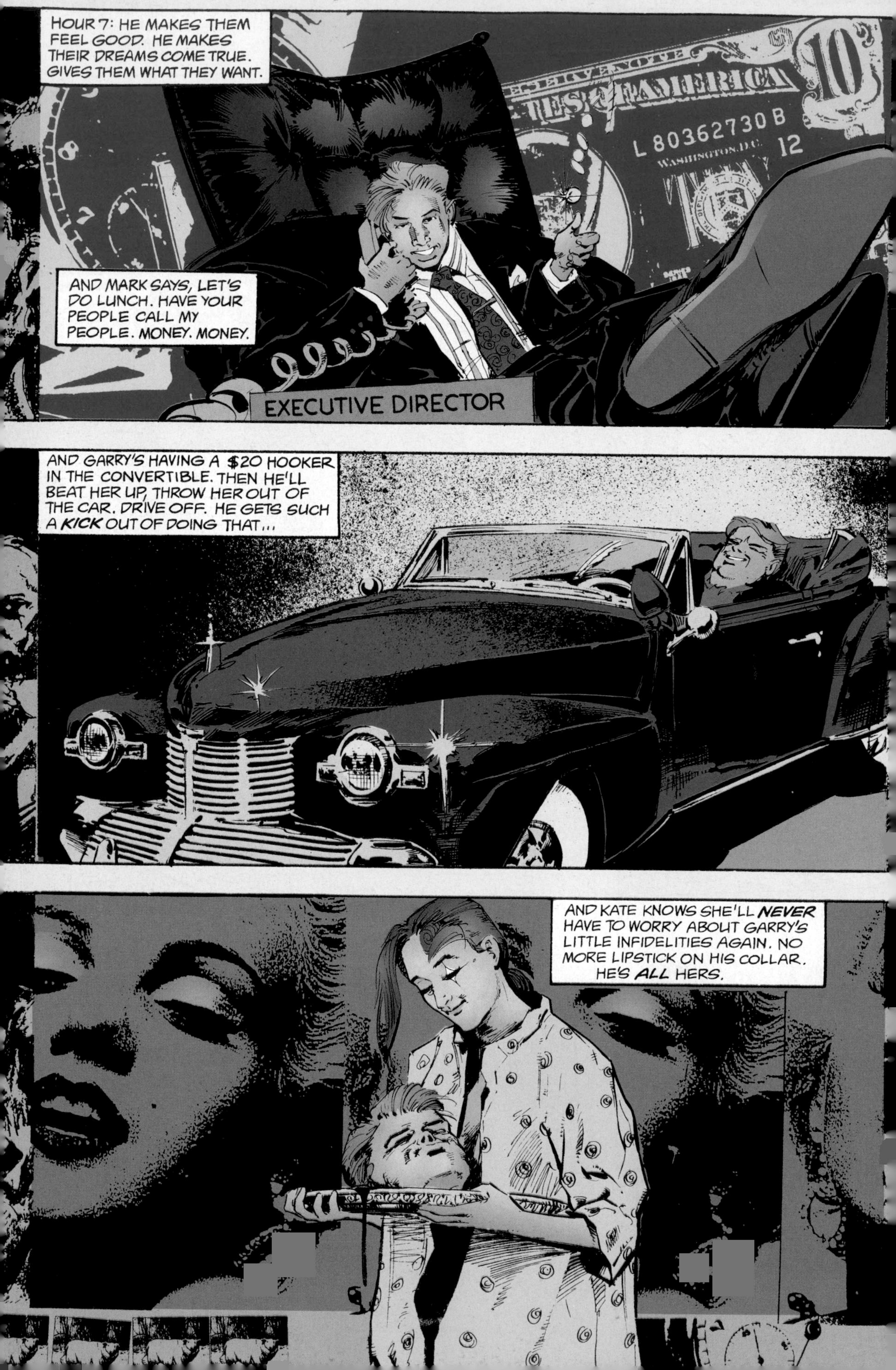
HOUR 7: HE MAKES THEM FEEL GOOD. HE MAKES THEIR DREAMS COME TRUE. GIVES THEM WHAT THEY WANT.
10
L 80362730 B
12
AND MARK SAYS, LET'S DO LUNCH. HAVE YOUR PEOPLE CALL MY PEOPLE. MONEY. MONEY.
EXECUTIVE DIRECTOR
AND GARRY'S HAVING A $20 HOOKER IN THE CONVERTIBLE. THEN HE'LL BEAT HER UP, THROW HER OUT OF THE CAR. DRIVE OFF. HE GETS SUCH A ***KICK*** OUT OF DOING THAT...
AND KATE KNOWS SHE'LL ***NEVER*** HAVE TO WORRY ABOUT GARRY'S LITTLE INFIDELITIES AGAIN. NO MORE LIPSTICK ON HIS COLLAR. HE'S ***ALL*** HERS.

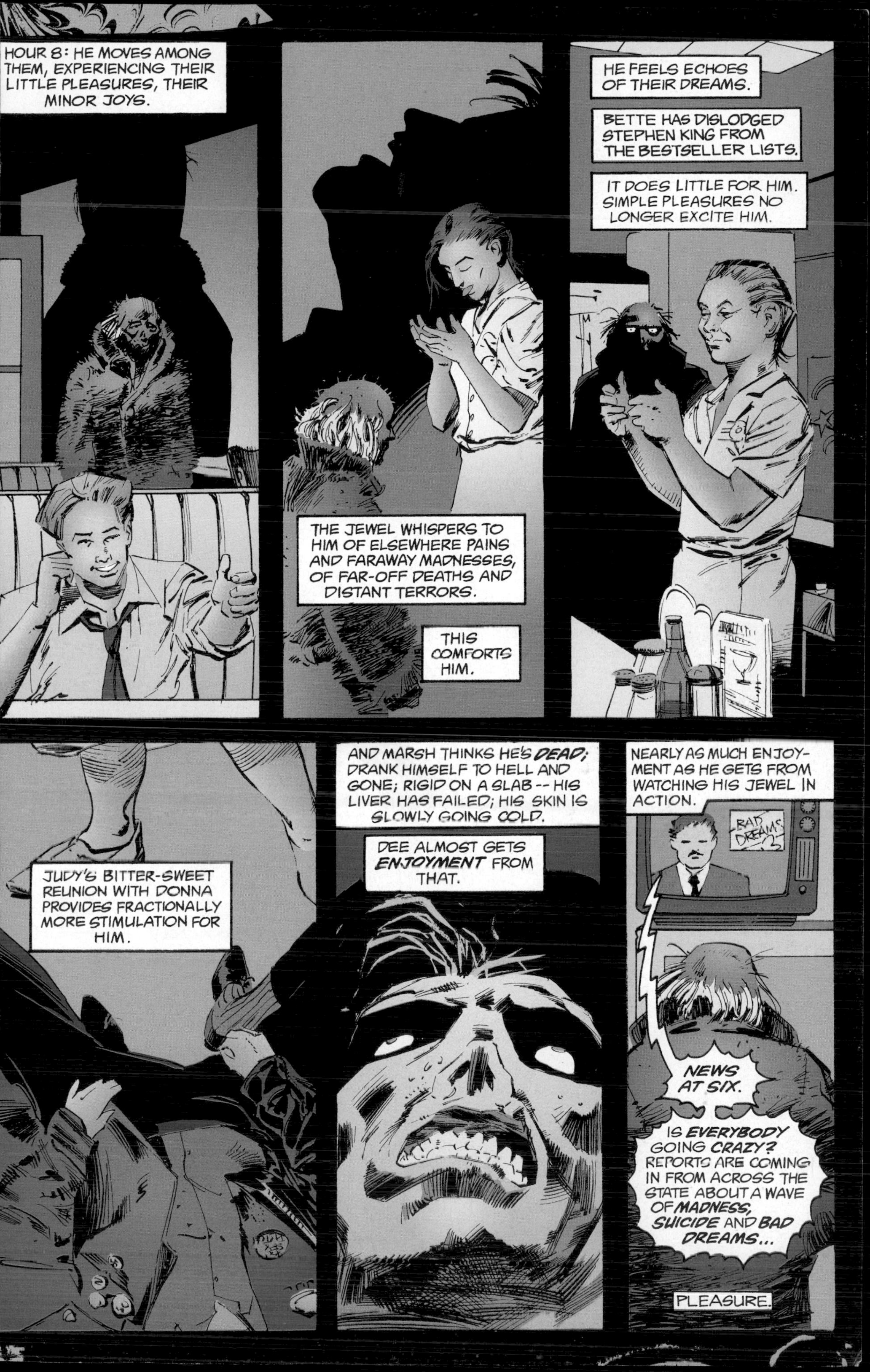
HOUR 8: HE MOVES AMONG THEM, EXPERIENCING THEIR LITTLE PLEASURES, THEIR MINOR JOYS.
THE JEWEL WHISPERS TO HIM OF ELSEWHERE PAINS AND FARAWAY MADNESSES, OF FAR-OFF DEATHS AND DISTANT TERRORS.
THIS COMFORTS HIM.
HE FEELS ECHOES OF THEIR DREAMS.
BETTE HAS DISLODGED STEPHEN KING FROM THE BESTSELLER LISTS.
IT DOES LITTLE FOR HIM. SIMPLE PLEASURES NO LONGER EXCITE HIM.
JUDY'S BITTER-SWEET REUNION WITH DONNA PROVIDES FRACTIONALLY MORE STIMULATION FOR HIM.
AND MARSH THINKS HE'S DEAD; DRANK HIMSELF TO HELL AND GONE; RIGID ON A SLAB -- HIS LIVER HAS FAILED; HIS SKIN IS SLOWLY GOING COLD.
DEE ALMOST GETS ENJOYMENT FROM THAT.
NEARLY AS MUCH ENJOYMENT AS HE GETS FROM WATCHING HIS JEWEL IN ACTION.
BAD DREAMS
NEWS AT SIX.
IS EVERYBODY GOING CRAZY? REPORTS ARE COMING IN FROM ACROSS THE STATE ABOUT A WAVE OF MADNESS, SUICIDE AND BAD DREAMS...
PLEASURE.

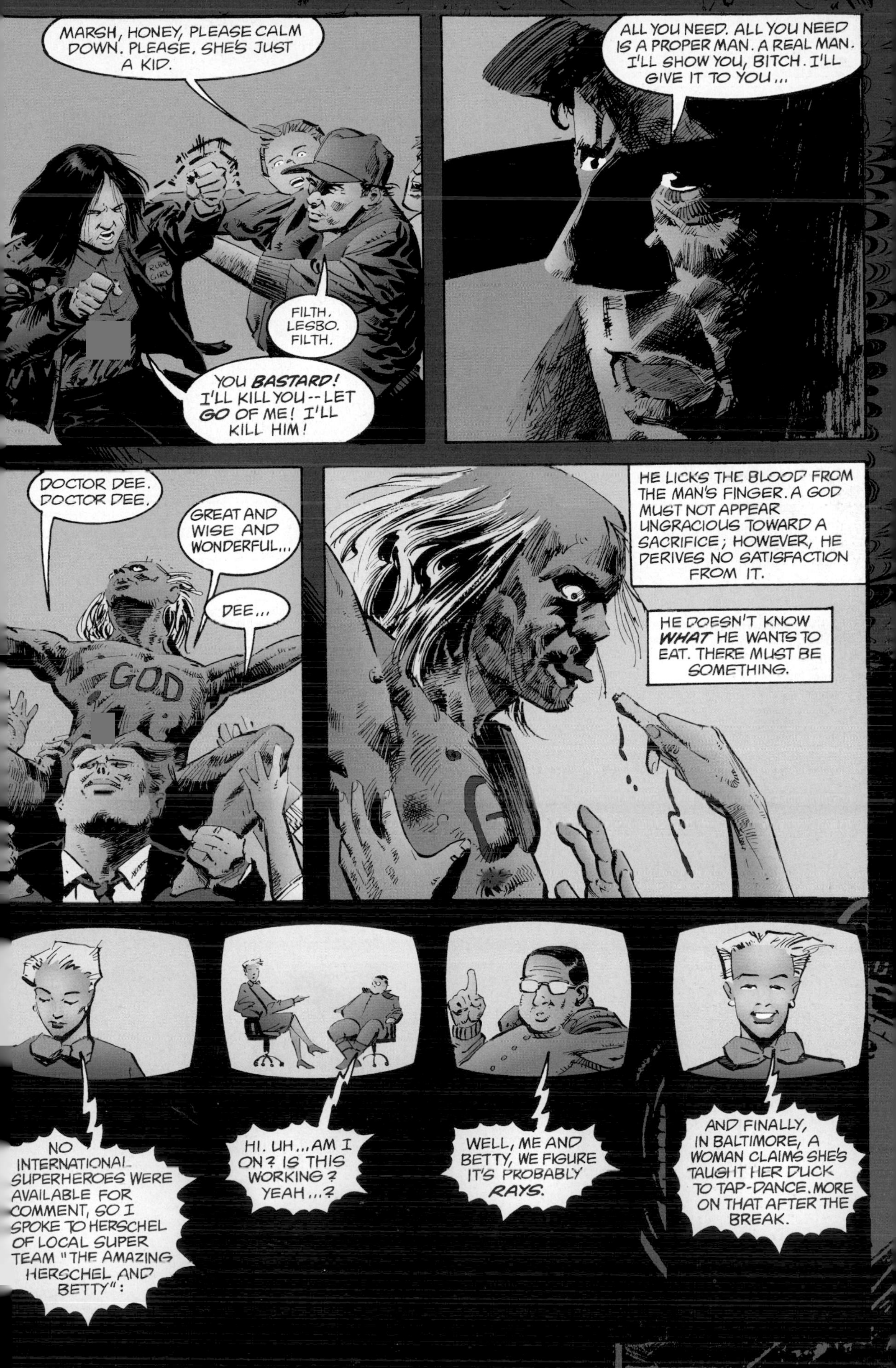
MARSH, HONEY, PLEASE CALM DOWN. PLEASE. SHE'S JUST A KID.
FILTH. LESBO. FILTH.
YOU **BASTARD!** I'LL KILL YOU -- LET **GO** OF ME! I'LL KILL HIM!
ALL YOU NEED. ALL YOU NEED IS A PROPER MAN. A REAL MAN. I'LL SHOW YOU, BITCH. I'LL GIVE IT TO YOU...
DOCTOR DEE. DOCTOR DEE.
GREAT AND WISE AND WONDERFUL...
DEE...
GOD
HE LICKS THE BLOOD FROM THE MAN'S FINGER. A GOD MUST NOT APPEAR UNGRACIOUS TOWARD A SACRIFICE; HOWEVER, HE DERIVES NO SATISFACTION FROM IT.
HE DOESN'T KNOW **WHAT** HE WANTS TO EAT. THERE MUST BE SOMETHING.
NO INTERNATIONAL SUPERHEROES WERE AVAILABLE FOR COMMENT, SO I SPOKE TO HERSCHEL OF LOCAL SUPER TEAM "THE AMAZING HERSCHEL AND BETTY":
HI. UH... AM I ON? IS THIS WORKING? YEAH...?
WELL, ME AND BETTY, WE FIGURE IT'S PROBABLY **RAYS**.
AND FINALLY, IN BALTIMORE, A WOMAN CLAIMS SHE'S TAUGHT HER DUCK TO TAP-DANCE. MORE ON THAT AFTER THE BREAK.

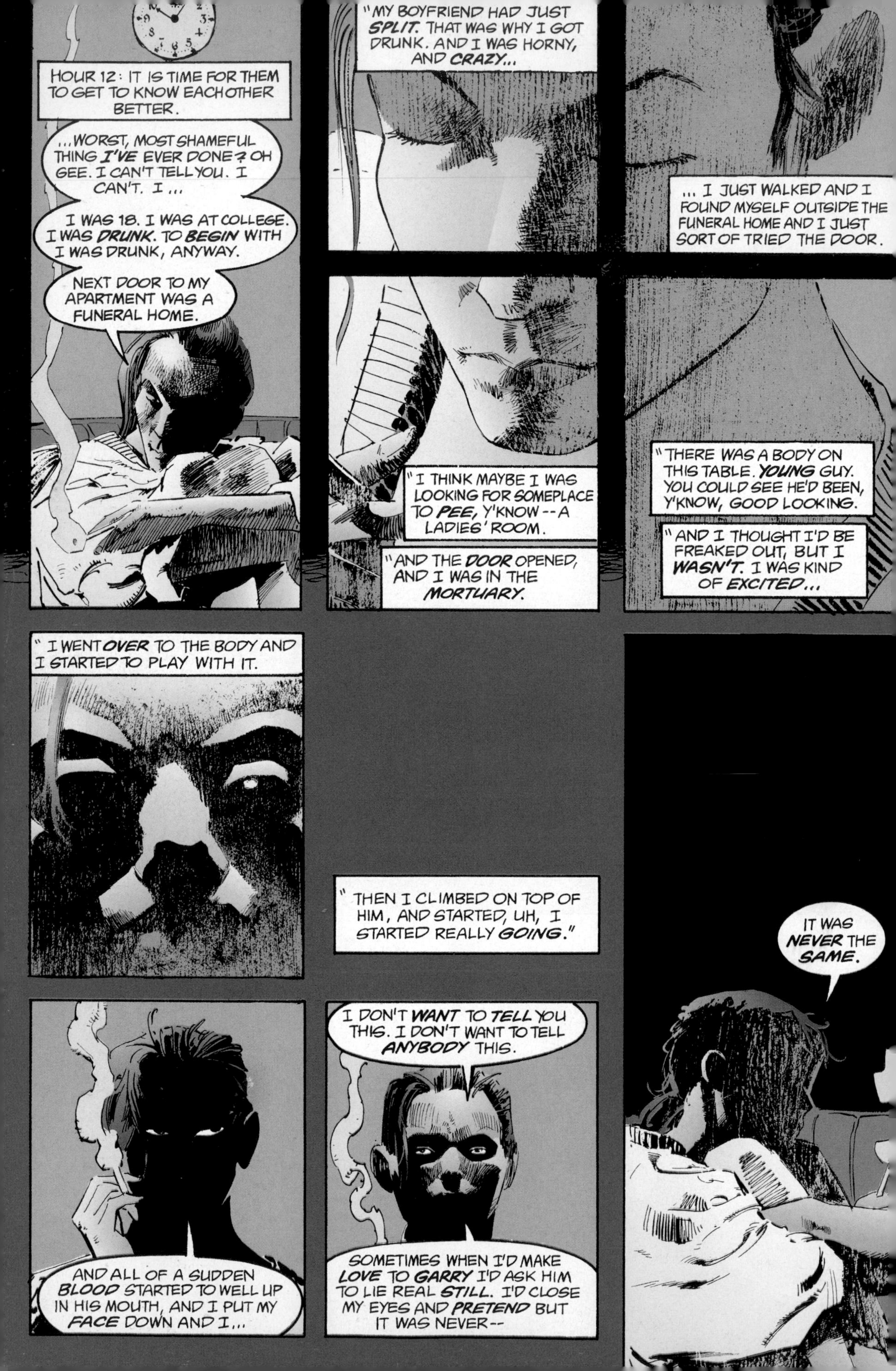
HOUR 12: IT IS TIME FOR THEM TO GET TO KNOW EACH OTHER BETTER.
...WORST, MOST SHAMEFUL THING I'VE EVER DONE? OH GEE. I CAN'T TELL YOU. I CAN'T. I ...
I WAS 18. I WAS AT COLLEGE. I WAS DRUNK. TO BEGIN WITH I WAS DRUNK, ANYWAY.
NEXT DOOR TO MY APARTMENT WAS A FUNERAL HOME.
"MY BOYFRIEND HAD JUST SPLIT. THAT WAS WHY I GOT DRUNK. AND I WAS HORNY, AND CRAZY...
... I JUST WALKED AND I FOUND MYSELF OUTSIDE THE FUNERAL HOME AND I JUST SORT OF TRIED THE DOOR.
"I THINK MAYBE I WAS LOOKING FOR SOMEPLACE TO PEE, Y'KNOW -- A LADIES' ROOM.
"AND THE DOOR OPENED, AND I WAS IN THE MORTUARY.
"THERE WAS A BODY ON THIS TABLE. YOUNG GUY. YOU COULD SEE HE'D BEEN, Y'KNOW, GOOD LOOKING.
"AND I THOUGHT I'D BE FREAKED OUT, BUT I WASN'T. I WAS KIND OF EXCITED...
" I WENT OVER TO THE BODY AND I STARTED TO PLAY WITH IT.
" THEN I CLIMBED ON TOP OF HIM, AND STARTED, UH, I STARTED REALLY GOING."
AND ALL OF A SUDDEN BLOOD STARTED TO WELL UP IN HIS MOUTH, AND I PUT MY FACE DOWN AND I...
I DON'T WANT TO TELL YOU THIS. I DON'T WANT TO TELL ANYBODY THIS.
SOMETIMES WHEN I'D MAKE LOVE TO GARRY I'D ASK HIM TO LIE REAL STILL. I'D CLOSE MY EYES AND PRETEND BUT IT WAS NEVER--
IT WAS NEVER THE SAME.

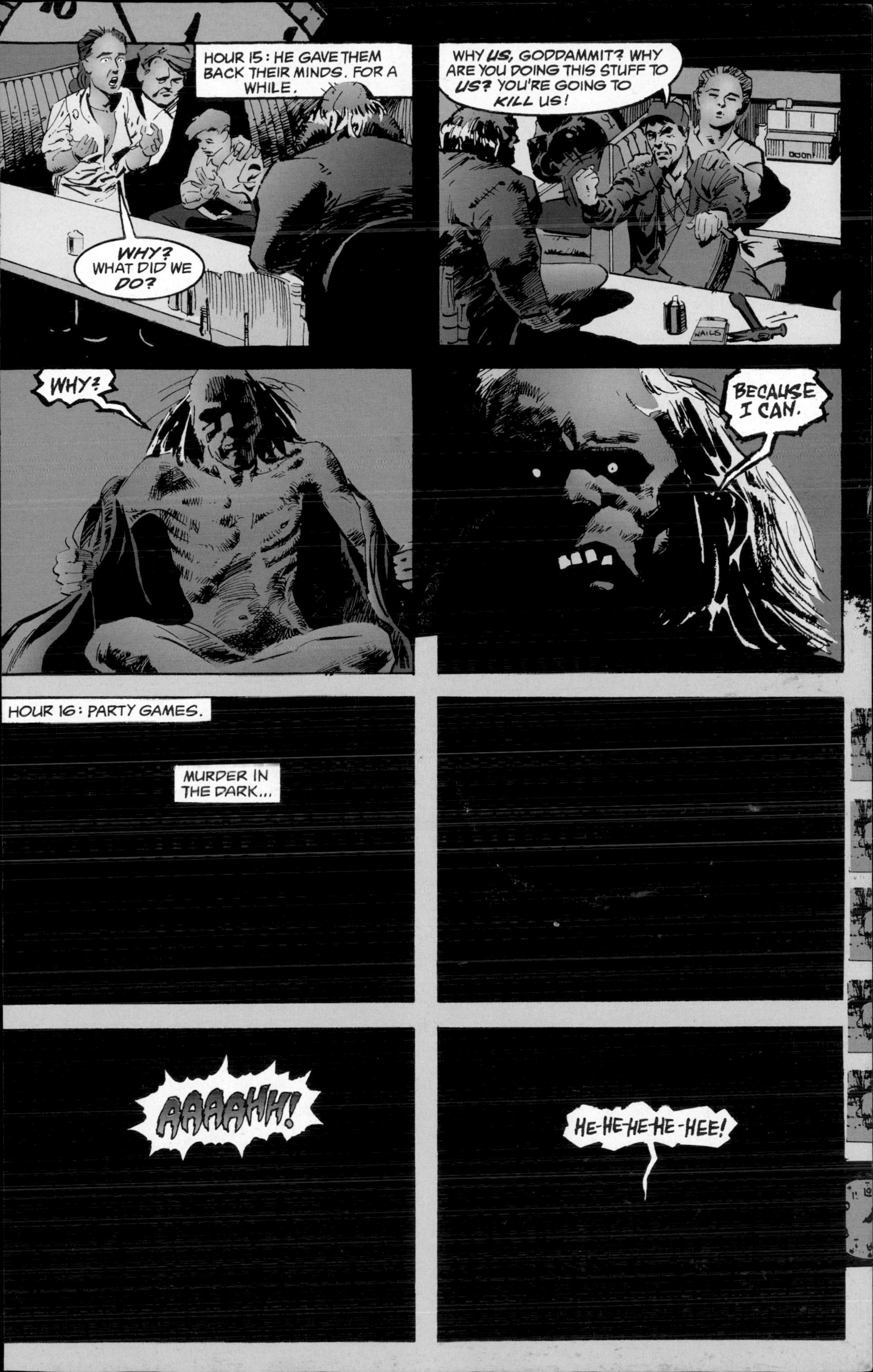
HOUR 15: HE GAVE THEM BACK THEIR MINDS. FOR A WHILE.
WHY? WHAT DID WE DO?
WHY US, GODDAMMIT? WHY ARE YOU DOING THIS STUFF TO US? YOU'RE GOING TO KILL US!
NAILS
WHY?
BECAUSE I CAN.
HOUR 16: PARTY GAMES.
MURDER IN THE DARK...
AAAAHH!
HE-HE-HE-HE-HEE!

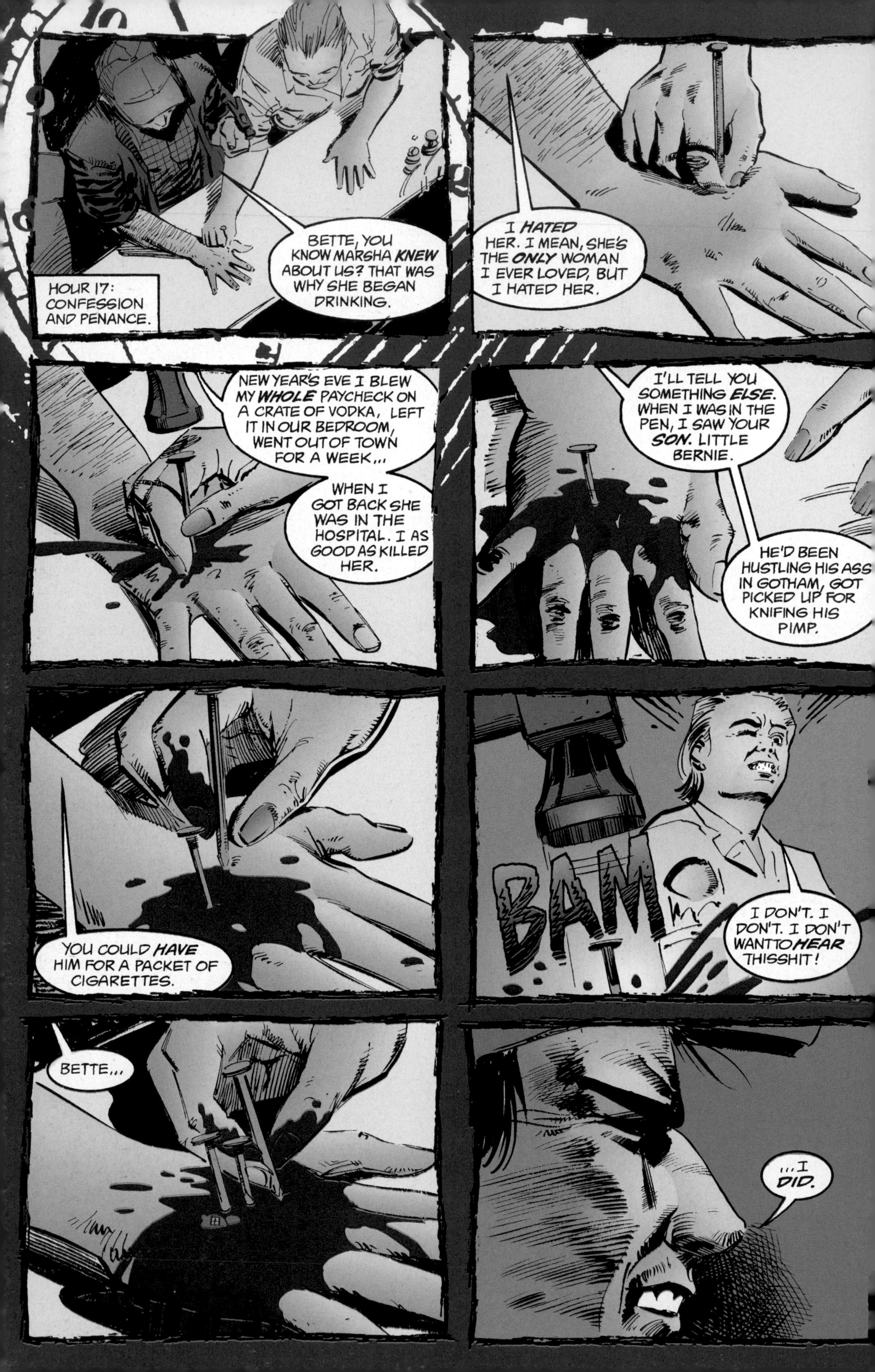
HOUR 17: CONFESSION AND PENANCE.
BETTE, YOU KNOW MARSHA KNEW ABOUT US? THAT WAS WHY SHE BEGAN DRINKING.
I HATED HER. I MEAN, SHE'S THE ONLY WOMAN I EVER LOVED, BUT I HATED HER.
NEW YEAR'S EVE I BLEW MY WHOLE PAYCHECK ON A CRATE OF VODKA, LEFT IT IN OUR BEDROOM, WENT OUT OF TOWN FOR A WEEK...
WHEN I GOT BACK SHE WAS IN THE HOSPITAL. I AS GOOD AS KILLED HER.
I'LL TELL YOU SOMETHING ELSE. WHEN I WAS IN THE PEN, I SAW YOUR SON. LITTLE BERNIE.
HE'D BEEN HUSTLING HIS ASS IN GOTHAM, GOT PICKED UP FOR KNIFING HIS PIMP.
YOU COULD HAVE HIM FOR A PACKET OF CIGARETTES.
BAM
I DON'T. I DON'T. I DON'T WANTTO HEAR THISSHIT!
BETTE...
...I DID.

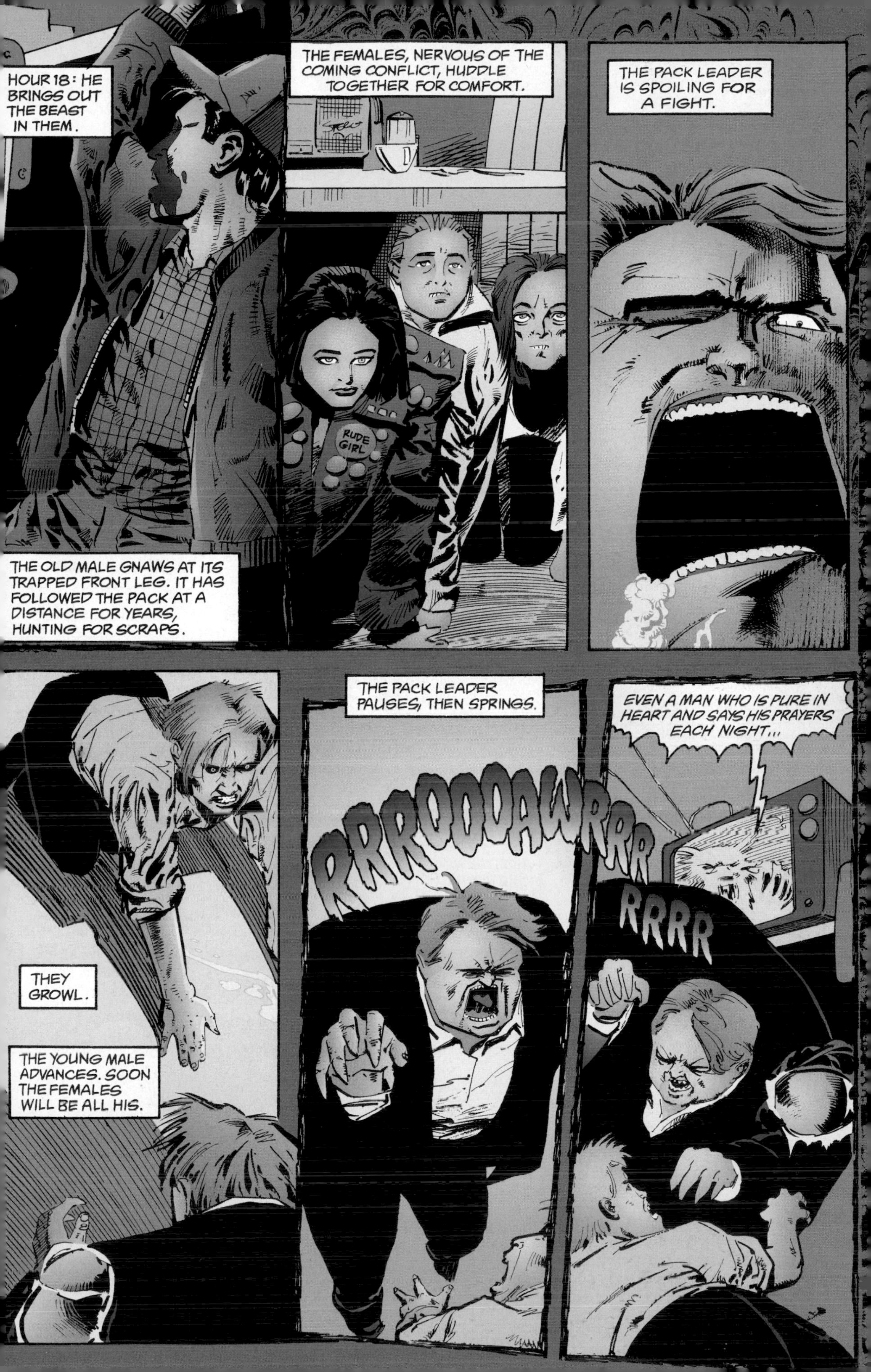
HOUR 18: HE BRINGS OUT THE BEAST IN THEM.
THE OLD MALE GNAWS AT ITS TRAPPED FRONT LEG. IT HAS FOLLOWED THE PACK AT A DISTANCE FOR YEARS, HUNTING FOR SCRAPS.
THE FEMALES, NERVOUS OF THE COMING CONFLICT, HUDDLE TOGETHER FOR COMFORT.
RUDE GIRL
THE PACK LEADER IS SPOILING FOR A FIGHT.
THEY GROWL.
THE YOUNG MALE ADVANCES. SOON THE FEMALES WILL BE ALL HIS.
THE PACK LEADER PAUSES, THEN SPRINGS.
RRROOOAWRRR
EVEN A MAN WHO IS PURE IN HEART AND SAYS HIS PRAYERS EACH NIGHT...
RRRR

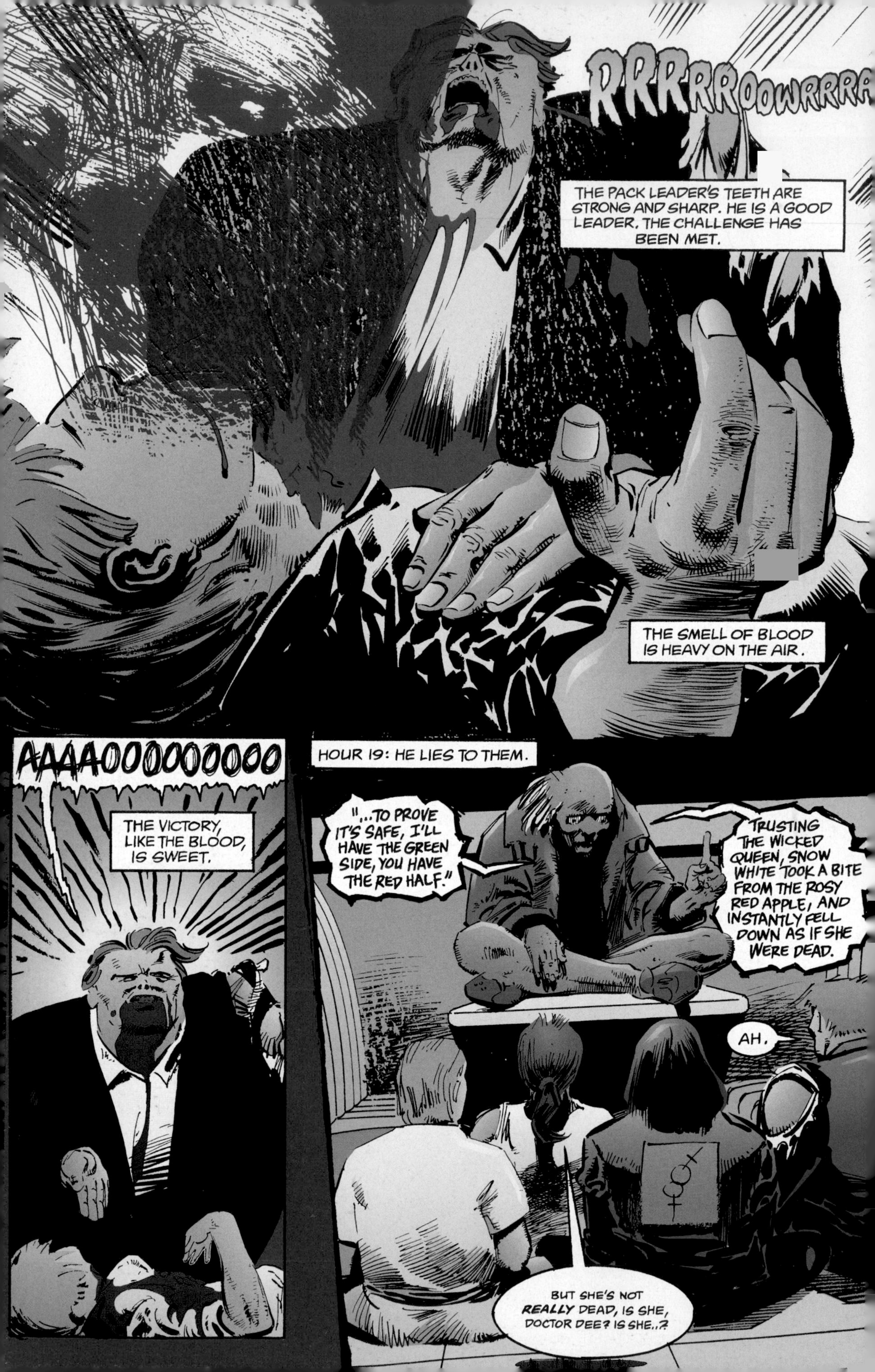
RRRRROOWRRRA
THE PACK LEADER'S TEETH ARE STRONG AND SHARP. HE IS A GOOD LEADER. THE CHALLENGE HAS BEEN MET.
THE SMELL OF BLOOD IS HEAVY ON THE AIR.
AAAAOOOOOOOOO
THE VICTORY, LIKE THE BLOOD, IS SWEET.
HOUR 19: HE LIES TO THEM.
"...TO PROVE IT'S SAFE, I'LL HAVE THE GREEN SIDE, YOU HAVE THE RED HALF."
TRUSTING THE WICKED QUEEN, SNOW WHITE TOOK A BITE FROM THE ROSY RED APPLE, AND INSTANTLY FELL DOWN AS IF SHE WERE DEAD.
AH.
BUT SHE'S NOT REALLY DEAD, IS SHE, DOCTOR DEE? IS SHE..?

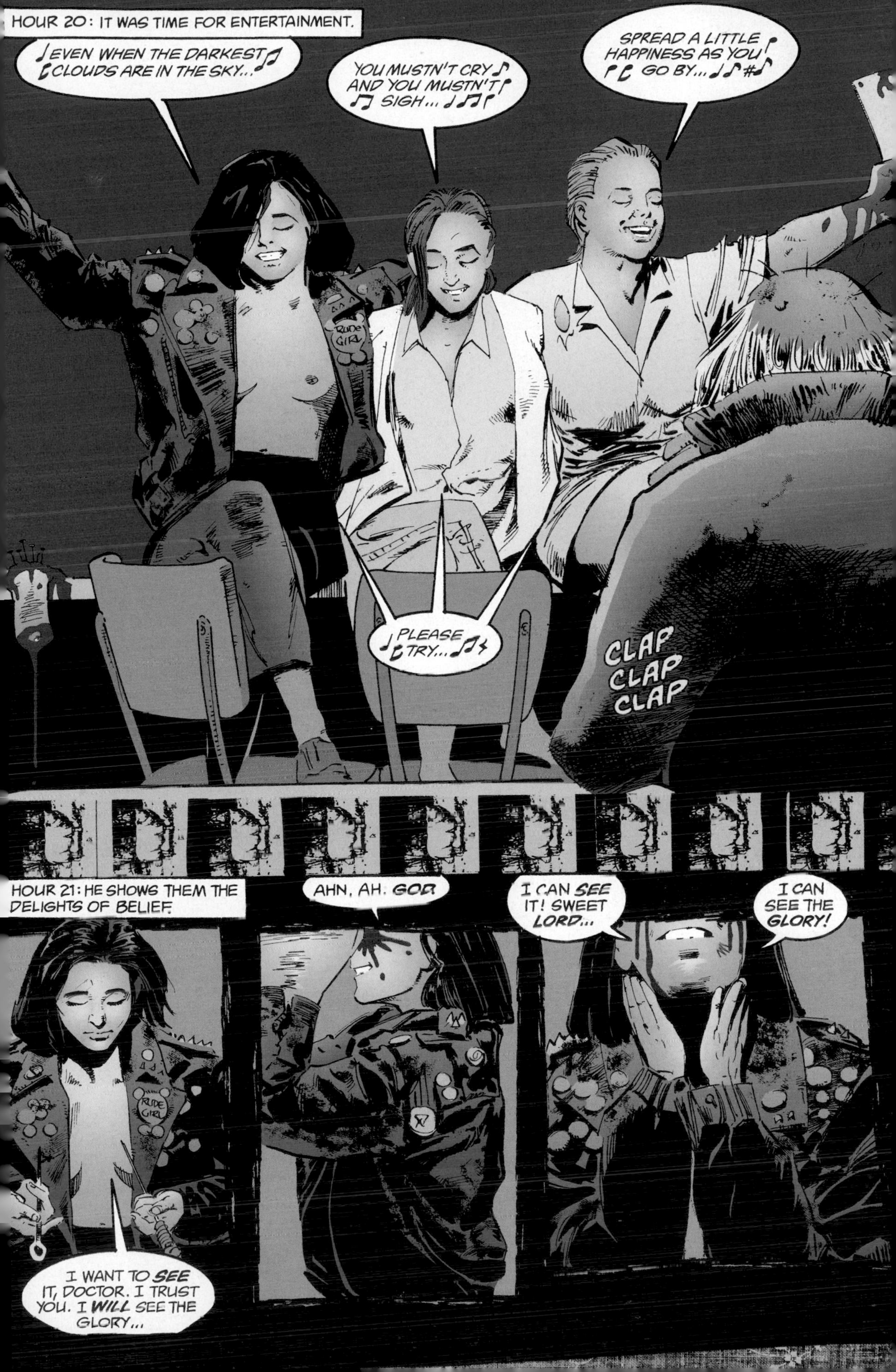
HOUR 20: IT WAS TIME FOR ENTERTAINMENT.
EVEN WHEN THE DARKEST CLOUDS ARE IN THE SKY...
YOU MUSTN'T CRY AND YOU MUSTN'T SIGH...
SPREAD A LITTLE HAPPINESS AS YOU GO BY...
PLEASE TRY...
CLAP CLAP CLAP
HOUR 21: HE SHOWS THEM THE DELIGHTS OF BELIEF.
I WANT TO SEE IT, DOCTOR. I TRUST YOU. I WILL SEE THE GLORY...
AHN, AH: GOD
I CAN SEE IT! SWEET LORD...
I CAN SEE THE GLORY!

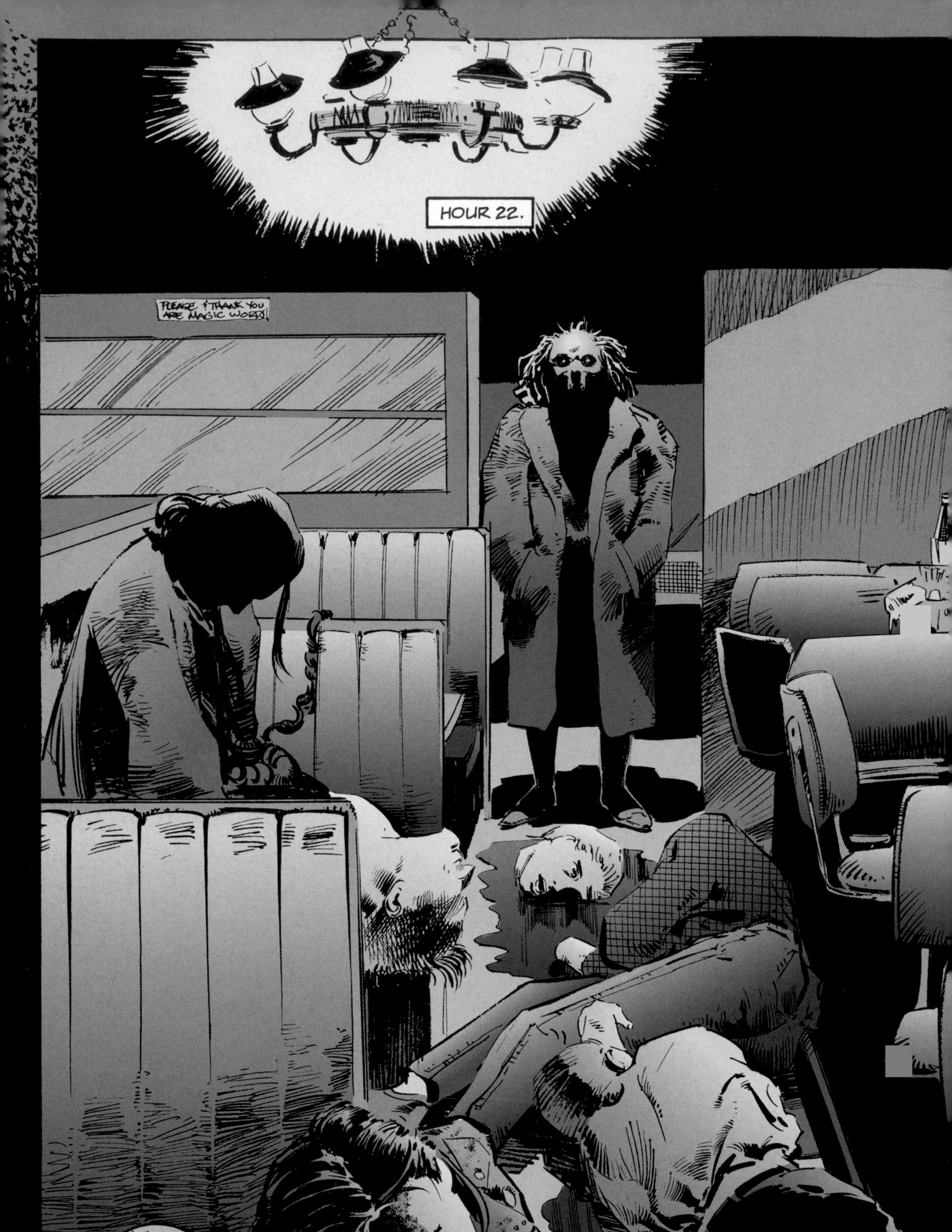
HOUR 22.
PLEASE & THANK YOU ARE MAGIC WORDS

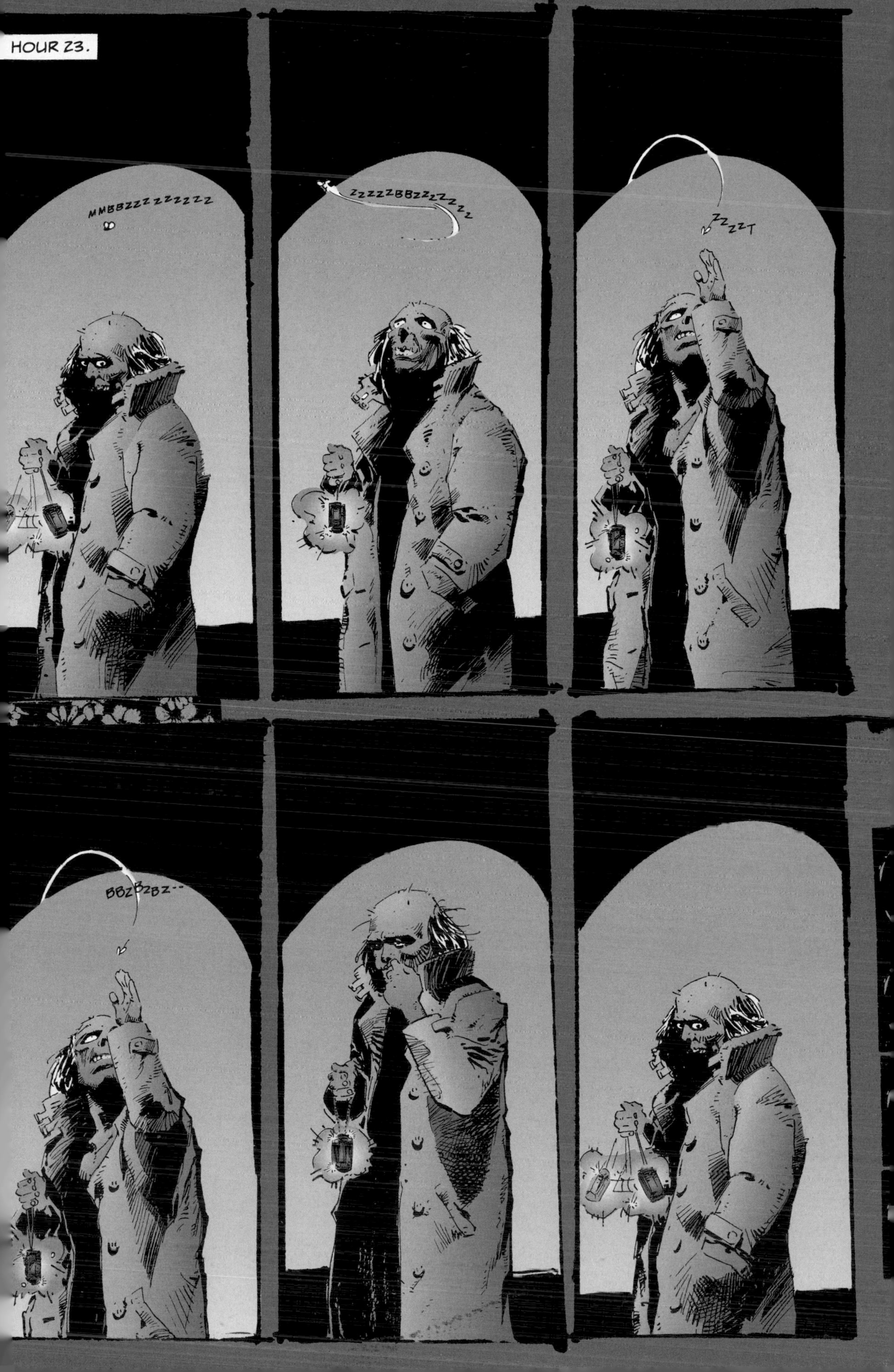
HOUR 23.
MMBBZZZZZZZZZZZ
ZZZZZBBZZZZZZZZ
ZZZZT
BBZBZBZ--

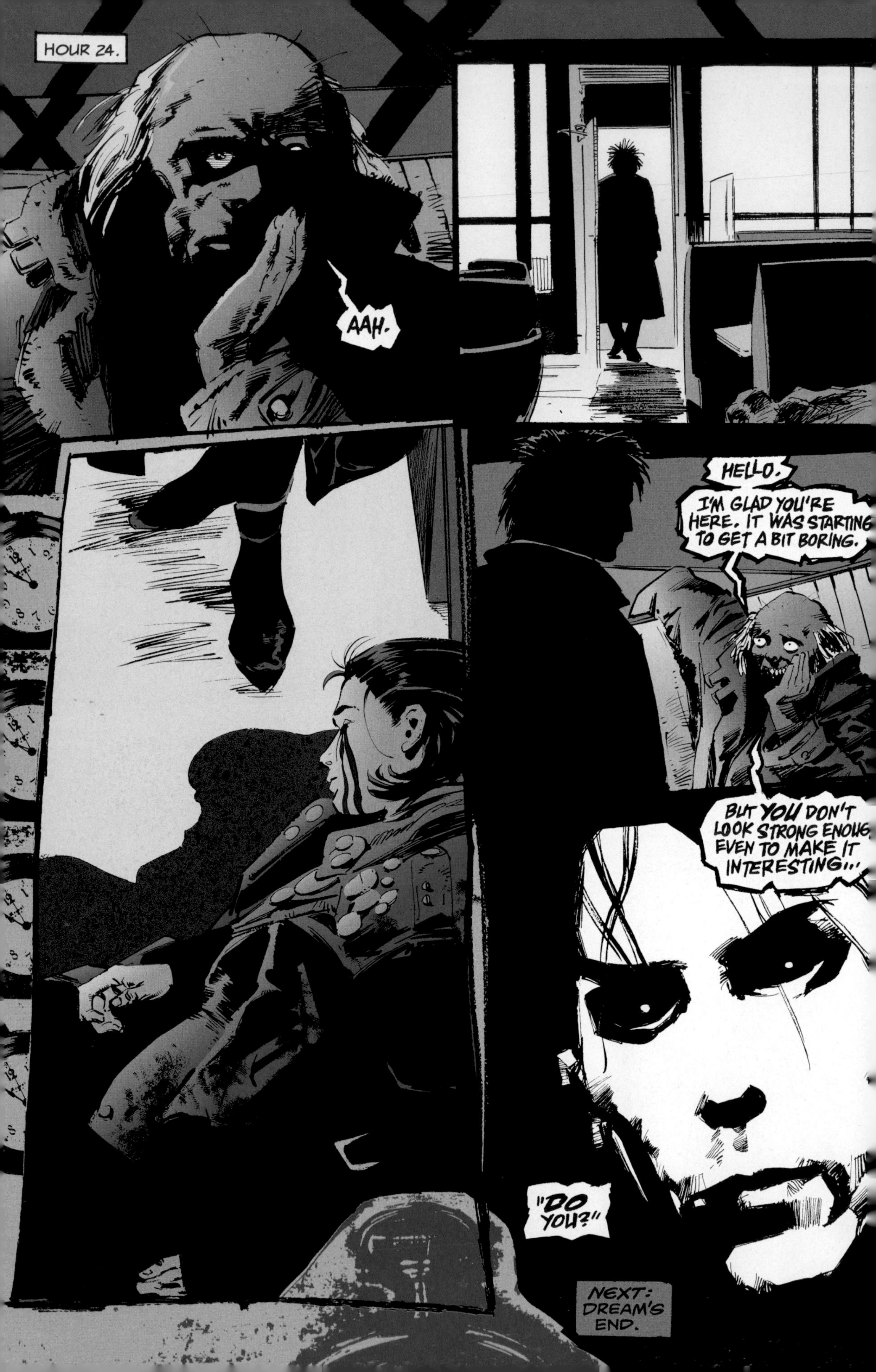
HOUR 24.
AAH.
HELLO.
I'M GLAD YOU'RE HERE. IT WAS STARTING TO GET A BIT BORING.
BUT YOU DON'T LOOK STRONG ENOUG EVEN TO MAKE IT INTERESTING...
"DO YOU?"
NEXT: DREAM'S END.

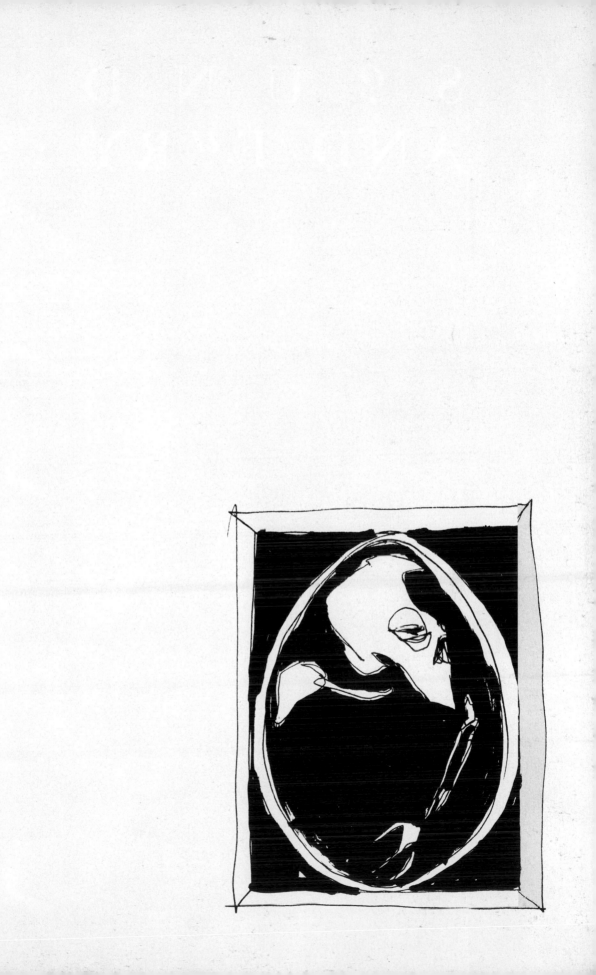

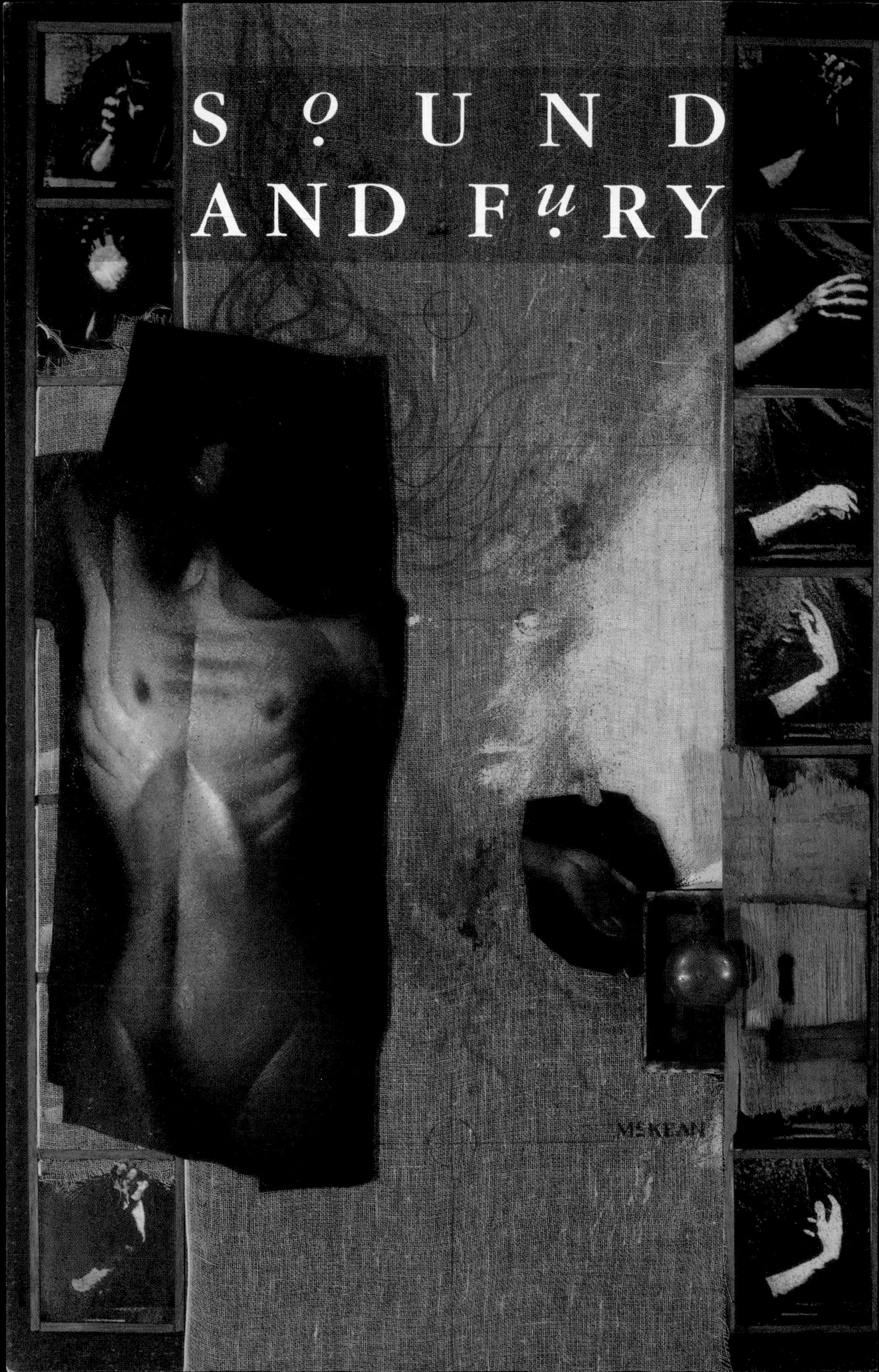
SOUND
AND FURY
McKEAN

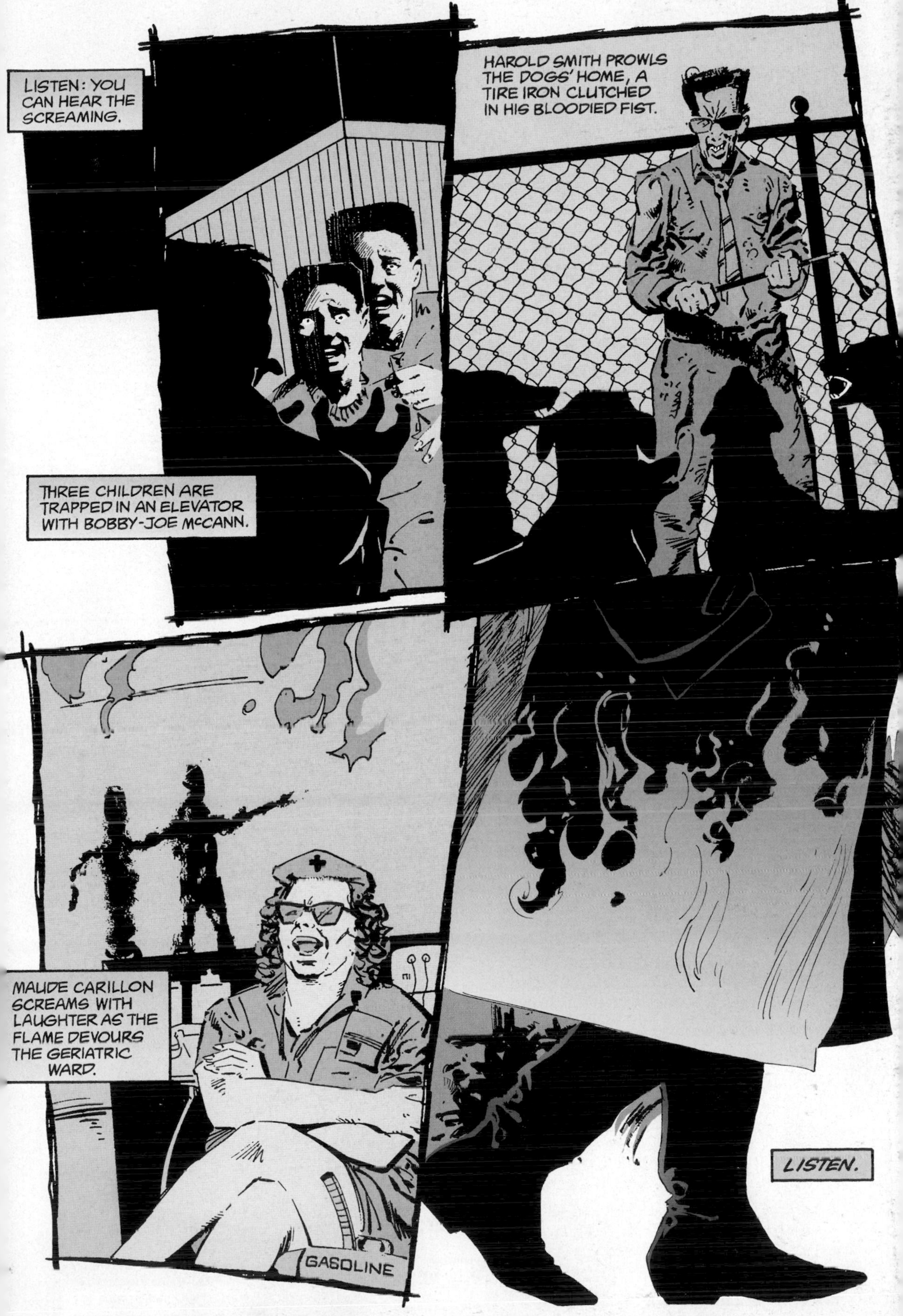
LISTEN: YOU CAN HEAR THE SCREAMING.
THREE CHILDREN ARE TRAPPED IN AN ELEVATOR WITH BOBBY-JOE McCANN.
HAROLD SMITH PROWLS THE DOGS' HOME, A TIRE IRON CLUTCHED IN HIS BLOODIED FIST.
MAUDE CARILLON SCREAMS WITH LAUGHTER AS THE FLAME DEVOURS THE GERIATRIC WARD.
GASOLINE
LISTEN.

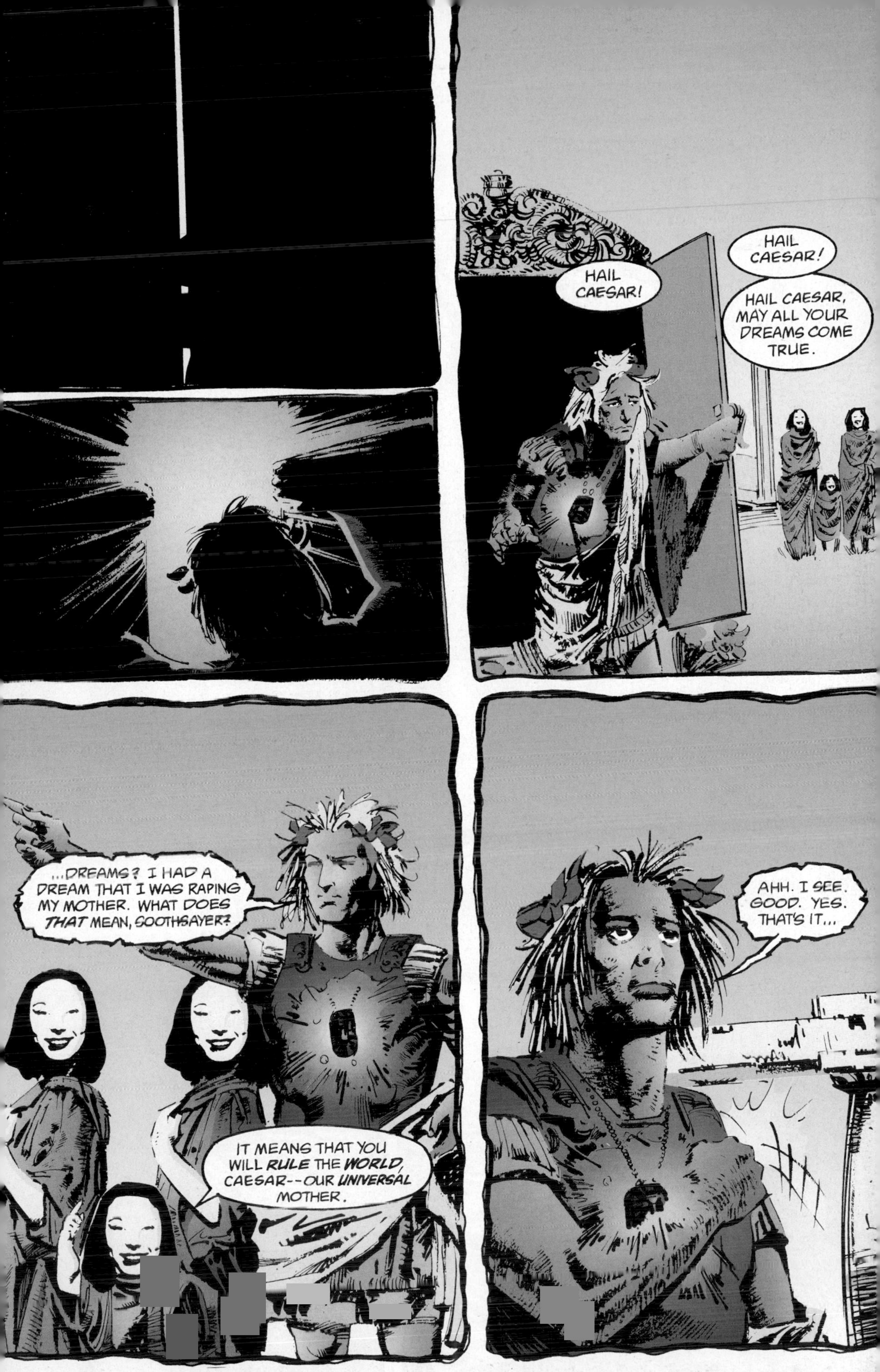
HAIL CAESAR!
HAIL CAESAR!
HAIL CAESAR, MAY ALL YOUR DREAMS COME TRUE.
...DREAMS? I HAD A DREAM THAT I WAS RAPING MY MOTHER. WHAT DOES *THAT* MEAN, SOOTHSAYER?
IT MEANS THAT YOU WILL ***RULE*** THE ***WORLD***, CAESAR--OUR ***UNIVERSAL*** MOTHER.
AHH. I SEE. GOOD. YES. THAT'S IT...

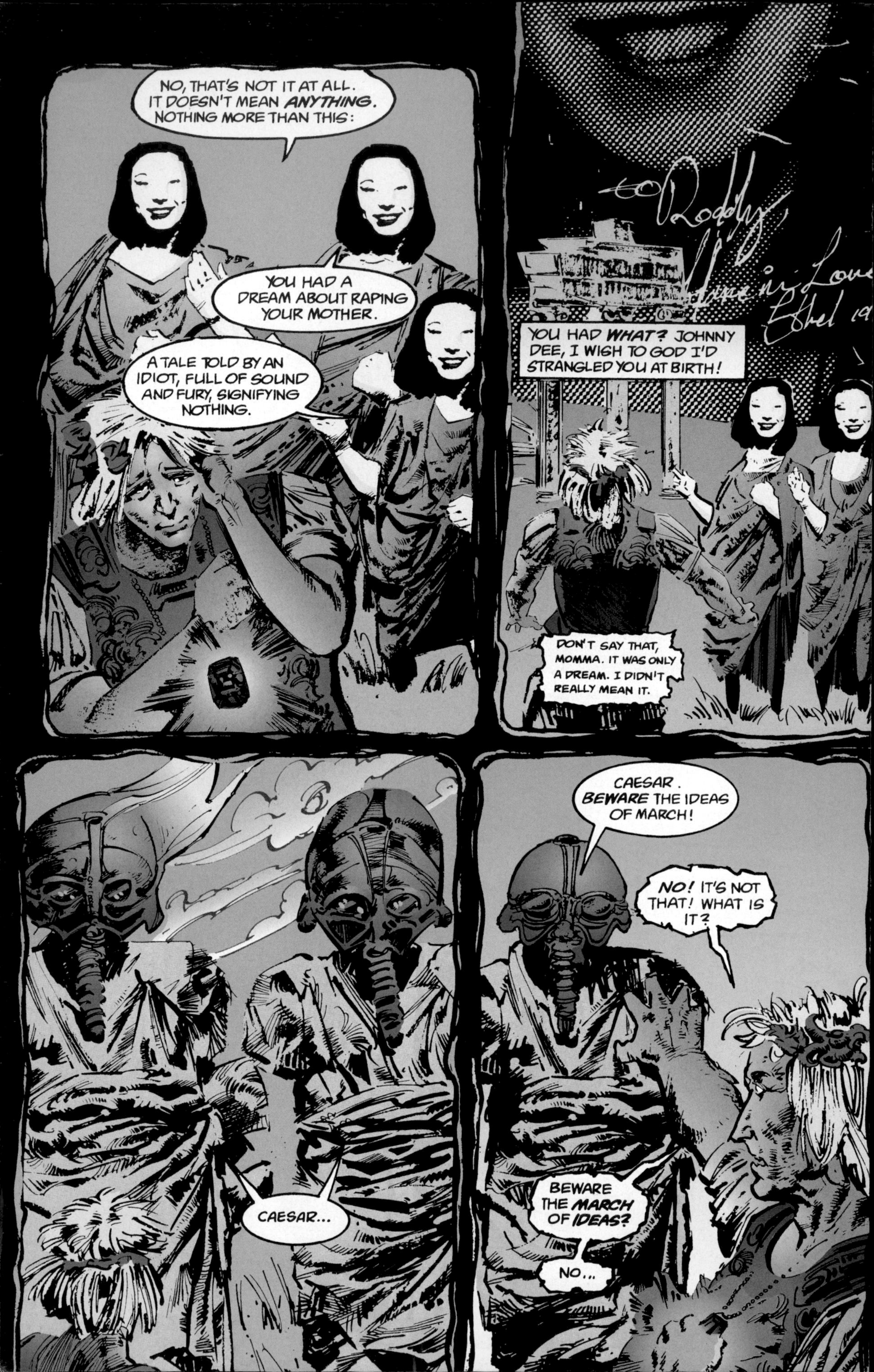
NO, THAT'S NOT IT AT ALL. IT DOESN'T MEAN ***ANYTHING***. NOTHING MORE THAN THIS:
YOU HAD A DREAM ABOUT RAPING YOUR MOTHER.
A TALE TOLD BY AN IDIOT, FULL OF SOUND AND FURY, SIGNIFYING NOTHING.
YOU HAD ***WHAT?*** JOHNNY DEE, I WISH TO GOD I'D STRANGLED YOU AT BIRTH!
DON'T SAY THAT, MOMMA. IT WAS ONLY A DREAM. I DIDN'T REALLY MEAN IT.
CAESAR...
CAESAR. ***BEWARE*** THE IDEAS OF MARCH!
NO! IT'S NOT THAT! WHAT IS IT?
BEWARE THE ***MARCH*** OF ***IDEAS?***
NO...

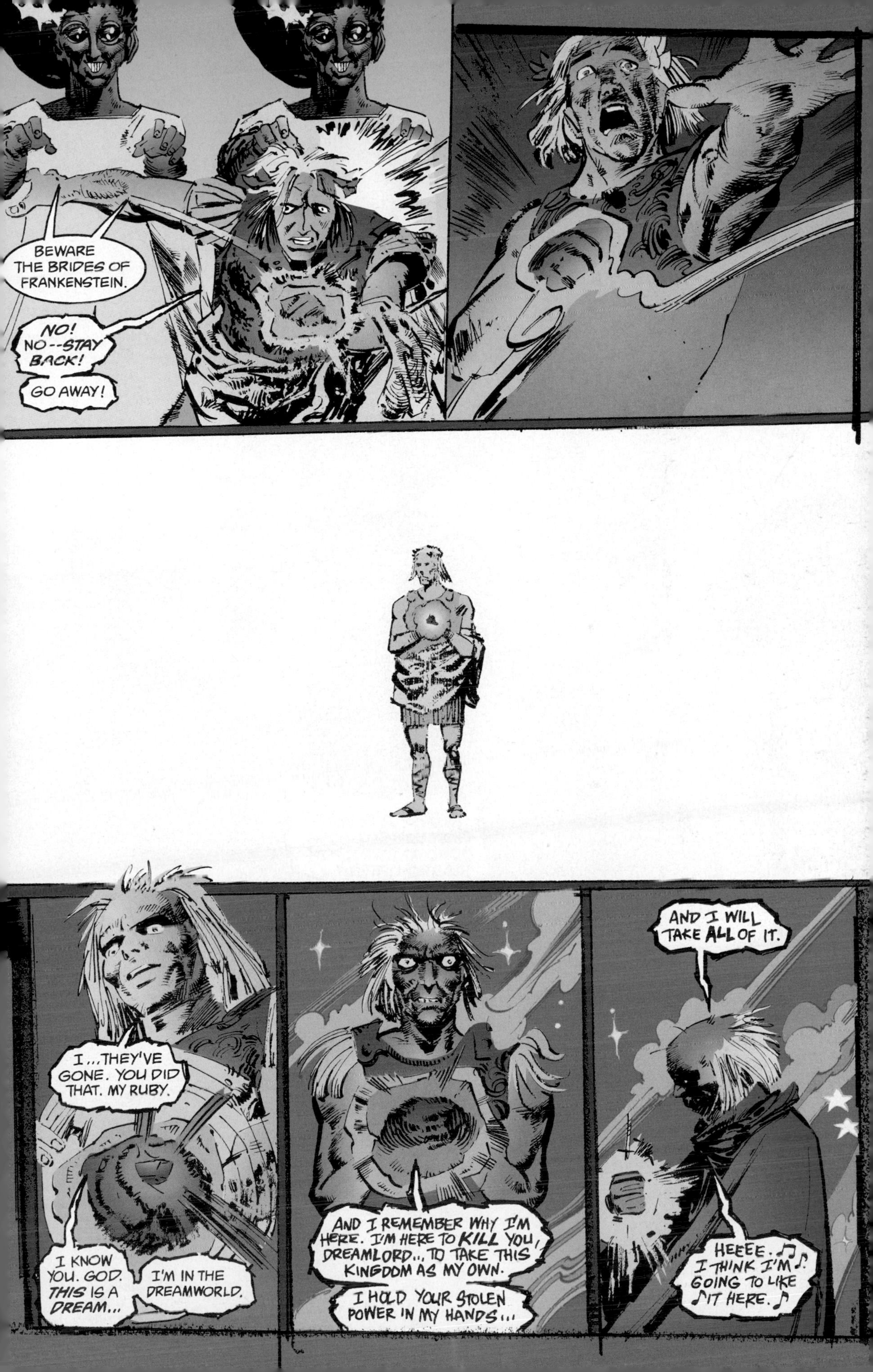
BEWARE THE BRIDES OF FRANKENSTEIN.
NO! NO--STAY BACK!
GO AWAY!
I...THEY'VE GONE. YOU DID THAT. MY RUBY.
I KNOW YOU. GOD. THIS IS A DREAM...
I'M IN THE DREAMWORLD.
AND I REMEMBER WHY I'M HERE. I'M HERE TO KILL YOU, DREAMLORD.., TO TAKE THIS KINGDOM AS MY OWN.
I HOLD YOUR STOLEN POWER IN MY HANDS...
AND I WILL TAKE ALL OF IT.
HEEEE. ♪♪ I THINK I'M ♪ GOING TO LIKE ♪IT HERE.♪

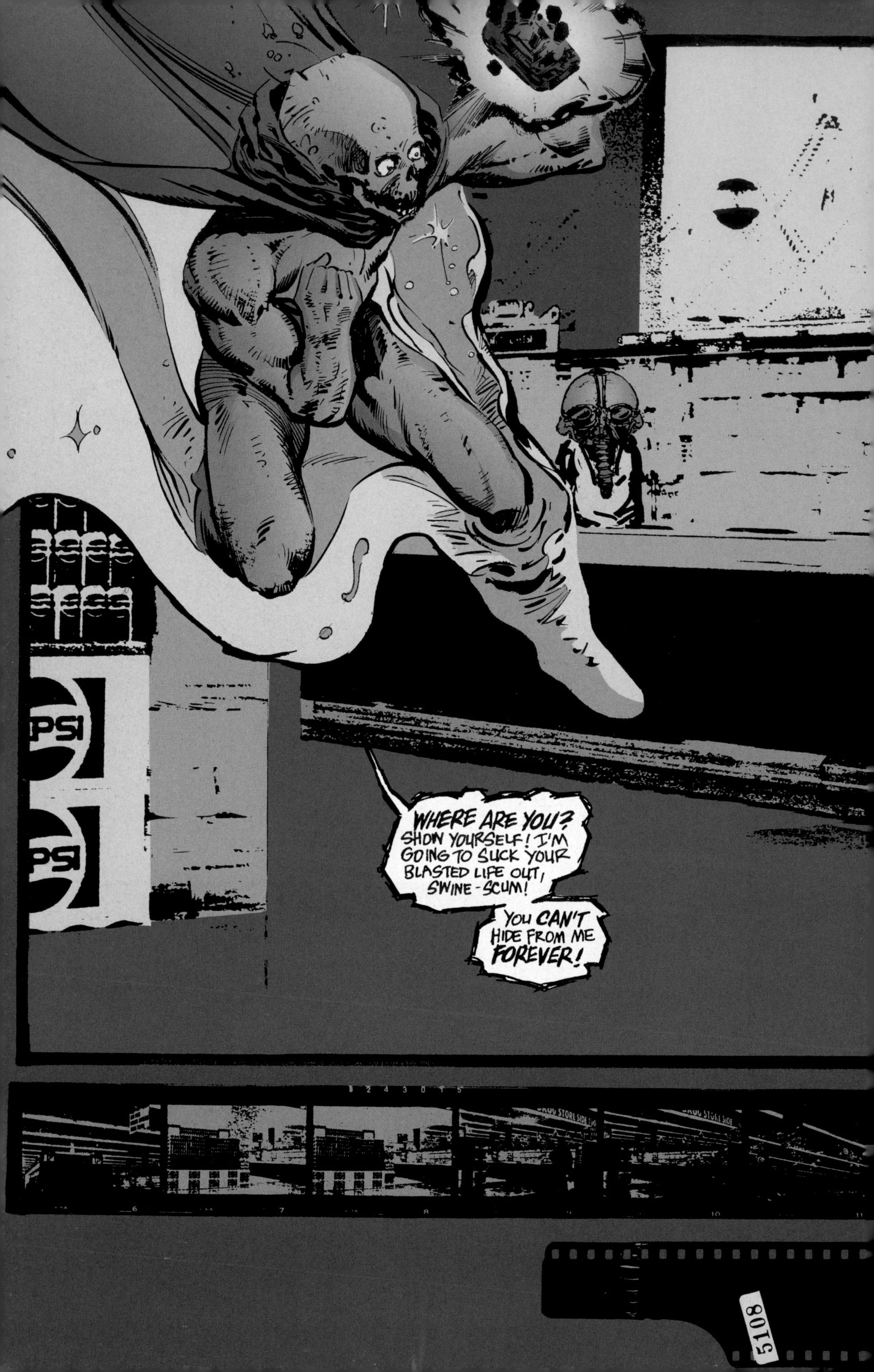
WHERE ARE YOU? SHOW YOURSELF! I'M GOING TO SUCK YOUR BLASTED LIFE OUT, SWINE-SCUM!
YOU CAN'T HIDE FROM ME FOREVER!
DRUG STORE SIDE
5108

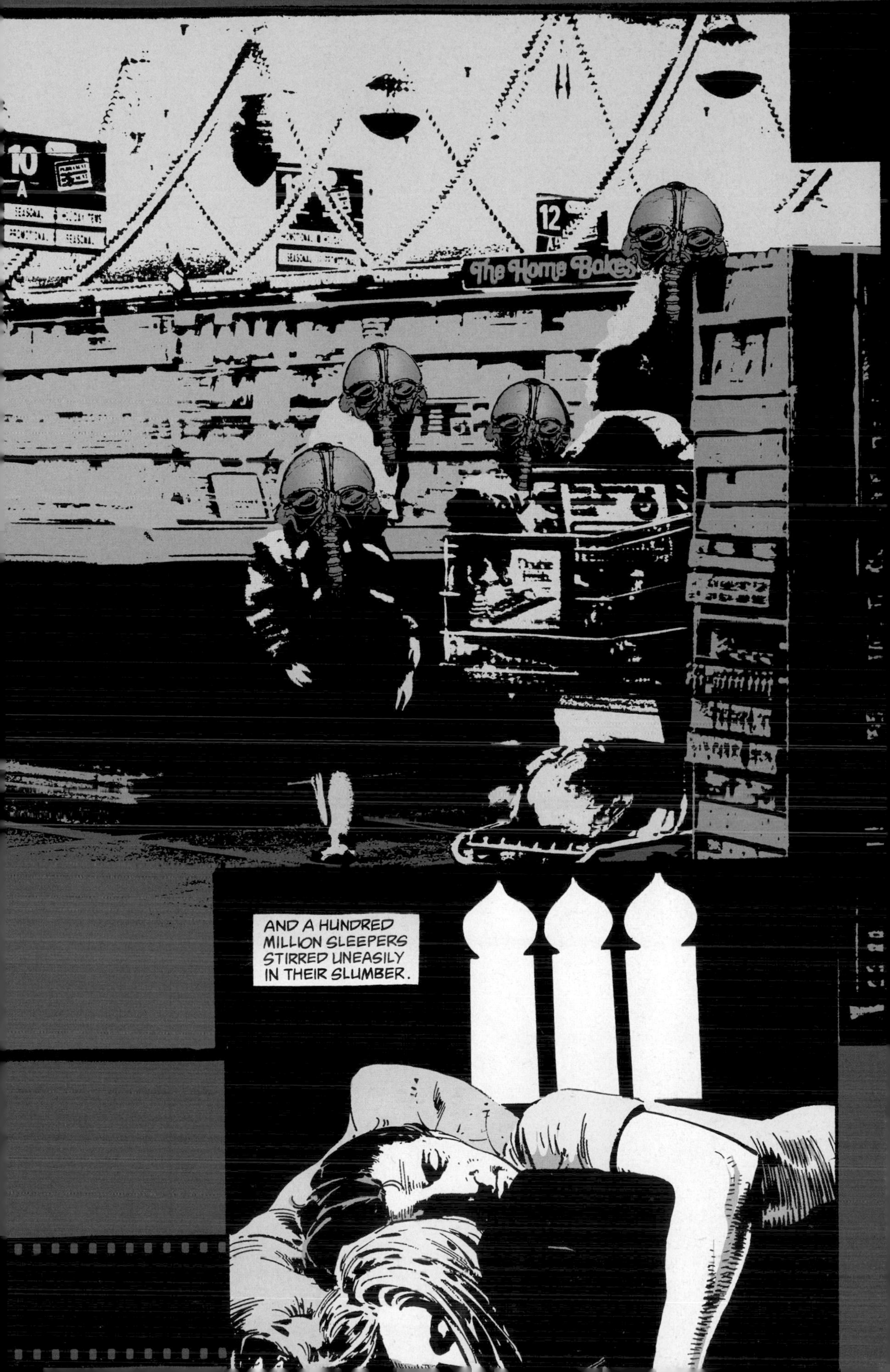
The Home Bakes
AND A HUNDRED MILLION SLEEPERS STIRRED UNEASILY IN THEIR SLUMBER.

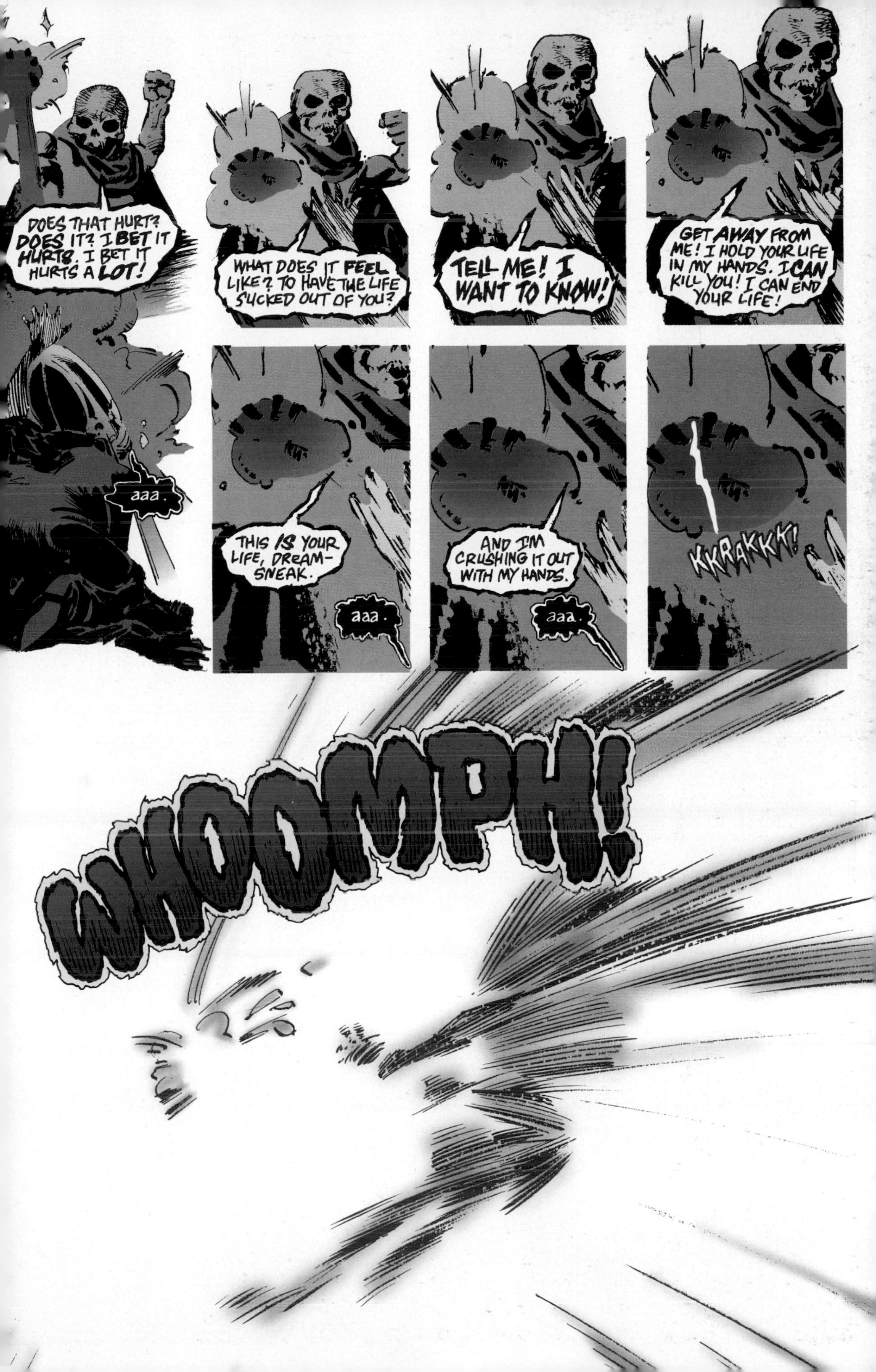
DOES THAT HURT? DOES IT? I BET IT HURTS. I BET IT HURTS A LOT!
WHAT DOES IT FEEL LIKE? TO HAVE THE LIFE SUCKED OUT OF YOU?
TELL ME! I WANT TO KNOW!
GET AWAY FROM ME! I HOLD YOUR LIFE IN MY HANDS. I CAN KILL YOU! I CAN END YOUR LIFE!
aaa.
THIS IS YOUR LIFE, DREAM-SNEAK.
aaa.
AND I'M CRUSHING IT OUT WITH MY HANDS.
aaa.
KKRAKKK!
WHOOMPH!

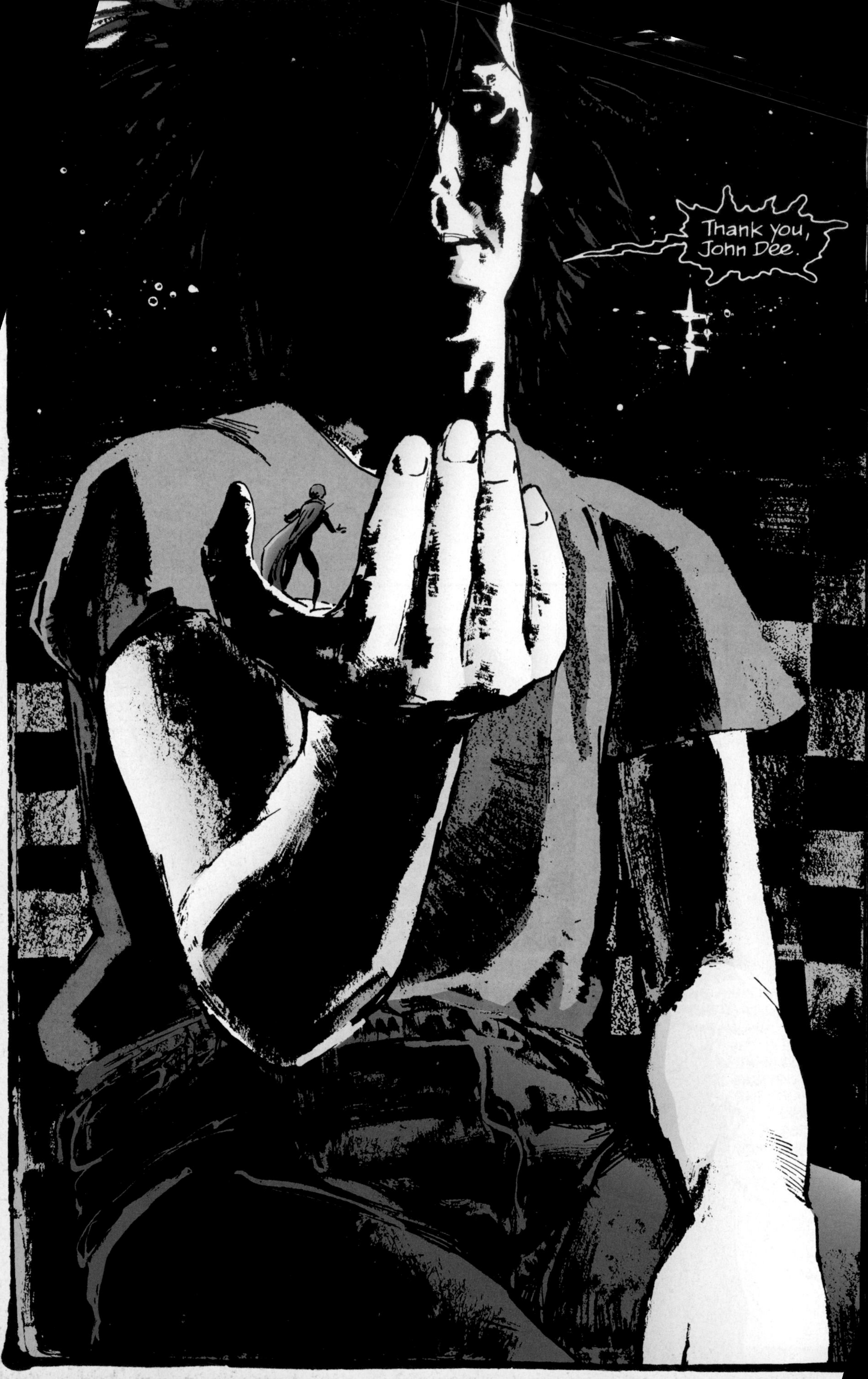
Thank you, John Dee.

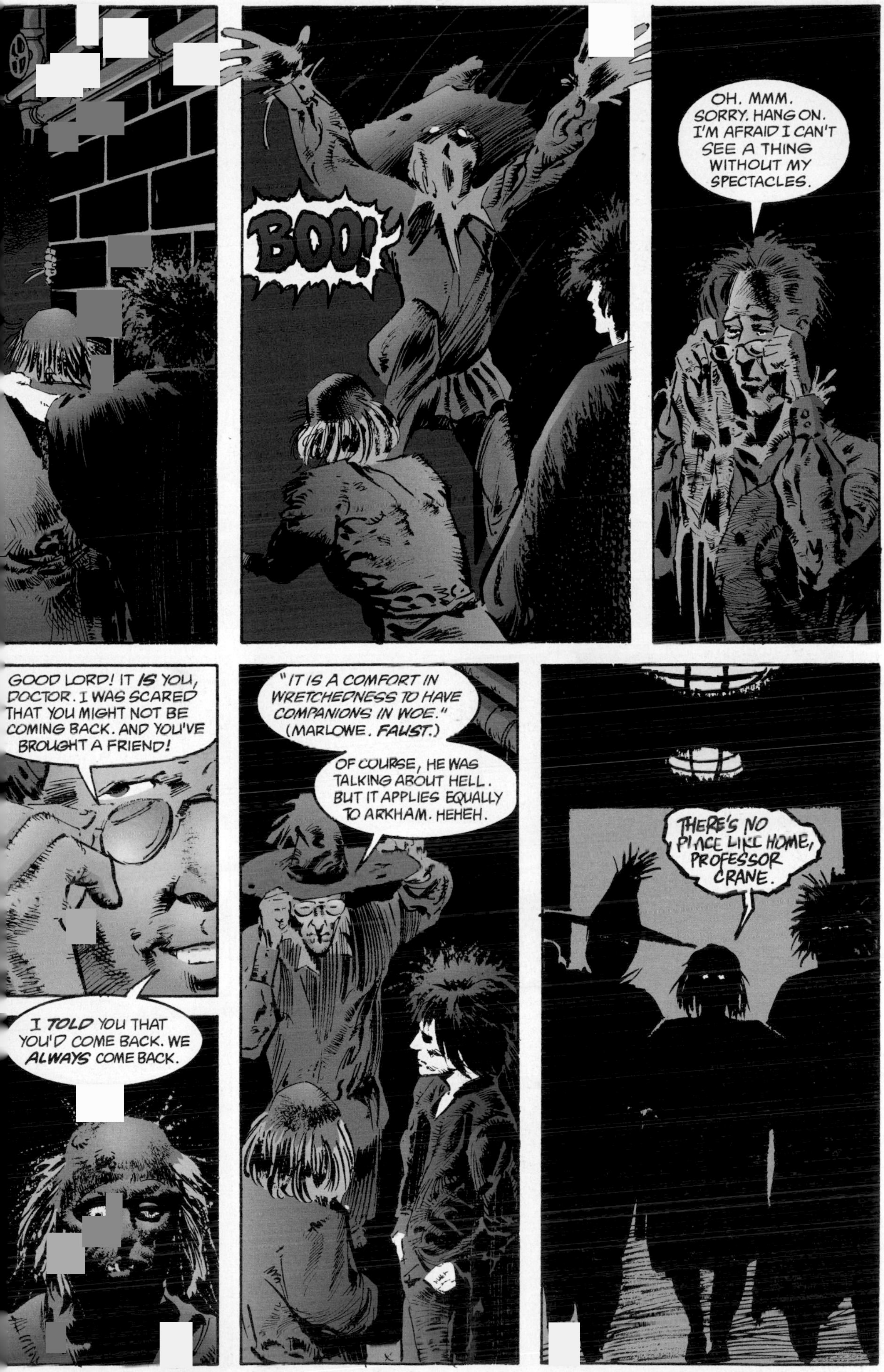
BOO!
OH. MMM. SORRY. HANG ON. I'M AFRAID I CAN'T SEE A THING WITHOUT MY SPECTACLES.
GOOD LORD! IT *IS* YOU, DOCTOR. I WAS SCARED THAT YOU MIGHT NOT BE COMING BACK. AND YOU'VE BROUGHT A FRIEND!
I *TOLD* YOU THAT YOU'D COME BACK. WE *ALWAYS* COME BACK.
"IT IS A COMFORT IN WRETCHEDNESS TO HAVE COMPANIONS IN WOE." (MARLOWE. *FAUST.*)
OF COURSE, HE WAS TALKING ABOUT HELL. BUT IT APPLIES EQUALLY TO ARKHAM. HEHEH.
THERE'S NO PLACE LIKE HOME, PROFESSOR CRANE.

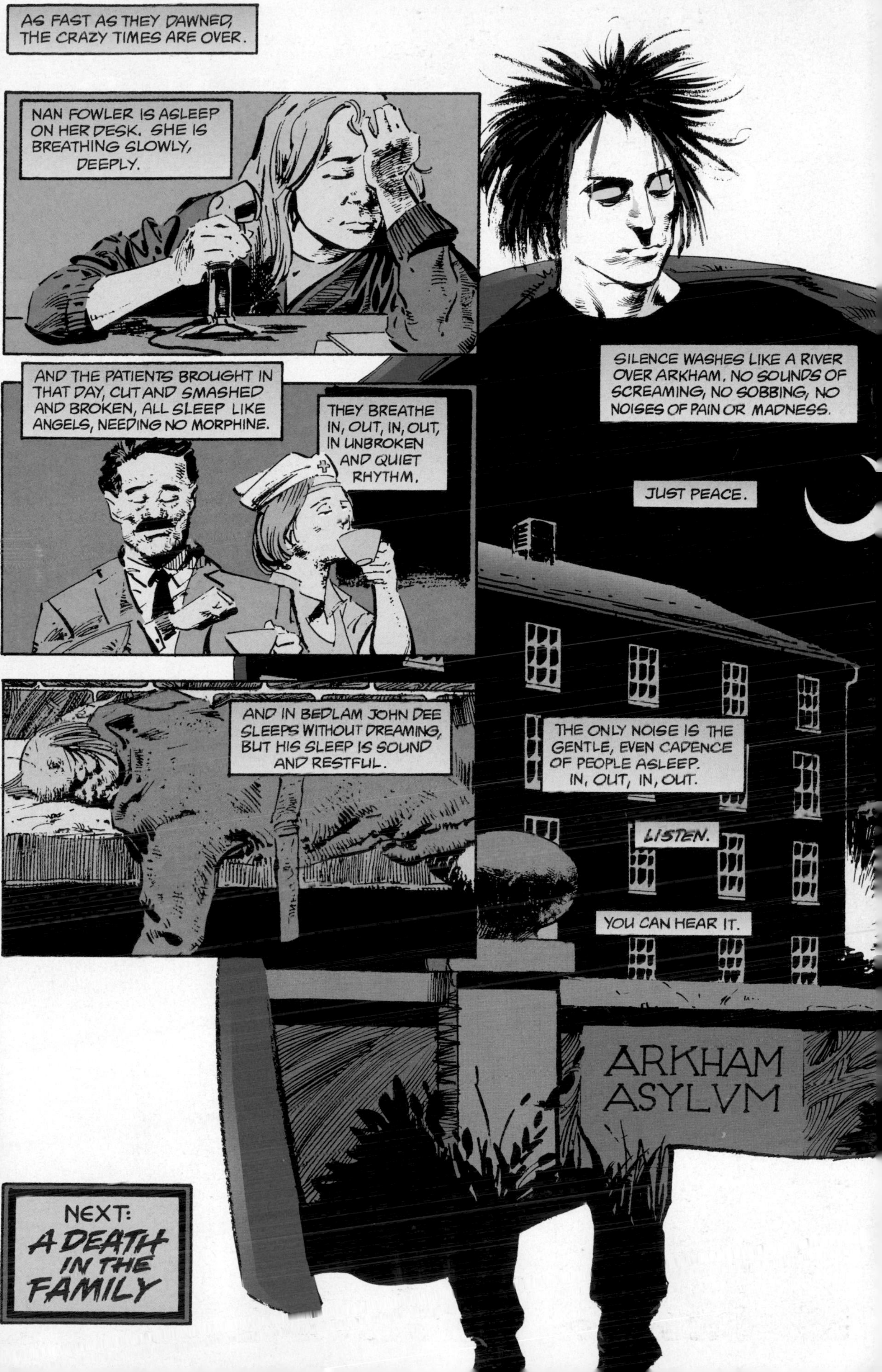
AS FAST AS THEY DAWNED, THE CRAZY TIMES ARE OVER.
NAN FOWLER IS ASLEEP ON HER DESK. SHE IS BREATHING SLOWLY, DEEPLY.
AND THE PATIENTS BROUGHT IN THAT DAY, CUT AND SMASHED AND BROKEN, ALL SLEEP LIKE ANGELS, NEEDING NO MORPHINE.
THEY BREATHE IN, OUT, IN, OUT, IN UNBROKEN AND QUIET RHYTHM.
AND IN BEDLAM JOHN DEE SLEEPS WITHOUT DREAMING, BUT HIS SLEEP IS SOUND AND RESTFUL.
SILENCE WASHES LIKE A RIVER OVER ARKHAM. NO SOUNDS OF SCREAMING, NO SOBBING, NO NOISES OF PAIN OR MADNESS.
JUST PEACE.
THE ONLY NOISE IS THE GENTLE, EVEN CADENCE OF PEOPLE ASLEEP. IN, OUT, IN, OUT.
LISTEN.
YOU CAN HEAR IT.
ARKHAM ASYLVM
NEXT: A DEATH IN THE FAMILY

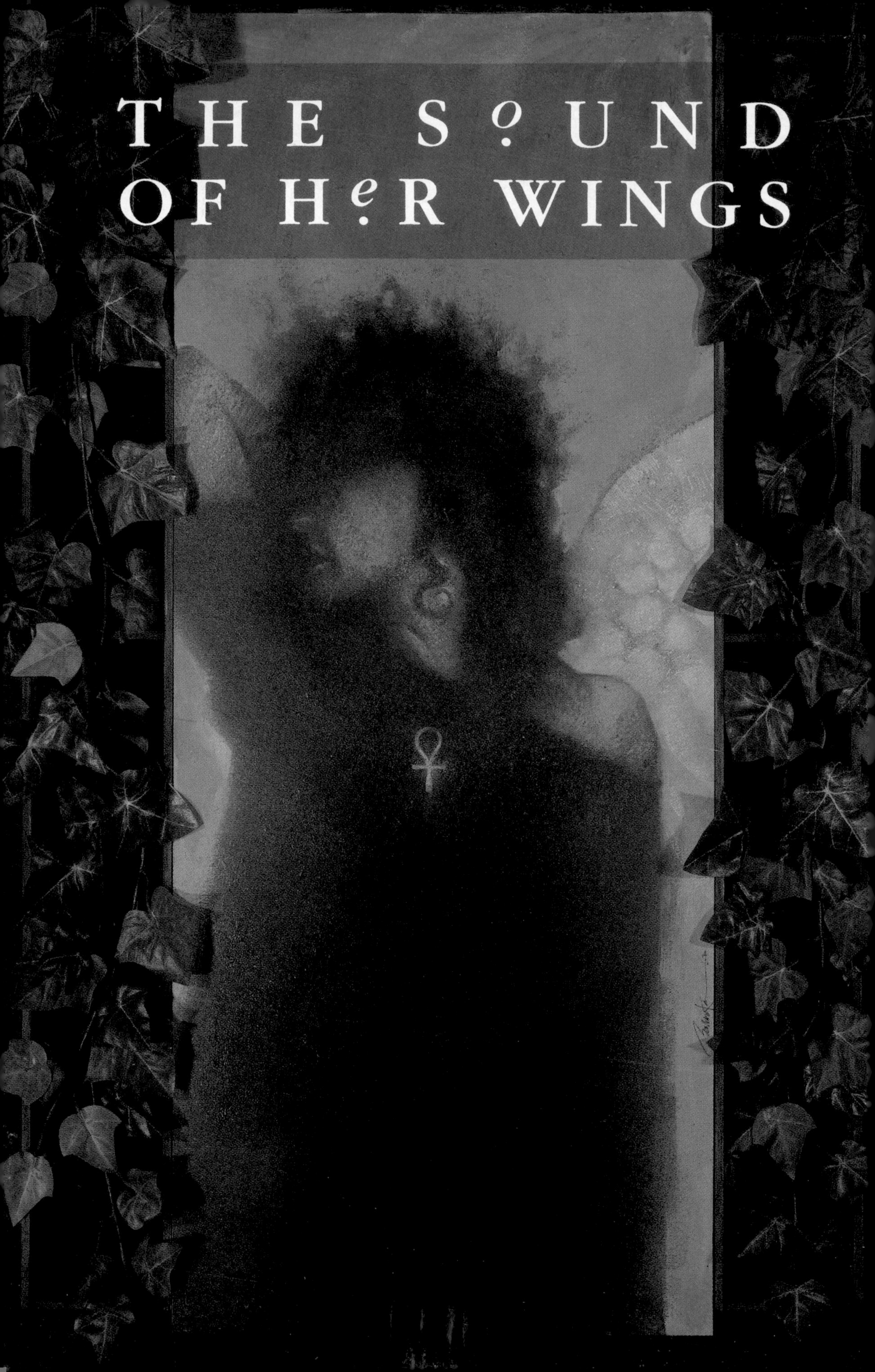
THE SOUND
OF HER WINGS

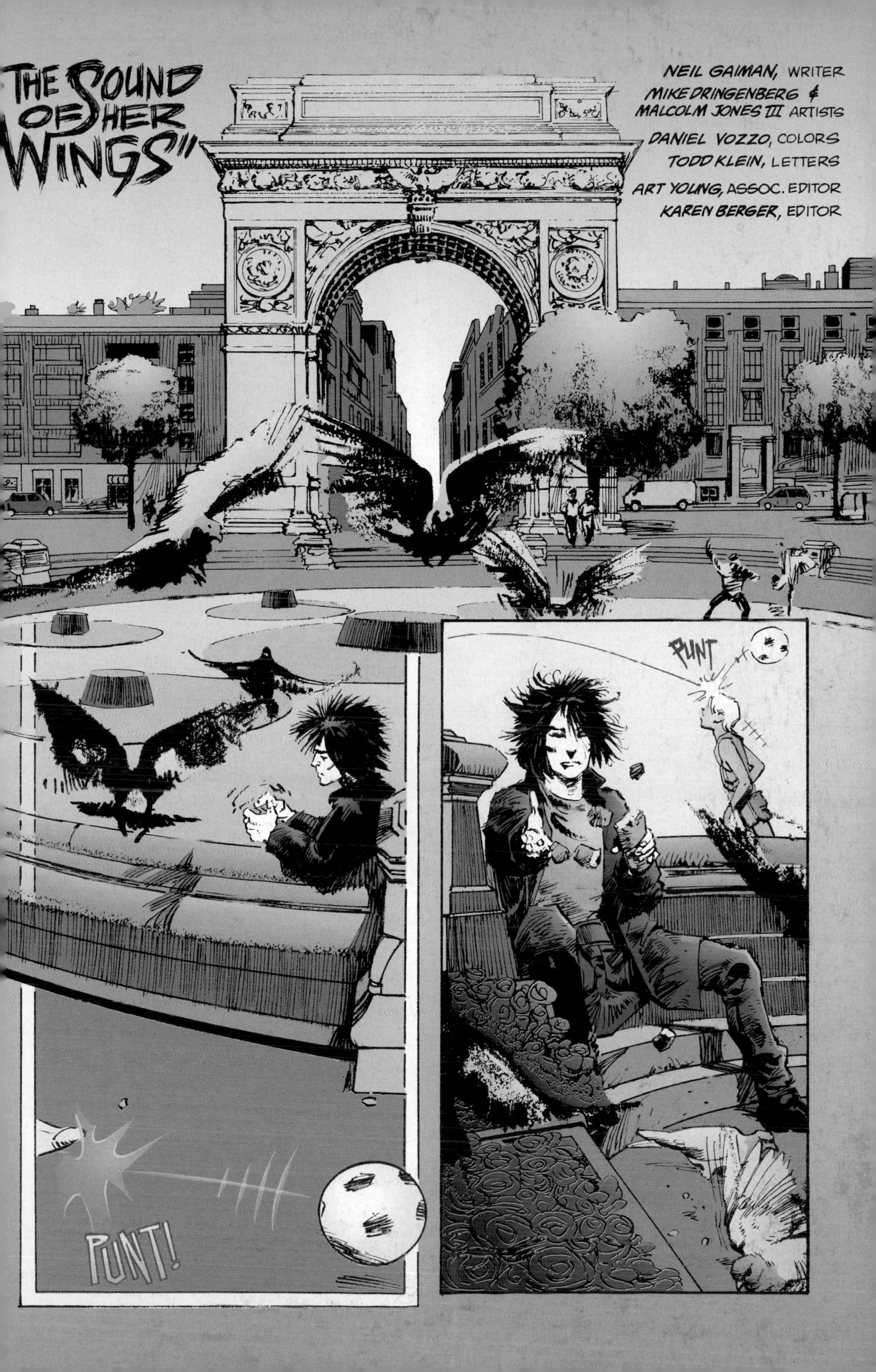

"THE SOUND OF HER WINGS"
NEIL GAIMAN, WRITER
MIKE DRINGENBERG & MALCOLM JONES III ARTISTS
DANIEL VOZZO, COLORS
TODD KLEIN, LETTERS
ART YOUNG, ASSOC. EDITOR
KAREN BERGER, EDITOR
PUNT!
PUNT

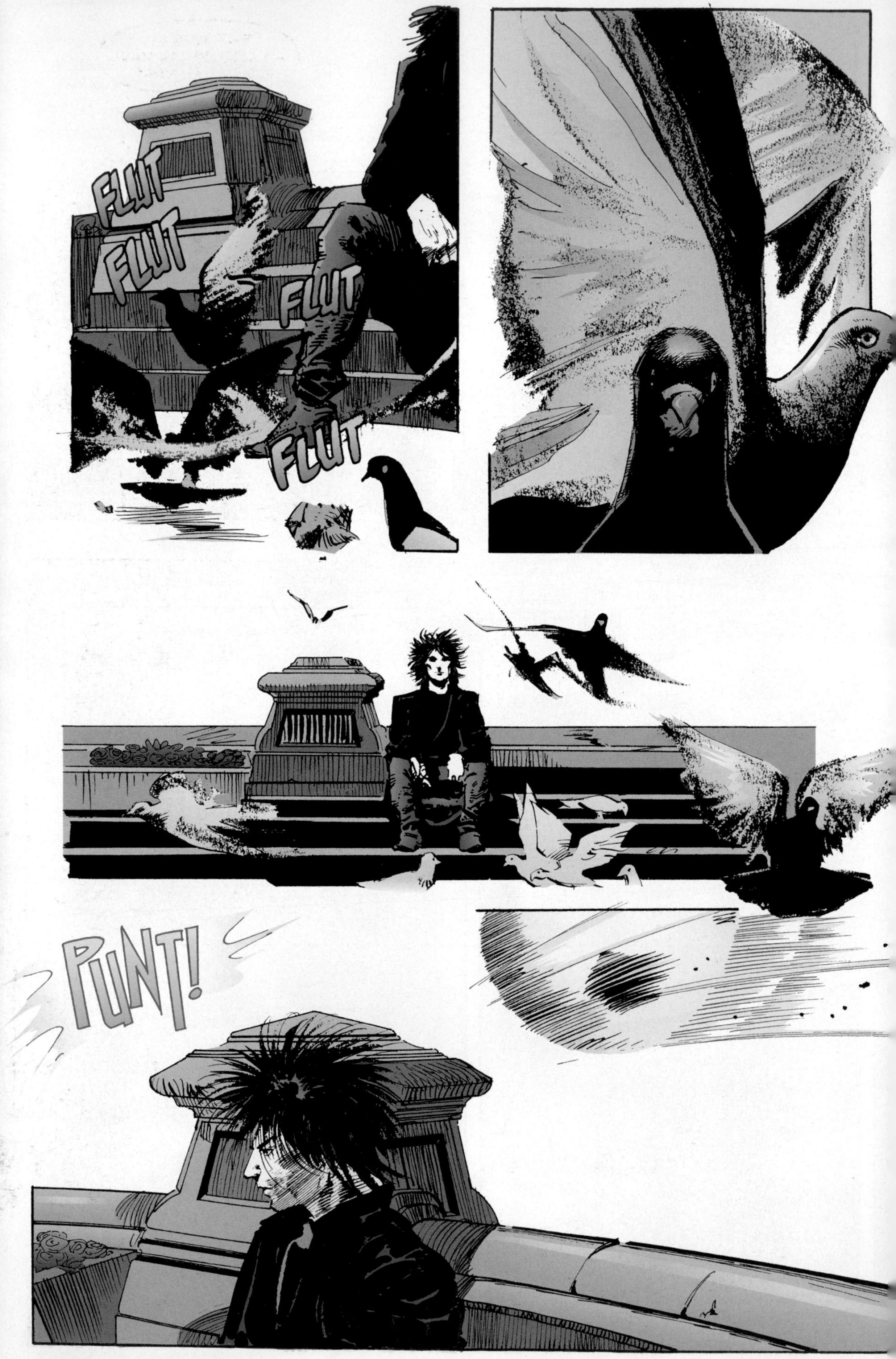
FLUT
FLUT
FLUT
FLUT
PUNT!

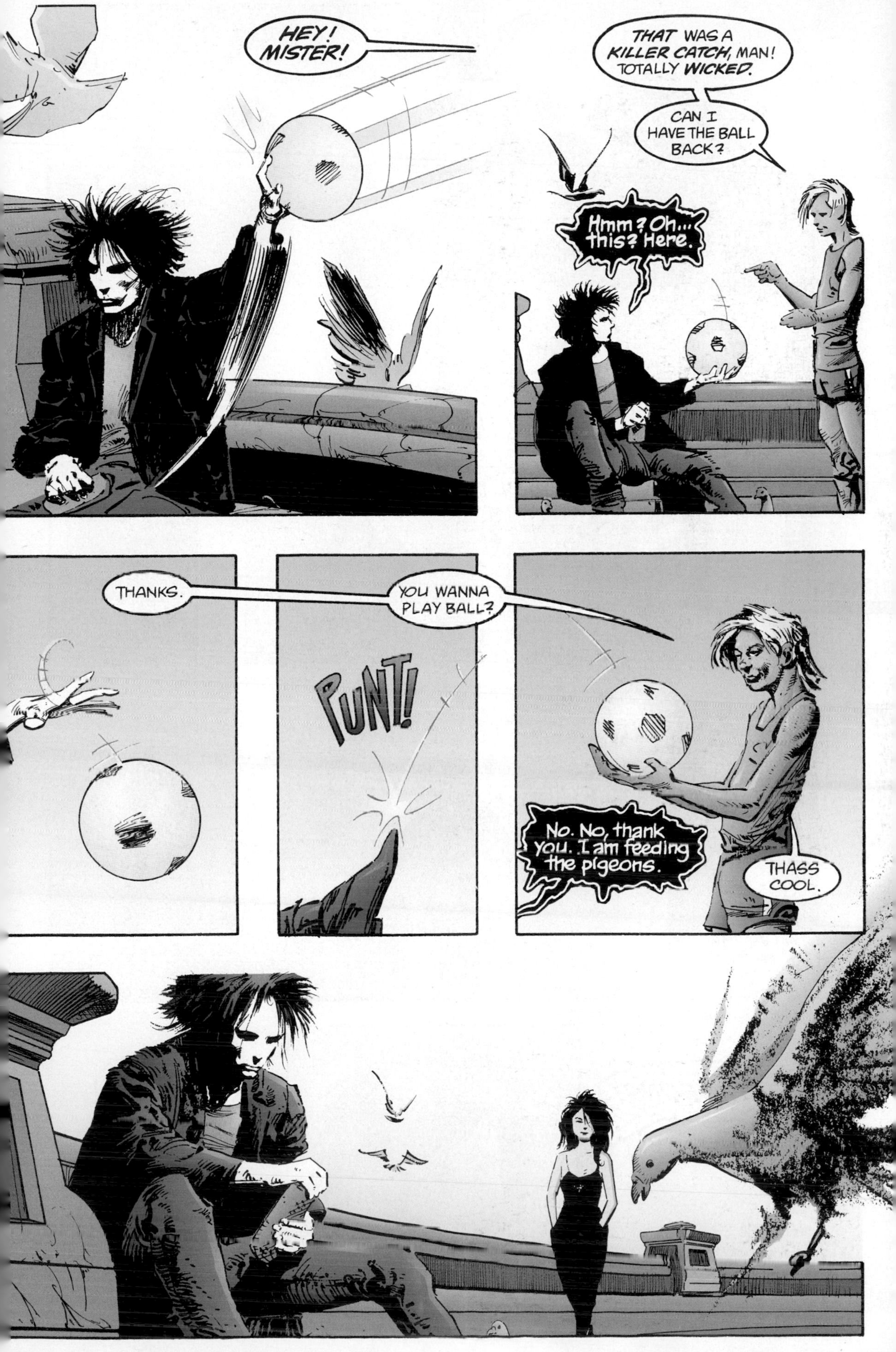
HEY! MISTER!
THAT WAS A KILLER CATCH, MAN! TOTALLY WICKED.
CAN I HAVE THE BALL BACK?
Hmm? Oh... this? Here.
THANKS.
YOU WANNA PLAY BALL?
PUNT!
No. No, thank you. I am feeding the pigeons.
THASS COOL.

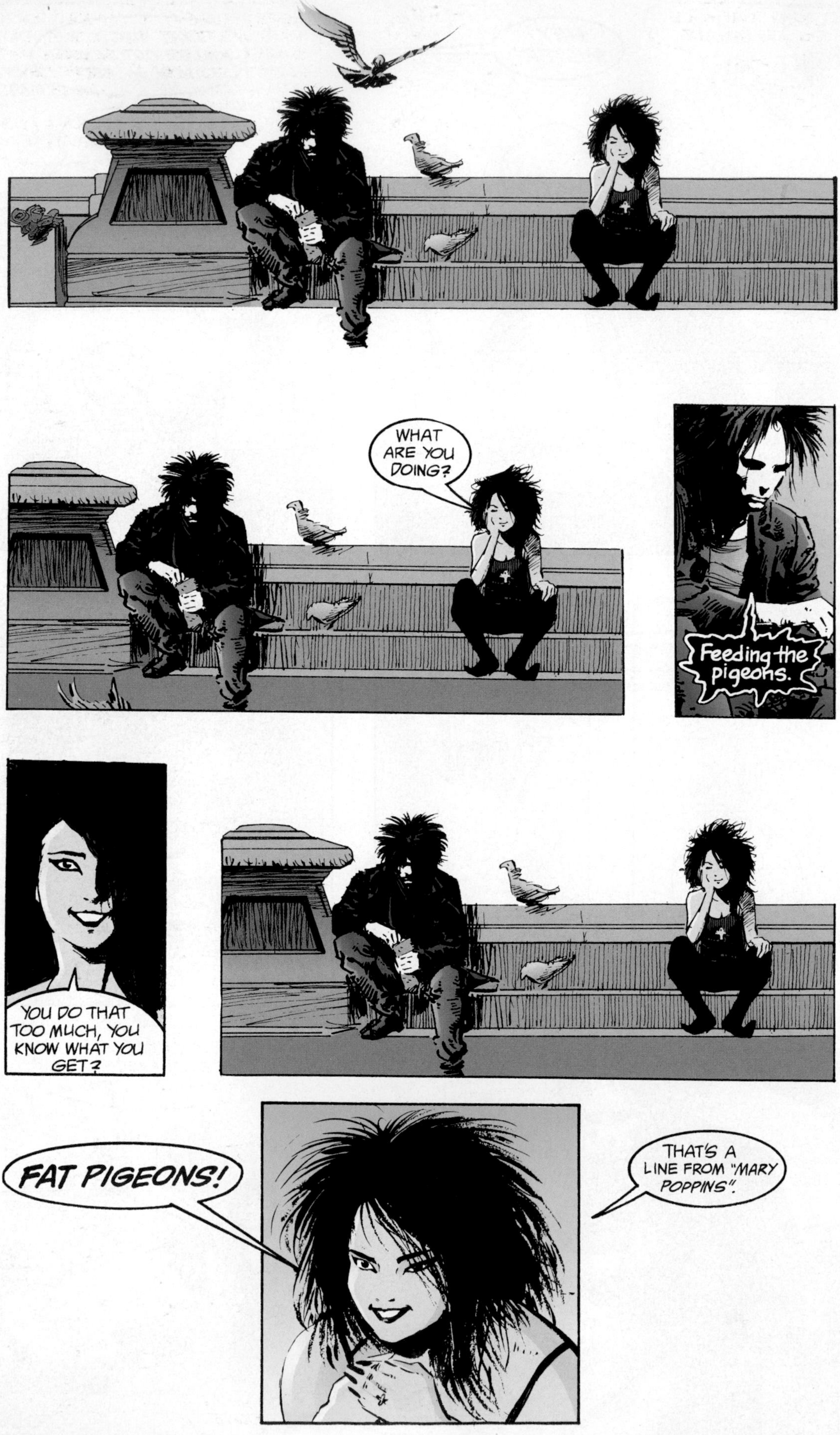
WHAT ARE YOU DOING?
Feeding the pigeons.
YOU DO THAT TOO MUCH, YOU KNOW WHAT YOU GET?
FAT PIGEONS!
THAT'S A LINE FROM "MARY POPPINS".

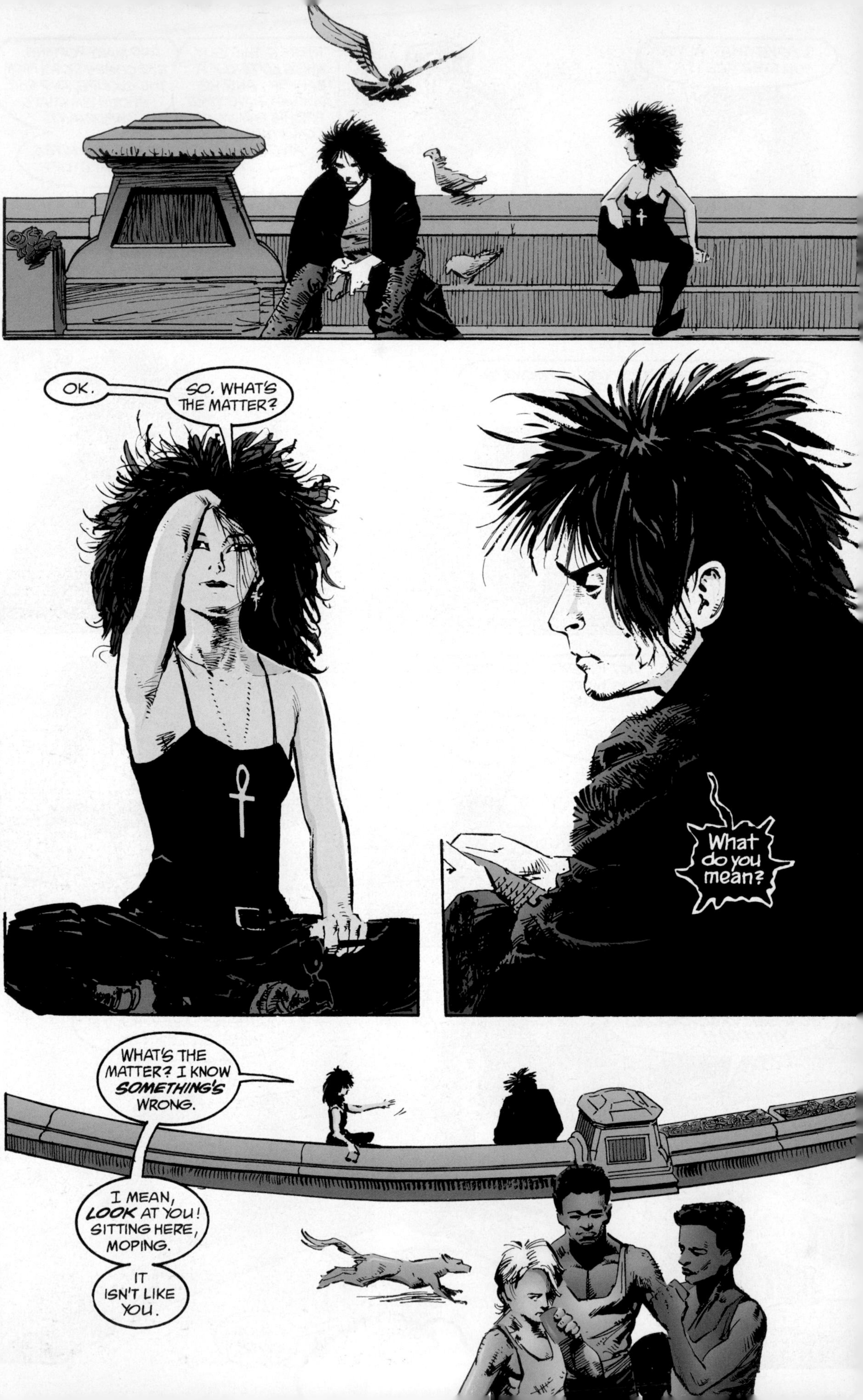
OK.
SO, WHAT'S THE MATTER?
What do you mean?
WHAT'S THE MATTER? I KNOW SOMETHING'S WRONG.
I MEAN, LOOK AT YOU! SITTING HERE, MOPING.
IT ISN'T LIKE YOU.

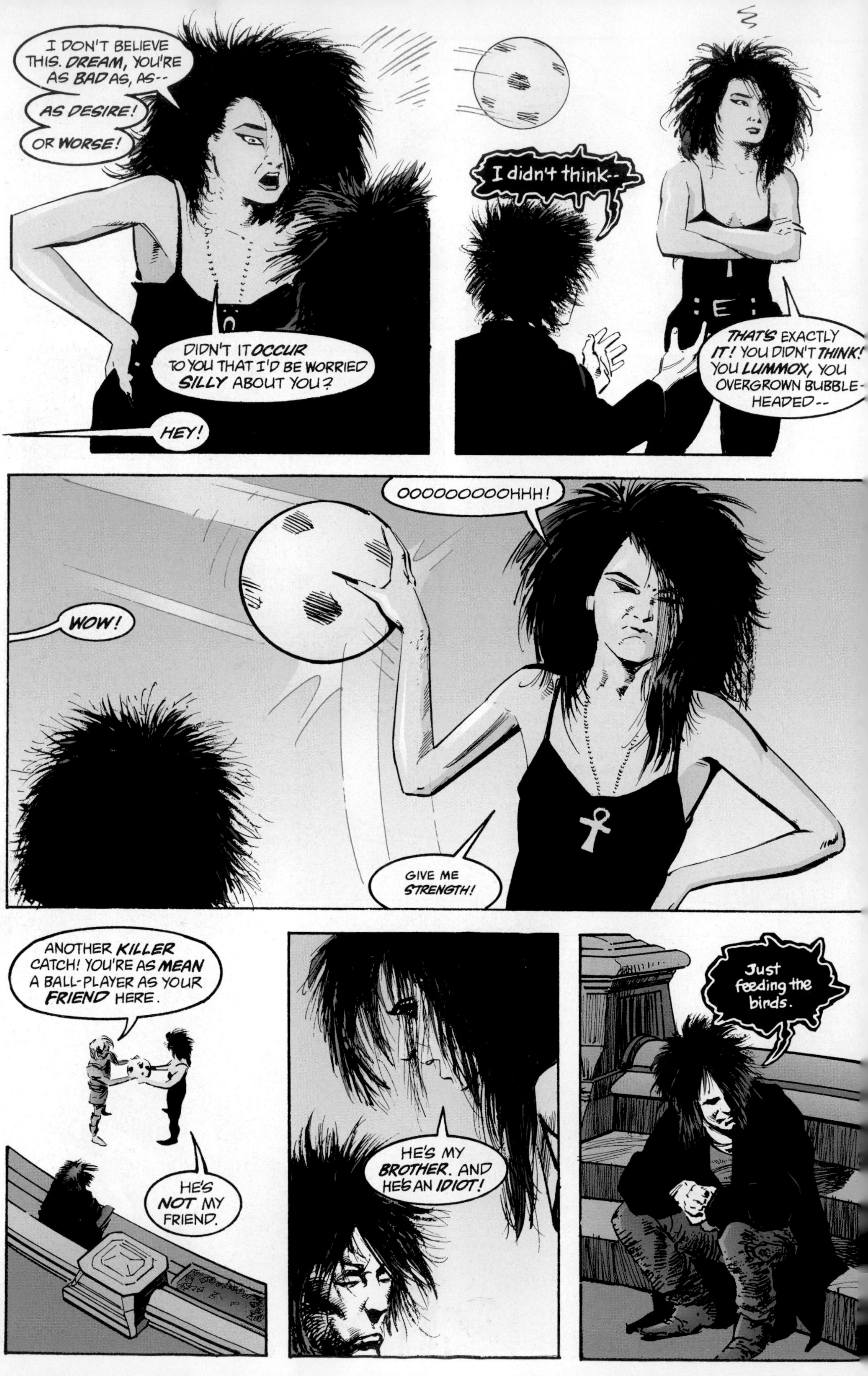
I DON'T BELIEVE THIS. DREAM, YOU'RE AS BAD AS, AS--
AS DESIRE!
OR WORSE!
DIDN'T IT OCCUR TO YOU THAT I'D BE WORRIED SILLY ABOUT YOU?
HEY!
I didn't think--
THAT'S EXACTLY IT! YOU DIDN'T THINK! YOU LUMMOX, YOU OVERGROWN BUBBLE-HEADED--
OOOOOOOOOHHH!
WOW!
GIVE ME STRENGTH!
ANOTHER KILLER CATCH! YOU'RE AS MEAN A BALL-PLAYER AS YOUR FRIEND HERE.
HE'S NOT MY FRIEND.
HE'S MY BROTHER. AND HE'S AN IDIOT!
Just feeding the birds.

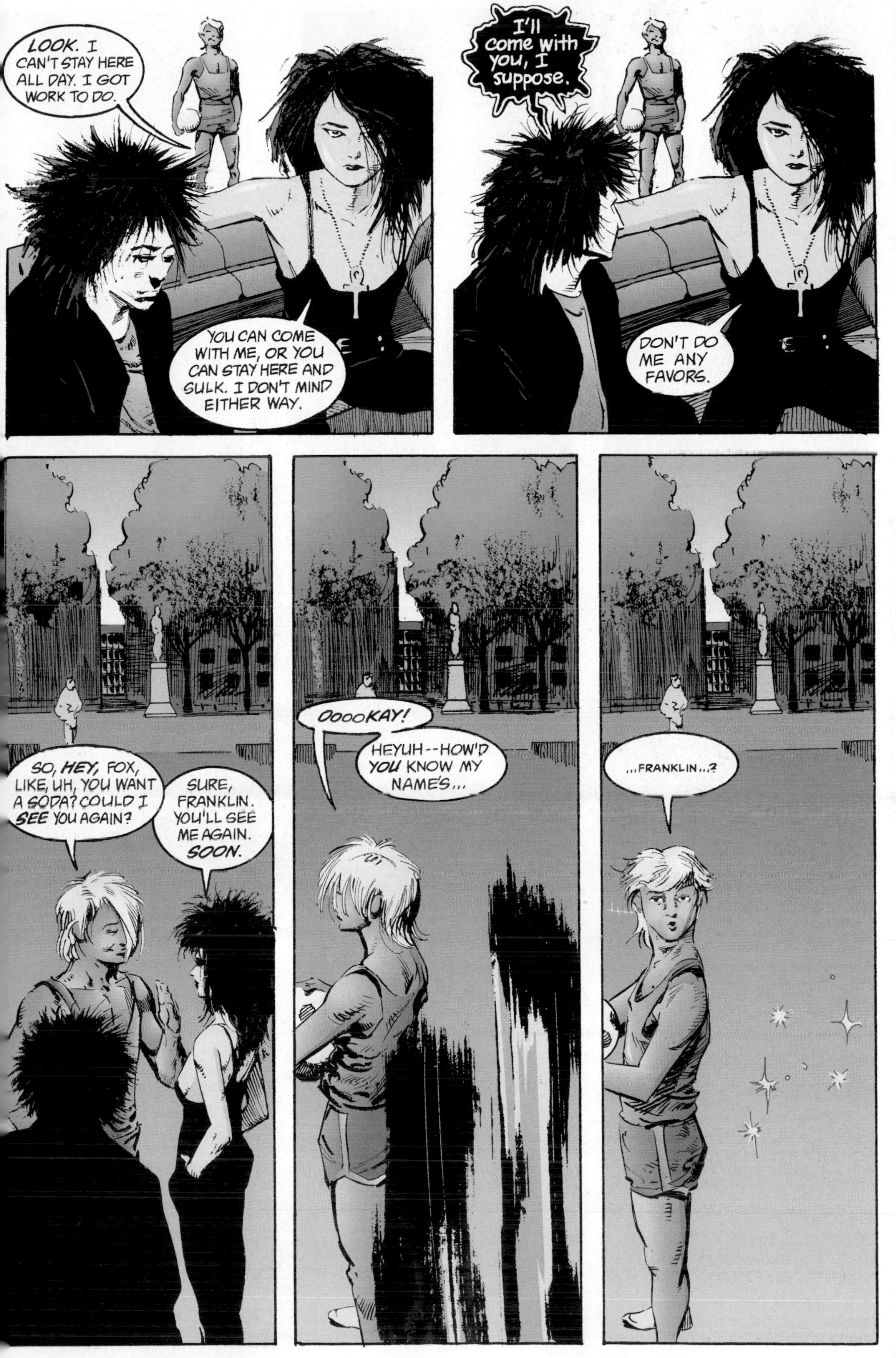
LOOK. I CAN'T STAY HERE ALL DAY. I GOT WORK TO DO.
YOU CAN COME WITH ME, OR YOU CAN STAY HERE AND SULK. I DON'T MIND EITHER WAY.
I'll come with you, I suppose.
DON'T DO ME ANY FAVORS.
SO, HEY, FOX, LIKE, UH, YOU WANT A SODA? COULD I SEE YOU AGAIN?
SURE, FRANKLIN. YOU'LL SEE ME AGAIN. SOON.
OOOOKAY!
HEYUH--HOW'D YOU KNOW MY NAME'S...
...FRANKLIN...?

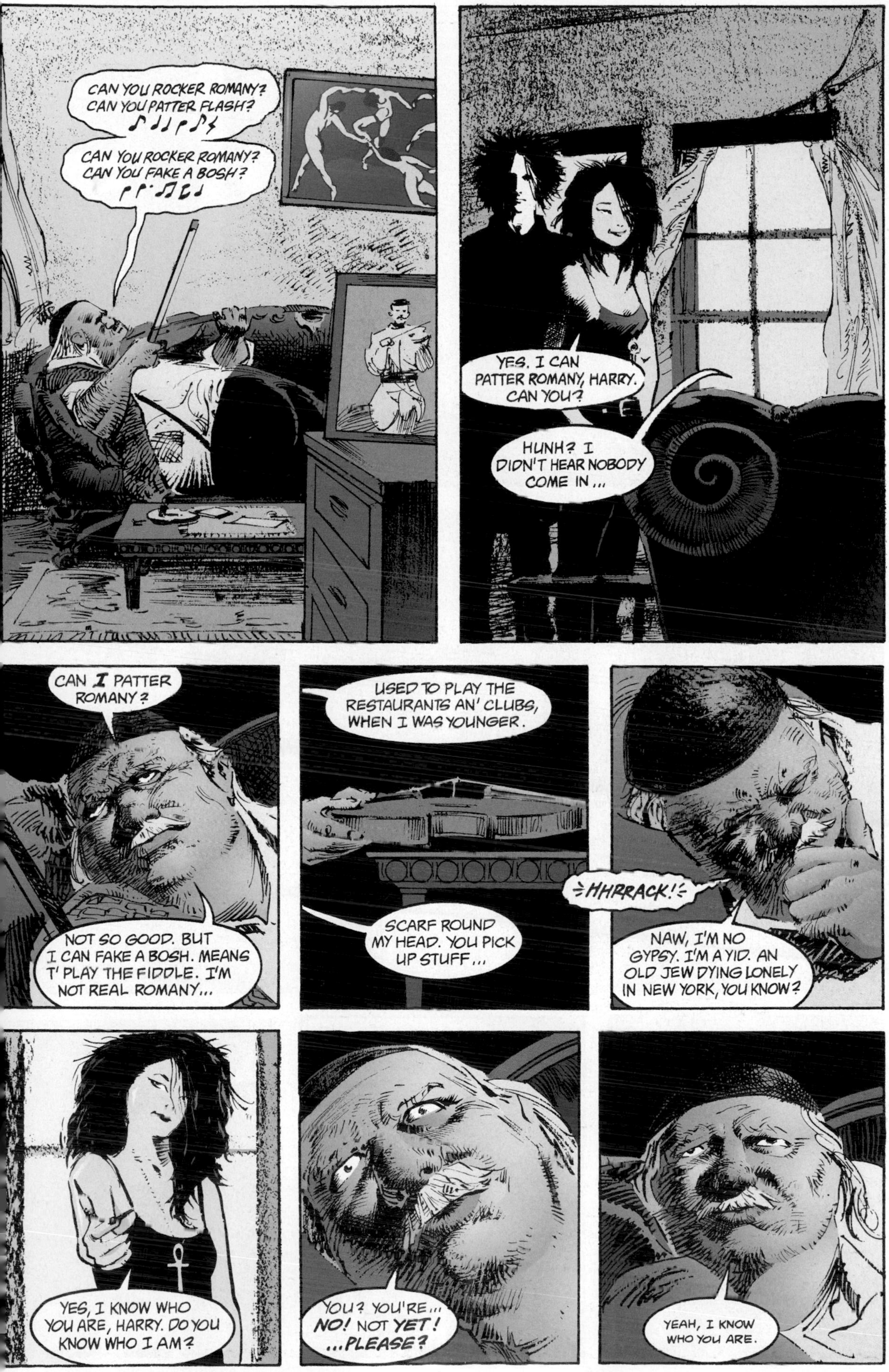
CAN YOU ROCKER ROMANY? CAN YOU PATTER FLASH?
CAN YOU ROCKER ROMANY? CAN YOU FAKE A BOSH?
YES. I CAN PATTER ROMANY, HARRY. CAN YOU?
HUNH? I DIDN'T HEAR NOBODY COME IN...
CAN *I* PATTER ROMANY?
NOT SO GOOD. BUT I CAN FAKE A BOSH. MEANS T' PLAY THE FIDDLE. I'M NOT REAL ROMANY...
USED TO PLAY THE RESTAURANTS AN' CLUBS, WHEN I WAS YOUNGER.
SCARF ROUND MY HEAD. YOU PICK UP STUFF...
HHRRACK!
NAW, I'M NO GYPSY. I'M A YID. AN OLD JEW DYING LONELY IN NEW YORK, YOU KNOW?
YES, I KNOW WHO YOU ARE, HARRY. DO YOU KNOW WHO I AM?
YOU? YOU'RE... **NO!** NOT **YET!** **...PLEASE?**
YEAH, I KNOW WHO YOU ARE.

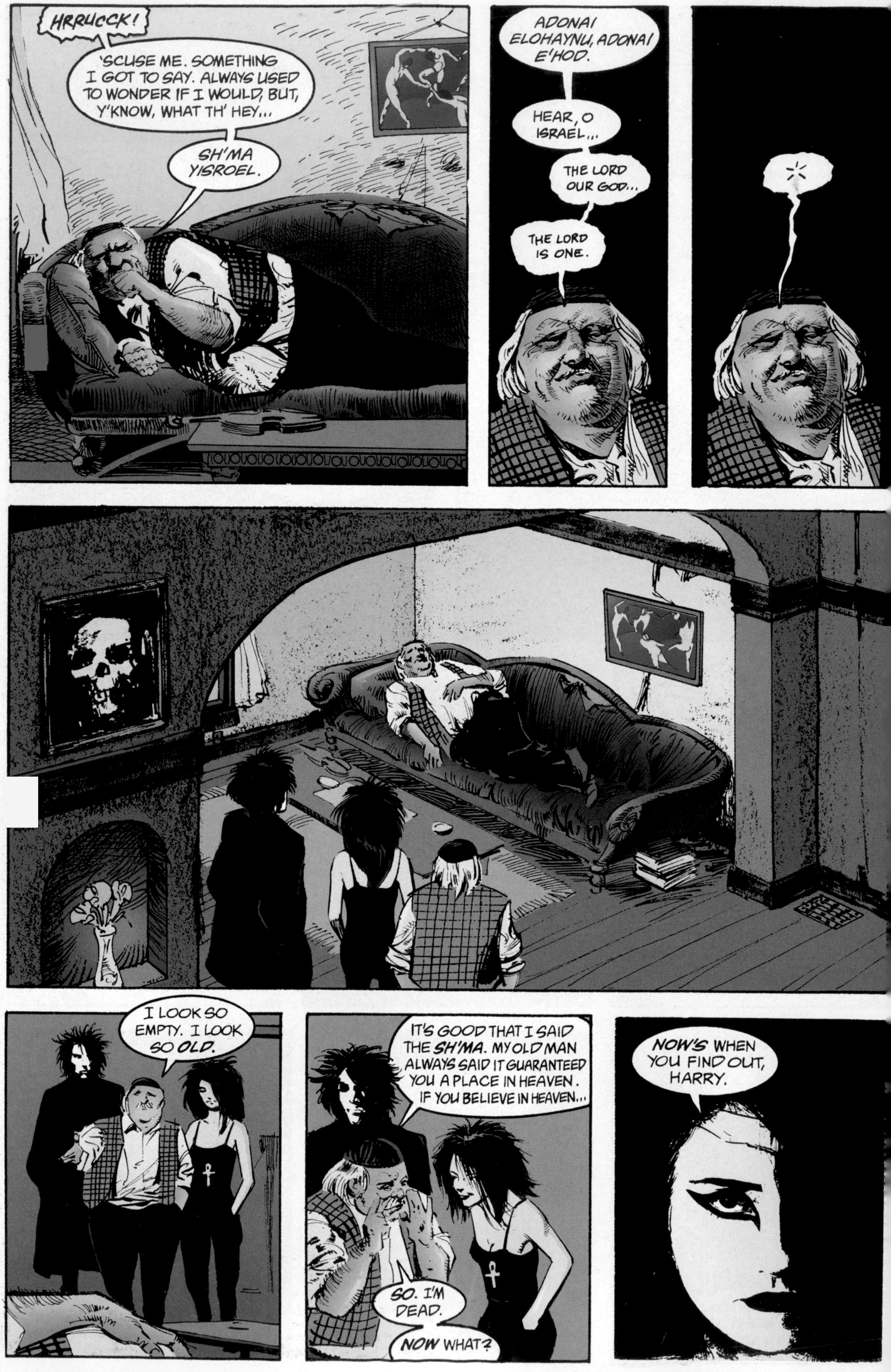
HRRUCCK!
'SCUSE ME. SOMETHING I GOT TO SAY. ALWAYS USED TO WONDER IF I WOULD, BUT, Y'KNOW, WHAT TH' HEY...
SH'MA YISROEL.
ADONAI ELOHAYNU, ADONAI E'HOD.
HEAR, O ISRAEL...
THE LORD OUR GOD...
THE LORD IS ONE.
I LOOK SO EMPTY. I LOOK SO OLD.
IT'S GOOD THAT I SAID THE SH'MA. MY OLD MAN ALWAYS SAID IT GUARANTEED YOU A PLACE IN HEAVEN. IF YOU BELIEVE IN HEAVEN...
SO. I'M DEAD.
NOW WHAT?
NOW'S WHEN YOU FIND OUT, HARRY.

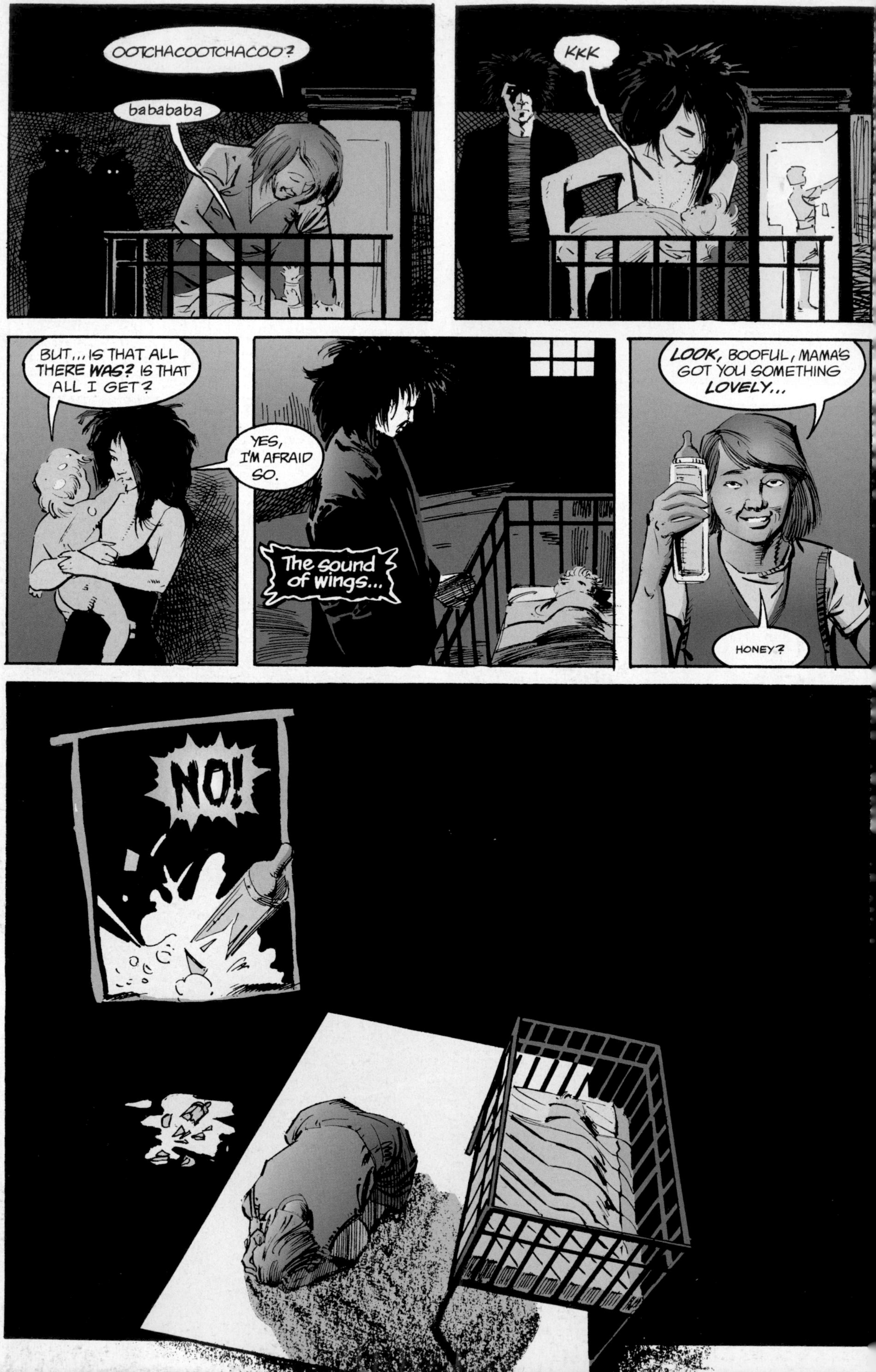
OOTCHACOOTCHACOO?
babababa
KKK
BUT... IS THAT ALL THERE WAS? IS THAT ALL I GET?
YES, I'M AFRAID SO.
The sound of wings...
LOOK, BOOFUL, MAMA'S GOT YOU SOMETHING LOVELY...
HONEY?
NO!

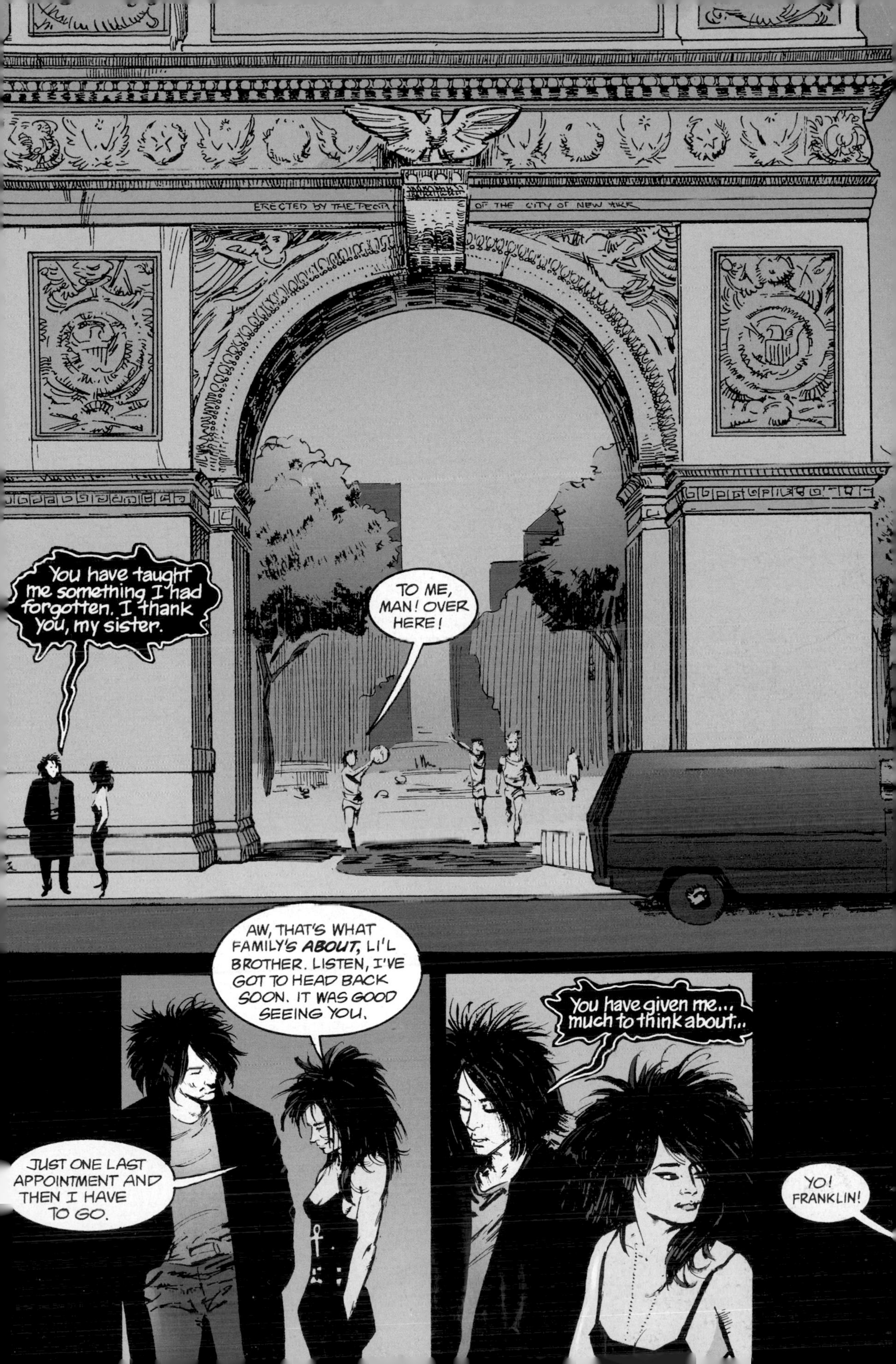
ERECTED BY THE PEOPLE OF THE CITY OF NEW YORK
You have taught me something I had forgotten. I thank you, my sister.
TO ME, MAN! OVER HERE!
AW, THAT'S WHAT FAMILY'S **ABOUT,** LI'L BROTHER. LISTEN, I'VE GOT TO HEAD BACK SOON. IT WAS GOOD SEEING YOU.
JUST ONE LAST APPOINTMENT AND THEN I HAVE TO GO.
You have given me... much to think about...
YO! FRANKLIN!

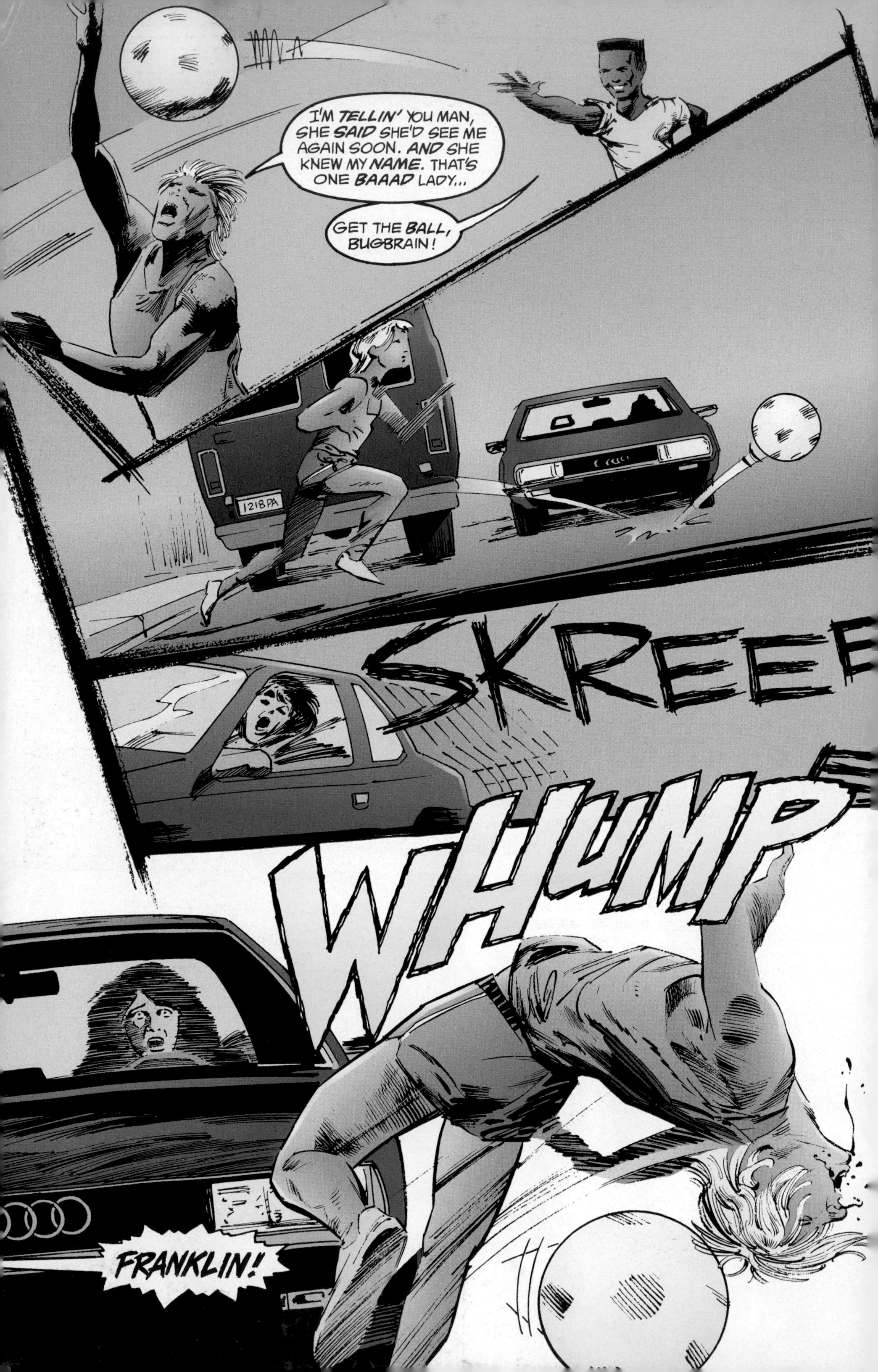
I'M TELLIN' YOU MAN, SHE SAID SHE'D SEE ME AGAIN SOON. AND SHE KNEW MY NAME. THAT'S ONE BAAAD LADY...
GET THE BALL, BUGBRAIN!
1218 PA
SKREEE
WHUMP
FRANKLIN!

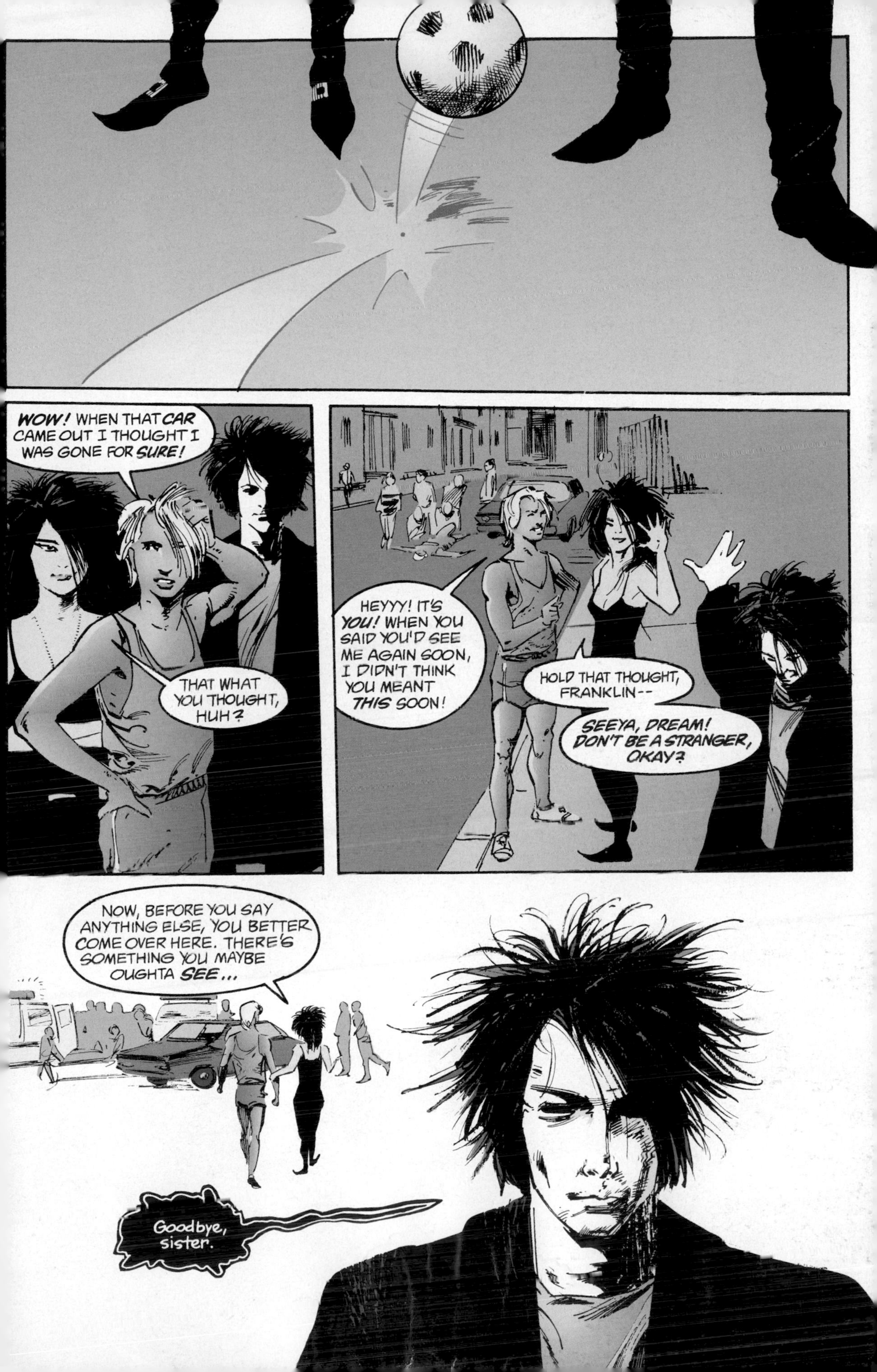
WOW! WHEN THAT CAR CAME OUT I THOUGHT I WAS GONE FOR SURE!
THAT WHAT YOU THOUGHT, HUH?
HEYYY! IT'S YOU! WHEN YOU SAID YOU'D SEE ME AGAIN SOON, I DIDN'T THINK YOU MEANT THIS SOON!
HOLD THAT THOUGHT, FRANKLIN--
SEEYA, DREAM! DON'T BE A STRANGER, OKAY?
NOW, BEFORE YOU SAY ANYTHING ELSE, YOU BETTER COME OVER HERE. THERE'S SOMETHING YOU MAYBE OUGHTA SEE...
Goodbye, sister.

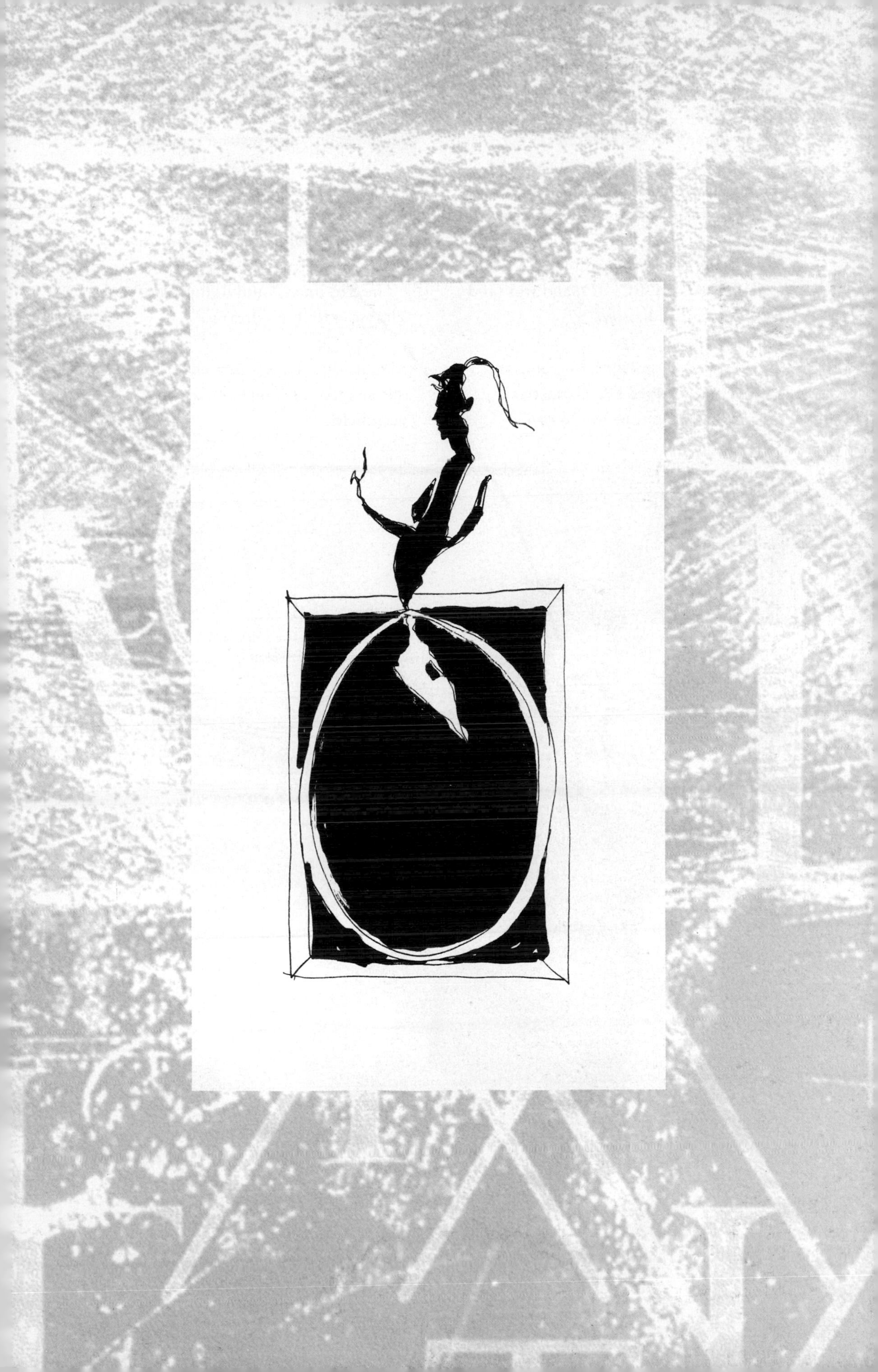

AFTERWORD

In September 1987 Karen Berger phoned me up and asked me if I'd be interested in writing a monthly title for DC. That was how it all started.

Karen was already my editor on a book called BLACK ORCHID, and was (and is) DC's British liaison.

She rejected all my initial suggestions (sundry established DC characters I thought it might be fun to revive from limbo), and instead reminded me of a conversation we'd had the last time she was in England — a conversation I'd almost forgotten — in which I'd suggested reviving an almost forgotten DC character, "The Sandman," and doing a story set almost entirely in dreams.

"Do it. But create a *new* character," she suggested. "Someone no one's seen before."

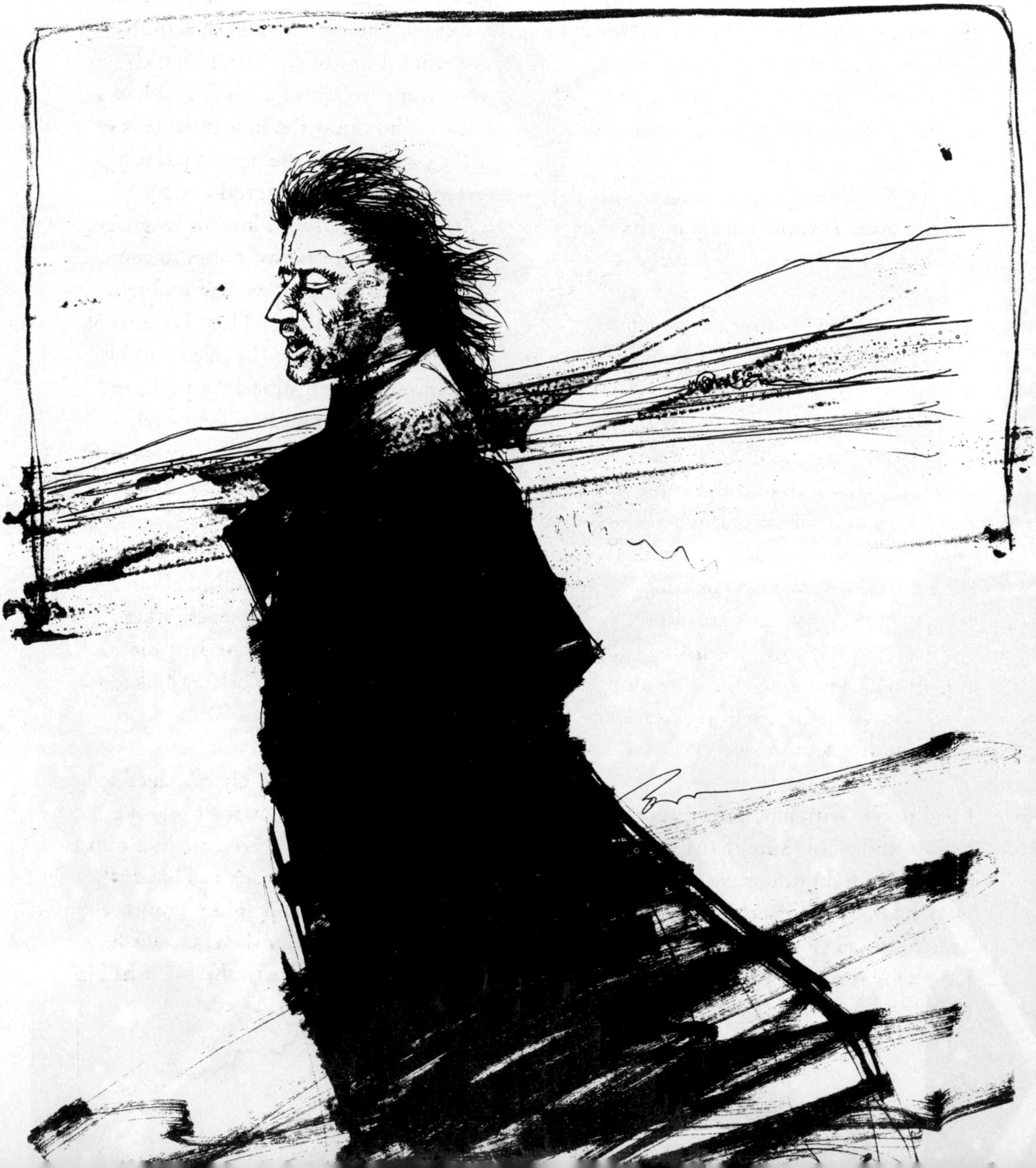

So I did. A year later the first issue of THE SANDMAN appeared in the stores. Put like that, it all sounds so simple.

I don't think it could have been, though. Not really.

Looking back, the process of coming up with the Lord of Dreams seems less like an act of creation than one of sculpture: as if he were already waiting, grave and patient, inside a block of white marble, and all I needed to do was chip away everything that wasn't him.

An initial image, before I even knew who he was: a man, young, pale and naked, imprisoned in a tiny cell, waiting until his captors passed away, willing to wait until the room he was in crumbled to dust; deathly thin, with long dark hair, and strange eyes: *Dream.* That was what he was. That was who he was.

The inspiration for his clothes came from a print in a book of Japanese design, of a black kimono, with yellow markings at the bottom which looked vaguely like flames; and also from my desire to write a character I could have a certain amount of sympathy with. (As I wouldn't wear a costume, I couldn't imagine him wanting to wear one. And seeing that the greater part of my wardrobe is black [It's a sensible colour. It goes with anything. Well, anything black.], then his tastes in clothes echoed mine on that score as well.)

I had never written a monthly comic before, and wasn't sure that I would be able to. Each month, every month, the story had to be written. On this basis I wanted to tell stories that could go anywhere, from the real to the surreal, from the most mundane tales to the most

outrageous. THE SANDMAN seemed like it would be able to do that, to be more than just a monthly horror title.

I wrote an initial outline, describing the title character and the first eight issues as best I could, and gave copies of the outline to friends (and artists) Dave McKean and Leigh Baulch: both of them did some character sketches and I sent the sketches along with the outline to Karen.

Fast forward to January 1988. Karen's back in England for a few days. Dave McKean, Karen and I met in London and wound up in The Worst French Restaurant In Soho for dinner (it had a pianist who knew the first three bars of at least two songs, the ugliest paintings you've ever seen on the wall, and a waitress who spoke no known language. The food took over two hours to come, and was neither what we had ordered, nor warm, nor edible). Then Dave went off to try to negotiate the release of his car from an underground car park, and Karen and I went back to her hotel room, devoured the complimentary fruit and nuts, and talked about Sandman.

I showed her my own notebook sketches of the character, and we talked about artists, throwing names at each other. Eventually Karen suggested Sam Kieth. I'd seen some of Sam's work, and liked it, and said so.

We rang Sam. Karen barely managed to convince him it wasn't a practical joke (and I completely failed to convince him I had actually seen his work and liked it), and she sent him a copy of the outline. He did a few character sketches, one of which was pretty close to the face I had in my head, and we got started.

Mike Dringenberg, whose work I'd seen and liked on *Enchanter*, came in to ink Sam's pencils. Dave McKean, my friend and frequent collaborator, agreed to paint (and, frequently, build) the covers. Todd Klein, possibly the best letterer in the business, agreed to letter, and Robbie Busch came in on colouring. We were in business.

The first few issues were awkward — neither Sam, Mike, Robbie nor myself had worked on a mainstream monthly comic before, and we were all pushing and pulling in different directions. Sam told us that he didn't want to carry on while drawing the third issue ("I feel like Jimi Hendrix in the Beatles," he told me. "I'm in the wrong band." I was sorry to see him go.) and with "24 Hours" Mike Dringenberg took over on pencils. The remarkable Malcolm Jones was now our regular inker.

Together we finished the first SANDMAN storyline, collected in this book.

There was a definite effort on my part, in the stories in this volume, to explore the genres available: "The Sleep of the Just" was intended to be a classical English horror story; "Imperfect Hosts" plays with some of the conventions of the old DC and E.C. horror comics (and the hosts thereof); "Dream a Little Dream of Me" is a slightly more contemporary British horror story; "A Hope in Hell" harks back to the kind of dark fantasy found in *Unknown* in the 1940s; "Passengers" was my (perhaps misguided) attempt to try to mix super-heroes into the SANDMAN world; "24 Hours" is an essay on stories and authors, and also one of the very few genuinely horrific tales I've written; "Sound and Fury" wrapped up the storyline; and "The Sound of Her Wings" was the epilogue and the first story in the sequence I felt was truly mine, and in which I knew I was beginning to find my own voice.

Rereading these stories today I must confess I find many of them awkward and ungainly, although even the clumsiest of them has something — a phrase, perhaps, or an idea, or an image I'm still proud of. But they're where the story starts, and the seeds of much that has come after — and much that is still to come — were sown in the tales in this book.

Preludes and Nocturnes; a little night music from me to you.

I hope you liked them. Good night.

Pleasant dreams.

Neil Gaiman
June 1991

BIOGRAPHIES

NEIL GAIMAN is currently living in a big, dark house in America with five cats, a large white dog and a number of awards from all over the world. He still does not understand how he came to be responsible for the feeding and domestic arrangements of these animals, nor, for that matter, what he is doing living in America. He has four beehives and many bees. He wears black leather jackets, black tee shirts and black jeans, and is now scared that one day he will wake up to find his wardrobe has become tweeds. He has written novels and comics and movies and TV and poems and an opera and he keeps an enormous blog, which is nothing like keeping bees at all. He enjoys old fountain pens and sushi.

SAM KIETH has drawn other people's characters, including the Sandman and Batman for DC Comics and Wolverine and the Hulk for Marvel Comics. He's also written and drawn for titles featuring characters of his own creation, the best known of which are probably THE MAXX, ZERO GIRL and FOUR WOMEN. He's currently creating a series of books for Oni Press involving a trout, magical creatures, toilet seats and, of course, dysfunctional relationships! Kieth also makes small weird movies out of his garage which no one sees, but he enjoys.

MICHAEL DRINGENBERG was born in France and grew up in Germany before emigrating to America in the early 1970s. He studied illustration and graphic design at the University of Utah and began illustrating books and comics before leaving college.

He met Neil Gaiman in 1988 and with him co-created the hugely popular and critically successful series THE SANDMAN.

Dringenberg's work as an illustrator continues, focusing on book jackets and, more recently, CD covers, exploring the relationship of sound and vision.

He likes cats and rain.

MALCOLM JONES III attended the High School of Art and Design and the Pratt Institute in New York City before making his comics debut in the pages of DC's YOUNG ALL-STARS. In addition to his celebrated work on THE SANDMAN, Jones contributed work to many other titles from both DC and Marvel, including BATMAN, THE QUESTION QUARTERLY, *Dracula* and *Spider-Man*. He died in 1995.

DAVE McKEAN has illustrated several award-winning comics, including the best-selling BATMAN: ARKHAM ASYLUM (written by Grant Morrison), MR. PUNCH, *Signal to Noise*, *Violent Cases* and the Newbery Medal-winning *The Graveyard Book* (all written by Neil Gaiman), *Slow Chocolate Autopsy* (written by Iain Sinclair) and his own *Cages*. His collected short stories *Pictures That [Tick]* won the Victoria & Albert Museum Book of the Year Award, and his short film *N[eon]* won overall first prize at the Clermont-Ferrand Film Festival.

McKean has illustrated, photographed and designed over 150 CD covers and hundreds of comic and book covers, including the entire SANDMAN series. He has worked on print and film projects with John Cale, Stephen King, the Rolling Stones, Lars Von Trier and SF Said, and created ad campaigns for Kodak, Nike, BMW Mini and Smirnoff, among others.

McKean also runs the jazz label Feral with top sax player Iain Ballamy, and has contributed production designs to the second and third Harry Potter films. Most recently, he directed the Jim Henson Productions film *MirrorMask*, which he co-wrote with Neil Gaiman. McKean lives in England's Kent countryside.

DANIEL VOZZO was born and raised in Brooklyn, New York. After spending most of the 1980s drumming for several rock-and-roll bands, he landed a job working in DC Comics' production department, where he helped develop a computer coloring department in 1989. He soon began to work freelance, coloring a number of titles for DC's Vertigo line.

He sings great in the shower and always holds the door open for people. Currently living in northern New Jersey, Vozzo continues to color comics and is once again playing music. He has also been working on fine-tuning his writing skills. When asked if he thinks he's good at writing, he insists that he has always had very good penmanship.

One of the industry's most versatile and accomplished letterers, TODD KLEIN has been lettering comics since 1977 and has won numerous Eisner and Harvey Awards for his work. A highlight of his career has been working with Neil Gaiman on nearly all the original issues of THE SANDMAN, as well as BLACK ORCHID, DEATH: THE HIGH COST OF LIVING, DEATH: THE TIME OF YOUR LIFE and THE BOOKS OF MAGIC.